CULTURES OF THE JEWS

Volume I:
Mediterranean Origins

CULTURES
OF THE JEWS

Volume I
Mediterranean Origins

A NEW HISTORY

EDITED BY

David Biale

SCHOCKEN BOOKS

NEW YORK

Library of Congress Cataloging-in-Publication Data

Cultures of the Jews : a new history / edited by David Biale.
v.   cm.
Originally published in 1 volume, 2002.
Includes bibliographical references and index.
Contents: 1. Mediterranean origins—2. Diversities of
diaspora—3. Modern encounters.
ISBN 0-8052-1200-0 (v. 1)—ISBN 0-8052-1201-9 (v. 2)—
ISBN 0-8052-1202-7 (v. 3)
1. Jews—History.   2. Jews—Civilization.   3. Judaism—History.
I. Biale, David, 1949–

DS102.95.C85 2006   909'.04924—dc22   2005049979

www.schocken.com

Book design by M. Kristen Bearse

Printed in the United States of America
First Edition
2   4   6   8   9   7   5   3   1

In memoriam

CONTENTS

LIST OF CONTRIBUTORS

DAVID BIALE is Emanuel Ringelblum Professor of Jewish History and Director of the Program in Jewish Studies at the University of California, Davis.

REUVEN FIRESTONE is Professor of Medieval Judaism and Islam and director of the Graduate School of Judaic Studies at Hebrew Union College–Jewish Institute of Religion in Los Angeles.

ISAIAH GAFNI is Sol Rosenbloom Professor of Jewish History at The Hebrew University of Jerusalem.

ERICH S. GRUEN is Gladys Rehard Wood Professor of History and Classics at the University of California, Berkeley.

RONALD HENDEL is the Norma and Sam Dabby Professor of Hebrew Bible and Jewish Studies at the University of California, Berkeley.

ODED IRSHAI is Senior Lecturer in Jewish History at The Hebrew University of Jerusalem.

ERIC M. MEYERS is Bernice and Morton Lerner Professor of Judaic Studies and Director of the Graduate Program in Religion at Duke University.

ILANA PARDES is Associate Professor of Comparative Literature at The Hebrew University of Jerusalem.

ACKNOWLEDGMENTS

The contributors to this work deserve the greatest thanks, not only for their own contributions but also for serving as equal partners with the editor, assisting in the selection of other contributors, and making invaluable suggestions to improve the work as a whole. Meeting twice as the project evolved—once in Berkeley at an early stage and later in Jerusalem—the authors read and criticized one another's chapters in a quest to find common ground without stifling individual voices. Rare it is in the humanistic disciplines that scholars, instead of working in isolation, come together for a shared purpose.

A special session at the 2001 World Congress of Jewish Studies in Jerusalem, organized at the initiative of Moshe Rosman, produced a lively debate over the work's governing hypotheses about Jewish culture. In the context of that session, Moshe's perceptive and critical reading of my general introduction contributed greatly toward refining that portion of the manuscript.

The origins of this work go back to a telephone conversation in 1995 with Arthur Samuelson, then the editor-in-chief of Schocken Books. Together, we developed the basic outlines of the project. Arthur participated as a full equal in the first conference of contributors and made a signal contribution by encouraging the authors to envision an audience beyond the academy. Arthur was succeeded some years later by Susan Ralston, who played no less important an editorial role. Susan entered the scene as the contributors submitted their chapters and her razor-sharp editor's pencil turned academic prose into much more accessible writing. Her advice, support, and good humor were indispensable in producing a coherent book from what had been piles of pages.

The members of the Editorial Advisory Board, whose names are listed elsewhere in this book, made many useful suggestions at different stages of the project's development. Two of them, William Brinner and Steven Zipperstein, deserve to be singled out for contributions beyond the call of duty, including reading and commenting on some of the chapters.

Abe Socher served as the project's editorial assistant and made many valuable comments on early drafts of chapters. Joe Socher did yeoman's duty as source checker. Julia Johnson Zafferano's careful copyediting assured consistency in spelling and style throughout the manuscript. Dassi Zeidel, at Schocken, coordinated much of the project, including the collection of illustrations. Susan Smith and Kathleen van Sickle deserve special thanks for their assistance in preparing the manuscripts. Carol Cosman translated Lucette Valensi's chapter from French, Murray Rosovsky translated Yosef Tobi's from Hebrew, and Azzan Yadin translated Ariel Hirschfeld's chapter, also from Hebrew.

Two foundations supported this work. The Koret Foundation of San Francisco helped underwrite the conferences that brought the contributors together. The Maurice Amado Foundation of Los Angeles subsidized the chapters on Sephardic, North African, and Middle Eastern Jewish cultures.

—DAVID BIALE
January 2002

Cofanetto (small casket or box), Ferrara (?), second half of the fifteenth century. Silver. (The Israel Museum, Jerusalem)

PREFACE: TOWARD A CULTURAL
HISTORY OF THE JEWS

DAVID BIALE

Sometime in the fifteenth century, a small silver casket was fashioned by an Italian Jewish craftsman known to us from his embossed signature on the lid as Jeshurun Tovar. The casket was intended as a wedding gift for a bride in northern Italy, probably to hold the keys to her linen closets.[1] On the lid of the casket are small dials indicating, in Hebrew numerals, quantities of different kinds of linen and clothing noted by their Italian names written in Hebrew characters: tablecloths, towels, men's shirts, women's chemises, handkerchiefs, knickers, and aprons or cloths for menstruation. It has been suggested that the purpose of this accounting system was to keep track of the items in characters unknown to the woman's Christian servants, although the Hebrew alphabet may also have been the only one that the woman or her Jewish servants could read. The nielloed front panel of the casket depicts three scenes of a Jewish wife fulfilling her cardinal religious duties: separating the *hallah* from the dough, lighting the Sabbath candles, and immersing herself in the ritual bath, which symbolized the separation of husband and wife during her menstrual period.[2]

What meaning does this intricate piece of craftwork have for understanding Jewish culture? Culture is an elastic term that can be stretched in many directions: indeed, the authors of the chapters in these volumes have each followed his or her own definitions. One way to define culture is as the manifold expressions—written or oral, visual or textual, material or spiritual—with which human beings represent their lived experiences in order to give them meaning.[3] But culture is more than just the literary or aesthetic products of a society. As one witty adage goes: "Culture is how we do things around here." From this point of view, culture is the practice of everyday life.[4] It is what people do, what they *say* about what they do, and, finally, how they understand both of these activities. If Jewish culture is broadly conceived along these lines, objects like the silver casket are as precious repositories of meaning as learned texts: the keys contained in it may unlock more doors than just those of linen closets. For example, the dresses worn by the three female figures on the casket are clearly similar to those worn in a somewhat earlier period in Italy by Christians as well as Jews. Yet the artistic themes themselves suggest a specifically Jewish culture. What, then, was the relationship between Jewish culture in that particular epoch and the culture of the non-Jews among whom the Jews lived? What can we learn from the casket about Jewish culture internally—especially, in this case, about the lives of Jewish women? Finally, can we speak of one Jewish culture across the ages or only Jewish cultures in the plural, each unique to its time and place? These are some of the questions that *Cultures of the Jews* will raise and attempt to answer.

The *Mekhilta,* one of the oldest rabbinic midrashim, tells us that the ancient Israelites were preserved as a distinct people in Egypt for four reasons: they kept their names; they maintained their language; they resisted violating the biblical sexual prohibitions (by which the midrash means that they did not intermarry); and they did not engage in "idle gossip" (*leshon ha-ra,* which the midrash understands as collaborating with the gentile government).[5] The *Mekhilta* nostalgically portrays the biblical Jews in Egypt as an "ideal" nation in exile. But from what we know of biblical times (and the Bible says nothing about the 430-year period in Egypt to which the midrash refers), this is an unhistorical portrait. Did the biblical Jews—or, more precisely, the Israelites, as they called themselves—resist foreign names, languages, and intermarriages? Quite the opposite. The name Moses itself is almost certainly of Egyptian origin; the Hebrew language borrowed its alphabet from the Phoenicians and is closely related to Ugaritic, the language of an earlier Canaanite culture (perhaps the earliest Hebrew ought to be called—tongue-in-cheek—"Judeo-Canaanite"); and the Bible is replete with intermarriages, from Joseph's marriage to the Egyptian Asnat to Bathsheba's marriage to Uriah the Hittite (not to speak of Solomon's many foreign wives). All the earmarks of "assimilation" can be found in the Bible itself.

Although it is not possible to date this rabbinic midrash precisely—it is probably from the late second or third century C.E.—the *Mekhilta's* cultural context was the Greco-Roman period, a period when all of these "prohibitions" were manifestly violated: Jews did adopt Greek names and the Greek language, intermarriage was not unknown, and some Jews did act as agents of or informers to the non-Jewish authorities. A stunning example of such interaction between Jewish and Greek culture was revealed in the excavations at Bet She'arim in the lower Galilee. An enormous third-century C.E. Jewish burial chamber at the site contains many sarcophagi decorated with a variety of mythological motifs, such as Leda and the swan, a favorite artistic theme from Greek mythology. Inscriptions in Greek are mixed with those in Hebrew. The Bet She'arim necropolis also contains the graves of rabbis contemporary with Judah the Prince, the compiler of the Mishnah, demonstrating that the cultural syncretism of the site was not alien to the rabbis themselves, despite the statements to the contrary in the *Mekhilta*. Did these Jews who shared a burial space—rabbis and others clearly of a wealthy class—believe in some fashion in the Greek myths portrayed on their tombs? Or, as seems more likely, were they adopting Greek motifs for their own purposes? What meaning did such images have for them, if not what they meant in Greek culture? Were they purely ornamental, or did the Jews graft onto them symbolic meanings consonant with their understanding of Jewish tradition?[6]

In the light of such findings as Bet She'arim, it is impossible to maintain the popular conception of rabbinic Judaism flourishing in splendid isolation from its Greco-Roman surroundings. We now know that the development of rabbinic culture involved the adaptation of legal principles and language from the Hellenistic and Roman worlds.[7] Although concerned with inoculating the Jews against contamination by pagan idolatry, the rabbis also made a clear distinction between images and idols. An image such as a statue of Aphrodite might be acceptable in a bathhouse but not in a pagan temple, where it functioned as an idol and was thus forbidden.[8] Similarly, Greek images might be incorporated into Jewish funerary practices, as at Bet She'arim, without this necessarily constituting adoption of their Greek meaning.

How should we label such adoption of non-Jewish culture? Does it suggest "assimilation" or, to use a less loaded term, "acculturation"? The Italian Jewish culture that produced our casket has frequently been described as one of the most assimilated or acculturated in all of pre-modern Jewish history. But perhaps the contemporary model of assimilation is misleading when applied to the Jews of Renaissance Italy.[9] Here was a traditional community intent on drawing boundaries between itself and its Christian neighbors but also able to adopt and adapt motifs from the surrounding culture for its own purposes. Indeed, the Jews should not be seen as outsiders who borrowed from Italian culture but rather as full participants in the shaping of that culture, albeit with their own concerns and mores. The Jews were not so much "influenced" by the Italians as they were one organ in a larger cultural organism, a subculture that established its identity in a complex process of adaptation and resistance. Jewish "difference" was an integral part of the larger mosaic of Renaissance Italy. Expanding beyond Renaissance Italy to Jewish history as a whole, we may find it more productive to use this organic model of culture than to chase after who influenced whom.

The findings at Bet She'arim—as well as our richly decorated silver casket— challenge another common misconception: that Jewish culture was hostile to the visual arts. The Jewish religion has traditionally been understood as a textual or written tradition in which visual images played a minor role at best. According to some interpretations, the second of the Ten Commandments, which prohibits all images of God, also prohibits, by extension, human images. But it is questionable whether such a prohibition ever really existed.[10] In the Middle Ages, illuminators of Jewish manuscripts were not shy about depicting human beings; the famous *Bird's Head Haggadah* and other Ashkenazic manuscripts from that period, in which people are portrayed with the heads of birds or other animals, are exceptions that prove the rule, and their meaning is still hotly debated.[11] Even within the textual tradition, there developed a particularly Jewish form of art, called micrography, in which the letters of a text were written in tiny characters that formed visual images.[12] In most cases, such as that of the casket, Jewish art involved an interaction between Jewish and non-Jewish motifs and artistic techniques. This interaction demonstrates how the culture of a minority group like the Jews can never be separated from that of the majority surrounding it.

Even in the earliest phases of Jewish history, the ancient Israelites were probably most often a minority among the Canaanite and other Near Eastern peoples who inhabited what the Bible itself calls "the Land of Canaan." In fact, the archaeological evidence suggests that many, if not most, of the Israelites were culturally and perhaps even ethnically descended from the Canaanites. As much as the authors of biblical monotheism tried to isolate the Israelite religion from the practices of their neighbors, it is now generally accepted among scholars of the biblical period that ancient Israel's cult, especially in its popular manifestations, was bound up with Canaanite polytheism.[13] The theological segregation of "Israelite" and "Canaanite" religions is just as mythic as the social and cultural segregation of the two peoples called "Israelite" and "Canaanite." The correct question may therefore not be the difference between "polytheism" and "monotheism" but rather how a theology that claims one, transcendent God nevertheless surreptitiously incorporated and transformed many of the elements of polytheism.

What was true for cult is true for culture. For every period of history, interaction with the non-Jewish majority has been critical in the formation of Jewish culture. Even those Jewish cultures thought to be the most insular adapted ideas and practices from their surroundings. A case in point are the medieval Ashkenazic Jews, whose culture is often considered to have been far more closed than the culture of the contemporaneous Sephardic Jews. Yet their spoken language was essentially that of their Christian neighbors. And, consider how the thirteenth-century German *Hasidim* (Pietists), whose ideals included segregation not only from Christians but also from nonpietistic Jews, adopted ascetic and penitential practices strikingly similar to those of the Franciscan Order from the same period.[14]

Rather than the *Mekhilta*'s explanation for why the Jews survived in exile—as well as in their own land—perhaps our supposition ought to be just the reverse: that it was precisely in their profound engagement with the cultures of their environment that the Jews constructed their distinctive identities. But this engagement involved two seeming paradoxes. On the one hand, the tendency to acculturate into the non-Jewish culture typically produced a distinctive Jewish subculture. On the other hand, the effort to maintain a separate identity was often achieved by borrowing and even subverting motifs from the surrounding culture.[15]

Language was one arena in which this complex process took place. Jews were remarkably adept at adopting the languages of their neighbors but also in reshaping those languages as Jewish dialects by adding Hebrew expressions: language was at once a sign of acculturation *and* cultural segregation. Yiddish, Ladino, and Judeo-Arabic (the latter is actually vernacular Arabic written in Hebrew characters) are the best known of these dialects, but there were many others. In the Greco-Roman world, Jews did not develop a Judeo-Greek, but they incorporated so many Greek words into both Hebrew and Aramaic that those languages, in Late Antiquity, must be considered "fusion" or "acculturated" languages (that is, languages strongly reflecting Greco-Roman culture).

The cases of Yiddish and Ladino are more complicated. Both started out as Jewish dialects of the local non-Jewish language: Middle High German (with some medieval French) for Yiddish, and Castilian Spanish for Ladino. But both took on a much more segregated quality when the Jews who spoke them migrated elsewhere. So, when the Ashkenazic or German Jews moved to Poland in the late Middle Ages, they did not develop a Judeo-Polish but rather absorbed some Slavic words into the Judeo-German that would come to be known as Yiddish. In Germany itself, the Jews continued to speak *ma'arav Yiddish* (Western Yiddish) into the early nineteenth century, long after the Germans themselves no longer spoke the German of the Middle Ages. Ladino was spoken by the Jews of the Iberian Peninsula, but it remained their language for half a millennium after the Expulsion in the Balkans, Greece, Turkey, and other areas of the Ottoman Empire; in these countries of "double exile," the Sephardim never developed Judeo-Greek or Judeo-Turkish. So, two processes were at work: first, intense linguistic acculturation in the early and high Middle Ages, and then, later, a kind of linguistic conservatism—the preservation of these earlier dialects as ever-more distinctive markers of difference from the surrounding cultures, at times even regarded as the "secret" languages of the Jews.

Only in modern times did the Diaspora Jewish languages begin to die out, replaced by the languages of the countries in which the Jews became citizens or by Hebrew, revived by the Zionist movement as a spoken language. Yet even in the modern process of linguistic acculturation, one can discern Jewish inflections in the way Jews wrote and spoke languages like German and English. In describing the translation of the Bible into German that they published in the 1920s, Franz Rosenzweig and Martin Buber used the word *Verdeutschung* rather than the standard German word for translation *(Übersetzung).*[16] *Verdeutschung* obviously means "a rendering into German," but it is also the Yiddish word for both translation into Yiddish and commentary (*teitsh ḥumesh* means something like "the Bible translated and explained in Yiddish"). It is doubly ironic that Yiddish refers to itself as *teitsh*—that is, German—and to translation into Yiddish as "to render into German." By using this rare German word with its Yiddish reverberations, Rosenzweig and Buber were hinting that one goal of the Bible translation was not so much to translate the Bible into "pure" German, as Martin Luther had, but to infuse German with the intonations of the original Hebrew and thus make it a "Jewish language." And they performed this linguistic magic with the very word they chose to describe their project.

Linguistic adaptation was part of a larger strategy of resistance in which the Jews asserted their identity in intimate interaction with the majority culture. The study of indigenous groups living under colonialism has enriched our understanding of how a politically subjugated people shapes its culture and identity.[17] This process involves both defending one's native traditions *and* incorporating and transforming the culture imposed by the colonial power. Both parties to these negotiations end up defining themselves through and against the other. Although the situation of the Jews as a minority was not precisely analogous to that of non-Western colonized peoples under Western imperialism, there is a similarity in the way Jewish identity developed in a rich dialectic with the identities of the non-Jewish majority: the category of "Jew" assumed and, indeed, produced the category *goy.*[18] The production of Jewish culture and identity in such circumstances can never be separated from the power relations between Jews and their neighbors.

A fascinating visual example of this process can be found in numerous Jewish medieval illuminated manuscripts. In 1215, the Fourth Lateran Council required that Jews wear identifying insignia, a piece of legislation purportedly motivated by fears of sexual relations between Jews and Christians. Among the distinctive forms of Jewish dress that one finds in the later Middle Ages is the hat, which assumed a variety of different shapes. In many Hebrew illuminated manuscripts, the Jews are depicted wearing these hats as a matter of course.[19] If the intention of the Christian rulers was to degrade the Jews, it seems evident from these pictures that the Jews did not feel degraded, for otherwise it is hard to imagine why they portrayed themselves—or commissioned Christian artists to portray them—wearing the distinctive hat in scenes of private or synagogue life. In a

later period, the age of emancipation, the Jewish hat came to be seen as humili-
ating. Yet, for the Jews of the Middle Ages, the way Christians commanded them
to dress became badges of their own identity, as much a part of their culture depicted in these manuscripts as the sacred words on their pages.

The Jewish minority often adopted non-Jewish beliefs or practices but in-
fused them with traditional Jewish symbols. For instance, the ritual—practiced
widely in many different communities—of the first day of school, during which
a young boy would eat honey in the shape of Hebrew letters, may have been enacted by the medieval Ashkenazic Jews in a way that responded to the new Christian dogma and rituals of the Eucharist.[20] And when the same Jews confronted
the Crusaders in 1096 with a messianic theology of blood vengeance—a theology that led some to slaughter their own children and commit suicide in order
to bring down the divine wrath on their persecutors—much of the language of
blood, sacrifice, and atonement, although rooted in earlier Jewish sources, resonates with similar Christian concepts from the time.[21]

The example of the Crusades suggests that the Jews did not interact with the
cultures of their non-Jewish neighbors only during peaceful times but also in
times of conflict. While much of this violence flowed from the majority toward
the minority, the street was not exclusively one-way. In the Middle Ages, Jews
also utilized violence, sometimes real and sometimes symbolic, to enforce the
boundaries that they, no less than Christians and Muslims, wished to maintain.
A particular instance of such ritualized violence was the custom of hanging an
effigy of Haman on a cross during Purim, thus demonstrating the Jews' contempt for Christianity.[22] Moreover, great cultural interchange, such as occurred
during the so-called Golden Age of Spain (roughly 1000–1400), did not preclude
such acts of real or symbolic violence.[23] Relations between the minority and the
majority cultures cannot, therefore, be so easily categorized as either peaceful
"symbiosis" or unrelieved antagonism, or, more broadly, as "golden ages" versus
"dark ages."

Jewish self-definition was, then, bound up in a tangled web with the non-
Jewish environment in which the Jews lived, at once conditioned by how
non-Jews saw the Jews and by how the Jews adopted and resisted the majority
culture's definition of them. For all that Jews had their own autonomous traditions, their very identities throughout their history were inseparable from that
of their Canaanite, Persian, Greek, Roman, Christian, and Muslim neighbors. An
old Arabic proverb claims that "Men resemble their own times more than the
times of their fathers." Viewed in this light, Jewish identity cannot be considered
immutable, the fixed product of either ancient ethnic or religious origins, but
rather to have changed as the cultural context changed.

But if Jewish identity changed according to differing historical contexts, can we speak at all of *a* Jewish history, a common narrative stretching from the Bible, through the Hellenistic and rabbinic periods, the Muslim and Christian Middle Ages, and into the modern period? Is there or was there *one* Jewish people with one history? Is there or has there ever been one Jewish religion called Judaism? Both high literary culture and material culture, from the way Jews dressed to the way they looked and behaved, from their natural landscapes to the architecture of their homes and communal institutions, differed radically from period to period and place to place. Culture would appear to be the domain of the plural: we might speak of Jewish *cultures* instead of culture in the singular.

And, yet, such a definition would be missing a crucial aspect of Jewish culture: the continuity of both textual and folk traditions throughout Jewish history and throughout the many lands inhabited by the Jews. The multiplicity of Jewish cultures always rested on the Bible and—with the exception of the Karaites and the Ethiopian Jews—on the Talmud and other rabbinic literature. In the Middle Ages, philosophical, legal, exegetical, and mystical traditions added to the edifice built on earlier textual foundations. This extraordinary library became the cultural legacy not only of the legal authorities and intellectuals who produced it but also of the people as a whole, as defining of Jewish identity as the diverse cultural interactions of which we have already spoken. To be sure, the Jewish library cannot be reduced to a single "essence." As the work of the great historian of Jewish mysticism, Gershom Scholem (1897–1981), taught us, myth and magic occupy as much room on its shelves as law and philosophy: Jewish religion—and, more broadly, Jewish culture—contain the rational *and* the irrational.

As the *Mekhilta*'s ideal of national isolation and purity demonstrates, the Jews throughout the ages *believed* themselves to have a common national biography and a common culture.[24] These beliefs are also an integral part of the history of Jewish culture because their very existence made them as true as the historical "facts" that seem to contradict them. The history of other national groups suggests how complicated the relationship is between the belief in the unity of the nation and historical reality. The Germans and the French, for example, only really became united peoples with a common language in the nineteenth century (although the French had a much older unified state, whereas the Germans did not). Yet the *idea* of a common French or German identity long preceded the historical reality and, indeed, contributed toward creating this reality. In a similar way, we can speak of a dialectic between, on the one hand, the *idea* of one Jewish people and of a unified Jewish culture, and, on the other, the history of multiple communities and cultures.

The role of rabbinic law in Jewish history demonstrates how this dialectic worked. The development of rabbinic law often appears to follow its own internal logic, with a sixteenth-century authority debating a twelfth-century predecessor as if both were in the same room. The legal innovations of a particular authority, often couched to appear as if they were really present in an earlier text, might seem to be utterly divorced from the culture, both Jewish and non-Jewish, in which the authority lived. Yet between the lines of this ethereal discourse, one often finds echoes of the external world, intruding and shaping the rulings of judges and scholars. In addition, the rigid fences of the law typically bent to include local customs (minhagim), unique to particular communities, which also reflected historical developments. And if rabbinic law can be considered the product of "elite" culture, "popular" culture exhibited the same dialectic: Jews throughout the world shared common beliefs—as well as actual books—about demons and how to ward them off. Yet these folk customs varied in their details from place to place, often reflecting the practices of the surrounding non-Jewish folk cultures. On both the elite and popular levels, then, the Jewish people were, at once, one *and* diverse.

Let us return to our silver casket as a case in point. A particular detail in the center of the frontal panel attracts our attention: the woman standing in the barrel-shaped ritual bath is naked. Does the presence of a nude woman on this object suggest that, following the predominant cultural values of the Italian Renaissance, the Jews of the time did not regard depiction of the unclothed human body as immodest, religiously unacceptable, or, perhaps, even erotic? Or, perhaps it *was* considered erotic, since the bed linens indicated by the dials on top of the box are connected with an act that Jewish law considered a suggestion of intimate marital relations: a wife making the bed for her husband (because during her menstrual period she was not allowed to make the bed).[25] Might, then, this image, appearing on a casket holding keys to the linen closet, serve to arouse her (or her husband) sexually? What does the casket teach us about attitudes toward the body among Italian Renaissance Jews? Was the woman who owned the casket aware of the discrepancy between rabbinic prohibitions of nudity and this particular image? Was her understanding of the images on the casket the same as that of her husband or of the casket's maker? What did the rabbinic authorities of the day think of such depictions? Do we have evidence here of divisions among the Italian Jews between a "secular" class and rabbinic authority or, perhaps, among the rabbis themselves?

Whatever the answers may be to these questions—and some will be found in the chapter on Jewish culture in the Italian Renaissance—it would be a mistake to assume that the maker and users of the casket necessarily intended to contradict the dictates of Jewish law. After all, the images were designed to remind the woman of the house of the primary commandments of her religious life. Rather, the cultural means by which people chose to represent and express rabbinic law changed from period to period and from context to context. Culture acted as a kind of expansive interpretation of the law, or, to put it differently, law was only one aspect of a wider culture that as much shaped the law after its own values as it was shaped by it. Instead of imagining an elite rabbinic culture coexisting perhaps uneasily with an opposing popular or nonlearned culture, we might see the two as much more tightly entangled with each other, for rabbis and other authorities often shared many of the cultural practices of the common folk, just as those who were not authorities incorporated "elite" culture into their own. The Talmud, for example, though the product of an elite class of rabbis in Palestine and Babylonia, contains much folklore, both Jewish and non-Jewish, suggesting that these rabbis were not walled off from the larger culture in which they lived. And in the Middle Ages the Talmud, while remaining a book studied by a small, male elect, came to shape popular Jewish culture, not only through its laws but also through its maxims and legends. While the terms "elite" and "popular" may still be useful in thinking about Jewish culture, it is equally important not to be seduced by such polar opposites and to recognize the common ground that existed between the two.

For the cultural historian, the intellectual elite does not exist in isolation, just as daily life does not remain in its own mute universe, unencumbered by intellectual reflection. Cultural history is an effort to see the connections between them. Those who produce cultural objects, whether written, visual, or material, can never be isolated from the larger social context, the everyday world, in which they live, just as those who belong to this larger world are not immune to the ideas and symbolic meanings that may be articulated by intellectuals. The relationship between text and context ought rather to be seen as the relationship between different types of texts, rather than between the "ideas" of elites versus the "material" reality of the wider society.[26] At times, those among the uneducated mobilized ideas, perhaps derived from old, subterranean traditions, to subvert the dominant discourse.[27] In the Jewish sphere, one might turn to folklore for such traditions or to the rabbinic responsa literature, which can provide not only a history of legal precedents and case law but also evidence of the actual beliefs and practices of Jews who lived their lives outside the *bet midrash* (the study hall) and the *bet din* (the rabbinic court), perhaps even in opposition to these venerable institutions.

An example of such subversion and of the complex relations between rabbinic and nonrabbinic culture for the same period as our silver casket are two prayer books copied by one of the leading rabbis of the day, Abraham Farissol. The first was commissioned by a man for his wife in Ferrara in 1478, and the second was ordered by a married woman in Mantua in 1480. In both cases, the morning blessings—when men traditionally thank God for "not making me a woman" and women thank God for making them "according to His will"— contain a radical revision: the prayer thanks God "for making me a woman and not a man."[28] Whose decision was it in the first case to change the blessings: the man who commissioned the work, or his wife? How did the woman in the second case decide to make this revision, and did she have the approval of her husband? We know nothing about the negotiations between the wealthy patrons and the learned rabbi who copied the books. Did Farissol resist the revision or, alternatively, did he perhaps suggest it? What more do these objects tell us about attitudes toward Jewish women in Renaissance Italy among the wealthy classes and among the rabbis? And, what meaning—if any—ought we assign to the fact that someone at a later point erased the names of the patrons from the title pages of the books?

Both the silver casket and these prayer books were objects intended for use by women. Introducing gender into the study of Jewish history is one way of including alternative voices and extending the scope of our inquiry from high or learned culture to the culture of everyday life. These objects suggest a cultural matrix for Italian Jewish women in the Renaissance that may have differed significantly from that of men of the time, but also from that of Jewish women in other periods and places. The woman who commissioned the prayer book was clearly educated enough to read Hebrew, as was the woman who owned the casket. Such details allow us to reconstruct at least some aspects of Jewish women's lives and thus to portray Jewish culture as much more diverse and heterogeneous than one might conclude from a study of rabbis or other learned men. Another example is the rich body of literature, written in Yiddish, that provided women with private prayers *(tehines)* about issues, such as the three cardinal commandments or conception and childbirth, specifically germane to their lives.[29]

Cultures of the Jews is therefore shaped by a broad definition of culture. As we have seen, this approach challenges such conventional distinctions as "unity" versus "diversity," "textual continuity" versus "cultural ruptures," "monotheism" versus "polytheism," "isolation" versus "assimilation," "golden ages" versus "dark ages," and "elite" versus "popular." Jewish history consisted of all these centripetal and centrifugal forces, and each coexisted with its opposite, to the point where the very opposition between them appears artificial and overly simplistic. More than just expanding our story to include what has been neglected, we will question these very dichotomies.

There is yet one more dichotomy that we need to examine: the opposition between "Homeland" and "Exile." The belief in a "Promised Land," the Land of Israel, lies at the core of the biblical narrative and subsequent Jewish thought; it is this belief, in barely secularized form, that animated the Zionist movement in its reestablishment of the Jewish state. Yet the Bible itself oscillates between the two. The Book of Genesis starts with exile from the Garden of Eden, and Abraham, almost immediately after arriving in the Land of Israel, goes "down" to Egypt. Exile and Return are the recurring motifs of the biblical text.[30] And, as we shall see repeatedly in this work, the Jews of many Diaspora communities, while holding onto the messianic vision of return to the Land, often saw in their own countries a remembrance of an ideal past and a taste of that messianic future: so it was that the Lithuanian Jews referred to Vilna as "the Jerusalem of Lithuania." So, too, the Jews of the Greco-Roman Diaspora, Sassanian Babylonia, Muslim al-Andalus, Christian Spain, and contemporary America seemed to feel at home in exile.

Even the modern return of the Jews to their historic homeland and the restoration of Jewish political sovereignty have not definitively resolved this dialectic between Land and Exile. The "national poet" of the Zionist movement, Ḥayyim Naḥman Bialik, perhaps the last person we might expect to endorse life in exile, described in an essay written in 1922 what he called the "Jewish dualism" of expansion and contraction, wandering and returning. He concludes with a startling prophecy:

After wandering for thousands of years and after endless changes and re-evaluations . . . after influencing the whole world and being influenced by it, we are now, for the third or fourth time, once again returning to our land. And here we are destined to fashion a culture sevenfold greater and richer than any we have heretofore created or absorbed. And who knows? Perhaps after hundreds of years we will be emboldened to make another exodus that will lead to the spreading of our spirit over the world and an assiduous striving towards glory.[31]

Rather than an end to Jewish wandering, the new nation of Israel may be only the latest phase in an eternal cycle of leaving and returning, Homeland and Diaspora. This, too, is an enduring theme in the cultural history of the Jews.

The ambiguous relationship today between Homeland and Exile, foreshadowed by Bialik, finds concrete expression in this work. For the first time, a collaborative history of the Jews includes an equal number of scholars from Israel and the Diaspora. Moreover, the lines between the two seem increasingly fuzzy. Many of the Israeli scholars were born and educated in the Diaspora (particularly the United States and Canada), while others born in Israel received their training in universities abroad. And, virtually all of the scholars currently based in the Diaspora have spent considerable periods in Israel, studying, teaching, or doing research. Jewish Studies as a field has become "globalized" and, though differences surely remain, the categories of Israel and Diaspora no longer occupy the central place in scholarly agendas they once held.

In the chapters that follow, scholars from many disciplines—archaeology, art history, ancient Near Eastern studies, cultural history, literary studies, and folklore—offer their answers to the questions raised in this introduction. Just as culture itself consists of many dimensions and facets, so there are many windows through which scholars may try to view this imprecise object of study. Instead of following one ironclad set of guidelines, each has been free to approach the subject with his or her own particular tools. The sum total of their diverse efforts constitutes a better or more approximate definition of Jewish cultures than does any one chapter.

This enterprise certainly does not exhaust its subject. For every major cultural formation discussed in these pages, a multitude of other approaches and other sources would be equally legitimate. Similarly, the reader should not expect to find an encyclopedia, with entries for every Jewish culture. We have attempted to identify the most significant and original cultures, often by subsuming regional variations under broader headings. The authors were also encouraged to frame their chapters with specific examples—a text, an artifact, or an anecdote—and undertake a "thick description" of them, as with our example of the Italian silver casket.

The questions we have posed in this study of Jewish culture are hardly new, and, indeed, every generation of scholars has asked them in one form or another. But the answers have not always been the same, because every generation weaves its image of the past out of the cloth of its present. In the past half-century, there have been two great, multivolume collaborative histories of the Jews, each a product of its own time and place. In the late 1940s, Louis Finkelstein of the Jewish Theological Seminary edited *The Jews: Their History, Religion and Contribution to Civilization*. The third volume of Finkelstein on the contribution of Jews to civilization takes an expansive view of culture, but it is primarily concerned with what its title suggests—the Jewish *contribution*—rather than with the mutual interaction between Jewish and non-Jewish cultures. Finkelstein makes it clear that he believes that the primary Jewish contribution to civilization was in religion, a view that dominates his understanding of Jewish culture and reflects rather accurately the self-definition of American Jewry in the late 1940s.

In the late 1960s, Haim Hillel Ben-Sasson edited *A History of the Jewish People*, three volumes written exclusively by scholars from the Hebrew University, published first in Hebrew and subsequently in English. The Ben-Sasson volumes are characterized by a distinct, if muted, nationalist teleology, reflecting the post-1967 atmosphere in Israel. Thus, Shmuel Ettinger, who wrote the chapter on modern Jewish history, concludes with the State of Israel. The authors emphasize the historical continuity of Jewish identity. In Ettinger's words: "One cannot overemphasize the tremendous force of historical continuity and of enduring conscious historical existence.... The Holocaust and the State of Israel are indisputable testimony to the fact that ... the communal and national uniqueness [of the Jews] has never ceased to be significant." Although some of the authors, notably Ben-Sasson in his medieval chapter, investigate cultural interaction, the work as a whole conveys a sense of Jewish difference and isolation.

Both of these collaborative histories were notably deficient in their treatment of the Ladino-speaking Diaspora and, especially in the modern period, of the Jewish communities of North Africa and the Middle East. Despite chapters on the Jews of Arab lands in the Middle Ages, these works were highly Eurocentric, reflecting the dominant intellectual tendencies of their times. This is a deficiency we have taken pains to correct. For the first time, these Jewish communities receive their due, a corrective that is particularly important given the growing influence of North African and Middle Eastern Jews on the politics and culture of the State of Israel.

The present work is also the product of a particular time. Ours is a self-conscious age, when we raise questions about old ideologies and "master" narratives and no longer assume as unchanging or monolithic categories like "nation" and "religion." Teleologies, whether national or religious, are harder to sustain, just as categories that were foundational for previous generations, such as Homeland and Exile, have lost their ideological edge. We have become acutely aware—and critical—of how we use these categories to construct the past; instead of accepting them as immutable and given, we try to see them too as products of historical contexts. We are conscious, perhaps more than any earlier generation, of how our contemporary culture and commitments influence the ways we view our historical subjects.

Our silver casket may once again demonstrate this point. As cultural historians, we are aware that we are viewing an object not intended for public display, which is its fate today in the Israel Museum. Perhaps the nudity of the woman portrayed in her ritual bath excited no curiosity or controversy when it was made precisely because the casket was intended for private, female use. Just as the Hebrew lettering on the lid may have been used to hide the number and type of the woman's linens from her Christian servants, so the casket itself, despite its revealing nakedness, is a kind of repository of secrets. We are like voyeurs peering into a world not our own and asking questions that are peculiarly modern. The cultural historian cannot ignore the gap that separates his or her investigations from the lived reality of those people—educated and uneducated, rich and poor, male and female—who have left us such artifacts. Our concerns may not have been theirs.

The task of the contemporary historian of Jewish culture is, then, paradoxical: to find commonalties between the past and present, but also to preserve all that is different and strange in that past. The singularly modern questions of Jewish identity—what is it that defines a Jew and where are the borders between what is and is not Jewish—preoccupy each of us as we reconstruct the variety of Jewish cultures. What it meant to be a Jew in biblical Canaan, Hellenistic Alexandria, sixteenth-century Poland, or nineteenth-century Morocco was certainly not the same as what it is today, nor were the questions we pose necessarily their questions. But by refracting our study of cultures past through such modern questions, those cultures appear at once more familiar *and* more alien. And by looking in the mirrors of the many and diverse Jewish cultures over the centuries, we may hope to see reflections of who the Jews were, what they are now, and, perhaps, some shards that they may use in fashioning what they will become.

NOTES

1. For a description of the casket, see Mordecai Narkis, "An Italian Silver Casket of the Fifteenth Century," *Journal of the Warburg and Courtland Institutes* 21 (1958): 288–95. See also Vivian Mann, *Gardens and Ghettos: The Art of Jewish Life in Italy* (Berkeley, 1989), 309–10; Elias Bickerman, "Symbolism in the Dura Synagogue," *Harvard Theological Review* 58, no. 1 (1965): 131–32; and Shalom Sabar, "Bride, Heroine and Courtesan: Images of the Jewish Woman in Hebrew Manuscripts of the Renaissance in Italy," *Proceedings of the Tenth World Congress of Jewish Studies*, Division D, vol. 2 (1990): 67.

2. The source for these commandments is m. Shabbat 2.6, which presents them negatively by stating that women die in childbirth for transgressions of these three laws. It should be noted that men are also subject to these laws. See Rachel Biale, *Women and Jewish Law* (New York, 1984), 40.

3. See Clifford Geertz, *The Interpretation of Cultures* (New York, 1973). For some critiques and expansions of Geertz, see Sherry B. Ortner, ed., *The Fate of Culture: Geertz and Beyond* (Berkeley, 1999), and James Clifford, *The Predicament of Culture: Twentieth-Century Ethnography, Literature, and Art* (Cambridge, Mass., 1988).

4. See Michel de Certeau, *The Practice of Everyday Life,* trans. Steven Rendall (Berkeley, 1984), and Michel de Certeau, *Culture in the Plural,* trans. Tom Conley (Minneapolis, 1997).

5. *Mekhilta,* Bo, parasha 5. The saying appears in a number of places in various forms in rabbinic literature: e.g., *Leviticus Rabba* 32.5; *Numbers Rabba* 13.19 and 20.22; Song of Songs Rabba 24.25, and *Tanhuma,* Balak 16.

6. For one view emphasizing a kind of mystical Judaism, see Erwin Goodenough, *Jewish Symbols in the Greco-Roman Period,* vols. 1–13 (New York, 1953–68). For a critique of Goodenough, see Bickerman, "Symbolism."

7. See Saul Lieberman, *Greek in Jewish Palestine,* 2d ed. (New York, 1965).

8. M. Avodah Zara 3.4. See the discussion of this problem in the chapter by Eric Meyers in this volume.

9. Roberto Bonfil has made a cogent case for this position in his *Jewish Life in Renaissance Italy,* trans. Anthony Oldcorn (Berkeley, 1994).

10. See Cecil Roth, *Jewish Art: An Illustrated History,* rev. ed. (London, 1971); Therese and Mendel Metzger, *Jewish Life in the Middle Ages: Illuminated Jewish Manuscripts of the Thirteenth to the Sixteenth Centuries* (New York, 1982); and Kalman Bland, *The Artless Jew: Medieval and Modern Affirmations and Denials of the Visual* (Princeton, 2000).

11. Ruth Mellinkoff has argued recently that such depictions of Jews were inserted by anti-Jewish Christian illuminators. See her *Antisemitic Hate Signs in Hebrew Illuminated Manuscripts from Medieval Germany* (Jerusalem, 1999). It seems hard to believe that the Jewish patrons who commissioned such works would have accepted these depictions if they were truly antisemitic. Nevertheless, Mellinkoff is convincing, following other Jewish art historians, in showing that there was no rabbinic prohibition on portraying the human face that might have led to the use of animal heads. The mystery remains unsolved.

12. See Stanley Ferber, "Micrography: A Jewish Art Form," *Journal of Jewish Art* 3–4 (1977): 12–24.

13. For a recent example, see Susan Ackerman, *Under Every Green Tree: Popular Religion in Sixth Century Judah* (Atlanta, 1992).

14. F. Y. Baer, "The Religious-Social Tendency of 'Sepher Hasidim' " (Hebrew), *Zion* 3, no. 1 (1938): 1–50.

15. See Marc Michael Epstein's fascinating study, *Dreams of Subversion in Medieval Jewish Art and Literature* (University Park, Pa., 1997).

16. See Martin Buber, *Die Schrift und ihre Verdeutschung* (Berlin, 1936), which contains essays by both Buber and Rosenzweig on the Bible translation.

17. See the collection of essays edited by Bill Ashcroft, Gareth Griffiths, and Helen Tiffin, *The Post-Colonial Studies Reader* (London, 1995).

18. See my "Confessions of an Historian of Jewish Culture," *Jewish Social Studies,* n.s. 1, no. 1 (Fall 1994): 40–51.

19. See an especially striking case in the *Bird's Head Haggadah:* one of the pages illustrating the "Dayanu" shows the Israelites in the desert collecting manna and receiving the law.

All have birds' heads on which are perched typical "Jew's hats." See the reproduction in Bazalel Narkis, *Hebrew Illuminated Manuscripts* (Jerusalem, 1969), 96–97. Another example in which human faces are shown with at least one figure wearing a "Jew's hat" at a Passover Seder is the *Darmstadt Haggadah* in ibid., 126–27. For a pictorial collection of such headgear, see "Head, Covering of the" in the *Encyclopaedia Judaica*. See also Raphael Straus, "The Jewish Hat as Cultural History," *Jewish Social Studies* 4 (1942): 59.

20. See Ivan G. Marcus, *Rituals of Childhood: Jewish Culture and Acculturation in the Middle Ages* (New Haven, Conn., 1996), as well as his chapter in Volume II of this work.

21. See Yisrael Yuval, "Vengeance and Damnation, Blood and Defamation: From Jewish Martyrdom to Blood Libel Accusations" (Hebrew), *Zion* 58, no. 1 (1993): 33–90.

22. See Elliott Horowitz, "The Rite to Be Reckless: On the Perpetration and Interpretation of Purim Violence," *Poetics Today* 15, no. 1 (Spring 1994): 9–54. See also his *Reckless Rites* (Princeton, 2001).

23. See David Nirenberg, *Communities of Violence: Persecution of Minorities in the Middle Ages* (Princeton, 1996).

24. See Ilana Pardes, *The Biography of Ancient Israel: National Narratives in the Bible* (Berkeley, 2000), and her chapter in this volume.

25. See the discussion in b. Ketubot 61a.

26. See Dominick LaCapra, *Rethinking Intellectual History: Texts, Contexts, Language* (Ithaca, N.Y., 1983), 116–17. LaCapra suggests that the relationship between ideas and context ought to be drawn using theories of intertextuality, since even the context is itself composed of texts.

27. Carlo Ginzburg, *The Cheese and the Worms: The Cosmos of a Sixteenth-Century Miller*, trans. John and Ann Tedeschi (Baltimore, Md., 1980).

28. The manuscripts are, respectively, 1478=JTSA MIC. 8255 (ms. JMC 16), 5b and 1480=JNUL 8°5492, 7a. See David Ruderman, *The World of a Renaissance Jew: The Life and Thought of Abraham Ben Mordecai Farissol* (Cincinnati, 1981), appendix, and Shalom Sabar, "Bride, Heroine and Courtesan," 68. I thank Sabar for drawing the text from the Jewish Theological Seminary Library to my attention. My student Yoel Kahn will be publishing his own study of these manuscripts in a work on the history of the morning blessings. Based on his examination of the manuscripts, he has concluded that the one from 1478 was written by Farissol, whereas the new version of the words in the one from 1480 was written in a different hand.

29. See Chava Weissler, *Voices of the Matriarchs* (Boston, 1998).

30. See Arnold Eisen, *Galut* (Bloomington, Ind., 1986).

31. Translation in Ḥayyim Naḥman Bialik, *Revealment and Concealment: Five Essays* (Jerusalem, 2000), 43–44. See also the afterword by Zali Gurevitch in which he describes Bialik as "the poet of exile."

CULTURES
OF THE JEWS

Volume I:
Mediterranean Origins

INTRODUCTION

DAVID BIALE

When and where does the first Jewish culture begin? Two deceptively simple questions whose answers remain shrouded in the mists of ancient Near Eastern history. Our sources are the Hebrew Bible and archaeological evidence, but these sources raise as many questions as they answer. The earliest mention of ancient Israel appears on a stele or victory monument of the Pharaoh Merneptah in the second half of the thirteenth century B.C.E. There the pharaoh boasts: "Israel is laid waste, his seed is no more." An inauspicious beginning for a people that was to last over three millennia after their proclaimed extermination! From this point on, the archaeological record becomes murky: we possess no external evidence of the Exodus from Egypt and ambiguous evidence for the subsequent conquest of Canaan. The archaeologists tell us that the material culture of ancient Israel differed little, if at all, from that of the Canaanites who inhabited the coastal plain; some have concluded that the Israelites *were* Canaanites who lived in the hill country between the Jordan River and the Mediterranean. According to this hotly contested opinion, the Exodus was a myth, because the Israelites never left the Land of Canaan.

And what of the Bible, which tells the familiar story of Abraham, whom God commands to leave Ur of the Chaldeans and go to the land of the Canaanites, whose possession he is promised? Does this mean that the "children of Israel," as they would later call themselves after the second name of Abraham's grandson, Jacob, originated in the fertile plains of Mesopotamia? The stories of the three patriarchs and their four wives certainly suggest such a connection. But then the Bible offers contradictory evidence. A gap of 400 (or, in another tradition, 430) years separates the Genesis stories from the emergence of the Israelite nation from slavery in Egypt. Why does the book that the Israelites themselves wrote—based, no doubt, on ancient traditions—contain no trace of memory for such a long period? Could it be that the stories of the patriarchs and matriarchs were independent tales added later to give a new and, even worse, a "slave" nation some venerable antiquity? The Exodus story itself admits that the nation left Egypt as a "mixed multitude" (Exodus 12:38), the very opposite of an ethnic or tribal group with a common lineage. Much later, the prophet Ezekiel would

thunder: "By origin and birth you are from the land of the Canaanites—your father was an Amorite and you're a Hittite" (Ezekiel 16:3).

These texts raise as many questions as do the archaeologists. Why would a nation preserve as canonical admissions of such a tainted genealogy? If the Exodus
was a myth, why would a nation invent such a disreputable story of slave origins?
If all nations are "imagined communities," ancient Israel has left us evidence of a
very conflicted imagination. Certain real historical events may well underlie
what some dismiss as literary myth. History and literature cannot be so easily
separated.

If, additionally, a culture is determined by the borders between "us" and
"them," the culture of biblical Israel was very poorly defended, because, even as
the nation was commanded to eradicate its neighbors ("you must doom them to
destruction: grant them no terms and give them no quarter"—Deuteronomy
7:2), both persons and ideas from those neighbors persistently appear and reappear in the Bible. An example is Uriah the Hittite, David's general and the first
husband of Bathsheba, who, once David had Uriah killed in battle, became
David's wife and was the mother of King Solomon. What was a Hittite doing as a
general in David's army if, as Deuteronomy 7 prescribes, the Hittites should
have been exterminated? Why does he have a name that suggests that he worships the God of Israel? And David himself, the great-grandson of a Moabite
woman, would also, according to a Deuteronomic law, have been forbidden
to enter "the assembly of God." These examples suggest that the boundaries
between Israelites and non-Israelites in the Land of Canaan were evidently
much fuzzier than we have traditionally believed. Categories of "ethnicity"
and "religion" may have meant something very different then than they mean
to us now.

To compound our difficulties, the biblical text itself—or, better, the disparate
and manifold collection of texts that we call the Bible—was not edited into the
form we have it until much later than the events it narrates. Even if, as seems
very likely, it was based on much older sources, it was not until after the destruction of the First Temple in 586 B.C.E., the Babylonian Exile, and the building
of the Second Temple (probably mid-fifth century B.C.E.) that the texts were
compiled and canonized. The Bible as we know it is a document of the Second Temple period, but exactly when it was redacted remains a mystery. So,
to speak of the culture of ancient or biblical Israel immediately raises the question of whether we are talking about the *actual* culture of those Israelites
described in the Bible, or, conversely, about how their culture was *imagined* by
later generations.

Since no single answer to this question will suffice, the first two chapters of
Volume I approach the task with different sets of tools. Ilana Pardes takes the

first six books of the Bible (the Torah plus Joshua) as the narrative expression of ancient Israel's history, regardless of when it was written or of how many sources it was composed. It is this collective biography that defines the Israelite nation—as well as the later Jewish people—but it is filled with conflict and contradiction. Ronald Hendel comes to a similar conclusion but from a consideration of ancient Israel in its Near Eastern context, at once an organic part of its neighborhood but also insistent on its uniqueness. Israelite and Canaanite cultures overlapped greatly, which was perhaps the reason that the Bible insisted so strongly on separating them.

The redaction of the Bible took place during the period when the Israelites became known as Jews, the inhabitants of *Yahud,* or Judaea. Who exactly were these Judaeans? The Second Temple period begins with Ezra the Scribe, who proclaims a ban on intermarriage between those who returned from the Babylonian Exile and the "peoples of the land." Some of these peoples were undoubtedly non-Israelites, but others, such as the Samaritans, believed themselves to be descendants of ancient Israel and worshipped, as their few surviving members do even today, the God of Israel. For Ezra, however, a Jew was a descendant of those who had gone into exile and returned, and he permitted none of the easy boundary crossing that evidently had taken place in the period of the First Temple. Ezra proclaimed an ethnic or even biological definition of the Jews, as a "holy seed" *(zera kodesh).* Yet his attempt at ethnic "purity" was honored more in the breach, because many who remained in exile or Diaspora, whether in Babylonia or Egypt, also considered themselves to be Jews. And a few centuries later, the Hasmonaean or Maccabean kingdom conquered and converted various peoples to the Jewish religion/nation. In fact, the evolution of a strict procedure of conversion probably began at this time and was finally codified by the rabbis in the second century C.E.

Thus, to be a Jew in antiquity involved elaborate juggling of religious, ethnic, and political affirmations. It meant that one worshipped the God who, unlike all the other gods, had no visual representation (which led some ancient "antisemites" to hold that the Jews were atheists, since their god could not be seen). It meant that one considered oneself an ethnic descendant of the ancient tribes of Israel even if, like King Herod, one's real ancestors were Edomites. And it meant one was a subject of a Jewish government in Jerusalem, though not if one lived outside of the Land of Israel (whose very borders, then no less than today, were never stable). The complexity of Jewish identity in the Second Temple period, and even later, rivals that of the modern age.

It was the encounter with the powerful culture of Hellenism that challenged the Jews to define themselves culturally. Unlike other imperialistic powers in the ancient world, the Greeks created a truly cosmopolitan or, in today's terms, a globalized culture: it was not necessary to be an ethnic Greek to partake of and identify with this culture. The process by which the Jews met this challenge was no less complex than the way they interacted with the earlier Canaanite cultures. Despite their own professions and the views of some outsiders, the Jews did not isolate themselves from this world culture but rather used its very riches to cultivate their singularity. Greece and Rome were, to be sure, at times the Jews' political and military enemies, but, culturally, there were startling similarities between them. Like the Romans, the Jews nourished a story of their origins that involved a lengthy journey, led by a hero, that eventually brought them to a new land that was also their ancestral patrimony. Like the Greeks, the Jews considered themselves an ethnic group, clearly distinguishable from the *barbaroi* (barbarians). But like the Greeks after Alexander's conquest of the Near East, and like the Romans later, they did not believe that their culture could only flourish on its native soil. Just as Hellenism and Roman culture might be transplanted to the far reaches of those empires, so the Jews, without an empire, scattered the seeds of their religion and culture throughout the Mediterranean basin, in part as they themselves migrated but also in part (the extent of which remains contested) by proselytism.

Once again, two chapters take up these themes: Erich Gruen considers the vast literature that the Jews produced primarily in Greek, and Eric Meyers weaves archaeological evidence from Palestine in the Persian to the Greco-Roman periods with the Hebrew and Aramaic literature produced by priests, rabbis, and other literati. In both material and literary culture, the confrontation with Hellenism produced new forms of Jewish culture and identity. The emphasis here is on the plural—*forms*—since the period was one of great pluralism, even factionalism, as dissident groups, such as the Dead Sea or Qumran communities, challenged the priestly establishment in Jerusalem, and as Diaspora communities, though still tied religiously to Jerusalem, experimented with their own interpretations of tradition. These new interpretations were not so much *influenced* by Greco-Roman culture as they were *part and parcel* of that culture.

It is frequently assumed that, with the destruction of the Second Temple by the Romans during the Great Jewish Revolt of 66–70 C.E., the fragmentation and diversity of the earlier period came to an end as the rabbis consolidated their hold on the definition of Jewishness. Although the destruction of the Temple was an event of enormous religious and political consequence, its cultural significance is less clear. The culture of the "rabbinic" period in Palestine continued to be dominated by Hellenism, and it did not lose its contentious diversity. The very term "rabbinic period" must be set in quotation marks, for it is only in historical hindsight that the rabbis loom so large. For many centuries, first under pagan Rome and then under Byzantine Christianity, the culture of the Jews reflected active interaction with both of these cultures. As in the Second Temple period, the question of what it meant to be a Jew might be answered in a variety of ways, despite the attempts by the rabbis to standardize identity.

Three chapters take up the diversity of Jewish culture in the period of Late Antiquity. Oded Irshai considers how the Jews of Palestine, still a sizable population, especially in the Galilee, responded to living for the first time under Christian rule, and how the boundaries between Judaism and Christianity continued to be quite porous. Isaiah Gafni takes up the culture of the Jews of Babylonia, an ancient community, as we have already noted, but one that began to feel a sense of its own intellectual and religious authority as the Palestinian Jewish community declined under Roman and Byzantine domination. It was these two communities that produced the two versions of the Talmud, the Babylonian and Jerusalem (or Palestinian). But a full understanding of the culture of these Jews requires going beyond the views of the rabbinic elite to consider other cultural centers, such as the synagogue, or the voices of the folk, preserved in rabbinic literature, and for whom rabbinic teachings may not yet have been normative. As an example of such an "alternative" Jewish culture that flourished far from the orbit of the Babylonian and Palestinian rabbis, Reuven Firestone treats the Jews of Arabia, the first to come into contact and confrontation with emerging Islam in the seventh century. Here, too, Jewish identity turns out to have been an intricate mixture of tribalism and religion, and Jewish culture was influenced by and also influenced that of the new Muslim religion.

A certain thematic unity therefore links the earliest with the latest Jewish cultures discussed in this volume, as the Jews in various contexts defined how they were different by using the very language and practices of their surroundings. Yet, unlike other ancient ethnic groups, the Jews had some singular qualities: although many others combined national and religious components in their identities, only the Jews—like Christians and Muslims—eventually came to worship a God who negated the existence of other gods. And the Jews developed a unique procedure for conversion to the Jewish *ethnos*, a possibility unknown to the ancient pagans, for whom an ethnic identity could not be adopted, even if one paid obeisance to a foreign god. "Jewishness" (an ethnic identity) came increasingly to be identified with "Judaism" (a religious credo), the latter probably developing in dialogue with nascent Christianity and leaving its mark on early Islam. Jewish culture at the end of our period thus made major contributions to the politics of ancient identity as Christians and Muslims came to dominate the Mediterranean basin, a domination that concludes Volume I and becomes central to Volume II.

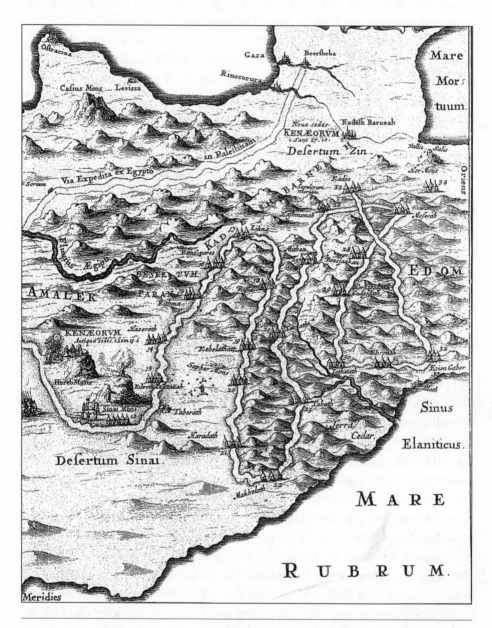

The map of wandering by Thomas Fuller, 1650. Detail.
(Courtesy Ilana Pardes)

IMAGINING THE BIRTH
OF ANCIENT ISRAEL:

National Metaphors in the Bible

ILANA PARDES

The Bible begins not with the culture of the Hebrews but with the origins of culture as such. The initial concern with the origin of civilization is already evident in the story of the Garden of Eden, where Eve and Adam acquire the first taste of "knowledge," but it is only in the account of the bold building of the Tower of Babel, East of Eden, that we get a fuller consideration of human culture. Humankind was once one, we are told, and "everyone on earth had the same language and the same words" (Genesis 11:1). But this era of cultural unity does not last for long. One day the people say to each other "Come, let us build us a city, and a tower with its top in the sky, to make a name for ourselves; else we shall be scattered all over the world" (11:4). In response to this challenge against heaven, God shatters the builders' dream of grandeur, confounds their language, and scatters them in all directions. Culture, however, is not destroyed. Rather, it assumes a different form. From now on its distinguishing mark is diversity and dispersion. From now on, its distinct site becomes the nation.

Of the many nations that "branch out" in the vast expanses of the earth, Israel is singled out. In the episode following the Tower of Babel, God demands that Abraham leave his birthplace (Ur of the Chaldeans) and go forth *(lekh lekha)* to the land shown to him. There, God assures him, "I will make of you a great nation, and I will bless you; I will make your name great" (Genesis 12:2). Abraham's migration to Canaan offers a new departure. Whereas the sinful homogeneous community of Babel failed, Abraham's descendants, the people God has chosen from a multitude of peoples, seem to hold much promise, destined as they are (unlike the builders of the Tower) to acquire a "great name."[1] The primary exile of the first patriarch, his capacity to part from his cultural origins, is construed as an essential rift, a prerequisite for the rise of the nation. Later, in Exodus, the people as a whole will follow a similar route, moving out of Egypt, wandering in the desert, and fashioning the cultural contours of the nation on their way to the Promised Land.

Dispersion and exile, however, do not lead to clear-cut borders between cultures. Languages intersect in unexpected ways. The very name "Babel," which commemorates the primary linguistic splitting, is also a cross-cultural product. Its meaning in Akkadian is presumably "the gate to the gods" *(bab iley)*, but in the course of the biblical story it is Hebraized via a pun when it is linked to the Hebrew root *blbl* (to confuse). Perhaps this interpretation of "Babel" is an attempt to mock the pretentious temples of Mesopotamia: the tower that was meant to lead to the gods leads only to confusion.[2]

But what turns out to be far more confusing is the lack of clear demarcation between the chosen and the non-chosen. As the history of the children of Israel unfolds, we discover that the rebellious quality of primeval culture does not dissipate once we move into the realm of the chosen ones. Quite the contrary: rebellion is one of the salient features of the chosen nation. The Israelites do not venture to construct brick temples whose tops reach heaven, but their idolatrous cravings betray a similar tendency to transgress sacred boundaries.

The question of national identity—the attempt to fathom the entangled relations between Israel and God, between Israel and other nations—is one of the most resonant and unresolvable questions in the Bible. In tackling it, the biblical text relies not on philosophical contemplation but rather on narrative. More specifically, it offers a narrative in which the nation is personified extensively. Any attempt to understand the history of the children of Israel, to fashion a conception of national identity, to grasp communal motives and fantasies, collective memories and oblivions, the Bible seems to suggest, requires a plunge into the intricate twists and turns of the individual life.

The nation—particularly in Exodus and Numbers—is not an abstract detached concept but rather a grand character with a distinct voice (represented at times in a singular mode) who moans and groans, is euphoric at times, complains frequently, and rebels against Moses and God time and again. Israel has a life story, a biography of sorts.[3] It was conceived in the days of Abraham; its miraculous birth took place with the Exodus, the parting of the Red Sea; then came a long period of childhood and restless adolescence in the wilderness; and finally adulthood was approached with the conquest of Canaan.

To be sure, a collective character is necessarily more heterogeneous and less predictable. The Pentateuch's account of national formation resists fixed definitions of the various phases in the nation's life cycle. Roughly speaking, chronology is maintained, and yet images of birth, youth, initiation, and suckling intermingle throughout. Thus, the distinct manifestation of national suckling appears only in Numbers 11, where Moses likens the people to a suckling infant in the wilderness, long after the grand-scale initiation at Sinai. But, after all, such boundaries are never that clear in individual biographies either. Infantile dreams may linger on and initiation is rarely exhausted in one rite.

National literatures were not common in the ancient world. Israel's preoccupation with its reason for being is exceptional in the ancient Near East.[4] In Greece and particularly in Rome, however, narratives concerning national origins are equally important.[5] Israel's history bears resemblance to the Roman one. It too involves a divine promise, individuation from a major civilization, a quest for lost roots, a long journey to what is construed as the land of the forefathers, and a gory conquest.[6] What makes the Bible unique is the extent to which the nation is dramatized. In the *Aeneid,* by way of comparison, the plot revolves round Aeneas. The wanderings between Troy and the promised new land are primarily Aeneas's wanderings: the people remain a rather pale foil. They engage in no conflict—either with Aeneas or the gods—that would grant them access to the central stage. The biblical text is significantly different in its rendering of national drama. Israel is a protagonist whose moves and struggles determine the map—so much so that 40 years of wanderings in the desert are added to the itinerary as a result of the people's protest against the official preference of Canaan over Egypt.

The fashioning of Israel as a character is a forceful unifying strategy, but the metaphor does not yield a homogeneous account of national formation. The biblical text reveals points of tension between different traditions regarding the nation's history and character. Even the nation's sexual identity is not stable. Although the Pentateuch shapes a male character, referring to the people as *am* (singular masculine noun), the Prophets, more often than not, represent Israel as female, using "Jerusalem" or "Zion" (feminine nouns) as alternative designations.

This essay focuses on the intricacies of national imagination in the Pentateuch, and as such it is concerned with the fashioning of a male character who is marked as God's firstborn son.[7] Double personification is at stake—of God and the nation—creating a familial link between the two.[8] If Rome's sacred origin is assured through the divine blood of its founding fathers—Aeneas is Venus's son, and Romulus and Remus are the offspring of Mars—in the case of Israel, the nation as a whole, metaphorically speaking, is God's son.[9] On sending Moses to Pharaoh to deliver the people, God proclaims: "Israel is My first-born son. I have said to you [Pharaoh], 'Let My son go' " (Exodus 4:22–23). The priority given to Israel by the Father represents a translation into national terms of the reversal of the primogeniture law—a phenomenon so central in the lives of the patriarchs. The late-born nation that came to the stage after all its neighbors had assumed their historical roles is elevated by God to the position of the chosen firstborn.[10]

Israel is a chosen nation, God's nation, but the reason for its chosen-ness remains obscure. It does not succeed in following traditional norms of male heroism, nor does it become an exemplary nation with high moral and religious standards. The more mature Israel, in the plains of Moab, on the threshold of Canaan, is far more established a community than the nascent nation on the way out of Egypt, but this by no means suggests that biblical historiography relies on the principle of progress. Whereas in the initial stages of the journey the children of Israel worship a Golden Calf in a carnivalesque feast, at the last station, just before crossing the Jordan river, they "cling" to Baal Peor (under the influence of Moabite women), adopting Canaanite religious practices with much enthusiasm. The Song of Moses, with its synoptic presentation of Israel's history, regards the nation as an ungrateful son whose conduct fails to improve over time: "Do you thus requite the Lord, O dull and witless people? Is not He the Father who created you, fashioned you and made you endure!" (Deuteronomy 32:6). Instead of appreciating God's vigilance, Moses claims, once the nation "grew fat" it used its new powers to "kick" (Deuteronomy 32:15).

What is most fascinating in the primary biography of ancient Israel is the ambivalence that lies at its very base, an ambivalence that is expressed so poignantly through the intense struggles between the Father (or Moses) and His people. The nation is both the chosen son and the rebel son, and accordingly its relationship with the Father is at once intimate and strained.

The fictional quality of the struggle between God and the nation does not preclude the historicity of the text. Israel's beginning is situated in historical times—in the days of the Exodus—rather than in a mythical "in illo tempore."[11] Similarly, God defines Himself, at Sinai and elsewhere, as the one who brought Israel out of Egypt—not as the Creator of primeval times. Even at moments when the biography of ancient Israel relies on mythical materials—primarily, on the myth of the birth of the hero and the myth of the hero's return—these are inextricably connected with a historiographical drive to record memorable past events and question their meaning. In the Bible, history and literature go hand in hand, more explicitly than in modern historiography, which is why it serves as a paradigmatic case for the examination of the narrative base of national constructions.[12]

NATIONAL BIRTH

The metaphor of birth is probably the most resonant anthropomorphic image in national narratives from antiquity to modern times. In fact, it is so resonant one tends to forget that nations are not born literally but are, rather, imagined in these terms. Every nation, however, has its own birth story, or birth stories. The book of Exodus provides an intriguingly complex representation of Israel's birth in keeping with the preliminary imaginings of the nation in Genesis. The opening verses of Exodus 1 make clear that God's reiterated promises to Abraham, Isaac, and Jacob—the grand national annunciation scenes of Genesis—are finally realized. The descendants of Jacob, whose names are listed solemnly, multiply at an uncanny pace and turn into a "mighty" nation: the nation of the "children of Israel."[13] "Israel" for the first time is not merely Jacob's second, elevated, name but rather a collective designation of a burgeoning community that "fills" the land. But then we discover that God's darker prophecy, in the covenant of the parts (Genesis 15:13), is equally fulfilled: Israel is born in a prolonged exile, against Pharaonic bondage.

Representing the birth of a nation is not a simple task. The imagining of this dramatic event in Exodus is facilitated by the interweaving of two biographies: the story of the birth of Moses, and that of the nation.[14] The fashioning of Israel as character, here as elsewhere, is inseparable from a complementary narrative strategy: the marking of individuals whose histories are paradigmatic. The nation's life story, in other words, is modeled in relation to the biographies of select characters.[15] Abraham, whose departure from Ur serves as prefiguration of the nation's exodus, is only the first exemplary figure. The heterogeneity of national imagination in the Bible depends on a variety of representatives. Fragments of the biographies of Isaac, of Jacob, the eponymous father, and even of Hagar, the Egyptian handmaid, whose affliction foreshadows the nation's enslavement in Egypt, are also linked in different ways to the nation's biography and take part in its construction.[16]

On the question of birth, Moses' story is of special importance. The analogy between the one and the multitude in this case is more immediate. Unlike the patriarchal biographies that pertain to a distant past and flicker over the chasm of time, Moses' birth occurs within the same historical setting. Moses is a national leader whose history blends with the history of the nation. He is one of many Hebrew babies persecuted by Pharaoh. His story, however, is marked as the exemplary account that sheds light on the collective birth story as it prefigures the deliverance of the nation as a whole from bondage.

Moses' birth story shares much in common with mythical birth stories. What characterizes the birth of a hero? The conception of the hero is usually impeded by difficulties such as abstinence or prolonged barrenness. During or before pregnancy there is a prophecy, or an oracle cautioning the father against the hero's birth; the father tries to shape a different future and gives orders to kill his new-born son; the babe is then placed in a basket or a box and delivered to the waves. Against all odds, however, the hero is saved by animals, or by lowly people, and is suckled by a female animal or by a humble woman. When full grown, he discovers his royal parents, takes revenge on his father, and, recognized by his people, finally achieves rank and honors.[17]

Moses' story is indeed compatible in many ways with this model: a threatened child, the exposure in the basket, the miraculous deliverance of the foundling, the two sets of parents, and the final acknowledgment of the hero's power.[18] But there is a significant difference: Moses' true parents are not the royal ones but rather the poor Hebrew slaves. At a moment of national birth, the inversion of the two sets of parents is not without significance. Moses' "true" parents are higher in rank despite their lowly position precisely because they are members of the chosen nation-to-be.

THE POLITICS OF BIRTH

The juxtaposition of Moses' story and that of the nation entails an adaptation of the myth of the birth of the hero on a national plane. Put differently, it enables the construction of a myth of the birth of the nation. Israel's birth, much like that of Moses, takes place against Pharaoh's will.

But the Israelites were fertile and prolific; they multiplied and increased greatly, so that the land was filled with them. A new king arose over Egypt who did not know Joseph. And he said to his people, "Look, the Israelite people are much too numerous for us. Let us deal shrewdly with them, so that they may not increase" (Exodus 1:9–10).

Interestingly, the expression *am beney yisrael* (the nation of the children of Israel) is first used by none other than Pharaoh. Pharaoh's anxieties over the safety of his rule enable him to perceive the rise of Israel long before the Hebrews themselves can. Intimidated by the growth of the Hebrews, Pharaoh orders that every son born shall be cast into the Nile "but let every girl live" (Exodus 1:22). Much has been written about his curious choice to get rid of the male babies alone, but with no consideration of the mythical background.[19] What is at stake here is an application of the exposure motif (a male motif to begin with) to a community of sons. Pharaoh, the ruler of the parent-nation, fears the power of a budding nation of rivals growing within Egypt. Parental anxieties—what will emerge from the teeming womb?—thus conflate with racist anxieties—will the others overbear?

Shiphrah and Puah, the two midwives whose names are associated with "beauty" (the former) and "birth sighs" (the latter), are the national correlate of Moses' female deliverers in Exodus 2.[20] Here too a curious detail in the text—the fact that two midwives are considered sufficient for a national massacre—can be explained in terms of the mythical context and the interrelations of the two biographies. The midwives, much like humble rescuers of heroes, choose to violate the king's decree and save the threatened newborns. They trick Pharaoh by telling him midwives' tales:

> So the king of Egypt summoned the midwives and said to them, "Why have you done this thing, letting the boys live?" The midwives said to Pharaoh, "Because the Hebrew women are not like the Egyptian women: they are vigorous. Before the midwife can come to them, they have given birth." (Exodus 1:18–19)

Shiphrah and Puah outwit Pharaoh by confirming his racist anxieties concerning the proliferation of the Hebrew slaves. Relying on a common racist notion, according to which the other is closer to nature, they claim that the Hebrew women need no midwives, for unlike Egyptian women, they are animal-like (ki hayot hena) and can give birth without professional help. There is an outburst of vitality out there, they seem to suggest, that cannot be yoked to the legal apparatus of the Pharaonic court. The recurrence of the term "midwife" in this brief episode—it appears seven times—highlights the power and courage of the two women.

Myth and history, however, are inseparable in this scene. The nation's birth story does not merely offer a mythical account of the rise of the nation but also a historical consideration of the concrete horrors of bondage.[21] Regulation and distortion of the process of reproduction is a mode of dehumanization that is all too well known from testimonies regarding other instances of slavery.

To reclaim birth in the context of slavery is a revolutionary act. It discloses hope for the newborn and the power to imagine a different future, one without bondage and tyranny; it means to reclaim subjecthood, to turn the birth of the oppressed into a meaningful historical event that needs to be recorded and narrated. The story of Israel's origins is one of trauma and recovery. The founding trauma in the nation's biography is bondage, the repression of birth. But then a process of recovery begins that entails the inversion of exposure from an antinatal act to a means of rescue. Yocheved casts her son into the Nile, but Moses' exposure is not meant to comply with Pharaoh's decree but rather to undo it. Similarly, the nation as a whole multiplies despite Pharaoh's tireless attempts to restrict its growth. "But the more they were oppressed, the more they increased and spread out" (1:12). The relation between affliction and growth is provocatively inverted. Pharaoh expected a reduction in the birthrate, but his harsh treatment of the Hebrews led to the opposite, to a mysterious increase.

"IN THY BLOOD LIVE"

In his explicit and rather graphic use of the metaphor of birth vis-à-vis the nation, Ezekiel sheds much light on the representation of national formation in Exodus. In a famous passage in Ezekiel 16, which relates the story of national birth, Jerusalem stands for the nation:

> As for your birth, when you were born your navel cord was not cut, and you were not bathed in water to smooth you; you were not rubbed with salt, nor were you swaddled. No one pitied you enough to do any one of these things for you out of compassion for you; on the day you were born, you were left lying, rejected, in the open field. When I passed by you and saw you wallowing in your blood, I said to you: "Live in spite of your blood." Yea, I said to you: "Live in spite of your blood." I let you grow like the plants of the field; and you continued to grow up until you attained to womanhood, until your breasts became firm and your hair sprouted. You were still naked and bare when I passed by you [again] and saw that your time for love had arrived. So I spread My robe over you and covered your nakedness. (4–8)

Israel was ruthlessly deserted by its parents at birth, soaking in blood helplessly without even receiving elementary postpartum care. The horrifying aspects of parental neglect are depicted in vivid detail. The newborn was not washed in water, her umbilical cord was not cut, her body was not salted (a practice that was apparently perceived as essential for the newborn's skin), nor was she swaddled. Then God passed by and adopted the neglected nation, adjuring Israel to live in her blood, to regard the marks of blood on her body as a source of life. What is more, He raised the nation and enabled its multiplication and growth. He provided her with the much-needed care and compassion that she lacked, washing the blood off her skin and furnishing her with excellent ornaments. Being a foundling nation is a traumatic experience but it ultimately turns out to be beneficial: it leads (as is the case in the myth of the birth of the hero) to the discovery of/by more distinguished parents and ensures the transition from rags to riches, or rather from nakedness to royal garments.

The story of the Exodus is indeed the story of Israel's rescue and adoption by a more distinguished Father who is not merely royal but divine as well. It is a Father who has the force to wash off the signs of a collective trauma, to turn a helpless late-born nation into a powerful chosen one. In Ezekiel, the adoption is construed as a marital bond between God and the nation, whereas in Exodus it entails a bond between the Father and His firstborn son.[22] In both cases the chosen-ness of Israel is defined in familial terms. The change in the representation of the nation's gender allows for a multifaceted treatment of the complex relation of Israel and God. Suffice it to say within the limited scope of this discussion that, whereas the representation of the nation as female accentuates the erotic aspect of the relationship, the father-son dyad is far more concerned with pedagogic issues as well as with the question of heroism.

REVENGE

Birth and revenge—or, rather, revenge fantasies—go hand in hand in birth myths. The hero's triumph over the "evil" father who tried to prevent his birth is a sign of utmost valor. A similar triumph may be traced in Exodus. Pharaoh, the anti-natal force with respect to both Moses and the nation, is defeated, at first by the ongoing multiplication of the Hebrews and then in a direct confrontation: the 10 plagues. Early commentators noted the gradual escalation of severity in the plagues, beginning with nuisances and pests, continuing with destruction of livestock and crops, and ending with the gravest of all—the death of human beings.

This last plague seems to represent the final push in Israel's delivery. It is the night of Passover. Pharaoh, who has refused to set the Israelites free, suffers from a symmetrical punishment. The Egyptian firstborn die while God's firstborn, Israel, is saved. The differentiation between the Egyptians and the Hebrews is now enhanced by means of blood. God demands that the children of Israel take the blood of the Paschal sacrifice and put it on the two door-posts and the lintel, where it will serve as "a sign for you: when I see the blood I will pass over you, so that no plague will destroy you when I strike the land of Egypt" (12:13).

The blood that marks the Israelites is not only apotropaic. Its location on the two side posts of the door evokes natal imagery.[23] The Israelites are delivered collectively out of the womb of Egypt. National birth, much like individual births (and all the more so in ancient times), takes place on a delicate border between life and death. It involves the transformation of blood from a signifier of death to a signifier of life. It also involves the successful opening of the womb, the prevention of the womb's turning into a grave. The term "opener of the womb" (peter reḥem) is introduced in Exodus 13:2 as a synonym for "firstborn." It appears in the depiction of the law regarding the firstborn, a law that is construed as a commemoration of the last plague: "Consecrate to Me every first-born; man and beast, the first issue of every womb among the Israelites is Mine." Although the term is not used explicitly with respect to the nation as a whole, this is precisely what is at stake in the context of the Exodus. The first opening of the womb (an act that is reminiscent of deflowering) is a unique and dangerous occurrence that requires divine vigilance. Those who do not deserve divine protection—namely, the Egyptians—find their death in the process, but Israel, God's firstborn, is consecrated as it opens the matrix.

Then comes the climactic moment of the delivery, which includes the ultimate revenge: the scene by the Red Sea.[24] Moses parts the waters at God's command. The Israelites walk upon land in the midst of the sea, and the Egyptian soldiers, who are pursuing them, drown as the waters return. The downfall of the parent nation seems total. Pharaoh, who wished to cast the Hebrew babies into the Nile, now finds his soldiers and fancy chariots sinking "like a stone" in the waters of the Red Sea.

"Did not old Pharaoh get lost, get lost, get lost in the Red Sea" marvels a famous African-American slave song. The song promises that power relations may change and conveys confidence in the possibilities of redemption. Even if the scene by the Red Sea is something of a slave fantasy—there is no evidence in Egyptian sources regarding such a defeat, nor did the great Egypt disappear from the map at this time—the importance of the moment lies in its carnivalesque spirit, in the reversal of hierarchies. The master falls and the oppressed spring to life.

From here on, time will be perceived differently. Everything will be measured in relation to the moment in which God delivered Israel from Egypt. "This month shall mark for you the beginning of the months; it shall be the first of the months of the year for you" (12:2). A new calendar is established with the birth of the nation as its point of departure. It is a revolutionary moment, a wondrous new beginning.[25] Slavery is left behind, and the intoxicating smell of freedom is in the air.

WONDER

God performs a variety of wonders in Egypt (the 10 plagues in fact are perceived as such), but the parting of the Red Sea seems to surpass them all. It marks the nation's first breath—out in the open air—and serves as a distinct reminder of the miraculous character of birth. Where there was nothing, a living creature emerges all of a sudden. If the myth of the birth of the hero accentuates the wonder of birth on an individual level, here the miracle is collective. Much like Moses, the nation is drawn out of the water against all odds. It is an intensified miracle: a wonder on a great scale. The two enormous walls of water, the ultimate breaking of the waters, and the exciting appearance of dry land all seem to represent a gigantic birth, a birth that is analogous to the creation of the world.

The parting of the waters evokes Genesis 1, and the "blast" of God's "nostrils" on the waters (Exodus 15:8) calls to mind the creation of Adam in Genesis 2:7: "The Lord God formed man from the dust of the earth. He blew into his nostrils the breath of life." Accordingly, God is defined as the "maker" of the nation *(am zu kanita)*, a term that otherwise is used only in the context of the creation (Exodus 15:16).

On witnessing this great wonder, the people as a whole burst out singing. The Song of the Sea, with its fast tempo, celebrates the singularity of the nation's miraculous delivery:

> Who is like You, O Lord, among the celestials; Who is like You, majestic in holiness, Awesome in splendor, working wonders! . . . For the horses of Pharaoh, with his chariots and horsemen, went into the sea; and the Lord turned back on them the waters of the sea; but the Israelites marched on dry ground in the midst of the sea. (15:11–19)

It is at once a breathtaking and breath-giving moment. All doubts and fears dissolve. Everything seems possible. Crossing the Red Sea is a leap of faith, a leap into life.

The birth of the nation involves a bewildering blurring of the boundaries between nature and history.[26] Nature participates in the shaping of this grand historical event, which is why the Song of the Sea is the Song of the Birth of the Nation. The sudden break in the rhythm of natural phenomena is used here to express the intense excitement of a nascent people.[27]

DIVINE MIDWIVES

Much has been written on the image of God as Warrior in the Song of the Sea in relation to other divine wars that hover in the background—above all, the crushing of the revolt of the sea by the Creator in the cosmic beginning (see Isaiah 51:9–10).[28] The image of the Warrior is indeed a central image in this song, but not the only one. God has feminine facets as well, though partially hidden.[29] Behind and against the "right hand" of the Warrior, one can detect a feminine hand: the strong magical hand of a grand Midwife drawing the newborn nation out of the depths of the sea, "the heart of the sea" (Exodus 15:8), into the world of the living, beyond the engulfing flood. God, as it were, follows in the footsteps of the two midwives who loom so large in the opening chapter of Exodus, though here the Israelites need to be rescued from the "mighty waters" of the Red Sea rather than the Nile.[30]

Ezekiel's depiction of the postpartum care that God bestows on the foundling nation reinforces the impression that the Father is something of a Midwife. The washing of the baby and the cutting of the umbilical cord were tasks usually performed by the midwife.[31] More important, they were at times, at least in Egyptian mythology, performed by divine midwives. A Middle Kingdom story records the miraculous birth of the first three kings of the Fifth Dynasty. The mother, Rudjedet, is attended at birth by four goddesses: Isis, Nephthys, Meskhenet, and Hekat. Each birth is represented in a similar manner:

> Isis placed herself before her [Rudjedet], Nephtys behind her, Hekat hastened the birth. Isis said: "Don't be so mighty in her womb, you whose name is 'Mighty.' " The child slid into her arms. . . . They washed him, having cut his navel cord, and laid him on a pillow cloth. Then Meskhenet approached him and said: "A king who will assume the kingship in this whole land."[32]

In the Bible, however, the mythical delivery is not merely that of a king but of an entire nation that is treated as if it were royal.

The fact that the Song of the Sea is sung by the women alone in the concluding lines of the scene adds yet another feminine touch to this miraculous birth. "Then Miriam the prophetess, Aaron's sister, took a timbrel in her hand, and all the women went out after her in dance with timbrels. And Miriam chanted for them: Sing to the Lord" (Exodus 15:20–21). Miriam, who stood between the reeds by the Nile watching over Moses' ark, orchestrating his deliverance, now dances by a Sea of Reeds (yam suf), with a timbrel in her hand, celebrating the redemption of the nation with an entire community of women.[33]

THE QUESTION OF NATIONAL IDENTITY

Nations may try to fashion a coherent conception of identity, or origin, to seek unity at points of clear disjunction, but their success can be only partial. The intertwined biographies of Moses and Israel poignantly disclose the difficulties in defining national identity for both the individual and the community. Moses' birth story differs from that of his heroic counterparts at another point as well. He is transferred back and forth between his Hebrew and Egyptian mothers. Yocheved places him in a basket at the Nile; he is found by Pharaoh's daughter, who then hands him back to Yocheved (believing her to be a wet nurse). Later Moses is brought back to the palace, where the princess adopts him and endows him with a name. He is raised in the palace but ultimately returns to his family and people.

The very fact that there are two sets of parents in the myth of the birth of the hero already intimates the difficulties involved in fashioning an identity. The myth addresses primary questions: Who am I? Who are my parents? Where do I come from? But the questions of origin become all the more complex when the two sets of parents pertain to two different nations. Moses' split national identity at birth will follow him for the rest of his life. When his first son is born in Midian, he chooses to name him "Gershom," saying, "I have been a stranger in a foreign land" (Exodus 2:22). His naming-speech relies on a pun that links the name "Gershom" with the word "stranger" (ger). But in what sense is Moses a stranger at this point—in relation to Midian (where Jethro's daughters regard him as an Egyptian), or Egypt (his words echo the oracular announcement of Israel's troubling future as "strangers [ger] in a land not theirs" in Genesis 15:13)?[34] Moses will devote the bulk of his life to constructing the concept of Canaan as homeland and will lead his people persistently toward the land of "milk and honey," but ultimately he will die in the wilderness, between Egypt and the Promised Land.

And the nation? Israel's lineage is far more complicated than Moses' family tree, but here too the multiple parental figures point to diverse national origins. The conflict between God and Pharaoh is but one expression of the issue. The nebulous identity of the two midwives is another case in point. Are the two midwives who deliver the Hebrew babies Egyptian or Hebrew? The problem stems from the indefinite use of the word "Hebrew" (ivriyot) in Exodus 1:16. If it is read as an adjective, then Shiphrah and Puah are Hebrew midwives. But the verse may mean that these are Egyptian midwives who specialize in delivering Hebrew women. Numerous commentators have tried to solve the problem. Thus, Josephus suggests that the king chose Egyptian midwives, assuming that they "were not likely to transgress his will." Similarly, Abarbanel claims that "they were not Hebrews but Egyptians, for how could he trust Hebrew women to put their own children to death." The midrash, on the other hand, perceived them as Hebrews and identified the two midwives with Yocheved and Miriam.[35] What these commentaries neglect to take into account is the significance of the indeterminate origin of the midwives, the extent to which the nation's story repeats the confusion about identity embedded in Moses' biography.

The children of Israel are torn between the two lands, between their deep ties to Egypt and their desire to seek another land. They were not raised in the Egyptian court, as Moses was, but nonetheless Egypt is more than just a site of trauma for them: it served, however partially, as a nurturing motherland, especially the luscious land of Goshen.

The birth of Israel entails a painful process of individuation from Egypt that is never fully resolved. Just before the parting of the Red Sea, God promises the children of Israel that they shall see the Egyptians no more (14:13). But the drowning of their pursuers does not lead to the effacement of Israel's strong longings for the land of Egypt. National identity is thus poised on the brink of a loss of identity.[36]

THE EMERGENCE OF THE NATIONAL VOICE: INTERNAL ANTI-NATAL FORCES

The nation's first words are delivered on the way out of Egypt. On seeing the Egyptian chariots pursuing them, the children of Israel cry out unto the Lord:

> And they said to Moses, "Was it for want of graves in Egypt that you brought us to die in the wilderness? What have you done to us, taking us out of Egypt? Is this not the very thing we told you in Egypt, saying, 'Let us be, and we will serve the Egyptians, for it is better for us to serve the Egyptians than to die in the wilderness'?" (Exodus 14:11–12)

National birth means gaining consciousness and the power of verbal expression. During their bondage in Egypt, the Israelites could only moan and groan. They were in a pre-verbal and pre-conscious state, unaware of God's providence. Or else their discourse was silenced (as they now claim), not deemed worthy of attention. Something changes with the Exodus. They acquire the capacity to verbalize their needs and cry out to the Lord through Moses. And yet the emergence of the voice of the nation is accompanied by anti-natal cravings. They use their new power of expression to convey their discontent, their desire to return to Egypt, to undo the birth of the nation. In a fascinating way they question the official biography. God here turns out to be not the Deliverer of the nation but rather the bearer of death, an abusive Father who seeks to kill His children in the wilderness. God now seems to be just as bad as, or even worse than, Pharaoh.

The children of Israel are masters of complaint. This is just their first complaint, but it initiates a long series of murmurings in the desert. It has the characteristic rhetorical questions, much anguish, and anger. The people evoke the land they left behind, obsessively ("Egypt" is mentioned five times in their grumbling), like an infant craving for a lost breast.[37] Egypt seems to have far more to offer than the desert—even its graves (and Egypt does indeed excel in its death culture) are more attractive than those available in the wilderness. The primary national biography is far from linear. Birth does not necessarily move the children of Israel unambiguously forward. Another forceful desire compels them to look back toward Egypt.

Pharaoh, then, is not alone in wishing to stop the birth of the nation. Anti-natal forces erupt from within as well. The Bible highlights the complexity of national formation in revealing counter-trends that challenge the very notion that the nation is an urgent, vital project. The people oscillate between a euphoric celebration of their deliverance—as after the parting of the Red Sea—and a continual questioning of the official consecration of national birth.

Before the Israelites actually leave Egypt, Moses turns the Exodus into a ritual to be cherished now and in days to come. He demands that they commemorate the event and pass the story on from one generation to another:

And Moses said to the people, "Remember this day, on which you went free from Egypt, the house of bondage, how the Lord freed you from it with a mighty hand: no leavened bread shall be eaten. . . . And you shall explain to your son on that day, 'It is because of what the Lord did for me when I went free from Egypt.' " (13:3–8)[38]

But the children of Israel choose to revere other memories. Against the recurrent injunction to remember the Exodus, they set up a counter-memory: a benevolent Egypt. Relentless, they persist in recalling life by the Nile, where they took pleasure in fleshpots and other Egyptian delights. Individuation from Egypt does not seem to be the only route. Memory can be shaped in a variety of ways.

Such counter-trends would seem to deflate national pride. Israel's heroism does not follow traditional perceptions of male courage. There is a good deal of fear of life in the nation's nascent voice and an acute horror of what lies ahead. God Himself often regrets having delivered the nation. The children of Israel do not succeed in fulfilling His expectations, and He never hesitates to express His disappointment in them. The people are blamed for being ungrateful, for forgetting even the unforgettable—the God who miraculously begot them (Deuteronomy 32:18). Of the numerous unflattering national designations God provides, the most resonant is His definition of Israel as "a stiff-necked people" (Exodus 32:9). The nation withholds its body from God and in doing so reveals a sinful lack of faith and an unwillingness to open up to the divine Word.

But then Israel's challenge to the national plans of Moses and God is not merely a sign of weakness. There is something about the stiff neck of the nation and the refusal to take national imaginings for granted that reveals an unmistakable force. The nation's very name, "Israel," means to struggle with God, and in a sense this is the nation's raison d'être. In this respect, the biography of the eponymous father, Jacob, is also relevant to the understanding of national birth. In the womb, Jacob struggles forcefully, trying to gain priority over his elder brother, Esau. Rebekah, who asks the Lord to explain the significance of the turmoil in her womb, is told: "Two nations are in your womb, Two separate peoples shall issue from your body; One people shall be mightier than the other; And the older shall serve the younger" (Genesis 25:23). We have seen the significance of the reversal of the primogeniture law on the national level, but what this primal scene equally emphasizes is the importance of the struggle for national formation. Not only the struggle with the other (Esau or Edom in this case) but also a struggle from within, a struggle with the Ultimate Precursor: God.[39] The uterine struggle between Jacob and Esau prefigures the momentous struggle with the angel. It is through wrestling in the night with a divine being that Jacob acquires the nation's name. "Your name shall no longer be Jacob, but Israel," says the divine opponent, "for you have striven with beings divine and human, and have prevailed" (32:29). Jacob does not become angelic as a result of this nocturnal encounter, but the struggle reveals a certain kind of intimacy with God that is unparalleled.

In its rendition of the ambivalence that characterizes the Father-son relationship, the primary biography of ancient Israel offers a penetrating representation of national ambivalence, making clear from the outset that the story of the nation is not a story without fissures and lapses. The nation, like the eponymous father, is the chosen yet unyielding son, and as such the history of its relationship with God is punctuated by moments of unfathomable violence and overwhelming intimacy. From the time of Israel's birth, mutual adoration and disappointment mark the bond of the nation and God, and this is true of later stages in the nation's life as well. The tension between God and the nation only increases as the nation becomes a restless adolescent in the wilderness.

THE SPIES IN THE LAND OF GIANTS

On the threshold of Canaan, in the wilderness of Paran, Moses sends 12 representatives, one from each tribe, to explore the Promised Land. "See what kind of country it is," Moses instructs them. "Is the soil rich or poor? Is it wooded or not?" (Numbers 13:18–20). After 40 days, the men—better known as the 12 spies—return with pomegranates, figs, and an enormous cluster of grapes borne by two men. Presenting the fruits to the people, they unanimously praise the fertility of the land: "We came to the land you sent us to," they say to Moses, "it does indeed flow with milk and honey, and this is its fruit" (13:27). The Mosaic image of the Promised Land as a land of milk and honey seems to be confirmed. But then a fissure opens up as 10 of the spies swerve from the official line and depict a land that has little to do with what had been promised. Canaan is more perplexing than anticipated: it is *both* good and bad, "fat" yet inhospitable. Despite the milk and the honey, they claim, it is a land "that devours its settlers. All the people that we saw in it are men of great size; we saw the Nephilim there . . . and we looked like grasshoppers to ourselves, and so we must have looked to them" (13:32–33). The home of the fathers, of Abraham, Isaac, and Jacob, turns out to be a strange land, a land of menacing giants, a land of others.

Of the 12 men only 2, Joshua and Caleb, are in favor of attempting the conquest of the land. The others advise against it, maintaining that the Israelites are incapable of overcoming the formidable Canaanites with their huge fortified cities. The people find the "evil report" of the 10 spies more convincing. They cry and protest, ready to stone their leaders yet again. The promise that lured them out of Egypt now seems a sham. "Let us head back for Egypt," they say to one another and turn their backs on Canaan (Numbers 14:4). God's wrath is kindled. The 10 spies die in a plague, and the desert generation as a whole is punished for its rebellious conduct. They do not deserve to enter the land, God declares, and condemns them to wander in the wilderness for 40 years—based on the number of the days in which the spies searched the land—until their carcasses fall down.

The map of the wanderings is drastically changed. Forty years of desert life are added, which means many more stations along the road. The voyage has a vertical dimension as well, with unmistakable symbolic implications. The Promised Land is set up high, the very opposite of Egypt. Egypt is a land one always "descends" to: Abraham and Sarah went down to Egypt (Genesis 12:10) when famine struck Canaan; Jacob and his sons, in their turn, did the same, settling down in Goshen with the help of Joseph. On hearing that Joseph has been devoured by a wild beast, Jacob, whose grief is immense, wishes to go down to *Sheol*, to the realm of the dead, with his beloved son (37:35), but ends up instead following him down to Egypt, the land of the monumental worship of the dead.[40] Egypt is not an underworld, strictly speaking, but it comes close to being one when it is seen as a house of bondage at the bottom of the world. The Exodus, for this very reason, entails a magnificent ascent: out of Egypt and up to Sinai, the mountain of God, and then to the Promised Land, home of the living and the free. Canaan is predominantly a mountainous land, far closer to God, as it were, than Egypt. The question the spies quarrel over is whether or not "to go up" to the Promised Land. While Joshua and Caleb insist that such a move is within their powers—"Let us by all means go up [alo na'ale], and we shall gain possession of it" (Numbers 13:30)—the others refuse to climb up impossible mountains in quest of a home that is possessed by others. Such heights seem to them more deadly than Egypt's lows.

The spies' story is a strange tale of no return, no homecoming. The hero's last trial—the final mark of his maturation—is to return home (older and wiser) after many years of wars and wanderings (which include, at times, a voyage to the underworld) and establish himself as a glorious leader, worthy of assuming the father's position. The *Odyssey* reminds us how difficult such homecoming may be. Agamemnon, who triumphed in the war against Troy, is murdered by his wife, Clytemnestra, on entering his palace, and Odysseus undergoes many hardships before and after he lands on the shores of Ithaca.

Biblical heroes are expected to return as well. Abraham and Sarah come back to Canaan after their sojourn in Egypt. The story of Jacob's homecoming to Canaan, however, is the most elaborate one. After 20 years of exile spent in Aram at the household of Laban, he sets out to return to his homeland at God's command. Jacob has a big family and much property by now—2 wives, 11 sons, many servants, and much cattle. He is no longer the helpless youth who ran away after stealing his elder brother's blessing, but nonetheless fear envelops him on the bank of the Jabbok, just before he crosses the border into Canaan:

> Then Jacob said, "O God of my father Abraham and God of my father Isaac, O Lord, who said to me, 'Return to your native land and I will deal bountifully with you'! . . . Deliver me, I pray, from the hand of my brother, from the hand of Esau; else, I fear, he may come and strike me down, mothers and children alike." (Genesis 32:10–12)

The blessing may be his, but the patrimony, that is, the power to hold it, is in the hands of Esau—or so it seems to Jacob on the eve of his return. The underlying fear is that the return will entail a regression to earlier times, when Jacob was indeed weaker than Esau, incapable of defending himself against the wrath of his elder sibling. Jacob, much like Odysseus, must refashion his identity in order to come back home safely. A mysterious "man" helps him do so. Wrestling in the night with the divine being, he acquires a new name, "Israel," which marks a break with the trickster that he was in the past and designates his new role as the nation's father.

The desert generation is even more confused and fearful about homecoming than was the eponymous patriarch. The discontinuities, or the fissures of identity, that characterize the return of the individual hero are far more pronounced in the case of collective identity, a construct whose unity is far more difficult to maintain. The wandering Israelites are skeptical about the very premise that Canaan is their homeland. The only land they wish to return to is Egypt. But they end their days in the wilderness, between Egypt and the Promised Land, returning to neither. They remain, in other words, in an in-between zone, between infancy and adulthood, in a prolonged phase of unsettling youth. Jeremiah depicts the desert years as a golden age, in which the nation followed God with the "devotion of youth" (*ḥesed ne'urim*, 2:2). Such "devotion," however, is shattered by moments in which the Israelites refuse to follow the Father and seek other routes.

The desire to return to Egypt is evident from the outset, but in Numbers 13 the people are ready to act on it. It is a moment of intense controversy that calls into question the official construction of Canaan as national home. To better understand the fracture, Moses' vision of the Promised Land needs to be explored further.

IMAGES OF THE LAND

Moses attempts to create what is so central to the formation of national belonging: a sense of home. He relies on two concepts: "the land of milk and honey," and "the land of the fathers." Home, for Moses, is a site where the mother—who is revealed solely via figurative language—provides space, and where the fathers provide the temporal dimension.

Let us begin with the fathers. The children of Israel spend 400 years (or 430, according to another tradition) in Egypt, oblivious of their past. It is left for Moses to evoke—or fashion—those long-buried memories of the three founding patriarchs, the divine promise, and the ancient patrimony far away. Just before the Exodus, Moses addresses the children of Israel in God's name, saying: "I will free you from the labors of the Egyptians and deliver you from their bondage.... I will bring you into the land that I swore to give to Abraham, Isaac, and Jacob, and I will give it to you for a possession" (Exodus 6:6–8). From the depths of misery, from "under the burdens" of bondage, God will lift them up to the land of promise, the land he swore (literally, "raised His hand") to give to their ancestors, to Abraham, Isaac, and Jacob. Moses offers the children of Israel a respectable lineage, the necessary cultural capital: three fathers who had the privileged position of the chosen, who won the favor of God and were deemed worthy of a promise and a heritage. They are models to be cherished and imitated for those who wish to be counted among the chosen.[41] To return to Canaan is thus defined as a return back home, as a quest for lost roots, a continuation of the glorious lives of the three founding patriarchs.

Moses creates continuity with a most suitable historical past. The promise that is given in the past is meant for the future, for the "seed" of the founding fathers, the nation-to-be. Much like the Trojan refugees in the *Aeneid* who discover (after a few mis-discoveries) that Italy, where they end up founding a new nation, is their ancestral home, so the Israelites discover that Canaan is their land from time immemorial.[42] Whether or not the "true origins" of the Israelites lie in Canaan, there is a significant breach of time between the patriarchs and the liberated Hebrew slaves, a breach that Moses denies as he sends spies to follow the route of their ancestors and explore the land that the latter possessed.

The plenitude conveyed by the image of a "land that flows with milk and honey" has been often noted, but little attention has been given to the choice of milk and honey in particular—that is, to the implied maternal facets of the representation of the land. The word "flow" *(zavat)* is usually used in the context of bodily fluids, reinforcing the notion that the land is a maternal body, with admirable flowing breasts. What Moses promises the children of Israel resembles an infantile dream of wish fulfillment, an image of a benevolent motherland whose milk is always available, flowing in abundance, intermingled with honey. The Promised Land, in other words, is imagined as a perfect mother with a perfect nature who can satisfy all the desires of the young nation: plenitude, pleasure, love, and security.

One needs to bear in mind, however, that in a sense the mother is a beloved as well, something that becomes all the more evident the closer the Israelites get to Canaan. The sexual dimension of milk and honey is revealed in the Song of Songs. "Sweetness drops From your lips, O bride; Honey and milk Are under your tongue" (4:11), says the lover to his beloved, while seducing her to open up her locked garden with its sealed fountain *(gan na'ul, ma'ayan ḥatum)*. To reach the Promised Land thus means to find the best of all feminine gardens: maternal nurturing coupled with erotic delights.

Joel's prophecy regarding the end of days illuminates the utopian connotations of the metaphor: "And in that day, The mountains shall drip with wine [the Hebrew word *asis* also stands for fruit juice], The hills shall flow with milk" (3:18; compare with Isaiah 66:9–13). Canaan is surely a concrete territory, but the historicity of the site does not preclude its mythical qualities. Much like the nation that calls it "home," the Promised Land has an imaginary dimension.

At first sight, however, Canaan does not seem like home sweet home. It definitely does not radiate the kind of warmth and familiarity one would expect. What the spies—the 10 rebellious ones—seem to claim is that the mother/bride who was to welcome them home turned out to be a great disappointment. Instead of supplying her sons and lovers with the goods, with the promised milk and honey, she threatens "to devour the inhabitants of the land" *(eretz okhelet yoshveha)*. Instead of being a source of nourishment, an object of desire, she is a perverse mother with cannibalistic impulses and an appetite of her own.

On the paternal front, the picture is not brighter. The fathers, or their traces, are simply absent. Their absence is all the more threatening in light of the fact that the land is packed with other nations. "Amalekites dwell in the Negeb region," say the spies. "Hittites, Jebusites, and Amorites inhabit the hill country;

and Canaanites dwell by the Sea and along the Jordan" (Numbers 13:29). There is no empty place in any direction. Neither God nor Moses conceals the fact that the land of the fathers is in the possession of others, but the promise includes divine intervention against the natives. "I will send an angel before you, and I will drive out the Canaanites, the Amorites, the Hittites, the Perizzites, the Hivites, and the Jebusites" (Exodus 33:2). And yet, upon seeing the inhabitants of the land, the possibility that they might vanish into thin air seems far less plausible. The land is truly theirs. No glimpse of continuity with the patriarchal tradition is to be seen on the horizon. The only past the spies evoke is pre-patriarchal. They depict the tall inhabitants of Canaan as *nefilim*, the legendary gigantic heroes of the antediluvian period who were considered to be the curious product of the couplings between the sons of God and the daughters of Adam (Genesis 6:2–4). The history of the patriarchs is provocatively eclipsed as another continuity between the *nefilim* and the inhabitants of Canaan is established. For the spies, the Promised Land is not merely an Old World awaiting their return. It resembles a threatening—though marvelous—New World whose relation to Israelite historiography is questionable.

NEW WORLDS

Travel accounts regarding the "discovery" of the New World can teach us much about the first encounter of the spies with the Promised Land. The relevance of the comparison did not escape William Bradford. In his report on the Pilgrims' first explorations of New England, he alludes to the story of the spies' expedition to Canaan. He writes of 16 armed men, under the conduct of Captain Standish, who ventured to explore the shore of Cape Cod. To their delight, they discovered buried Indian baskets full of corn, which they hastened to bring back to the ship. "And so like the men of Eshcol [the cluster of grapes], carried with them of the fruits of the land and showed their brethren, of which, and their return, they were marvelously glad and their hearts encouraged."[43]

One of the characteristic features of the discoverers' accounts is their emphasis on the wonder experienced on seeing the new landscapes. Such wonder was so great at times that it generated narratives of a superlative mode in which the immeasurability of the sights was celebrated. An exemplary case is Columbus's account of Española: "It is very fertile to a limitless degree, . . . it has many good and large rivers which is marvelous; and its mountains are most beautiful of a thousand shapes, and all are accessible and filled with trees of a thousand kinds and tall, and they seem to touch the sky."[44]

Just such wonder is evident in the spies' depiction of the exceptional fertility of Canaan, with its big lush fruits, samples of a different agriculture and a different climate, unknown back in the irrigated flatlands of Egypt.[45] Here too, nature is beyond measure, and particularly the grapes, not to mention the interminable flow of milk and honey. The surpassing of measure includes the inhabitants of the land as well. Three different terms are used to underline the unusual stature of the men they encountered: *anshey midot* (men of great stature), *beney anak* (sons of giants), and *nefilim* (the primordial gigantic heroes). And as if all these synonyms were not enough, they go on to explain that "we looked like grasshoppers to ourselves, and so we must have looked to them."

The spies' words disclose the projection at work. They move swiftly from their own perspective to that of the giants, never considering the possibility that the latter may have a different worldview. The midrash already noted the phenomenon when conjecturing God's response to the spies: "I take no objection to your saying 'We looked like grasshoppers to ourselves' but I take offense when you say 'so we must have looked to them.' How do you know how I made you look to them? Perhaps you appeared to them as angels?"[46]

The shock at the sight of the other and the fantasies and projections created as a result are a familiar feature in European descriptions of the natives of the New World. The natives were often depicted as utterly strange in their appearance and customs. The most powerful fantasy, however, operative in all early encounters in the New World, was cannibalism. In part, it was a matter of misinterpreting different eating habits and unfamiliar non-Christian religious rituals, but it also had to do with a more deep-seated anxiety about losing one's identity in the other.[47]

The fear of cannibalism hovers over the travel account of the spies as well. The land as a whole is described as a cannibalistic (m)other who swallows up her children. And even the representation of the giants is colored in similar hues insofar as grasshoppers are known as the smallest edible animal, according to biblical law (see Leviticus 11:22).

There are, however, significant differences between the biblical explorers and the "discoverers" of the New World. In the account of the spies, unlike Columbus's *Diario*, there is more fear than wonder, although in both cases one finds an intriguing mixture of the two. Whereas Columbus, Cortés, and the American Pilgrims seize the lands they explore ravenously, the spies—who perceive themselves as inferior in size and power to the natives—recommend avoiding the conquest of Canaan. Bradford surely smooths out the subversive aspect of the tale in contriving a "happy ending" to the story. According to his narrative, Captain Standish and his men return from the shore with the fruits of the land (the corn) and all were "marvelously glad" and much "encouraged." But the biblical spies are neither encouraged nor encouraging. They come to uncover the secrets of the land, to uncover "her nakedness," to use Joseph's definition of spying (on accusing his brothers of spying on Egypt), but are overwhelmed by the giants who possess her.[48]

The giants, strangely enough, seem to represent not only the indigenous Canaanite population but also a distorted image of the patriarchs. The fathers and the others blend at points. The fact that the giants turn up, of all places, in the area of Hebron, the burial site of Abraham, Isaac, and Jacob (see Genesis 23), reinforces this notion, as if they were tall ghosts of the distant forefathers who have risen from their grave in the cave of Machpela to haunt their descendants.[49] Note that the term *refa'im*, associated with the giants of Hebron in Deuteronomy 2:11, makes an analogous connection: it stands both for a legendary pre-Israelite community in Canaan and for the ghosts of the underworld.[50] Canaan, far more than Egypt, seems from the spies' point of view a shadowy frightful realm, dominated by the dead. Voyages to the underworld to speak with the dead (of the kind found in *The Epic of Gilgamesh* or in the *Odyssey*) are impossible within the biblical framework, where *Sheol* remains a secluded realm below, beyond narrative, but at times mythical overtones seep into the text, hinting at a more dramatic underworld behind the scenes.

On seeing the giants, the spies sense their powerlessness. They seem to shudder at the thought that they will never "grow up" or reach such stature.[51] The tradition Moses had invented for them has a dark side. If they really had such glorious ancestors, how could they follow in their footsteps? Canaan is the land of the "grown-ups," which means that there is no room in it for them. But then their reluctance to enter the world of adults is also a challenge to the underlying presuppositions of adulthood. Adulthood entails conquest and a mode of heroism they find hard to accept.

THE QUESTION OF HEROISM

The desert generation is not a generation of warriors. On hearing the spies' report, the people lift up their voice and cry:

> The whole community broke into loud cries, and the people wept that night. All the Israelites railed against Moses and Aaron. "If only we had died in the land of Egypt," the whole community shouted at them, "or if only we might die in this wilderness! Why is the Lord taking us to that land to fall by the sword? Our wives and children will be carried off! It would be better for us to go back to Egypt!" (Numbers 14:1–3)

Fighting with giants is the dream of every warrior. (David, who managed to triumph over the giant Goliath, is exemplary in this connection.) But the wandering Israelites do not find such dreams attractive. They worry about the horrifying outcome of war, the possibility that their wives will be captured and their children will be as prey in the hands of the enemy. They refuse to endanger their lives. Although Moses insists that there is no other home but Canaan, the desert generation wonders about the validity and value of the newly discovered memories of the Promised Land. And wondering means wandering—being in exile.

CARCASSES IN THE WILDERNESS

God's response is harsh. "Ten times" they have "tried" Him, and He is tired of their complaints (Numbers 14:22). First they rejected His laws, then His manna, and now the land He had designated for them. Once again, as in the episode of the Golden Calf, God is ready to annihilate the nation on the spot and fashion another via Moses, but Moses manages to dissuade Him. And yet the pardon is only partial. The people are by no means exempt from punishment. In His wrath, God chooses to take their request literally:

> Say to them: "As I live," says the Lord, "I will do to you just as you have urged Me. In this very wilderness shall your carcasses drop. Of all of you who were recorded in your various lists from the age of twenty years up, you who have muttered against Me, not one shall enter the land in which I swore to settle you—save Caleb son of Jephunneh and Joshua son of Nun. Your children who, you said, would be carried off—these will I allow to enter; they shall know the land that you have rejected. But your carcasses shall drop in this wilderness, while your children roam in the wilderness for forty years, suffering for your faithlessness, until the last of your carcasses is down in the wilderness." (Numbers 14:28–33)

Given that dying in the wilderness seemed preferable to them than waging war on the Canaanites, He'll grant them their wish. They will die in the wilderness, not immediately, but within 40 years of wanderings. The depiction of their death is blunt and gruesome. It sounds like an elaborate sonorous curse, voiced repeatedly. They will not simply die in the desert but rather "drop dead," or, in biblical idiom, their "carcasses will drop," with nothing to soften the blow, without, one suspects, the elementary right of the dead: burial.[52] Instead of going up to Canaan, they will fall as low as one can get. Their death will be total, their bodies will be wasted completely (*ad tom pigrekhem*) in the arid desert, leaving no room to hope for a change of fate. The Promised Land will remain forever beyond their reach.

The children of the desert generation, however, the very children they feared would fall prey, will ultimately enter Canaan and settle there. Whereas the parents are doomed to "know" what it means to thwart God (Numbers 14:34), their offspring will have the privilege of "knowing" the Promised Land.[53] Their only suffering will be caused not by God but rather by the burden of their parents' "whoredoms," which they will need to bear for many years until the carcasses of the desert generation fall apart, setting them free.

THE CLUSTER OF GRAPES:
NEW SITES ON AN OLD MAP

Greek mythology tells of Persephone, Demeter's daughter, who yielded to Hades' offer and took a few seeds of pomegranate on leaving him. As a result, she was doomed to return every year to the underworld for four months. Something similar happens to the spies. In picking the fruit of the Promised Land, they become part of it, regardless of their fears and reservations. According to a parenthetical comment of the narrator, we learn that the place where they had found the fruit, "That place was named the wadi Eshcol [cluster] because of the cluster that the Israelites cut down there" (Numbers 13:24).

Naming is a mode of discursive appropriation that is an integral part of every conquest.[54] The spies are not the agents of naming; it is not they who call the brook Eshcol. And yet their story participates in the appropriation of Canaan. In taking the fruit, they commit themselves to the land of milk and honey and disclose their underlying desire to conquer it, to taste its fruits, to make new marks on the ancestral map: to imprint the name "Eshcol" alongside "Hebron," the burial site of the patriarchs.

The desert generation, despite itself, craves for a home of its own, free of oppression and shame. They yearn for it to the extent that, right after the conflict over the spies' report, they regret having rejected Canaan and decide to wage war with the Amalekites and the Canaanites: "Early next morning they set out toward the crest of the hill country, saying, 'We are prepared to go up [hinenu ve'alinu] to the place that the Lord has spoken of, for we were wrong' " (Numbers 14:40). Now they finally want to go up the mountain and seek the promise, but it is too late. Moses warns them that, because of their sin, God will not stand by them in battle. They insist on trying. As expected, they lose. The Amalekites and the Canaanites who dwell in that hill come down and smite them (45). It is an aborted attempt to climb up the mountain that marks their ongoing ambivalence with respect to Canaan.

The spirit of the desert generation unsettles future generations as well. Even when the Israelites finally invade Canaan, the wandering does not fully stop. Exile piles up on exile. The Promised Land continues to be regarded throughout biblical times with some ambivalence, never to be seen as a truly stable home, nor as the only center of holiness.[55] "I accounted to your favor the devotion of your youth, Your love as a bride—How you followed Me in the wilderness, In a land not sown," says Jeremiah in the name of God to Israel (2:2). In this verse, Jeremiah ventures to claim that the desert offers a youthful passion the Promised Land lacks. He realizes, with his wandering precursors, that a land that is not "sown" leaves more room for dreaming than a tilled land.

In Numbers 16, Moses is challenged once again, this time by Dathan and Aviram who ask: "Is it not enough that you brought us from a land flowing with milk and honey to have us die in the wilderness, that you would also lord it over us?" (16:13). They provocatively turn *Egypt* into the land that flows with milk and honey, calling into question Moses' authority and national vision. Their punishment is not without significance: the earth of the desert "opens" her "mouth" and swallows them up. They "go down alive into Sheol," the realm of the dead (16:30). Canaan is not inherently a land of milk and honey, nor is it the only land with cannibalistic tendencies. Any land can be both. Any land can be both the home of the living and the home of the dead. It all depends on the eye of the spy.

JOSHUA: THE REVISED VERSION

In Joshua 2, we are given a revision of Numbers 13 that accentuates the antithetical character of the first expedition to Canaan. Joshua sends two spies to explore Jericho before approaching his first target in Canaan. Joshua, as one recalls, supported the official line already in Numbers. It was he and Caleb who inverted the claim of the other 10 spies in describing the inhabitants of Canaan as "bread" (Numbers 14:9) that could be eaten up easily. And indeed, 40 years later, Joshua sets out to "devour" the Promised Land and force the cannibalistic mother back to her position as an object of desire, whose only role is to provide her hungry children with the milk and honey they long for.

Joshua's spies reach Jericho and lodge in the house of the prostitute Rahab. The King of Jericho tries to catch them, but Rahab hides them in the roof of the house, explaining her motives to the men at length:

> I know that the Lord has given the country to you, because dread of you has fallen upon us, and all the inhabitants of the land are quaking before you. For we have heard how the Lord dried up the waters of the Sea of Reeds for you when you left Egypt. (Joshua 2:9–10)

She goes on to request that, once they conquer the city, they will not harm her family. The giants have disappeared and so has the mythical aroma. This time it is not the spies whose hearts fall at the sight of the inhabitants but rather the natives who "quake" at the prospect of an Israelite invasion: a significant departure from the previous tale.

Rahab is a key figure in the drama. Her theophoric name, which means "God has broadened" or "will broaden" (like the name "Rehavia"), intimates that she serves as an opening of sorts, a gate to the Promised Land.[56] Put differently, Rahab, who resides at the city wall, points to the way in which the "fortified cities" of Canaan may be penetrated. With the scarlet rope that she ties as a sign on her window (the same rope with which she helped the two spies escape), she makes clear that Jericho, like the other cities of Canaan, is not as impenetrable as it may seem at first sight: There is a breach in the wall and a hopeful red rope in the window.[57]

The conquest of the land goes hand in hand with sexual conquest. Rahab offers her body in addition to strategic suggestions. There is no detailed description of the affair; it is simply intimated via the word "lie," which means both "to lodge" and "to have sexual relations." Whereas the spies in Numbers merely pluck the fruit but do not eat it (and the sexual connotations of fruit-eating are all too well known from the days of Eden), in Joshua 2 the spies "lie" with an inhabitant of the new land while hiding in her protective home. The nation is "mature" enough, as it were, to conquer. The people do not shy away from sexuality or from possessing the land; they are willing to break through the fortified walls of Jericho and demand their patrimony.

CROSSING THE JORDAN

The history of ancient Israel is replete with meaningful repetitions, intimating that nothing is random: every event is connected to a whole gamut of other incidents. Some links are explicit, others less so, but all point to a divine hand above that shapes the course of events below, however incomprehensible the nation's route may be. When the children of Israel finally cross the Jordan River, their crossing is modeled—most conspicuously—on the wondrous parting of the Red Sea. Here too they walk on dry land in the midst of water, here too the waters return to their place as the crossing ends. And as if these recurrent motifs were not clear enough, an explicit statement by Joshua follows:

For the Lord your God dried up the waters of the Jordan before you until you crossed, just as the Lord your God did to the Sea of Reeds, which he dried up before us until we crossed. Thus all the peoples of the earth shall know how mighty is the hand of the Lord, and you shall fear the Lord your God always. (Joshua 4:23–24)

It is a moment of rebirth, an initiation rite that marks Israel's coming of age. Much as Jacob's initiatory crossing of the Jabbok (after struggling with the divine being) recapitulates his uterine struggle with his elder brother Esau, so the nation's crossing of the Jordan evokes the natal imagery of the primary parting as it fashions a new birth, a transition into another phase. The rite of passage by the Jordan River may not be as exhilarating as the one by the Red Sea (we do not hear the people singing), but it clearly reveals a tremendous change in the nation's position: no longer a multitude of runaway slaves, a nascent nation, but an established community, with the Ark of the Covenant at its midst, with priests who lead the ceremonial crossing, and with 40,000 soldiers ready to wage war on Jericho, the first city to be conquered.

The final note of this initiatory ceremony takes place on the other side of the Jordan, after the crossing has been completed. Twelve stones are taken from the river and placed together to commemorate the occasion of the passage of the 12 tribes into Canaan. At this liminal site, all the men are circumcised together (circumcision is a very common practice in initiation rites) by means of sharp knives made of flint. Joshua chooses to call the place Gilgal, and God provides the explanation: "Today I have rolled away *[galoti]* from you the disgrace of Egypt" (Joshua 5:9). The pun on which this naming-speech relies associates the name Gilgal with the root *glh*. The cutting of the foreskin, on the threshold of Canaan, is seen as God's rolling off the disgrace of Egypt, the turning of a new national page, far away from the humiliation of bondage.

But this national rite of passage is not a magical coming of age in which the foundling nation suddenly matures into an invincible upright hero and acquires cultural individuation and dominance. The yielding of the Israelites to the seduction of the daughters of Moab just before the crossing, much like the inclusion of Rahab's household within the Israelite camp right after the crossing, indicates that Israel is not that successful in "dwelling apart," not even on entering a land of its own.

The shadow of exile hovers on the threshold of Canaan. If Israel fails to erase the traces of previous cultures from the Promised Land, Moses warns, and defiles its home with idolatrous rites of the sort adopted in the plains of Moab, that which God planned to do to the Canaanites will be enacted upon them (Numbers 33:56). The Israelites will be dispossessed at once.

Biblical historiography points to the complexity of national imagination. It offers penetrating renditions of national ambivalence, resisting the temptation of endorsing idealized epic narratives of devoted ancestors who had no qualms. It offers a daring representation of national formation, where conflicting views of the nation are placed side by side, where exhilarating moments of collective creativity are juxtaposed with moments of immense despair and appalling violence, where the fragility of concepts such as "chosen-ness" and "promise" is an ongoing concern. The nation is the privileged site of cultural production in the Bible, but its privileged position by no means exempts it from critique.

NOTES

1. For more on the relation between the stories of the Tower of Babel and Abraham, see Martin Buber, *On the Bible* (New York, 1982), 30–31.

2. See Umberto Cassuto, *Commentary on Genesis I: From Adam to Noah* (1944; reprint, Jerusalem, 1961).

3. I take the concept of "national biography" from the inspiring study by Benedict Anderson, *Imagined Communities: Reflections on the Origin and Spread of Nationalism* (London, 1981), 204–6.

4. For an extensive discussion of the question of national literature in the ancient Near East, see Moshe Greenberg, *Understanding Exodus* (New York, 1969), 12–13.

5. For more on Greek foundation stories, see Irad Malkin, *Religion and Colonization in Ancient Greece* (Leiden, 1987). On Roman national identity, see Erich Gruen, *Culture and National Identity in Republican Rome* (Ithaca, N.Y., 1992).

6. On the comparison between the Bible and the *Aeneid,* see Moshe Weinfeld, *The Promise of the Land: The Inheritance of the Land of Canaan by the Israelites* (Berkeley, 1993), 1–21, and Yaakov Licht, *Ta'anat ha-kinun ha-mikra'it: Shenaton lemikra u-lecheker ha-mizrach ha-kadum* (Jerusalem, 1980), 98–125.

7. It is only in the Prophetic texts that the nation is construed as God's wife. For a cogent analysis of the husband-wife metaphor, see Moshe Halbertal and Avishai Margalit, *Idolatry* (Cambridge, Mass., 1992), 9–36.

8. Much has been written on the anthropomorphic character of God by scholars as diverse as Yehezkel Kaufmann, *The Religion of Israel* (New York, 1972); Phyllis Trible, *God and the Rhetoric of Sexuality* (Philadelphia, 1978); and Jack Miles, *God: A Biography* (New York, 1995). In most of these cases, however, the concomitant personification of the nation has not received much attention.

9. This is an interesting monotheistic revision of the divine lineage attributed to heroes in polytheistic traditions. No biblical hero could be defined as God's son (that would make Him far too anthropomorphic), but the nation as a whole may acquire such a status precisely because it is more clearly a metaphoric affiliation.

10. Greenberg, *Understanding Exodus.* For more on the biblical treatment of Israel as a "young" nation, see Amos Funkenstein, *Perceptions of Jewish History* (Berkeley, 1993), 50–53.

11. Funkenstein, *Perceptions,* 51. See also Yosef Haim Yerushalmi, *Zachor: Jewish History and Jewish Memory* (Seattle, 1982).

12. Much has been written on the intricate interrelations of literature and history in biblical narrative. See the insightful studies of Robert Alter, *The Art of Biblical Narrative* (New York, 1981), and David Damrosch, *The Narrative Covenant: Transformations of Genre in the Growth of Biblical Literature* (San Francisco, 1987).

13. For more on the link between the opening of Exodus and the promises and blessings of Genesis, see Umberto Cassuto, *A Commentary on the Book of Exodus* (Jerusalem, 1967), 7–9.

14. My analysis of the interrelations between the birth story of Moses and that of the nation is indebted to the insightful observations of James Nohrnberg, "Moses," in *Images of Man and God: Old Testament Short Stories in Literary Focus,* B. O. Long, ed. (Sheffield, Engl., 1981), 35–57. Nohrnberg, however, focuses on the representation of Moses rather than that of Israel.

15. The midrash noticed this structuring and defined it as *ma'aseh avot siman lebanim* (the deeds of the fathers are a sign for their children).

16. For more on the intertextual links between the story of Hagar and that of the nation, see Phyllis Trible, *Texts of Terror: Literary Feminist Readings of Biblical Narratives* (Philadelphia, 1984), 9–36, and Yair Zakovitch, *And You Shall Tell Your Son: The Concept of the Exodus in the Bible* (Jerusalem, 1991).

17. I rely on Otto Rank's list of recurrent motifs in *The Myth of the Birth of the Hero* (New York, 1932). Rank refers to a variety of myths—from the birth legend of Saragon, the third-millennium B.C.E. king of Akkad, to the renowned story of Oedipus's exposure, and the tale of Remus and Romulus, the legendary founders of Rome. Biblical scholarship mostly focused on the Mesopotamian version of the "Legend of Saragon," regarding it as a possible source of influence on the biblical writers. The relevant section of the text reads as follows, as quoted in Nahum Sarna, *Exploring Exodus: The Origins of Biblical Israel* (New York, 1986), 30: "Saragon, the mighty king, king of Agade, am I. / My mother was a high priestess, my father I knew not . . . / My mother, the high priestess, conceived; in secret she bore me. / She set me in a basket of rushes, with bitumen she sealed my lid. / She cast me into the river which rose not over me. / The river bore me up and carried me to Akki, the drawer of water. / Akki, the drawer of water, lifted me out as he dipped his ewer. / Akki, the drawer of water, took me as his son and reared me." One could add another story of Egyptian mythology to the list: that of Horus among the bulrushes. See my discussion on the interrelations of the birth stories of Moses and Horus in *Countertraditions in the Bible: A Feminist Approach* (Cambridge, Mass., 1992).

18. See Sigmund Freud, *Moses and Monotheism,* trans. Katherine Jones (1939; reprint, New York, 1967), 3–15.

19. See D. Zeligs, *Moses: A Psychodynamic Study* (New York, 1986).

20. For more on the names of the two midwives, see Cassuto, *Commentary on the Book of Exodus,* 13–14.

21. For more on the political aspects of enslavement in Exodus, see Michael Walzer, *Exodus and Revolution* (New York, 1985).

22. It is noteworthy that Ezekiel provides a different account not only of the nation's gender but also of its place of birth and primary lineage. "Thy birth and thy nativity is of the land of Canaan," he claims, "thy father was an Amorite and thy mother an Hittite" (16:3). He regards the Amorites and Hittites (closely connected with the Canaanites according to biblical ethnography) as parent-nations (rather than Egypt) because he is interested in raising a more immediate concern—Israel's distinctiveness (or lack thereof) vis-à-vis the neighboring nations of Canaan. The Exodus tradition, however, is still present in the scene, because God's second passing by seems to take place in Egypt. See Moshe Greenberg, *Ezekiel 1–20* (Garden City, N.Y., 1983).

23. See Nohrnberg, "Moses," 46.

24. "Red Sea" is a well-established mistranslation. *Yam suf* actually means "Reed Sea."

25. For more on calendars and revolutions, see Walter Benjamin, *Illuminations* (New York, 1969), 261.

26. See Martin Buber, *Moses: The Revelation and the Covenant* (Atlantic Highlands, N.J., 1988), 75–76.

27. See Robert Alter, *The Art of Biblical Poetry* (New York, 1985), for a fascinating analysis of the literary aspects of the Song of the Sea.

28. See Cassuto, *Commentary on the Book of Exodus,* 177–79.

29. For more on the feminine metaphors of God, see Trible, *God and the Rhetoric of Sexuality.* Trible, however, does not consider the Song of the Sea in this connection.

30. Perhaps God is a cross between the midwives and Pharaoh's daughter.

31. Sarna, *Exploring Exodus,* 24.

32. Quoted in G. Robins, *Women in Ancient Egypt* (Cambridge, Mass., 1993), 82.

33. For more on Miriam's role in this scene, see the essays by F. Dijk-Hemmes and by Carol Meyers in *Feminist Companion to Exodus-Deuteronomy,* A. Brenner, ed. (New York, 1994), 200–206, 207–30.

34. For an extensive consideration of the etymology of the name "Gershom," see Sarna, *Exploring Exodus,* 37.

35. Nehama Leibowitz offers an insightful analysis of the various traditions regarding the two midwives in *Studies in Shemot,* trans. Aryeh Newman (Jerusalem, 1981), 31–38.

36. Julia Kristeva, *The Kristeva Reader* (New York, 1986), 304.

37. Leibowitz, *Studies,* 245.

38. On the injunction to remember the Exodus, see the illuminating discussion in Yerushalmi, *Zachor.*

39. Esau is the eponymous father of Edom. "Edom," in fact, is another name for Esau, at-

tributed to him (according to Gen. 25:30) for gulping down the red *[adom]* stew Jacob prepared for him.

40. Alter, *The Art of Biblical Narrative,* 170–71. For more on Egypt as an underworld of sorts, see J. Ackerman, "Joseph, Judah, and Jacob," in *Literary Interpretations of Biblical Narratives,* K. R. Gros Louis, ed., with J. S. Ackerman (Nashville, Tenn., 1982), 92. Thomas Mann provides an elaborate reading of Joseph's descent to Egypt as a descent to the underworld in *Joseph and His Brothers,* trans. H. T. Lowe-Porter (New York, 1934).

41. On ancestors and the nation, see Ernst Renan, "What Is a Nation?" in *Nation and Narration,* H. Bhabha, ed. (London, 1992), 19.

42. For more on the conflicting traditions regarding the origins of Rome, see Gruen, *Culture and National Identity in Republican Rome.*

43. William Bradford, *Of Plymouth Plantation* (New York, 1967), 65–66.

44. On the representations of the New World, see Stephen Greenblatt, *Marvelous Possessions: The Wonder of the New World* (Chicago, 1991).

45. In Deuteronomy, one finds an interesting comparison between Egyptian and Canaanite agriculture: "For the land that you are about to enter and possess is not like the land of Egypt from which you have come. There the grain you sowed had to be watered by your own labors, like a vegetable garden; but the land you are about to cross into and possess, a land of hills and valleys, soaks up its water from the rains of heaven" (11:10–11).

46. *Numbers Rabbah* 16:2, *Tanhuma B. Numbers* 66.

47. Greenblatt, *Marvelous Possessions,* 136.

48. Interestingly, in the texts of the New World one finds a similar notion of the nakedness of the land. By the 1570s, as Louise Montrose shows, "allegorical personifications of America as a female nude with feathered headdress had begun to appear in engravings and paintings, on maps, and title pages, throughout Europe." In *New World Encounters,* S. Greenblatt, ed. (Berkeley, 1993), 179.

49. The notion that the choice of Hebron had something to do with the burial site of the fathers is evident in BT Sota 34. According to this tradition, Caleb visited the fathers' graves during the expedition and asked the deceased to help him in his struggle against the other spies.

50. See Shamaryahu Talmon, *Literary Studies in the Hebrew Bible: Form and Content* (Jerusalem, 1993), 76–90.

51. See Bruno Bettelheim, *The Uses of Enchantment: The Meaning and Importance of Fairy Tales* (New York, 1977).

52. See Jacob Milgrom, *Commentary on Numbers* (Philadelphia, 1990), 114.

53. Ibid., 115.

54. See Tzvetam Todorov, *The Conquest of America: The Question of the Other,* trans. R. Howard (New York, 1984), and Greenblatt, *Marvelous Possessions,* for extensive discussions on naming and the New World.

55. On the ongoing ambivalence vis-à-vis the Promised Land, see the thought-provoking

discussion in Zali Gurevitch and Gideon Aran, "Never in Place: Eliade and Judaic Sacred Space," *Archives de Sciences Sociales des Religions* 87 (Sept. 1994): 135–52.

56. See G. Boling and E. Wright, *Joshua* (Garden City, N.Y., 1982), 145.

57. In Hebrew one can discern wordplay between "rope" and "hope," given the double meaning of *tikvah, tikvat chut hashani.*

SELECTED BIBLIOGRAPHY

Alter, Robert. *The Art of Biblical Narrative.* New York, 1981.

Bal, Mieke. *Death and Dissymmetry: The Politics of Coherence in the Book of Judges.* Chicago, 1988.

Buber, Martin. *Moses: The Revelation and the Covenant.* Atlantic Highlands, N.J., 1988.

———. *On the Bible.* New York, 1982.

Damrosch, David. *The Narrative Covenant: Transformations of Genre in the Growth of Biblical Literature.* San Francisco, 1987.

Douglas, Mary. *In the Wilderness: The Doctrine of Defilement in the Book of Numbers.* Sheffield, Engl., 1993.

Freud, Sigmund. *Moses and Monotheism.* Trans. Katherine Jones. 1939. Reprint, New York, 1967.

Greenberg, Moshe. *Understanding Exodus.* New York, 1969.

Halbertal, Moshe, and Avishai Margalit. *Idolatry.* Cambridge, Mass., 1992.

Josipovici, Gabriel. *The Book of God: A Response to the Bible.* New Haven, Conn., 1988.

Nohrnberg, James. *Like unto Moses: The Constituting of an Interruption.* Bloomington, Ind., 1995.

Pardes, Ilana. *The Biography of Ancient Israel: National Narratives in the Bible.* Berkeley, 2000.

———. *Countertraditions in the Bible: A Feminist Approach.* Cambridge, Mass., 1992.

Sarna, Nahum. *Exploring Exodus: The Origins of Biblical Israel.* New York, 1986.

Schwartz, Regina. *The Curse of Cain: The Violent Legacy of Monotheism.* Chicago, 1997.

Trible, Phyllis. *God and the Rhetoric of Sexuality.* Philadelphia, 1978.

———. *Texts of Terror: Literary Feminist Readings of Biblical Narratives.* Philadelphia, 1984.

Walzer, Michael. *Exodus and Revolution.* New York, 1985.

Weinfeld, Moshe. *The Promise of the Land: The Inheritance of the Land of Canaan by the Israelites.* Berkeley, 1993.

Yerushalmi, Yosef Haim. *Zachor: Jewish History and Jewish Memory.* Seattle, 1982.

Gold pendant representing the great Syrian goddess Kadesh,
Ugarit (Ras Shamra), thirteenth century B.C.E.
(Louvre Museum, Paris. Photo: Chuzeville.
© Réunion des Musées Nationaux / Art Resource, New York)

ISRAEL AMONG THE NATIONS:

Biblical Culture in the Ancient Near East

RONALD S. HENDEL

". . . Yahweh, the God of all the earth"
—Hebrew inscription from Khirbet Beit Lei
(SIXTH CENTURY B.C.E.)[1]

After defeating King Og of Bashan, whom biblical tradition remembers as a giant,[2] Moses and the Israelites camp in the plains of Moab, east of the Jordan River. Frightened at their numbers, the king of Moab summons the foreign seer Balaam to curse this people, but instead of a curse, Balaam pronounces God's blessing. As Balaam tells the story:

> *From Aram has Balak summoned me,*
> *the king of Moab from the eastern mountains,*
> *"Come, curse Jacob for me,*
> *come, condemn Israel!"*
> *But how can I curse what God has not cursed,*
> *how can I condemn what Yahweh has not condemned?*
> *For I see them from the top of the mountains,*
> *from the hills I gaze upon them.*
> *Behold, it is a people dwelling apart,*
> *not counting itself among the nations.*
> *Who can count the dust of Jacob,*
> *who can number the dust-cloud of Israel? (Numbers 23:7–10)[3]*

Balaam perceives that Israel is a unique people whom God has blessed, a people set apart from the usual run of ancient Near Eastern nations.

My theme is taken from Balaam's description of Israel as "a people dwelling apart, not counting itself among the nations." Israel was a nation and a culture of the ancient Near East, yet it saw itself as different and somehow incommensurate with the other nations. On one level, this sense of uniqueness is far from unique: it is the root of nationalism and ethnicity in its many forms.[4] The Greeks denoted non-Greeks as barbarians *(barbaroi)* because they did not speak Greek, the language of civilized people. The Egyptians referred to themselves as "people" *(rmt),* implicitly—and sometimes explicitly—evoking the nonpeoplehood of others. But, on another level, the ancient Israelite claim to uniqueness was more forceful than most peoples' and more central to its self-definition.[5] Indeed, it is arguable that this claim to uniqueness was in some measure self-fulfilling, enabling the Jewish people to outlive all the other cultures of the ancient Near East. By persisting in its claim to uniqueness, and by routinizing this claim in its cultural habits, the Jewish people made that uniqueness a historical reality. The fact of its being alive today, roughly three millennia later, seems to ratify Balaam's perception that this is a people apart.

The boundaries that biblical culture set about itself were in a sense more permanent and decisive than those of its ancient peers. Elsewhere in the ancient Near East, one could identify one's own gods and religious practices with those of other nations.[6] For example, the Egyptians could adopt Canaanite gods and their mythology into the Egyptian religious system simply by equating them with native gods (Baal = Seth; El = Ptah; etc.). The standard formula of international treaties required that both parties' gods participate as witnesses, acknowledging a degree of communication and mutual recognition among the gods of different cultures. Although the names, languages, and local practices might differ, there was a consciousness of a basic cultural translatability in the ancient Near East. Ancient Israel seems to have been the exception to this rule.[7] Israelite writings from the earliest period repeatedly sound the theme of nontranslatability, of the birth of something new and different.

The choice of the seer Balaam to announce this basic difference reveals some interesting aspects of Israel's claim to uniqueness. Balaam is a foreigner—he is identified as an Aramean from the eastern mountains—and we now know that he was a figure of some repute in other neighboring cultures. In 1967 a Dutch excavation at Tell Deir Alla, not far from the plains of Moab, discovered an inscription from the eighth century B.C.E. that relates "the account of Balaam, son of Beor, the man who was a seer of the gods."[8] The language of this inscription is a Northwest Semitic dialect not hitherto known, sharing some distinctive features with Ammonite and Aramaic. This is an inscription of one of Israel's neighbors, showing us the continuity of religious and literary traditions—and their dramatis personae—in the West Semitic cultural sphere. Balaam, it seems, was an exemplar of the virtuous foreign seer. His dual status as a true seer and a foreigner makes him an apt figure to proclaim the uniqueness of Israel in the biblical narrative. As a foreigner, he is not prone to Israelite partisanship, and as an inspired seer, he speaks only the truth. But the fame of Balaam in West Semitic traditions shows that Israelite traditions were not unique—that is, they shared a common root and repertoire with Israel's neighbors. The voice of Balaam subtly proclaims that Israel was not wholly a nation apart.

In contrast to this early portrait of Balaam, later biblical traditions had trouble assimilating the idea of him as a virtuous foreign seer. The doctrine of cultural and religious uniqueness, which Balaam announces, led perhaps inevitably to a reevaluation of his character. In later biblical writings, this righteous gentile is recast in the common stereotype of the dangerous and/or stupid foreign Other. In the Priestly source—dating from roughly the sixth century B.C.E.[9]—Moses blames Balaam for inciting Israelite men to have sex with foreign women, a grievous sin in God's eyes, and Balaam dies in battle as his just punishment (Numbers 31:8, 16). In a later postexilic supplement to the story, Balaam is derided as more stupid than his donkey, since even the donkey can see the angel of God (Numbers 22:22–35).[10] The foreign seer who sees truly has been transformed into an agent of sin and a blindly blundering fool. These are typical biblical tropes for the foreign Other: obtuse, seductive, and/or evil. The bitter side of Israel's claim to uniqueness is revealed by its inability to preserve Balaam's virtue in its narrative traditions. The righteousness of the foreign seer was lost in translation.

Interestingly, the chief exceptions to the disparagement of foreigners in the Bible are foreign women. Tamar in Genesis 38, Rahab in Joshua 2, Jael in Judges 4–5, and Ruth in the book of her name are the paradigm examples of the righteous foreigner, and all are women. This situation turns the table on Balaam's sin of inciting Jewish men to have sex with foreign women, because in at least two out of these four instances, the virtuous act of the foreign women involves having sex with Jewish men. (The Rahab story is ambiguous on this issue, though she is a prostitute by profession.) Tamar's seduction of Judah and Ruth's seduction of Boaz result in the restoration of an Israelite lineage that would otherwise have been lost—the lineage that produces King David. Without their exceptional actions, the line of Judah would have been forfeit, and David would have never been born. The virtues of these foreign women have to do with their preservation of the tribal patriline. Because they are foreigners, their virtues are extraordinary, and their seduction of Jewish men is, in these cases, a moral good. Tamar and Ruth are the antitheses to the late portrayal of Balaam.

The Bible presents many ways of defining and negotiating the boundaries between Israel and the foreign nations. In this chapter, I will address some of the ways that biblical culture approached the differences between Israel and its Others. The questions involved (Who is an Israelite? What are the distinctive structures of Israelite religion? What are the implicit boundaries of Israelite culture?) are both historical and hermeneutical: they touch upon what really happened in the history of ancient Israel *and* how these events and circumstances were interpreted in the biblical writings. But first a caveat—history does not come neat or plain in these writings; the Hebrew Bible consists in large part of interpretations and reflections on history—more a midrash on the times than the times themselves. But, of course, this is part of what makes the Bible a timeless book. Interpretation or commentary is, as Gershom Scholem observed, part of the essence of Judaism.[11] This process of making sense of texts begins in the interpretations and contested meanings within the Hebrew Bible.

One of these conflicts of interpretation, we shall see, concerns the nature of Israel's relations with its foreign Others. Balaam's statement is not the last word on Israel's distinctiveness in the Hebrew Bible. A dialectic of sharing and distancing, of inclusion and estrangement, characterizes biblical culture from its earliest sources to its most recent.

THE EXODUS AND THE CULTURAL
CONSTRUCTION OF ISRAEL

The origins of Israel in history are obscure. In the year 1207 B.C.E., the Egyptian pharaoh Merneptah stated in a royal inscription that he had conquered Israel (among other peoples) in a military campaign through Canaan. The key line reads in Egyptian: "Israel is laid waste, his seed is no more."[12] Merneptah overstated the case, as was conventional in royal inscriptions, since Israel continued to exist. In spite of its pharaonic hyperbole, the Merneptah stele provides the earliest textual evidence outside of the Bible for Israel's existence as a people in the Near East.

The archaeological evidence shows that, beginning in the late thirteenth century B.C.E.—around the time of this inscription—there was significant population expansion in the central highlands of the land of the Canaanites.[13] This new group of highland settlers was presumably the people Merneptah called Israel—or possibly Israel was one of several groups in the highlands at this time. The settlements excavated by archaeologists share a number of similar cultural features. They are small, unwalled villages, some probably no more than the dwellings of extended families. There are no signs of social stratification or permanent military establishments. The material culture in general is a local, rural development of Canaanite culture.

This evidence indicates that early Israel was largely a local culture, a variant of regional Canaanite or West Semitic cultural traditions. If this was so—if Israel was a frontier society in the now habitable highlands—then how did being an Israelite differ from being a rural Canaanite or an Ammonite or a Moabite? (Ammon and Moab were neighboring cultures coming into being at roughly the same time as Israel.) This essential question concerns the construction of ethnic identities and cultural boundaries in this period.

Recent research has demonstrated that culture and ethnicity are more matters of belief and custom than they are proof of common descent. In the memorable title of one such study, nations or ethnic groups are "imagined communities,"[14] imagined into existence by those who believe in the group and participate in its social interactions. In the case of ancient Israel, the imagination that flows into the construction of a cultural identity is, at least in part, preserved for us in the biblical portrayal of Israel's origins. The most important of these imaginative constructs are the stories of the Exodus-Sinai-Wanderings period, related in the books of Exodus through Deuteronomy.

These stories can be regarded not only as a national biography, in Ilana Pardes' evocative phrase,[15] but also as a historical engine for the construction of cultural identity. That is, the stories not only narrate the life of a nation but also functioned in historical time as a key agent in the formation of the nation they narrate. Early Israel included, in the words of the biblical story, "a mixed multitude" (Exodus 12:38). Many of the people who settled in the early highlands community would have fit this description; they probably included peasant farmers and pastoralists, fugitives and bandits, and escaped slaves. How did they become incorporated into a cohesive social community? In no small part this transformation of identity was created by shared belief in a common story: the Exodus from Egypt, the revelation at Sinai, the wanderings in the wilderness, and the passage as a unified people into the Promised Land. These stories, in their aggregate, constitute a collective rite of passage for the people of Israel, transforming a mixed multitude from their former identity as slaves in a foreign land into a new identity as a free people—God's people—in a land of promise and plenty.[16]

Even if some or many of these formative events did not really happen in the way that they are told, they were—and still are—felt and understood to be a shared memory of a collective past. Such stories of an epic past function as a symbolic shaper of community, joining people together around a common ethnic, cultural, and religious identity. The celebrations and tales of the Exodus create and periodically reaffirm this common identity. The most obvious example is the Passover meal, the Seder, which includes the retelling of the Exodus story as an expression of the continued collective significance of the deliverance from Egypt. Jewish identity, from its beginnings to the present day, is formed in no small part by the recitation of these stories.

The function of ethnic identity-formation bound up with these stories is at times directly indicated in the biblical writings. In the midst of the plague narratives, God tells Moses that he is performing these deeds "so that you will tell your children and your children's children how I dealt with Egypt and how I brought my signs upon them, so that you [plural] will know that I am Yahweh" (Exodus 10:2). Knowing God's power and identity seems to be the point of these deeds and the point of preserving their memory in stories. But knowing God's identity also has a social correlate—knowing that Israel is God's people. This is emphasized in God's repeated promise: "I will be your God and you will be my people." In his command that the Israelites recount the story to their children and grandchildren, God seems to acknowledge that the stories of his great deeds on behalf of his people are a narrative that binds the people together as a cohesive religious community (12:24–27, 13:8). The command to tell these stories in each generation is, in a sense, a self-fulfilling command that constructs the cultural identity of its primary audience.

The cultural boundaries of early Israel were, at least in part, constructed by the dissemination of stories about the deliverance of Israel from Egyptian bondage and the birth of a free people in the Promised Land. It is important to note that even Israelite settlers who had never been slaves in Egypt could easily participate in this narrative memory, because Egypt had been the overlord of Canaan for several centuries previously (ca. 1500–1200 B.C.E.). Egyptian rule during this period had often been harsh, including the regular export of Canaanites to Egypt to serve as slaves.[17] With the waning of the Egyptian empire in Canaan, the memory of oppression and slavery and the concomitant memory of deliverance to freedom would have resonated in the drama of the Exodus story.[18] By adopting this story as their own, the villagers in the highlands became Israelites, and a mixed multitude crystallized its collective identity as the people of Yahweh.

GENEALOGY AND DIFFERENCES

One of the ways that the ancient Israelites joined together was by forming genealogical alliances. In so doing, they defined who was an Israelite and who was an outsider. The difference between inside and outside inevitably became charged with moral difference, with the insiders superior to the outsiders. This is a universal human trait, egoism on a national scale.

Sigmund Freud once commented, somewhat diffidently, on the reasons that closely related peoples disparage one another:

> I once interested myself in the peculiar fact that peoples whose territories are adjacent, and are otherwise closely related, are always at feud with and ridicul-

ing each other. . . . I gave it the name of "narcissism in respect of minor differences," which does not do much to explain it.[19]

This trait of cultural narcissism is strongly at work in the genealogical stories
in the Bible, primarily in Genesis, in which the relations between Israel's ancestors and the ancestors of other nations are recounted. In these stories, the cultural boundaries of Israel are continually endangered by the presence of the
ancestors of other peoples, and the Israelites survive the slings of fortune by
varying means—including virtue, guile, and divine intervention. Before we turn
to these stories, let us examine more closely the importance of genealogies and
genealogical narratives in the construction of cultural identity.

A genealogy shows, in a memorable way, who is related to whom. In many
small-scale societies, including early Israel, genealogical relations are the internal boundaries of society. That is, person X and person Y are both members of
the same society because, at some level of the national or tribal genealogy, they
descend from a common ancestor. The degree of distance from the common ancestor determines the particular status of the relationship between the two persons. For example, in a patrilineal society such as ancient Israel (where descent is
measured on the male side), two siblings are related because of a common father, two cousins by a common grandfather, two members of the same clan by a
common ancestor of the clan, two tribesmen by a common ancestor of the tribe,
and two Israelites by common descent from the ancestor Israel, father of the
twelve tribes. The closer the common ancestor to the generation of X and Y, the
closer their relationship to each other. The degree of closeness determines their
mutual obligations and responsibilities.

The idiom of descent or genealogy is itself a cultural construction; that is, one
does not need to be related by blood to be genealogically related. It is a regular
rule in patrilineal societies that women enter into their husband's lineage at
marriage. At times in the Bible, we can see whole clans or villages changing their
places in the genealogy because of a change of historical circumstances. For example, the clans or villages of Hetzron and Carmi are both sons of Reuben in
some texts (Genesis 46:9; Exodus 6:14; cf. 1 Chronicles 5:3) but are elsewhere
listed as sons of Judah (1 Chronicles 4:1). This shift in genealogical affiliation
probably provides a glimpse of tribal history, as Reubenite clans were absorbed
into Judah. Even foreign villages and clans can become Israelite and enter the genealogy. The foreign clan of Jerahmeel later became a clan of Judah, again reflecting the tribal expansion of Judah and the absorption of foreign clans into its
lineage (cf. 1 Samuel 27:10 and 1 Chronicles 2:9, 25). A group can change its status
from outsider to insider by assuming a new social identity and entering the ge-

nealogy. One's place in the genealogy is a sign of cultural self-definition more
than it is a sign of biological descent.

With the social function and historical fluidity of genealogies in mind, let us
see how they are used in the Bible to mark the boundary between inside and
outside, between Israel and the nations. In Genesis, these boundaries are fragile
and contentious. The legal status of the firstborn son to carry the main line
of the genealogy is highly contested, most obviously between Jacob and Esau
but also between Sarah and Hagar (on behalf of their sons, Isaac and Ishmael),
Perez and Zerah, Joseph and his brothers, and even Cain and Abel. Usually the
younger son prevails and the older son is denigrated in some way, as if the firstborn were unworthy of carrying the lineage that issues in the people Israel. In
these lineage conflicts, the Israelite ancestors are extolled and the ancestors of its
cultural neighbors disparaged. Although the genealogical stories acknowledge
Israel's relatedness to its neighbors, the relationship is colored by various stereotypes of the Other. Through a dialectic of structural opposition, Israel asserts in
its genealogical stories that it is a righteous and civilized people, in contrast to
the foreigners who more often than not are seen as creatures of nature: wild, stupid, sexually licentious, or violent.

In the primeval narratives of Genesis 1–11, three peoples are singled out for
genealogical derision: the Kenites, the Canaanites, and the Babylonians. Cain
(originally *Qayn*) is clearly, by his distinctive name, the eponymous ancestor of
the tribe of Kenites (originally *Qayni*).[20] Cain, of course, is a fratricide whom
God curses to wander without home or refuge (Genesis 4:12). This is an attribution of a shameful, violent ancestral origin. The Israelites, in contrast, are descended from Adam and Eve's third and youngest son, Seth. The next people
disparaged are the Canaanites, whose ancestor is Canaan. He is cursed for his father's sexual transgression—"Ham, Canaan's father, saw his father's nakedness"—
and is consigned to servitude (9:20–27). Canaan's curse in this story is, as Rashi
noted, a justification for God's decision to reassign the land of Canaan to the
children of Israel. This, too, is a shameful origin for this foreign people and a
warrant for Israelite domination. The third people disparaged in the primeval
narratives is Babylon, whose city becomes a watchword of cultural arrogance
and disaster (11:1–9). The Tower of Babel story deflates the cultural pretensions
of Babylonian civilization. In all three of these ethnographic tales, a foreign people is colored with shameful origins.

In the patriarchal narratives of Genesis 12–50, the genealogical contrast of
wild foreigners with the civilized precursors of Israel is both heightened and
complicated. The three generations of the patriarchs—Abraham, Isaac, and
Jacob—each portray a different set of genealogical oppositions. In the first,

Abraham's righteousness is contrasted with his nephew Lot's flaws. Lot's most egregious fault occurs in Genesis 19, when he offers his daughters to the lustful townsmen of Sodom in an attempt to protect his guests. In an apt and shameful turnabout, his daughters later seduce Lot, and they become pregnant and bear the ancestors of Moab and Ammon (19:30–38). Lot's incest with his daughters is a grievous sin, which stains the ancestry of the peoples of Moab and Ammon. Although Israel is related to its Transjordanian neighbors and is at times on good terms with them, these peoples are denigrated by their ancestors' shameful sexual origins.

The next generation juxtaposes Ishmael, the son born of the slave woman Hagar, and Isaac, the son born of Abraham's wife, Sarah. Ishmael, who is cast out at Sarah's insistence, becomes the ancestor of the Arab peoples. Although an angel of God gives him the promise of a great nation, the angel also promises that "he will be a wild ass of a man, his hand against everyone, and everyone's hand against him" (Genesis 16:12). Later, Ishmael prospers as a hunter in the wilderness and marries an Egyptian woman (21:20–21). The story of Ishmael gives a mixed portrait: he is blessed by God, but he ends up as a predator on the outskirts of civilization, violent as a wild ass and marrying a foreign woman. In terms of the story, Ishmael—and, by implication, his descendants—are less civilized than the line of his younger half-brother, Isaac.

It is illuminating to note how Islamic and Christian traditions later revise the structural opposition of Abraham's two sons in accord with their cultural and genealogical preferences. In post-koranic Islamic tradition, Ishmael is exalted as the beloved son whom Abraham almost sacrifices, and Ishmael and Abraham together build the holy shrine of the Kaaba in Mecca.[21] In the New Testament, Paul identifies the child of the promise, Isaac, as the symbolic precursor of the Christians, and the slave's child, Ishmael, as the symbolic precursor of the Jews (Galatians 4:22–31). In all three Abrahamic religions, the genealogical process of cultural self-definition is at work in the portrayal of Abraham's sons.

The third generation of the patriarchal lineage in Genesis contrasts Jacob, the younger son, with Esau, the firstborn. Whereas Jacob is a smooth man—a term that applies both to his body and to his deceptive stratagems[22]—his brother Esau is hairy, a wild man like Ishmael, more at home in the wilderness than in human settlements. "When the boys grew up, Esau was a man skilled in hunting game, a man of the open country; but Jacob was a civilized [literally, 'pure, whole'] man, dwelling in the tents" (Genesis 25:27). Esau is a man of nature, in contrast to Jacob, the man of culture.[23] Esau's brutish simplicity makes him an easy mark for Jacob's wiles when he sells his birthright for a bowl of lentil soup (25:29–34). At the end of this tale, Esau does not even seem to realize what he has done: "He ate and he drank and he rose up and he walked away"—he is a man who thinks with his belly.[24] Because Jacob is the intelligent one—and is favored by his intelligent mother—he also tricks his father and obtains the patriarchal blessing and promise (27). Later he resourcefully wins from God the name Israel (32:29), sealing his identity as Israel's ancestor. By contrast, Esau is identified as the ancestor of Edom because he is unable to think of the correct name for the lentil soup, referring to it stupidly as "this red red stuff" (*ha'adom ha'adom ha-zeh* [25:30]). In these stories, the Edomites are collectively stereotyped by their simple and brutish ancestor.

In the processes of genealogical self-definition expressed in these stories, the foreign Other is generally described as, to varying degrees, uncivilized or immoral. One would expect that the hero of the Israelite patriline is, in contrast, civilized and just. Such is the case with Abraham versus Lot and, perhaps, Isaac versus Ishmael (though Isaac is not a major character). But the case of Jacob versus Esau is more complicated, because Jacob, while clearly civilized, is not wholly moral. There is a slippage in the case of Israel's eponymous ancestor.

Jacob is morally challenging—a man of culture, but not a man consistently presenting the best face of human culture. His wiles (and his mother's) win him the birthright and patriarchal blessing. But he pays for his trickery when Laban substitutes his firstborn daughter Leah for the younger daughter Rachel on Jacob's wedding night (Genesis 29:23). In this turnabout, the father tricks the son-in-law in a manner that mirrors the son's earlier trick of his own father. The older child is now substituted for the younger, and Laban justifies the deception in words heavy with irony: "It is not done in our place to give the younger before the firstborn" (29:26). Later, in Genesis 37, Jacob's sons avenge themselves on their precocious younger brother, Joseph, and deceive their father by cleverly manipulating Joseph's special cloak. This trick also echoes Jacob's deception of his father, which involved wearing his brother's best clothes. Jacob pays the price for his tricks several times over, though he retains his status as the eponymous ancestor, Israel. Even Esau seems to grow in maturity by the end of the story (see Genesis 33), while Jacob is still a trickster in old age (see his deception of Joseph in Genesis 48), in spite of having grown wiser.

In the stories of Jacob/Israel, the cultural narcissism of genealogical self-definition is turned, at least in part, into a self-representation of impropriety and guilt. The complexities of the Jewish soul are foreshadowed by this ambiguous characterization. On the one hand, Jacob/Israel is the man of the promise and blessing, who has "striven with God and with men and has prevailed" (Genesis 32:29). On the other hand, he suffers for his triumphs and pays a price for taking the name "Israel." Though he prevails, he also limps (32:32).

THE CANAANITE MATRIX

The prophet Ezekiel, in a message of divine wrath against Israel, castigates its genealogical origins: "Your origins and birth are from the land of the Canaanites.
Your father was an Amorite, and your mother was a Hittite" (Ezekiel 16:3). Formulated in the same idiom as the genealogical stories discussed above, this is an
attribution of shameful origins, leading to the application of the proverb "Like
mother, like daughter" to Israel's infidelity (16:44). Although this genealogical
insult is intended to inspire shame and guilt, it also seems to be a fairly accurate portrayal of Israel's origins. There is a deep ambivalence in Ezekiel's angry
speech—even though there were marked continuities between Canaanite and
Israelite culture, the principle of nontranslatability applies. Anything Canaanite
is foreign and abominable in the prophet's eyes.

The extent of the Canaanite matrix of Israelite culture has become clearer
over the past several decades. The twin turning points have been the archaeological finds about Israel's origins discussed above, and the discovery of religious
texts from the ancient city of Ugarit on the coast of modern Syria, beginning in
the 1930s and continuing to the present day.[25] Ugarit was a flourishing Canaanite
city-state in the Late Bronze Age (1500–1200 B.C.E.), and most of the texts come
from this period, which was immediately prior to the rise of Israelite civilization
farther to the south.

The texts from Ugarit are in a language (called Ugaritic) closely related to Hebrew. They tell stories whose themes, diction, and characters are often familiar
from the Bible. For example, the following passage from the Ugaritic myth of
Baal stands in close relation to a passage from the book of Isaiah written over
half a millennium later:

> *When you killed Litan, the fleeing serpent,*
> *finished off the twisting serpent,*
> *the mighty one with seven heads,*
> *the heavens withered and drooped.*[26]

> *On that day, Yahweh will punish*
> *with his fierce, great, and mighty sword*
> *Leviathan, the fleeing serpent,*
> *Leviathan, the twisting serpent,*
> *he will slay the dragon of the sea. (Isaiah 27:1)*

In this instance, as in many others, the Ugaritic and biblical texts draw on a common West Semitic cultural tradition. The monster Litan/Leviathan (variants of the same name) is destined to die at the hand of the great Divine Warrior, Baal at Ugarit and Yahweh in Israel. In Isaiah 27, this myth is projected into the future, when all the forces of chaos will be defeated, and God's rule will be established forever. The defeat of chaos at the dawn of time will recur at the dawn of the hoped-for new era.[27] In the comparison of these two passages, we can see plainly the continuities and the transformations of tradition in Canaan and Israel.

Israelite culture inherits and transforms not only the mythology of the Divine Warrior but also the stories and traits of other figures of the Canaanite pantheon. Perhaps the most surprising survivals and transformations belong to the mythologies of El and Asherah, the father and mother of the Canaanite gods. In the Bible and in several recently discovered Hebrew inscriptions, we can see how aspects of these deities were woven deeply into Israelite conceptions of the divine.

El is the high god of the Canaanite pantheon at Ugarit. His name simply means "God."[28] El is described as wise and gracious; he is called "El, the kind and compassionate one." He is an elderly god with a gray beard and is depicted in reliefs and statuary seated on a royal throne. His image is comparable to the description of the God of Israel in Daniel 7:9: "As I looked, thrones were set up, and the Ancient of Days sat down. His garment was white as snow, and the hair of his head was [white as] pure wool." In other Canaanite and Phoenician texts, El is called "creator of earth," just as the God of Israel is called "El most high, creator of heaven and earth" by Abraham (Genesis 14:22).[29] El is the father of the gods, who are appropriately called the "Children of El" *(banu ili)*, just as the subordinate deities or angels in the Bible are called the "Children [or Sons] of God [El]" *(beney el, beney elohim,* and similarly). El lives on a mountain or, alternately, at the "source of the two seas." Similarly, the God of Israel dwells on a mountain (Sinai or Zion), and his divine garden ("Eden, the garden of God" on "the holy mountain of God" in Ezekiel 28:13–14) is the source of the four rivers (Genesis 2:10). In name, character, and locale, Canaanite El and the God of Israel are closely affiliated.

El is also the "Father of Humans" and "Creator of Creatures," and he blesses his favored worshipers by granting them sons when they lack heirs. The similarities to the biblical stories of the creation of Adam and the granting of sons to Abraham and the other patriarchs are apparent. The decrees of El, promulgated from his mountain home, also remind us of the laws that the God of Israel grants from His holy mountain. The Law at Sinai, in some respects, echoes old cultural memories of the wise decrees of El. Even the name "Israel" *(yisra'el)* seems originally to mean "El rules." The fact that Israel's God is often simply called "El," as for example in the titles *el olam*, "El the Ancient One" (Genesis 21:33), or *el shaday*, "El the One of the Mountain" (17:1, etc.), underscores the continuity of divine traits shared by Canaanite El and the God of Israel.[30]

The mother of the gods in the Ugaritic texts is Asherah, whose name derives from the word for "trace, path, or place."[31] She is the "Creatress of the Gods" and is probably referred to as the "Holy One." As El's wife, she effectively appeals for his blessing on behalf of other gods. In the Baal myth, she approaches El for his permission to grant Baal a palace, using sweet and well-balanced words:

Coin depicting sacred place of Tyre with incense, altar, standing stones, and tree. The inscription below reads "ambrosial stones." (British Museum, London)

> *Lady Asherah of the sea replied:*
> *"Your decree, O El, is wise,*
> *your wisdom is eternal,*
> *a fortunate life is your decree."*[32]

With such elegant poetic diction—including the interwoven sounds and sense of *taḥ muka* (your decree), *ḥakamu* (wise), and *ḥakamuka* (your wisdom)—El easily accedes to her request.

Asherah is also a beneficent goddess for her earthly worshipers. The wise King Kirta makes an oath to Asherah at one of her temples, promising great tribute if Asherah grants success to his quest for a wife.

> *They arrived at the holy shrine of Asherah of Tyre,*
> *and of the goddess of Sidon.*
> *There the noble Kirta made a vow:*
> *"As Asherah of Tyre lives,*
> *and the goddess of Sidon,*
> *if I take Hurraya into my house*
> *if I bring the maiden to my court,*
> *I will give double her [weight?] in silver,*
> *triple her [weight?] in gold."*[33]

This passage shows that Asherah had local shrines and worshipers, and that she was appealed to for her blessings, including matters of marriage and the accompanying expectation of offspring. Such matters seem appropriate for the wife of El and mother of the gods.

In the Bible, Asherah is known as a goddess who was imported into Israel from Phoenician culture. (Phoenicia was a direct descendant of old Canaanite culture.) The dread Queen Jezebel seems to have brought the "prophets of Asherah" into Israel from her Phoenician homeland (1 Kings 18:19). The evil king Manasseh is said to have erected some sort of statue to Asherah in the Jerusalem Temple (2 Kings 21:7), and there were special rooms in the Temple where women wove embroidered garments for this statue (2 Kings 23:7).[34] The Queen Mother Maacah is also said to have made an "abominable thing" for Asherah (1 Kings 15:13), which suggests some sort of statue or image. It is interesting that these references to the worship of Asherah are restricted to royal families, who are thereby marked as wicked and corrupt.[35]

Elsewhere in the Bible, Asherah (or asherah, with small "a") is used as a word referring to a wooden pole or tree that is part of the cultic furniture of the local shrines in Israel.[36] This "asherah" is a common noun, not a personal name, and, perhaps curiously, has a masculine plural ending. It is not clear whether this asherah-object was conceived as a symbol of the goddess Asherah or whether it had become somehow denatured as a holy symbol of the God of Israel. The prominence of holy trees in various foundation stories of local shrines—including Shechem ("the oak of the Teacher" in Genesis 12:6, probably the same as "the oak in the sanctuary of Yahweh" in Joshua 24:26), Beersheba ("a tamarisk tree," Genesis 21:33), and Ophrah ("a terebinth tree," Judges 6:11)—suggests a diversity of Israelite interpretations of the symbolism of trees at shrines. In these texts, the sacred trees are an unproblematic part of ordinary Israelite worship. In Deuteronomy and other related texts (discussed below), the holy trees, asherahs, and related cultic objects are castigated as foreign abominations, along with the local shrines themselves.

The discovery of several Hebrew inscriptions from the eighth century B.C.E. that mention Asherah—or asherah—has highlighted the prominence of this goddess and/or holy object in ancient Israelite religion.[37] From a local shrine at Kuntillet Ajrud, a stop on an ancient trade route in the northern Sinai, come the following inscriptions on pots and plaster, some quite fragmentary:[38]

1. "I bless you by Yahweh of Samaria and by his asherah."

2. "... by Yahweh of Teman and by his asherah."

3. "I bless you by Yahweh of Teman and by his asherah. May he bless you, protect you, and be with my lord forever."

4. "... let them say, 'By Yahweh of Teman and by his asherah ... May Yahweh do good'...."

Another inscription from the same general period, from a rock tomb at Khirbet el-Qom, also mentions Asherah:[39]

5. "May Uriah be blessed by Yahweh, my protector, and by his asherah. Deliver him...."

These inscriptions share the same general blessing formulas that we find in the Bible and other Hebrew inscriptions, with the notable addition of the appeal to "his asherah" (*šrth*, which can be vocalized in biblical style as *asherato*). But who or what is "his asherah"? There are several possible ways to read this reference, and none is entirely satisfactory.

The simplest way to construe "his asherah" is as a reference to the wooden pole or tree that was part of a shrine. This would cohere with the references to the local cults of Yahweh: "Yahweh of Samaria" (the capital city of the northern kingdom), and "Yahweh of Teman" (probably a reference to the region of Kuntillet Ajrud—*teman* means "south"). Each of these local shrines plausibly had an asherah-object or sacred tree beside its altar. This object is perhaps called upon here as an aspect of the sacred presence of Yahweh that is manifested in these places. The "asherah," in this reading, is a symbol of Yahweh's presence, not a separate deity. This coheres with the requests that follow in three of the blessings, in which it is Yahweh alone who acts: (3) "May he bless you, protect you, and be with my lord forever"; (4) "May Yahweh do good . . ."; and (5) "Deliver him. . . ." All of these verbs are in the masculine singular, clearly referring to Yahweh.

A slightly more difficult construction is to read "his asherah" as the goddess Asherah, appealed to in these blessings as a distinctive deity and object of worship. In this reading, Asherah is Yahweh's wife, just as she was El's wife in Canaanite religion. The chief problem for this reading is that the pronominal suffix, "his," is not used for proper names in classical Hebrew. To see the goddess clearly in these blessings requires that the blessing formula be ungrammatical, which seems unlikely. A way around this grammatical objection is to read "asherah" as a generic word for "goddess," which is plausible but not elsewhere attested.

A third way to read this reference combines the meanings of the asherah-object and the goddess Asherah. The reference may be to the asherah-object, but the object may have been generally understood to be a symbol of the goddess. In this reading, the goddess is implicit in the object. There can be no grammatical objection to this reading, but it still encounters some difficulty in the absence of the goddess in the invocations following, which are limited to the masculine sin-

gular, "may *he* bless you, protect you," etc. One way out of this difficulty would
be to see Asherah as a mediating deity between the worshiper and Yahweh, who
is the effective bestower of blessing.

We still do not possess a conclusive understanding of these blessings "by
Yahweh and his asherah." One way or another, however, it seems to shed further light on the Canaanite matrix of Israelite religion. Matrix literally means
"womb," from the Latin word for "mother." Perhaps in the legacy of Asherah
in Israelite religion, we see the trace of the Mother of the Gods in the worship
of Yahweh, who, though male, is the one who grants the "blessing of breasts
and womb" (Genesis 49:25). Asherah's blessing persists in some measure in the
character of this God and his A/asherah.

RITUAL BOUNDARIES: THE BODY, FOOD, TIME

Israelite religion and culture were not monolithic. There were, to borrow William James's phrase, varieties of religious experience in ancient Israel.[40] Recent scholarship has brought to light regional, chronological, and sociological
differences in religious practices and beliefs. One of the primary sociological differences is that between family religion and state religion, which at times clashed
in the turmoil and social upheavals of Israelite history.[41] Family religion centered
on marriage, offspring, and good fortune—as exemplified in the family stories
of the patriarchs and others. State religion often centered on national wars and
the ideologies of kings—as exemplified in many of the narratives of Judges,
Samuel, and Kings.

In the differences between the one religion and the other, we find the natural
locations of the legacies of El, the gracious god of the fathers, and Baal, the Divine Warrior. In the patriarchal stories, God is a beneficent divine patriarch; in
the national battles of the Exodus and Conquest, he is a warrior and king. For
example, the patriarch Jacob blesses his son Joseph by "the God of your fathers,
who helps you, the God of the mountain [literally, 'El, the One of the Mountain'], who blesses you" (Genesis 49:25).[42] This is the god of family religion. But
in the context of great national events, such as after God's victory at the Red Sea,
the divine portrayal is in a different register: "Yahweh is a warrior" and "Yahweh
will rule forever and ever" (Exodus 15:3, 18). The two divine "types" emerge in
these differing social contexts.

Although the varying internal boundaries in Israelite religion and culture
suggest a real cultural pluralism,[43] there were also external boundaries that de-
marcated, more or less clearly, where Israelite culture began and ended. These
external boundaries determined whether or not one was an Israelite. One such

common cultural ground was, of course, language, though there is evidence of dialectal variation within Hebrew.[44] Another source of shared identity was the recitation of traditional stories of the past, such as the Exodus story discussed above. A third source was the web of genealogies, in which one's family and clan were explicitly related to everyone else in the lineages of Israel. And fourth was the body of shared rituals. In the practices of everyday life, Israelites enacted their cultural identity in symbolic actions, whether offering animal sacrifice at local shrines, making pilgrimages on the major festivals, or undergoing rites of healing or passage.

A range of ritual practices served to mark the implicit boundaries of cultural identity. Some of these were identical in origin to the practices of neighboring peoples, but over time they came to be understood, by insiders and outsiders, as distinctively Israelite. Among these many acts, three that were—and still are— singled out as distinctive are circumcision, food laws, and observance of the Sabbath. The domains of these practices—the body, food, and time—are exemplary for showing the effective symbolism of rituals as markers of cultural boundaries.

The Body In ancient Israel, a patrilineal society, the male body was ritually marked by circumcision, called a "sign of the covenant" (Genesis 17:11).[45] By so marking the male organ of procreation, each Israelite family was covered with a sacred sign. Various kinds of symbolism—patrilineal descent, sexual fertility, male initiation, cleansing of birth impurity, and dedication to God—are intermingled in this mark. It has been elegantly described as "the fruitful cut."[46]

For this bodily mark to serve as a cultural boundary, there must be contrasting male bodies that lack it—the uncircumcised. Curiously, the evidence indicates that most of the males in Israel's immediate vicinity were also marked by circumcision. The prophet Jeremiah informs us that many of the peoples of the ancient Near East practiced circumcision, including "Egypt, Judah, Edom, the Ammonites, Moab, and all the desert dwellers who clip the corners of their hair" (Jeremiah 9:25). Textual and pictorial evidence from outside the Bible also indicate that the practice went back thousands of years.[47] The only males among Israel's immediate neighbors who lacked this mark were newcomers—the Philistines.

The Philistines were peoples from the Greek Aegean region who invaded and settled in the eastern Mediterranean shortly after 1200 B.C.E., precisely the period of the cultural formation of Israel in the highlands of southern Canaan.[48] The Philistines, with their superior technology, became the dominant political and military force of the region, as recalled in the stories of Samson, Saul, and David. This was probably the major impetus in the transformation of Israel from a tribal society to a unified kingship, with a permanent standing army. The Philistines were the dominant foreign Other in this crucial period, and their male bodies were uncircumcised.

In the biblical stories about this period, the term "uncircumcised" is often used as a synonym for "Philistine" (e.g., Judges 15:18; 1 Samuel 14:6, 31:4). In David's lament over Saul and Jonathan, killed in battle against the Philistine army, he cries:

> Do not tell it in Gath
> Do not recount it in the streets of Ashkelon,
> Lest the daughters of the Philistines rejoice,
> Lest the daughters of the uncircumcised exult. (2 Samuel 1:20)

It is interesting to note in this regard that the bride-price Saul had earlier requested of David was a hundred Philistine foreskins (1 Samuel 18:25). By this means, Saul managed not only to endanger David's life but also potentially to refashion the Philistines, reconstituting them as circumcised men.

It appears that the origin of circumcision as a cultural boundary of the Jews was facilitated by the dangerous presence of the uncircumcised Philistines.[49] Uncircumcision as a sign of the dangerous and dominant Other was later associated with the Assyrians and Babylonians, and later still the Greeks. Perhaps in response to the hegemony of these foreign powers, ancient Israel developed the belief that the uncircumcised had a particularly gloomy place reserved for them in Sheol, the underworld, alongside the unburied (Ezekiel 28:10, 31:18, 32:19–31). To have a foreskin was to be barbarous, cruel, and doomed to the "death of the uncircumcised."[50]

Curiously, the cultural boundaries drawn by this opposition between circumcised and uncircumcised—involving the contrast of civilization versus barbarism—are in tension with those constructed in the genealogical stories discussed above. Circumcision was a shared cultural trait of other neighboring peoples (Ammonites, Moabites, Edomites, Phoenicians, Arameans, etc.), who were thus grouped on the inside of this boundary. A kinship with these people as similarly circumcised and therefore civilized is implicit.

By this logic, a foreign people could become kin of the Israelites on the condition of their being circumcised. So Jacob's sons say to the Hivites of Shechem: "Only on this condition will we agree with you (to marry our sister), if you become like us, to have every male among you circumcised" (Genesis 34:15). Jacob's sons don't intend to go through with the bargain, but their pledge seems to show how the rite worked as a cultural boundary in matters of kinship. To be circumcised—or to be a daughter of a circumcised father—is to be a potential Israelite. Thus, David can marry an Aramean princess (2 Samuel 3:3); Solomon can wed an Egyptian princess (1 Kings 3:1) along with Moabite, Ammonite, Edomite, Phoenician, and Hittite women (1 Kings 11:1); Ahab marries the Phoenician Jezebel (1 Kings 16:31); and Chilion marries the Moabite Ruth (Ruth 1:4)—they are all eligible brides on account of their male kin's circumcision. This ritual logic was apparently later overruled by the postexilic ban on intermarriage with "the peoples of the land" (Ezra 9–10; Nehemiah 10:31, 13:23–27). In this revision of custom, national boundaries replaced the older ritual boundaries. Or, to be more precise, the nation or ethnos replaced the tribal system as the locus for kinship relations.[51]

The expansive cultural boundaries of circumcision seem to be restricted to the children of Abraham in God's covenant with Abraham in Genesis 17, in which circumcision is a sign of the covenant. This is a Priestly text, probably written around the sixth century B.C.E. This mark, which previously was a general sign of West Semitic culture, crystallized into one of the most prominent boundary markers of Jewish identity. At some time during the Second Temple period, the rite became obsolete in other West Semitic cultures.[52] By this fruitful cut, the identity of the Jewish male body—and the Jewish social body—came to be distinguished from the bodies of other cultures.

Food   Another daily reminder of cultural identity is food. Ethnic foodways develop in varying degrees in different cultures, but food is always a sign of home—certainly in Judaism. What one eats and with whom one shares food are visible expressions of social bonds and boundaries. The biblical food laws are, like circumcision, reminders of God's covenant with Israel. The theological issue is holiness, as God commands in the conclusion to the food laws in Leviticus: "You shall be holy, for I am holy" (11:45). To be holy with respect to food means to eat what is allowed and to abstain from what is prohibited. As the anthropologist Mary Douglas demonstrated in her classic essay "The Abominations of Leviticus," the biblical food laws have to do with boundaries—cultural, theological, and conceptual.[53]

The earliest trace of these food laws in Israelite material culture comes from the era of Philistine hegemony, the same period when circumcision seems to have become an ethnic boundary marker. Recent archaeological excavations of early Israelite and Philistine sites show a remarkable contrast in the presence and absence of pig bones. The archaeologist Lawrence Stager reports that "In the highland villages [of early Israel] of the Iron I period, the bones of pigs are rare or completely absent, but in Philistia they constitute a significant proportion of excavated faunal remains."[54] This contrast is not explicable on ecological grounds; it rests, rather, on cultural ones. The archaeological evidence indicates that pig production was scarce in West Semitic culture,[55] but in Mycenaean Greek culture pigs were a valued source of meat. The Philistine preference for pork was apparently imported from their Aegean homeland. It was arguably the catalyst for the explicit avoidance of this food in early Israelite culture.[56]

With this dietary law, as with the rite of circumcision, a general West Semitic practice crystallized into a mark of Israelite cultural identity. The dangerous presence of the Philistines was the foil for the formation of a "counter-identity" in Israel; a traditional foodway became transformed into a theological and cultural affirmation. Holiness was endangered by taking pork into the Israelite body, just as Philistine culture was a threat to the wholeness of the Israelite social body. The ritual boundaries of the Israelite meal celebrated and maintained the boundaries of society.

Time The way that time is measured is another mark of cultural boundaries and group authority. Judaism, Christianity, and Islam each have different religious calendars, counting time from different foundational events (creation, the birth of Christ, the exodus from Mecca). In biblical writings, time is marked according to key moments such as the Exodus or the reigns of Israelite kings. In the later era of the Second Temple, the Essenes proclaimed their cultural boundaries by advocating a calendar based on the solar year, in contrast to the traditional lunar (or lunisolar) calendar.[57] The high priest of Jerusalem even seems to have journeyed to Qumran to discipline the wayward community for deviating from the official calendar. Since then, Jewish groups and authorities have continued to vie over calendrical issues, such as the beginning of the day, the times and durations of festivals, and intercalation.

One of the distinctive ritual marks in biblical time is the Sabbath. It is, like circumcision, a "sign of the covenant" (Exodus 31:12–17), and, like the food laws, it is a matter of holiness. God commands: "You shall keep the Sabbath, for it is holy to you" (31:14, similarly 20:8–11). Just as God rested on the seventh day of creation, Israel shall rest every seventh day. Time becomes sacred, periodically, in this fruitful temporal cut.

The institution of the Sabbath is an Israelite innovation, as is the division of time into weeks.[58] It is impossible to tell when this system was invented, but a Hebrew inscription of the seventh century B.C.E. mentions the Sabbath,[59] and it is prominent in writings of the eighth-century prophets.[60] It is plausible that such a mark of temporal distinctiveness—involving cultural and religious difference—derived from an early era of Israelite culture, perhaps the same formative period when circumcision and food laws began to be ritual identity-markers. At minimum we can say that the Sabbath was an important pre-exilic institution.[61]

The divisions of time, along with demarcations in foodways and the body, have long marked the external boundaries of the Jewish body politic. In ancient Israel, these were part of the growing system of ritual practices that served to display the inclusions and exclusions of Israelite cultural identity. Such clear external boundaries have long provided a protective cover for the plurality of religious experience within Judaism.

REVISIONISM AND TRADITION

Ancient Israel shared many cultural features with its neighbors in the Near East. In matters of ethics, law, architecture, medicine, poetry, theology, and ritual, Israel belonged to a family of West Semitic cultures.[62] Differences certainly existed, and these were made emblematic of a perception of cultural uniqueness, of a people dwelling apart. Yet, as we have seen, differences also existed within Israelite culture. Over time, some of these internal differences were felt by some to be problematic. Certain biblical authors came to reject some of the ancient customary features of Israelite religion, labeling them as foreign and therefore corrupt and irreligious. Native practice was reinterpreted as a foreign assault on Israel's cultural boundaries, following the idiom of the dangerous and seductive Other.

During the eighth to sixth centuries B.C.E., a powerful revisionist movement developed among various prophets, priests, and sages. The result was a far-reaching upheaval in the boundaries and structures of Jewish identity. An argument began that has not yet ceased on what Judaism is, and who is an authentic Jew.

The first such critic known to us is Hosea, who prophesied in the Northern Kingdom in the mid-eighth century B.C.E. He abhorred many of the religious practices, institutions, and beliefs of his day. Prominent among these were the major northern shrines at Gilgal and Bethel (which he mockingly called Beth-Aven, "house of wickedness"):

Do not come to Gilgal,
and do not go up to Beth-Aven,
and do not swear: "As Yahweh lives." (Hosea 4:15)

These shrines and their cultic practices—including sacrifices[63] and oaths—were illegitimate in Hosea's eyes. He also objected to the multiplicity of local religious shrines, which typically featured sacrificial altars, standing stones, and

holy trees or asherah-objects. He associates the worship at these shrines with illicit sex and promiscuity:

> On the mountaintops they make sacrifices,
> and on the hills they burn offerings;
> Beneath oaks, poplars, and terebinths
> whose shade is good.
> That is why their daughters have illicit sex,
> and their daughters-in-law commit adultery. . . .
> And they too turn aside with prostitutes,
> and sacrifice with sacred whores.[64] (Hosea 4:13–14)

The equation of religious and sexual misconduct provides the background
for the cautionary story of Hosea's marriage to a prostitute (Hosea 1 and 3) and
the metaphor of Yahweh's marriage to promiscuous Israel (Hosea 2).[65] The language of sexual misconduct—whether historically accurate or not—gives Hosea
a broad brush to paint Israel's depravity.[66]

But when we look at earlier portraits of Israelite religious practice, the local
shrines are depicted as perfectly orthodox and innocuous. For example, Abram's
first act when he enters the Promised Land is to build such a shrine:

Abram traveled across the land to the site of Shechem, to the Oak of the
Teacher. The Canaanites were then in the land. And Yahweh appeared to
Abram and said, "To your descendants I will give this land." And he built there
an altar to Yahweh, who had appeared to him there. (Genesis 12:6–7)

Abram next builds an altar on a hill between Bethel and Ai, and he prays to
Yahweh there (Genesis 12:8). Later Yahweh appears to Jacob at Bethel, and Jacob
makes a vow and erects a standing stone to mark it as a holy site: "And this rock,
which I have set up as a standing stone, will be a temple [lit. "house"] of God
[beth elohim]" (Genesis 28:21). From these and many other examples, we can see
that these were normal shrines in the Yahwistic cult. Why should Hosea disparage them with such a blanket denunciation?

There were probably many factors at play in the prophet's rejection of the
legitimacy of the local shrines, but one was likely the fact that these were cultic
features shared with Israel's neighbors. Local shrines with altars, standing stones,
and trees were a common phenomenon in West Semitic culture, probably going
back to the Stone Age.[67] Phoenician coins clearly depict the iconography of such
shrines (Figure 1). One of Hosea's objections is that the shrines were devoted to

"Baal" (or "the Baals"), even though he admits that the sacrifices and oaths were offered to Yahweh.[68] The repudiation of the local shrines with "the Baals" seems, at least in part, to follow the same logic of nontranslatability that we saw above in the castigation of the seer Balaam. A trait that is shared with non-Israelites is damned as foreign and illicit, and it is redescribed as conducing to illicit sex.

Baruch Halpern has described this phenomenon, which Hosea begins and which bears fruit in Deuteronomy and other biblical books, as "the elite redefinition of traditional culture."[69] The old religious practices and ideas—which shared features with neighboring cultures—were derided as alien, foreign, and corrupting. The new religious elite developed a critique that at times extended to all traditional forms of religious ritual, setting in its place the primacy of individual ethics and interior piety. This critique, when implemented following the reforms of Kings Hezekiah and Josiah, transformed the local aspect of Israelite religion from family religion to personal, interior devotion.[70] Hosea captures the direction of this movement by posing ritual and ethics as antithetical, a contrast that would have seemed strange and radical to most Israelites:[71] "For I desire love, not sacrifices, / knowledge of God rather than burnt offerings" (Hosea 6:6).

The old practices are empty, and inner religion becomes ascendant. This gives rise to Jeremiah's later formulation of the "new covenant," which is purely interior: "I will put my teaching within them, and I will write it in their hearts, so that I will be their God, and they will be my people" (Jeremiah 31:32).

According to the biblical accounts, the elimination of the local shrines was adopted as public policy by Kings Hezekiah and Josiah (2 Kings 18 and 23).[72] Among the circumstances that made possible the rejection of these shrines and the uprooting of traditional religious practice was the devastation wrought by the Assyrians in the Judaean countryside in the campaign of 701 B.C.E.[73] With only Jerusalem left, the decision to abolish local shrines and transform kin-based religion was perhaps inevitable: the Assyrian armies had already done the work of demolition. In the wake of this calamity, Jerusalem and its Temple became the primary locus of Israelite religion.

More than any other biblical book, Deuteronomy (composed in the seventh–sixth centuries B.C.E.) defines the new course of Judaism as a religion of interior choice and commitment.[74] The object is to love God and to obey the law that God has planted in our hearts. Priests, prophets, and other religious intermediaries are rarely mentioned; rituals are mere reminders of God's gracious laws. God is transcendent and One, not a multiplicity of local phenomena, as might be gathered by the multiplicity of shrines. (Note the local divine titles "Yahweh of Samaria" and "Yahweh of Teman" discussed above.)[75] These emphases of Deuteronomy are aptly captured by the Shema:

Hear, O Israel, Yahweh our God, Yahweh is One. You shall love Yahweh, your God, with all your heart, with all your soul, and with all your might. These things that I command you today shall be upon your hearts. You shall repeat them to your children, and you shall speak of them when you sit in your house, when you walk on the way, when you lie down, and when you rise up. (Deuteronomy 6:4–7)

This is classic Jewish spirituality, nurtured by Deuteronomy and transmitted through the centuries.

The obverse side of this interior spirituality is the condemnation of the old shrines as foreign and corrupting, inevitably leading to sex with foreigners.[76] Rather than be seduced by foreign culture, Moses in Deuteronomy commands the Israelites to destroy it:

This is what you shall do to them: pull down their altars, break their standing stones, cut up their wooden pillars [asherahs], and burn their idols in fire. For you are a holy people to Yahweh your God. Yahweh your God has chosen you to be His precious people, over all the peoples on the face of the earth. (Deuteronomy 7:5–6)

The language of cultural distinctiveness is here joined to the alienation of native tradition. The local shrines are now defined as foreign Canaanite snares, on the far side of Israelite identity. Because Israel is different, it must spurn the practices of the nations. Thus, the old-time religion became stigmatized as the foreign Other. Only Jerusalem, "the site that Yahweh your God will choose" (Deuteronomy 12:5, cf. 1 Kings 8:16), is hallowed as the place of God's true name.

Deuteronomy's revisionism ushers in a new Jewish theology and identity. God is transcendent, uncontained by heaven and earth, having no shape or form, "for you saw no form when Yahweh spoke to you on Horeb out of the fire" (4:15). He demands that Israel love and obey him, each by his or her free choice: "Choose life . . . by loving Yahweh your God" (30:19–20). Wherever one is—whether in Jerusalem or not—God is there: "If you look there for Yahweh your God, you will find Him, if you seek with all your heart and soul" (4:29). Yahweh's law, which is wise and perfect, exists within the individual: "It is not too wonderful for you or too distant . . . but the word is very close to you, it is in your mouth and your heart, to do it" (30:14). And as God is wise and profound, so is His people, as the nations—obtuse no more—proclaim: "This great nation is indeed a wise and profound people" (4:6). Thus do the nations add their assent to the revision of the traditional structures of Judaism. For a brief moment, the foreign nations, like the early portrayal of Balaam, are truthful seers of Israel's wisdom.

The *way* that Deuteronomy revises Jewish tradition is also fraught with significance. The book is presented as Moses' farewell discourse to Israel, in which he recounts the instructions that God gave to him at Mount Horeb.[77] Moses recalls that God said to him: "As for you, stand here before Me so that I may tell you all the commands, the laws, and the statutes that you will teach them" (Deuteronomy 5:28). Forty years later, on the threshold of the Promised Land, Moses finally teaches the Israelites "all that Yahweh had commanded him concerning them" (Deuteronomy 1:3) at the holy mountain. By means of this narrative frame, the book of Deuteronomy authorizes its version of Israelite laws and traditions as *torah misinay,* "Torah from Sinai," to use the later rabbinic term (though it is "Torah from Horeb" in this case). Deuteronomy begins a process that will become central in rabbinic Judaism: attributing all revisions and interpretations of biblical law and religion to the original revelation at Sinai.[78]

Deuteronomy makes interpretation of the law a fundamental way of constructing Jewish culture, and it does so by placing its interpretation in the foundational setting of God's revelation at the holy mountain. In this process, the Torah becomes an interpreted artifact, with the chain of Mosaically authorized interpretations stretching to the horizon. A later rabbi drew out some of the more extravagant consequences of this idea: "Torah, Mishnah, Talmud, and Aggadah—indeed, even the comments some bright student will one day make to his teacher—were already given to Moses on Mount Sinai."[79] All interpretation is always already there in the initial revelation at Sinai. From the precedent of Deuteronomy, interpretation has become both essential and interminable in Jewish culture. Every new boundary or relationship, every freshly redrawn inclusion or exclusion, are already implicit in God's original discourse, according to this ancient hermeneutical key. As a fascinating text from the Talmud puts it: "What is Torah? The interpretation [lit. "midrash"] of Torah" (BT Kiddushin 49a–b). Revision has come home to roost.

CONCLUSION: NEIGHBORS AND FENCES

Robert Frost famously observed that "good fences make good neighbors." A clear sense of the differences between oneself and others can conduce to a true neighborly relationship. But fences are often barbed, and a moral difference tends to inhere in the separation of inside from outside. Such is the case in many of the instances of genealogical, ritual, narrative, and revisionist self-definition in ancient Israel. Moral claims are often asserted in the differentiation of the collective self from the Other, of Israel from the nations.

Some biblical writings protested against this process of drawing the boundaries so that Israel is, by definition, on the side of the good and the nations on the side of evil. They pointedly confused and problematized these simple moral boundaries, providing a legacy of cultural self-critique within Judaism. I have mentioned above the stories of foreign women—Tamar, Rahab, Jael, and Ruth— who are, as Judah says, "more righteous than I" (Genesis 38:26). The book of Job presents a uniquely righteous man who is a foreigner (from "the land of Uz").[80] Job, like Abraham, argues with God about issues of morality, though the outcome is more ambiguous than in Abraham's case. Most important, the classical prophets also tended to criticize the ethnocentric claims of Israel. Amos warns: "Are you not like the children of the Cushites to me, O children of Israel, declares Yahweh? Did I not bring Israel out of the land of Egypt, and the Philistines from Caphtor, and Aram from Kir?" (Amos 9:7). This universalizing tendency offset the ethnocentrism implicit in a "chosen people" and created the potential for a powerful cultural critique, one of the great legacies of the biblical prophets.[81] The prophetic writings are not fond of the cultural fences that divide neighbor against neighbor.

The moral problem of nationalism and ethnic boundaries is most directly addressed in the book of Jonah, in which the reluctant prophet is angry and despondent when Yahweh forgives the people of Nineveh:

> This seemed like a great evil to Jonah, and he was very angry. He prayed to Yahweh, saying, "O Yahweh, isn't this what I said when I was in my own land, and why I earlier fled to Tarshish? For I know that you are a gracious and compassionate God, slow to anger, abundant in kindness, and renouncing evil. Now, Yahweh, take my life from me, for I would rather die than live." (Jonah 4:1–2)

In the end, Yahweh teaches Jonah his lesson, that the nations are precious in God's eyes and that cultural narcissism is irrational and immoral. Notably, in view of the prominence of humor in later Jewish self-critique, God accomplishes this with a dash of humor. God's final comment—and the last word in the book—refers to the "many cattle" (4:11) who too had fasted and worn sackcloth alongside the Ninevites (3:7–8).[82] The comic image of penitent cows drives home the point that Israel has no intrinsically superior claim to God's love than the other nations. Or even their cows.

Biblical Israel shows many faces in its relations with its neighbors and fences in the ancient Near East. It is a member of a larger cultural family but a self-consciously unique member of that family. It constructed its self-image out of the rich traditions of prior ideologies, narratives, and rituals, but it made something new out of the old worlds.[83] One of the leitmotifs in modern biblical scholarship has been the recovery of the cultural context of ancient Israel, allowing us the opportunity to read the biblical writings anew. When read in the context of the ancient Near East, the Bible shows itself to be more complex, variegated, and even self-contradictory than we knew before. Moral and philosophical issues are debated in this book, and often they are not settled. Cultural identities are constructed in one part, only to be deconstructed in another. A culturally and historically alive Bible may be unsettling to some, for whom its meanings require the stable sediment of tradition. But tradition is itself unstable, and interpretation goes on, without end.

NOTES

1. R. Hestrin et al., eds., *Ketovot Mesaprot* (Jerusalem, 1973), 94. On the difficulties of this text, see P. D. Miller, Jr., "Psalms and Inscriptions," *Supplements to Vetus Testamentum* 32 (1981): 320–22.

2. According to Deuteronomy 3:11, Og was the last of the *rephaim*, the aboriginal giants of Canaan, and his huge iron bed (or iron coffin) was on display at Rabbah, the capital city of Ammon. Its dimensions were 13½ feet (9 cubits) long by 6 feet (4 cubits) wide. It is possible that the tradition of the giant stature of the aboriginal Canaanites was inferred from the huge ruined walls of Middle Bronze Age (2200–1500 B.C.E.) tells, combined with old traditions of the quasi-divine Rephaim; see H. Rouillard, "Rephaim," in *Dictionary of Deities and Demons in the Bible*, K. van der Toorn, B. Becking, and P. W. van der Horst, eds., 2d ed. (Leiden, 1999), 692–700.

3. This passage belongs to the oldest stratum of biblical poetry; see S. Morag, "Layers of Antiquity: Some Linguistic Observations on the Oracles of Balaam" (Hebrew), in S. Morag, *Mehkarim bi-leshon ha-Mikra* (Jerusalem, 1995), 45–69.

4. See A. D. Smith, *The Ethnic Origins of Nations* (Oxford, 1986); B. Anderson, *Imagined Communities: Reflections on the Origin and Spread of Nationalism*, rev. ed. (London, 1991).

5. P. Machinist, "The Question of Distinctiveness in Ancient Israel: An Essay," in *Ah, Assyria . . . Studies in Assyrian History and Ancient Near Eastern Historiography Presented to Hayim Tadmor*, M. Cogan and I. Ephal, eds. (Jerusalem, 1991), 196–212; P. Machinist, "Outsiders or Insiders: The Biblical View of Emergent Israel and Its Contexts," in *The Other in Jewish Thought and History: Constructions of Jewish Culture and Identity*, L. J. Silberstein and R. L. Cohn, eds. (New York, 1994), 35–60.

6. J. Assmann, *Moses the Egyptian: The Memory of Egypt in Western Monotheism* (Cambridge, Mass., 1997), 44–47.

7. Ibid., 2–3.

8. Deir Alla I.1. See J. A. Hackett, *The Balaam Text from Deir Alla* (Chico, Calif., 1984), and S. Ahituv, *Asupat Ketovot Ivriyot* (Jerusalem, 1992), 265–86.

9. On the methods involved in dating the biblical sources, see R. E. Friedman, *Who Wrote the Bible?* (San Francisco, 1997), and D. M. Carr, *Reading the Fractures of Genesis: Historical and Literary Approaches* (Louisville, Ky., 1996).

10. A. Rofé, *Introduction to the Composition of the Pentateuch* (Sheffield, Engl., 1999), 93–94; A. Rofé, *Sefer Bilam* (Jerusalem, 1979), 49–57.

11. Gershom Scholem, "Revelation and Tradition as Religious Categories in Judaism," in Gershom Scholem, *The Messianic Idea in Judaism and Other Essays on Jewish Spirituality* (New York, 1971), 289–90: "Not system but *commentary* is the legitimate form though which truth is approached. . . . Commentary thus became the characteristic expression of Jewish thinking about truth."

12. P. K. McCarter, Jr., *Ancient Inscriptions: Voices from the Biblical World* (Washington, D.C., 1996), 48–50. For the whole text, see M. Lichtheim, *Ancient Egyptian Literature, Vol. II: The New Kingdom* (Berkeley, 1976), 73–77. For a recent discussion, see J. R. Huddlestun, "Merneptah's Revenge: The 'Israel Stela' and Its Modern Interpreters" (forthcoming).

13. See the recent syntheses of L. E. Stager, "Forging an Identity: The Emergence of Ancient Israel," in *The Oxford History of the Biblical World*, M. D. Coogan, ed. (New York, 1998), 123–75; I. Finkelstein, "The Great Transformation: The 'Conquest' of the Highlands Frontiers and the Rise of the Territorial States," in *The Archaeology of Society in the Holy Land*, 2d ed., T. E. Levy, ed. (London, 1998), 349–65; and W. G. Dever, "The Late Bronze–Early Iron I Horizon in Syria-Palestine: Egyptians, Canaanites, 'Sea Peoples,' and Proto-Israelites," in *The Crisis Years: The 12th Century B.C. from Beyond the Danube to the Tigris*, W. A. Ward and M. S. Joukowsky, eds. (Dubuque, Iowa, 1992), 99–110.

14. Anderson, *Imagined Communities*.

15. See chapter 1 in this volume and Ilana Pardes, *The Biography of Ancient Israel: National Narratives in the Bible* (Berkeley, 2000).

16. On the Exodus stories as a symbolic rite of passage, see R. L. Cohn, *The Shape of Sacred Space* (Chico, Calif., 1981), 7–23; R. S. Hendel, "Sacrifice as a Cultural System: The Ritual Symbolism of Exodus 24:3–8," *Zeitschrift für die Alttestamentliche Wissenschaft* 101 (1989): 375–79; and W. H. C. Propp, *Exodus 1–18* (New York, 1999), 35–36.

17. D. B. Redford, *Egypt, Canaan, and Israel in Ancient Times* (Princeton, 1992), 221–27.

18. For further details, see B. Halpern, "The Exodus from Egypt: Myth or Reality?" in *The Rise of Ancient Israel*, H. Shanks, ed. (Washington, D.C., 1992), 86–113, and R. S. Hendel, "The Exodus in Biblical Memory," *Journal of Biblical Literature* 120 (2001): 601–22.

19. Sigmund Freud, *Civilization and Its Discontents*, trans. J. Riviere (New York, 1958), 64.

20. The Kenites are mentioned in only a handful of biblical passages: Joshua 15:57; Judges 4–5; Judges 1:16; 1 Samuel 15:6, 27:10, 30:29; and 1 Chronicles 2:55. See B. Halpern, "Kenites," in *The Anchor Bible Dictionary*, D. N. Freedman, ed. (New York, 1992), 4: 17–22.

21. R. Firestone, *Journeys in Holy Lands: The Evolution of the Abraham-Ishmael Legends in Islamic Exegesis* (Albany, N.Y., 1990).

22. R. S. Hendel, *Epic of the Patriarch: The Jacob Cycle and the Narrative Traditions of Canaan and Israel* (Atlanta, Ga., 1987), 84, 128.

23. Ibid., 128–31.

24. See R. Alter, *The Art of Biblical Narrative* (New York, 1981), 42–45.

25. The major studies are F. M. Cross, *Canaanite Myth and Hebrew Epic: Essays in the History of the Religion of Israel* (Cambridge, Mass., 1973), and M. S. Smith, *The Early History of God: Yahweh and the Other Deities in Ancient Israel* (San Francisco, 1990). Translations of the major religious texts are available in S. Parker, ed., *Ugaritic Narrative Poetry* (Atlanta, Ga., 1997); W. W. Hallo, ed., *The Context of Scripture: Vol. I: Canonical Compositions from the Biblical World* (Leiden, 1997), 239–375; M. D. Coogan, *Stories from Ancient Canaan* (Philadelphia, 1978); and J. B. Pritchard, ed., *Ancient Near Eastern Texts Relating to the Old Testament*, 3d ed. (Princeton, 1969), 129–55.

26. M. Dietrich, O. Loretz, and J. Sanmartín, eds., *The Cuneiform Alphabetic Texts from Ugarit, Ras Ibn Hani and Other Places* (Münster, 1995), 1.5.1–4.

27. Biblical allusions to the defeat of chaos monsters in primeval times include Psalms 74:13–14 (the vanquished monsters are Sea, Dragons, Leviathan), Isaiah 51:9–10 (Rahab, Dragon, Sea), and Job 40–41 (Leviathan and Behemoth). See J. Day, *God's Conflict with the Dragon and the Sea: Echoes of a Canaanite Myth in the Old Testament* (Cambridge, Engl., 1985).

28. On El in Canaan and Israel, see Cross, *Canaanite Myth*, 13–75; Smith, *Early History of God*, 7–12; and W. Herrmann, "El," in van der Toorn et al., eds., *Dictionary of Deities*, 274–80.

29. A Hebrew inscription from the eighth or seventh century B.C.E. reads "[El], creator of earth" (a trace of the *lamed* is readable). See P. D. Miller, "El, The Creator of Earth," *Bulletin of the American Schools of Oriental Research* 239 (1980): 43–46, and Ahituv, *Asupat Ketovot*, 22–23.

30. The term *shadday* is also used, in the plural, to denote the gods of the Deir Alla inscription (see n. 8 above). These gods are the *shaddayin*, the "mountain ones."

31. On Asherah in Canaan and Israel, see Smith, *Early History of God*, 80–114; J. Day, "Asherah in the Hebrew Bible and Northwest Semitic Literature," *Journal of Biblical Literature* 105 (1986): 385–408; S. M. Olyan, *Asherah and the Cult of Yahweh in Israel* (Atlanta, Ga., 1988), 1–37; and N. Wyatt, "Asherah," in van der Toorn et al., eds., *Dictionary of Deities*, 99–105, and references.

32. Dietrich et al., eds., *Cuneiform Alphabetic Texts*, 1.4.4.40–43.

33. Ibid., 1.14.197–206.

34. On the *battim* woven for Asherah, cf. Akkadian *betatu*, "a decoration used on garments and leather objects" (*Chicago Assyrian Dictionary* [Chicago, 1956–92], s.v.), and note the comparable function of the *bet pirishti*, "a room in the Babylonian temple complex which was used to house the vestments of priests and the garments used to clothe the statues of deities" (L. T. Doty, "Akkadian bet pirišti," in *The Tablet and the Scroll: Near Eastern Studies in Honor of William W. Hallo*, M. E. Cohen, D. C. Snell, and D. B. Weisberg, eds. [Bethesda, Md., 1993], 87–89).

35. On the theme of cultic purity and impurity among Israel's monarchs in the books of Kings, see B. Halpern, *The First Historians: The Hebrew Bible and History* (San Francisco, 1988), 220–28.

36. On the biblical passages, see especially Olyan, *Asherah*, 3–22.

37. The literature on these inscriptions is vast; see, e.g., the thorough treatments and reviews of literature in O. Keel and C. Uehlinger, *Gods, Goddesses, and Images of God in Ancient Israel* (Minneapolis, 1998), 210–48; S. Wiggins, *A Reassessment of 'Asherah': A Study According to the Textual Sources of the First Two Millennia* B.C.E. (Neukirchen, Germany, 1993); and W. Dietrich and M. A. Klopfenstein, eds., *Ein Gott allein? JHWH-Verehrung und biblischer Monotheismus im Kontext der israelitischen und altorientalischen Religionsgeschichte* (Göttingen, 1994). See also n. 31 above.

38. Ahituv, *Asupat Ketovot*, 152–60.

39. Ibid., 111–13. Some of the words are indistinct or overwritten, and there are other possible readings.

40. W. James, *The Varieties of Religious Experience: A Study in Human Nature* (New York, 1902).

41. See K. van der Toorn, *Family Religion in Babylonia, Syria and Israel: Continuity and Change in the Forms of Religious Life* (Leiden, 1996), and R. Albertz, *A History of Israelite Religion in the Old Testament Period* (Louisville, Ky., 1994), 1: 25–39, 94–103, 186–95.

42. Reading *el shadday*, "God (El), the One of the Mountain," with the Samaritan Pentateuch and the Syriac Peshitta (the Septuagint also reads *el*); the Masoretic text reads *et shadday*, "with the One of the Mountain." The poetic parallelism of this line strongly supports reading *el* here rather than the preposition *et* (which is found predominantly in prose); the Masoretic text has apparently suffered a small scribal error.

43. See, e.g., M. Weippert, *Jahwe und die anderen Götter: Studien zur Religionsgeschichte des antiken Israel in ihrem syrisch-palästinischen Kontext* (Tübingen, 1997), 1–24, and S. Ackerman, *Under Every Green Tree: Popular Religion in Sixth-Century Judah* (Atlanta, Ga., 1989).

44. For one such dialectal variation, see R. S. Hendel, "Sibilants and šibbolet (Judges 12:6)," *Bulletin of the American Schools of Oriental Research* 301 (1996): 69–75.

45. M. Fox, "Sign of the Covenant: Circumcision in the Light of the Priestly *ôt* Etiologies," *Revue biblique* 81 (1974): 557–96.

46. H. Eilberg Schwartz, *The Savage in Judaism: An Anthropology of Israelite Religion and Ancient Judaism* (Bloomington, Ind., 1990), 141–76.

47. The earliest evidence is from ca. 2800 B.C.E. in Syria; see J. Sasson, "Circumcision in the Ancient Near East," *Journal of Biblical Literature* 85 (1966): 473–76; W. H. C. Propp, "The Origins of Infant Circumcision in Israel," *Hebrew Annual Review* 11 (1987): 355; and R. de Vaux, *Ancient Israel: Its Life and Institutions* (New York, 1961), 46–48.

48. L. E. Stager, "The Impact of the Sea Peoples in Canaan (1185–1050 BCE)," in *The Archaeology of Society in the Holy Land*, T. E. Levy, ed. (London, 1995), 332–48.

49. This is suggested in passing by Stager in ibid., 344.

50. Propp, "Origins of Infant Circumcision," 363–66.

51. On this transformation, see S. J. D. Cohen, *The Beginnings of Jewishness: Boundaries, Varieties, Uncertainties* (Berkeley, 1999), 241–62.

52. Josephus, *Antiquities*, 13.257–58 (Edom), 318 (Ituria/Yeter); Judith 14:10 (Ammon). On the significance of circumcision in the Hellenistic and Roman periods, see Cohen, *Beginnings of Jewishness*, 39–49, 120–25, and J. J. Collins, "A Symbol of Otherness: Circumcision and Salvation in the First Century," in J. J. Collins, *Seers, Sybils and Sages in Hellenistic-Roman Judaism* (Leiden, 1997), 211–35.

53. Mary Douglas, "The Abominations of Leviticus," in Mary Douglas, *Purity and Danger: An Analysis of the Concepts of Pollution and Taboo* (London, 1966), 41–57. See also Mary Douglas, "Deciphering a Meal," in Mary Douglas, *Implicit Meanings: Essays in Anthropology* (London, 1975), 249–75, and Mary Douglas, *Leviticus as Literature* (Oxford, 1999), 134–75.

54. Stager, "Forging an Identity," 165; see also Stager, "Impact of the Sea Peoples," 344.

55. On the general rarity of pork production in the Levant in the second and first millennia B.C.E., see B. Hesse, "Pig Lovers and Pig Haters: Patterns of Palestinian Pork Production," *Journal of Ethnobiology* 10 (1990): 195–225.

56. Stager, "Impact of the Sea Peoples," 344.

57. See S. Talmon, "The Calendar of the Covenanters of the Judean Desert," in S. Talmon, *The World of Qumran from Within: Collected Studies* (Jerusalem, 1989), 147–85, and J. C. VanderKam, *Calendars in the Dead Sea Scrolls: Measuring Time* (London, 1998).

58. W. W. Hallo, *Origins: The Ancient Near Eastern Background of Some Modern Western Institutions* (Leiden, 1996), 127–35 and references.

59. Ahituv, *Asupat Ketovot*, 98–99 (the Yavneh Yam letter).

60. E.g., Amos 8:5, Hosea 2:13, and Isaiah 1:13, each in the context of a critique of public injustice or immorality, implying that the Sabbath was a well-entrenched religious tradition by this time.

61. M. Z. Brettler offers cogent counterarguments to the view—originally rooted in religious apologetics—that circumcision and the Sabbath only became signs of Israelite identity after the exile (Brettler, "Judaism in the Hebrew Bible? The Transition from Ancient Israelite Religion to Judaism," *Catholic Biblical Quarterly* 61 [1999]: 436–38).

62. See the excellent survey in J. J. M. Roberts, "The Ancient Near Eastern Environment," in *The Hebrew Bible and Its Modern Interpreters*, D. A. Knight and G. M. Tucker, eds. (Chico, Calif., 1985), 75–121.

63. The prohibition, "do not go up" *(al-ta'alu)* in the second line is also a wordplay on "do not sacrifice."

64. The sense of *kedeshot*, lit. "sacred women," in parallel with "prostitutes," is uncertain; see K. van der Toorn, "Cultic Prostitution," in Freedman, ed., *Anchor Bible Dictionary*, 5: 510–13, and the next note.

65. M. J. W. Leith, "Verse and Reverse: The Transformation of the Woman, Israel, in Hosea 1–3," in *Gender and Difference in Ancient Israel*, P. L. Day, ed. (Minneapolis, 1989), 95–108; P. A. Bird, " 'To Play the Harlot': An Inquiry into an Old Testament Metaphor," in P. A. Bird, *Missing Persons and Mistaken Identities: Women and Gender in Ancient Israel* (Minneapolis, 1997), 219–36.

66. On adultery and nymphomania as metaphors for idolatry, see M. Halbertal and A. Margalit, *Idolatry* (Cambridge, Mass., 1992), 9–20.

67. T. N. D. Mettinger, *No Graven Image? Israelite Aniconism in Its Ancient Near Eastern Context* (Stockholm, 1995), 168–91.

68. See B. Halpern, "The Baal (and the Asherah) in Seventh-Century Judah: Yhwh's Retainers Retired," in *Konsequente Traditiongeschichte: Festschrift für Klaus Baltzer zum 65. Geburtstag*, R. Bartelmus et al., eds. (Fribourg, 1993), 115–54. Halpern argues that the "baals" in such denunciations often refer to the "heavenly host," i.e., the angels. On the denigration of the angels in biblical writings of this period, see also A. Rofé, *Ha-Emunah bi-Melakhim be-Yisrael* (Jerusalem, 1979).

69. B. Halpern, "Sybil, or the Two Nations? Archaism, Kinship, Alienation, and the Elite Redefinition of Traditional Culture in Judah in the 8th–7th Centuries B.C.E.," in *The Study of the Ancient Near East in the Twenty-First Century*, J. S. Cooper and G. M. Schwartz, eds. (Winona Lake, Ind., 1996), 291–338.

70. Van der Toorn, *Family Religion*, 375.

71. R. S. Hendel, "Prophets, Priests, and the Efficacy of Ritual," in *Pomegranates and Golden Bells: Studies in Biblical, Jewish, and Near Eastern Ritual, Law, and Literature in Honor of Jacob Milgrom*, D. P. Wright, D. N. Freedman, and A. Hurvitz, eds. (Winona Lake, Ind., 1995), 185–98.

72. P. K. McCarter, Jr., "The Religious Reforms of Hezekiah and Josiah," in *Aspects of Monotheism: How God Is One*, H. Shanks and J. Meinhardt, eds. (Washington, D.C., 1997), 57–80.

73. B. Halpern, "Jerusalem and the Lineages in the Seventh Century B.C.E.: Kinship and the Rise of Individual Moral Liability," in *Law and Ideology in Monarchic Israel*, B. Halpern and D. W. Hobson, eds. (Sheffield, Engl., 1991), 41–49; Halpern, "Sybil," 311–21.

74. On the date of Deuteronomy and its religious innovations, see M. Weinfeld, *Deuteronomy and the Deuteronomic School* (Oxford, 1972), esp. 191–243; Halpern, "Sybil," 327–37; and B. M. Levinson, *Deuteronomy and the Hermeneutics of Legal Innovation* (New York, 1997).

75. On the issue of multiple manifestations of Yahweh, see McCarter, "Religious Reforms," 57–80.

76. On the key texts, see G. N. Knoppers, "Sex, Religion, and Politics: The Deuteronomist on Intermarriage," *Hebrew Annual Review* 14 (1994): 121–41.

77. The name of God's mountain fluctuates between Sinai (in J and P sources of the Pentateuch) and Horeb (in the E source and Deuteronomy). On these sources, see R. E. Friedman, *Who Wrote the Bible?* (New York, 1987).

78. On the exegetical issues raised by Deuteronomy, see M. Fishbane, *Biblical Interpretation in Ancient Israel* (Oxford, 1985), 435–40, and Levinson, *Deuteronomy*, 15–17.

79. Midrash Tanḥuma 2.58b; trans. Scholem, "Revelation and Tradition," 289.

80. The land of Uz (Job 1:1) is probably to be located on the Arabian peninsula; see E. A. Knauf, "Uz," in Freedman, ed., *Anchor Bible Dictionary*, 6: 770–71.

81. See the illuminating discussion of M. Walzer, *Interpretation and Social Criticism* (Cambridge, Mass., 1987), 67–94.

82. Note that the object of the command "let them pray" (Jonah 3:8) can also be construed as including the cows; see J. M. Sasson, *Jonah* (New York, 1990), 257.

83. R. S. Hendel, "Worldmaking in Ancient Israel," *Journal for the Study of the Old Testament* 56 (1992): 3–18.

SELECTED BIBLIOGRAPHY

Albertz, R. *A History of Israelite Religion in the Old Testament Period.* 2 vols. Louisville, Ky., 1994.

Coogan, M., ed. *The Oxford History of the Biblical World.* New York, 1998.

Cross, F. M. *Canaanite Myth and Hebrew Epic: Essays in the History of the Religion of Israel.* Cambridge, Mass., 1973.

Day, P. L., ed. *Gender and Difference in Ancient Israel.* Minneapolis, 1989.

King, Philip J., and Lawrence E. Stager. *Life in Biblical Israel.* Louisville, Ky., 2001.

Miller, P. D. *The Religion of Ancient Israel.* Louisville, Ky., 2000.

Pedersen, J. *Israel: Its Life and Culture.* 2 vols. London, 1926–40.

Shanks, H., ed. *Ancient Israel: From Abraham to the Roman Destruction of the Temple.* 2d ed. Washington, D.C., 1999.

Smith, M. S. *The Early History of God: Yahweh and the Other Deities in Ancient Israel.* San Francisco, 1990.

van der Toorn, K. *Family Religion in Babylonia, Syria and Israel: Continuity and Change in the Forms of Religious Life.* Leiden, 1996.

Greek motifs decorating the cave walls of a Jewish burial chamber in Tell Maresha,
in southern Judaea, illustrate the adaptation of Hellenic symbols in Second Temple Judaism.
(Israel Antiquities Authority, Jerusalem)

HELLENISTIC JUDAISM

ERICH S. GRUEN

Alexander the Great burst like a thunderbolt upon the history of the Near East. Within a dozen years in the late fourth century B.C.E., he humbled the mighty Persian Empire, marching its length and breadth, defeating its armies, toppling its satraps, terminating its monarchy, and installing a Greek hegemony from the Hellespont to the Indus. It was a breathtaking achievement—and on more than just the military front. The conquests of Alexander provided a springboard for the expansion of Greek culture in the lands of the eastern Mediterranean. That world would never be quite the same again.

No direct confrontation occurred between the great Macedonian conqueror and the Jews of Palestine. Fanciful tales sprang up later in which Alexander paid homage to the high priest in Jerusalem and Yahweh sanctioned his subjugation of Persia. None of them has a basis in fact. Palestine was of small interest to the king who captured the great fortress of Tyre, then marched straight to Egypt and subsequently to Mesopotamia, on the way to the heartland of the Persian Empire. Judaea was spared—and largely ignored.

The long-term impact on Jewish culture, however, was momentous. Jews had hitherto lived under a Persian yoke, a light one and a relatively benign one. The centers of royal power lay at a great distance, in Susa and Persepolis, with little direct effect upon the society of the Jews. A major change occurred with the coming of the Greeks. Alexander's vast holdings splintered after his death, as his powerful marshals divided and fought fiercely over the territories he had claimed. In the new configurations of the Hellenistic kingdoms, Greco-Macedonian dynasts held sway, and Hellenism became the culture of the ruling class in the major cities and states, both old and new, of the Near East—in places like Sardis and Ephesus, Alexandria and Antioch, in Babylon, Tyre, and Sidon, and in the coastal communities of Palestine.

The political constellation affected Jews everywhere. Palestine itself came under the control of the Ptolemies of Egypt for about a century after Alexander's death, and, when power shifted in the region, the land entered the hegemony of the Seleucid monarchs of Syria from the beginning of the second century B.C.E. The Maccabean rebellion ushered in a Jewish dynasty, the Hasmonaeans, fol-

lowed by the house of Herod, who provided ostensibly indigenous rule. But the
Hasmonaeans, in fact, governed only under the shadow of the Seleucids, and
the Herodians under the shadow (sometimes more than the shadow) of Rome.
The Hellenistic monarchies continued to reckon Palestine within their sphere of
influence, and Rome later undertook to supply its own governors of the region.
In the Diaspora, Jews everywhere lived in circumstances where pagan power
held sway. Through most of the third and second centuries B.C.E., the Ptolemies
exercised authority in Egypt and usually in Cyprus and Cyrene; the Seleucids
held power in Syria, Phoenicia, and at least nominally in the lands across the Euphrates; the Attalids ruled in Pergamum and extended their influence elsewhere
in Asia Minor where a diversity of dynasts struggled for control; and in Greece
itself contending forces from Macedon and various states and federations kept
the Jews of their region in a politically subordinate position. The subsequent
dominance of Rome in the eastern Mediterranean, beginning in the late second
century B.C.E., brought Jews, among others, into direct contact with Roman governors, officialdom, and imperial power.

The Jewish Diaspora, to be sure, did not await Alexander. Jews had certainly
found their way to Syria, to Egypt, and to the lands of the Tigris and Euphrates
well before. But the arrival of the Greeks proved to be an irresistible magnet.
Jews migrated to the new settlements and expanded communities in substantial
numbers. A Greek diaspora had brought the Jewish one in its wake. Within a few
generations, Jews had installed themselves in an astonishing array of places all
around the Mediterranean and beyond. If one can believe the author of 1 Maccabees, composed in the late second century B.C.E., they could be found not only
in Syria, Egypt, the Parthian empire, and throughout the cities and principalities
of Asia Minor, but even in Greece itself, in various islands of the Aegean, and
in Crete, Cyprus, and Cyrene.[1] This remarkable dispersal impressed itself even
upon pagan writers like Strabo, who commented that the Jewish people by his
day (late first century B.C.E.) had moved into almost every city and that hardly a
place remained where they had not made their presence felt.[2]

The consequences are readily discernible. Jews became exposed to and thoroughly engaged with the Greek culture that prevailed in the various communities in which they settled. And not only in the Diaspora. Greek towns sprang up
in Palestine itself, from Akko to Gaza on the Mediterranean coast, in the Lower
Galilee, and in various sites on both sides of the Jordan.[3] Hence, even the Jews
of Judaea could not and did not isolate themselves altogether from the pervasive aura of Hellenism. For many Jews, especially in the Diaspora, the close
contact with the institutions, language, literature, art, and traditions of Hellas
reached the point where they lost touch with Hebrew itself. The translation of
the Hebrew Bible into Greek, probably in Alexandria sometime in the third or

second century B.C.E., reflects the needs of Jews settled abroad for several generations for whom Greek was the primary, perhaps sole, language and for some of whom education gave greater familiarity with Plato than with Moses. The Jewish involvement with Hellenism in the period from Alexander the Great to the destruction of the Second Temple in 70 C.E. was a central, even a defining, characteristic.

But the involvement is rife with ambiguities. Indeed, ambiguity adheres to the term "Hellenism" itself. No pure strain of Greek culture, whatever that might be even in principle, confronted the Jews of Palestine or the Diaspora. Transplanted Greek communities mingled with ancient Phoenician traditions on the Levantine coast, with powerful Egyptian elements in Alexandria, with enduring Mesopotamian institutions in Babylon, and with a complex mixture of societies in Anatolia. The Greek culture with which Jews came into contact comprised a mongrel entity—or rather entities, with a different blend in each location of the Mediterranean. The convenient term "Hellenistic" signifies complex amalgamations in the Near East in which the Greek ingredient was a conspicuous presence rather than a monopoly.

The tombs of Bnei Hezir (on left) and Zechariah (in center) in Jerusalem's Qidron Valley (probably first century C.E.) exhibit the appropriation by the Jewish elite of Greek architectural forms. (Israel Antiquities Authority, Jerusalem)

"Judaism," it need hardly be said, is at least as complex and elastic a term. The institution defies uniform definition. And changes over time, as in all religions, render any effort to capture its essence at a particular moment highly problematic. "Hellenistic Judaism" must have experienced considerable diversity, quite distinct in Alexandria, Antioch, Babylon, Ephesus, Cyrene, and Jerusalem. Simplistic formulations once in favor are now obsolete. We can no longer contrast "Palestinian Judaism" as the unadulterated form of the ancestral faith with "Hellenistic Judaism" as the Diaspora variety that diluted antique practices with alien imports. Hellenism existed in Palestine—and the Jews of the Diaspora still held to their heritage. Each individual area struck its balance differently and experienced its own peculiar level of mixture. It is essential to emphasize that Jews were not obliged to choose between succumbing to or resisting Hellenism. Nor should one imagine a conscious dilemma whereby they had to decide how far to lean in one direction or another, how much Hellenism was acceptable before they compromised the faith, or at what point on the spectrum between apostasy and piety they could comfortably locate themselves.

A different conception is called for. Many Diaspora Jews and even some dwelling in Hellenistic cities of Palestine after a generation or two were already confirmed Greek speakers and integrated members of communities governed by pagan practices and institutions. They did not confront daily decisions on the degree of assimilation or acculturation. They had long since become part of a Hellenic environment that they could take as a given. But their Judaism remained intact. What they needed was a means of defining and expressing their singularity within that milieu, the special characteristics that made them both integral to the community and true to their heritage.

JEWISH CREATIONS IN GREEK GENRES

How does one locate the boundaries between the cultures? The issue put in that form is itself problematic. The very metaphor of boundaries, even permeable boundaries, begs the question. The Jews, it might better be said, redefined their heritage in the terms of Hellenistic culture itself. They engaged actively with the traditions of Hellas, adapting genres and transforming legends to articulate their own legacy in modes congenial to a Hellenistic setting. At the same time, they recreated their past, retold stories in different shapes, and amplified the scriptural corpus itself through the medium of the Greek language and Greek literary forms. The challenge for the Jews was not how to surmount barriers or cross boundaries. In a world where Hellenic culture held an ascendant position, they strove to present Judaic traditions and express their own self-definition through the media of the Greeks—and to make those media their own.

This refashioning can be illustrated in a number of ways. Tragic drama is perhaps the quintessential Greek medium. This did not render it off-limits to the Jews. Quite the contrary. In one instance at least (and it can hardly be the only one), a Jewish writer named Ezekiel tried his hand in that genre, probably in the second century B.C.E. Working within the tradition of classical tragedy, influenced particularly by the plays of Aeschylus and Euripides, Ezekiel produced his own dramas, one of which—or at least a substantial portion of one—survives. The theme, however, is not drawn from Greek mythology or from the titanic clashes within Greek royal houses of distant and legendary antiquity. Ezekiel turned instead to material from his own people's legacy. The extant text, the *Exagoge,* is based on the story of Moses leading the Israelites out of Egypt. The choice of that tale clearly indicates an appeal to pride in national history and tradition produced in the most characteristically Hellenic mode.[4]

Ezekiel hewed closely to the narrative line contained in the Book of Exodus. He cast it in different form, of course, employing the conventions of the Greek theater, writing monologues and dialogues, keeping the battle scenes and the gore offstage, even bringing on the trusty messenger's speech to summarize events that transpired between dramatic episodes. But his tale diverges little from the biblical version. It was not Ezekiel's purpose to raise any doubts about the authority or adequacy of the Scriptures. The Septuagint, the Greek version of the Hebrew Bible, served as his text, and he conveyed its narrative faithfully. But Ezekiel was not wedded to it irrevocably. In a few key instances, he added new material to the mix. And they supply important clues to the tragedian's intent.

One item in particular merits special notice. Ezekiel inserted a remarkable scene that has no biblical prototype. Moses, in dialogue with his father-in-law, reports a puzzling dream in which he had a vision of a great throne high upon a summit extending to the cleft of heaven. There a noble man sat with diadem and a great scepter, summoned Moses to him, handed him the scepter and diadem, and departed from the throne. From that spot Moses had a view of the whole earth, both below it and above the sky, and a multitude of stars fell on their knees. Moses' father-in-law provides a most heartening interpretation of the dream: it is a sign from God that Moses will lift up a great throne, will issue judgments, and will serve as guide to mortals; the vision of the whole world, things both below and beyond God's firmament, signifies that Moses will perceive what is, what has been, and what will be.[5] This striking passage corresponds to nothing in the Book of Exodus. Indeed, no other tale anywhere in literature ascribes a dream vision to Moses. Furthermore, the very idea of a dream by a Hebrew figure rendered intelligible by a non-Hebrew figure is unparalleled. Ezekiel plainly aimed to capture his readers' attention here.

Greek tragedy could supply precedents of a sort. Certainly Attic plays include dream visions in sufficient quantity. And some approximations can be found in the Bible: a few fortunate figures received visions of God in their dreams, and still fewer actually glimpsed a throne. But nothing is quite like the sight seen by Moses in *Exagoge*. Nowhere does God relinquish his seat to anyone else.

The creativity of Ezekiel should receive its due. In the Book of Numbers, God announces that, though he reveals himself to others in visions and dreams, he speaks to Moses directly, face to face, without enigmatic messages.[6] Ezekiel chose to ignore or sidestep that message. It seemed a small price to pay. The playwright had a powerful scene in mind: the forecast of Moses' future through a dramatic dream that gave him access to divinity. Ezekiel employed forms and material drawn both from Greek literature and from Jewish traditions, but he shaped them to convey an original conception. The dramatist not only intensifies the grandeur of Moses but also reconceives Moses' relationship with God.

Moses encounters a "noble man" with scepter and diadem on the great throne that extends to Heaven. The image here plainly presents God as sovereign power, ruler of the universe. The celestial realm appears as analogous to royal governance on earth. God beckons to Moses to approach the throne, then bids him sit upon it, hands over the scepter and diadem, and departs. The meaning can hardly be that God has relinquished universal dominion. Rather, Ezekiel directs attention to the analogy. Moses' ascension to the throne and acquisition of royal emblems signals his appointment as the Lord's surrogate in governing the affairs of men. That meaning is reinforced when Moses' father-in-law interprets the dream. His reference to the great throne, to the exercise of jurisdiction, and to the leadership of men had clear resonance to the contemporaries of Ezekiel. Moses' role as executor of God's will on earth, with absolute authority, is modeled on royal rule in the Hellenistic realms.

Ezekiel deftly combined familiar conventions with striking novelty to create a complex portrait. He nowhere disputes or denies the biblical account. But the admixture of the dream episode both magnifies the Moses figure and renders it more accessible to the dramatist's own society. He expressed the powers of the Hebrew prophets in terms that applied to Greek seers. And he draped Moses in the emblems of royal power that would carry direct relevance to those who lived in the era of the great monarchies. The author reinvents the position of Moses on the model of Hellenistic kingship while making him the model and precursor of Hellenistic kingship itself. God places Moses upon his own throne, a symbolic assignment of universal authority, to sit in judgment and be a guide for all mortals. Those lines have telling significance: they betoken the application of the Law as a pattern for all nations. The Israelite hero thus becomes a beacon for humankind, a representative of the divinity on earth, described in phraseology that struck responsive chords among Ezekiel's Hellenic or Hellenized compatriots.

The tragic poet held scriptural authority in awe. But that did not prevent him from occasionally improving upon it. His most inventive scenes gave heightened force to Jewish traditions by commingling them with features arising from Greek culture and society. God's elevation of Moses to glory signified a royal dominion familiar to Hellenistic readers and a universal message that Jews could claim as their own. Ezekiel had effectively commandeered a preeminent Greek genre and deployed it as a source of esteem for his Jewish readership.

Jewish writers also adapted another and even more venerable Greek medium: epic poetry. Extant fragments are scanty and tantalizing—but also informative and illuminating. Record survives of a second-century-B.C.E. epic poet named Theodotus, whose remaining verses treated the tale of the rape of Dinah by Shechem and the consequent destruction of the Shechemite city by Dinah's brothers Levi and Simeon, the sons of Jacob.[7] The poet had obviously imbibed Hellenic culture and enjoyed thorough familiarity with Homeric language and epic technique. But he took as his text, at least in the surviving lines, an episode recorded in Genesis 34.

The biblical account has Jacob return to Canaan, after his lengthy absence in the land of Laban, and reach the city of Shechem. His daughter Dinah wanders into the city, only to be seized and ravished by the like-named Shechem, son of the ruler, Hamor. The event sets matters rapidly in motion. Shechem may have been initially overcome by lust, but he soon aims to make an honest man of himself. He obtains the intercession of his father, who speaks to Jacob about arranging a wedding. Hamor indeed goes well beyond that initial request. He generously proposes a host of marriage alliances between Jacob's people and his own, and makes his land and possessions available to the newcomers. The sons of Jacob, however, outraged at the defilement of Dinah, plot deception and revenge. They consent to the uniting of the peoples but only on condition that the Shechemites circumcise themselves, because intermarriage with the uncircumcised would be intolerable. Hamor and Shechem readily agree, and their example is swiftly followed; within a short time all the males in Shechem are circumcised. That provides the opportunity for Dinah's brothers. While the Shechemites still suffer the effects of the surgery, Levi and Simeon swoop down upon them, murder every male, loot the city, and carry off the women and children. The underhanded scheme and the ruthless butchering of a compliant people sits ill with Jacob. He rebukes his sons for making him vulnerable to the hostility of his neighbors. And he never forgives them. On his deathbed, he curses Levi and Simeon for their resort to the sword and their reckless yielding to animus and anger.[8] The tale hardly casts the Israelites' actions in the best possible light.

Theodotus's version adheres to the basic narrative but turns it in quite a different direction.[9] Both his elaborations and his omissions set the events in contrasting colors. Theodotus kept his eye on the Genesis narrative throughout. Nothing in his account stands in flagrant contradiction to it. But he felt free to embroider or suppress matters, thus giving a distinctive slant and allowing for an alternative meaning.

The epic poet blended Greek elements with the Hebrew legend. Theodotus identified Shechem's founder with the son of Hermes, a feature that linked the city's story to *ktisis* (colonial foundation) tales and Greek mythology.[10] And he has the divine impetus for the attack on Shechem delivered through an oracular forecast, in Hellenic fashion.[11] The pagan trimmings were plainly congenial to the auditors of Theodotus's epic rendition of the Scriptures.

More important divergences, however, lay elsewhere. The biblical tale casts a cloud on the Israelites. Shechem's act of rape, to be sure, is hardly exemplary conduct, nor is it condoned in Genesis. But the young man hastens to make amends; his father is magnanimous toward Jacob's people; and the Shechemite males unhesitatingly subject themselves to circumcision—a stunning display of neighborliness. Yet it earns them only massacre, pillage, and captivity, the result of deception and a sneak attack. Theodotus puts a different twist on the tale. God implants the thought of revenge in the minds of Simeon and Levi. And the Shechemites get what they deserve, because they are a godless and disreputable people, maimed by God to set them up for the slaughter by Jacob's sons. Theodotus leaves out any calculated ruse on the part of the Hebrews. Nor does he suggest that the Shechemites had circumcised themselves and were still recuperating when attacked—although Hamor did encourage them to do so. The poet also omits any reproach or dissent from Jacob. The retaliation for Dinah's disgrace goes unquestioned.

What significance do these changes bear? Theodotus's revisions of Genesis do not so much excoriate the Samaritans as exculpate the Hebrew forefathers. The alterations are subtle rather than radical. Theodotus forbears from demonizing the Shechemites. In the poem, Hamor receives Jacob in welcoming fashion and provides him with land—thus going one better than the biblical version, which has Jacob purchase the lot.[12] Hamor further graciously meets Jacob's conditions and undertakes to persuade his people to circumcise themselves. Theodotus holds close to the biblical text here.[13] He avoids contradiction or challenge, let alone any suggestion of undermining the authority of the Bible. The selective omission had greater effect. No hint of duplicity on the Israelites' part, no actual circumcision by the Shechemites, no attacks while they were disabled, and no censure by Jacob of his sons. This rendition smoothed out some rough spots in the Genesis narrative. Theodotus's tale nowhere contravened the Scriptures; it left the Shechemites' behavior ambiguous but cleared the Hebrew leaders of acting deceptively, passed over their internal friction, and set the outcome as the execution of the divine will. Even though the fragments are few, they exhibit the skill of a Jewish poet employing a Hellenic genre to refashion his own people's history.

Epic poetry evidently had an audience among Hellenistic Jews. At least one other writer composed in that mode: the poet Philo, of uncertain date, a few of whose verses have reached us, produced a poem of substantial size with the title "On Jerusalem."[14] What survives may constitute no more than a tiny fraction of the whole. The few extant lines treat only Abraham, Joseph, and the waters of Jerusalem. And even they are expressed in tortured language enveloped in studied obscurity, with a variety of arcane allusions.[15] But a number of the preserved verses suggest that Philo, like Theodotus, may have endeavored to enhance the luster of the patriarchs.

Philo's inflated vocabulary, however pompous and pretentious, could serve that purpose. He hails Abraham in words either invented or refashioned as "widely famed," "resplendent," and "abounding in lofty counsels." He applies to the patriarch some striking terms to arrest the attention even of highly cultivated Jews conversant with the epic language of Hellenic literature.[16] Joseph receives comparable elevation. Philo depicts him not only as prophetic interpreter of dreams but also as holder of the scepter on the thrones of Egypt, a man who discloses the secrets of fate in the stream of time.[17] His extravagant language was more than mere bombast. Like Theodotus, Philo employed the genre to expand upon Scripture.

The re-inscription of biblical legend in Hellenic form had multiple manifestations. Perhaps the most extraordinary, however, came in the romantic story *Joseph and Aseneth*. This tale moves in a realm quite distinct from those discussed above, that of novelistic fantasy. Genesis provides barely a pretext for this invention. The Scriptures report only that Pharaoh gave to Joseph as his wife Aseneth, daughter of Potiphar the priest of On, and that she subsequently bore him two children.[18] All else is embellishment. And *Joseph and Aseneth* embellishes in style.

The genre of the work has evoked discussion and controversy. Noteworthy affinities exist with Greek romances like those of Chariton, Heliodorus, Achilles Tatius, or Xenophon of Ephesus. One can, to be sure, find differences and contrasts. The erotic features usually prominent in Greek novels are subordinated in the first part of *Joseph and Aseneth* and altogether absent in the second. Parallels can also be found in Jewish fiction of contemporary or near-contemporary eras, like Judith, Esther, and Tobit. The mutual interactions and influences cannot be traced. But there is little doubt that *Joseph and Aseneth* emerged in the literary climate that also produced and encompassed the Hellenic novel.[19]

A summary of the yarn would be apposite. Joseph, gathering grain in the course of his duties as Pharaoh's agricultural minister at the outset of seven plenteous years, reaches the territory of Heliopolis. There he encounters the eminent priest Pentephres and his beautiful 18-year-old daughter Aseneth. The maiden, however, like Puccini's Turandot, scorns all men and rudely rejects suitors from noble houses in Egypt and royal families elsewhere. Pentephres immediately proposes to betroth Aseneth to the righteous, powerful, and pious Joseph. But Aseneth recoils in anger: she will have nothing to do with one who is a stranger in the land, a shepherd's son from Canaan, sold as a slave and imprisoned as an adulterer. The arrogant girl will accept marriage only with the son of Pharaoh. When she spies Joseph from her bedroom window, however, Aseneth is smitten—and overcome with self-reproach. Joseph in turn has his own reasons for reluctance. He first fears that Aseneth is yet another predatory female determined to bed him, like Potiphar's wife and a host of others. And then he recoils from Pentephres' arrangement on other grounds. The purist devotee of a sole deity will have no congress of any kind with an idolatress. Aseneth will have to mend her ways and acknowledge the true god.[20]

The maiden turns her religious life around at a stroke. Much weeping and wailing ensue as she repents of former heresies, removes all the idols from her home, and falls to fasting and mourning, self-flagellation and humiliation, uttering desperate prayers to her newly found god, seeking forgiveness for past sins and rescue from the fury of spurned divinities. Aseneth's prayers are answered. An angel of the Lord materializes, offers her absolution, and bids her prepare for a wedding. Pharaoh himself presides over the ceremonies, places crowns on the heads of the couple, and sponsors a spectacular banquet that lasts for seven days. The marriage is consummated, and Aseneth subsequently produces two sons as Joseph's legacy.[21]

The happy ending, however, has not yet come. A second part of the tale, quite different from the love story, moves the narrative in a new direction. Internal friction shows itself both in the Hebrew patriarch's household and in that of Pharaoh. Joseph's brothers Simeon and Levi take joy in the company of Aseneth, while other brothers feel only envy and hostility. Further, Pharaoh's son determines to take her by foul means, enlisting certain of the brothers in his nefarious enterprise. They lead Egyptian armed men in an ambush of Aseneth and her entourage, and plots are hatched to murder Joseph and his sons, while the heir to the Egyptian throne prepares to assassinate his own father. All the schemes, of course, are foiled. Benjamin, now a strapping lad of 18, protects Aseneth and launches 50 stones, each of which fells an Egyptian, including Pharaoh's off-spring. His brothers wipe out the remaining foes. And when the wicked brothers make a final effort to slay Benjamin and Aseneth, their swords fall miraculously to the ground and dissolve into ashes. Aseneth then intervenes to urge forgive-ness and concord. The peace-loving Levi stays Benjamin's hand when he at-tempts to finish off Pharaoh's helpless son. In gratitude, Pharaoh prostrates himself before Levi. The aging, ailing ruler subsequently turns his kingdom over to Joseph, bestowing upon him the diadem that signals royal authority. And Joseph goes on to reign as monarch of Egypt for 48 years.[22]

So ends the narrative, an agreeable and entertaining one. In fact, it consists of two narratives, a love story followed by an adventure tale, the two only loosely connected. The work has generated immense discussion, most of it concerned with language, date, provenance, genre, and audience of the text.[23] We focus here on a different matter of broader consequence: the relation between Jew and gen-tile in the Diaspora. An initial impression might suggest that the tale pits the two cultures against one another. Joseph's insistence upon the purity of the faith and the pollution of idolatry, Aseneth's abject debasement and thorough break with her past to achieve absolution, the rigorous separation of Hebrews and Egyp-tians, and the favor of God supporting the faithful against the idol worshippers all seem to suggest a stark dichotomy between the forces of good and evil. But the breakdown is not so simple and the polarity not so sharp. Friction exists after all *within* each of the two communities. Joseph's brothers engage in poten-tially murderous activities against one another, and Pharaoh's son plots the as-sassination of the king. The fact that the wedding of Joseph and Aseneth takes place under the auspices of Pharaoh, who had not himself become a convert, holds central symbolic significance. The enemies of the faithful were forgiven, harmony and reconciliation followed, and the gentile ruler presided over the union of the Hebrew patriarch and the daughter of an Egyptian priest. The fable plainly promotes concord between the communities. Equally important, it as-serts the superiority of Jewish traditions and morality—even against some Jews themselves.

Joseph exudes power and authority, more strikingly in this work than in Genesis or any other Hellenistic elaboration. The author of *Joseph and Aseneth* introduces Pentephres as chief of all satraps and grandees in the realm.[24] Yet, when he learns of Joseph's imminent visit, he is beside himself with excitement and goes to every length in preparing his household to receive so eminent a

guest—one to whom he refers as "powerful man of God." Pentephres breath-
lessly describes Joseph to his daughter as ruler of all the land of Egypt and
Pharaoh's appointee as all-powerful governor.[25] Joseph then enters the gates of
his host's estate in a royal chariot, resplendent in purple robes and a gold crown
with precious stones. Pentephres and his entire family hasten to prostrate themselves. The text could not make plainer the fact that, no matter how lofty was the
position of Pentephres in the court and in the realm, he was far below the station
of Joseph the Jew.[26] His crown radiated with 12 golden rays, emblematic of a sun
god.[27] Aseneth's prayer to the Lord describes Joseph as beautiful, wise—and
powerful.[28] Joseph himself emphasizes his stature by dismissing Pentephres'
offer to provide a wedding banquet. He would have none other than Pharaoh
perform that task.[29] At the conclusion of the narrative, the dying Pharaoh presents him with the diadem, and Joseph reigns as king of Egypt for five decades.[30]
This goes well beyond the biblical tale and probably beyond any subsequent
Hellenistic version of it.

The superiority of the Hebrews, their character, faith, and traditions, constitutes a central theme of the work. Joseph's contemptuous refusal to have a meal
with Egyptians deliberately reverses the biblical passage that has the Egyptians
shun any table occupied by Hebrews.[31] Aseneth's smashing of idols and her abject submission to the Lord accentuate the inferiority of her native religion.
Pharaoh makes obeisance to Joseph's god when he conducts the wedding ceremony.[32] The second segment of the narrative demonstrates that the authority of
the Hebrews is physical as well as spiritual. Pharaoh's son acknowledges that
they are powerful men, beyond all others on the face of the earth.[33] And, in a
climactic scene, Pharaoh descends from the throne to prostrate himself before Levi, who had spared his defeated son.[34] The harmonious relationship between Jews and gentiles stands at the core of the tale, but it is achieved only
through the Egyptians' affirmation of the Hebrews' distinctiveness. This novel,
therefore, fits a pattern that can be discerned again and again. Jews appropriated
a genre familiar in the Hellenic cultural world, crossed conventional boundaries,
underscored commonalties, but reiterated the special eminence they claimed for
themselves.

Jewish writers in Greek entered still another realm preeminently associated
with the Hellenic achievement: historiography. Here again, as in other modes,
they utilized the conventions to present or to expand upon biblical material.
They had no desire to compete with Greeks in recording the exploits of other
peoples—let alone of the Greeks themselves. But they saw the virtue of borrowing the methodology to reproduce their own past.

A certain Demetrius saw the advantages. He is one of the first Hellenistic

Jews, perhaps *the* first (around the late third century B.C.E.), to venture into the arena of the historians. He is frequently called "Demetrius the Chronographer," a somewhat unfair label. His interest in chronological matters is clear enough. But the extant fragments of his work evince broader concerns.[35]

Demetrius composed an account, historical in form, that treated material in Genesis and Exodus. Three fragments at least, perhaps as many as five, attest to it. A sixth is ascribed to a work entitled *On the Kings in Judaea* and concerns subjects deriving from 2 Kings. Demetrius's attention was captured by problems and puzzles for which he could offer solutions. So, for instance, he addresses the issue of how Jacob managed to father 12 children in just seven years. The schedule is tight, but Demetrius works out a timetable that includes all 12, produced by four different mothers.[36] Similarly, he confronts the question of why Joseph fed Benjamin five times what he offered his other brothers and bestowed four times the amount of clothing upon him. He supplies an answer: Leah had seven sons, Rachel but two; hence Benjamin's five portions plus Joseph's two evened the balance. The disproportion appears in Genesis, but the explanation is Demetrius's.[37] When the historian moves on to Moses, he grapples with another puzzle: how is it that Moses could marry Zipporah, who like him traced her descent from Abraham, if Moses was six generations distant from the patriarch and Zipporah was seven? Demetrius's reconstruction answers the question: Isaac was already married when Abraham married Keturah and had a second son, who was thus of the same generation as the son of Isaac from whom Zipporah descended—a solution Demetrius evidently developed from a piecing together of biblical testimonies and some shrewd calculations.[38] And he also tackles a very different issue in the Exodus story: how did the Israelites, who left Egypt unarmed, manage to secure weapons in the desert? An easy answer: they appropriated the arms of Egyptians who drowned in the sea. The conclusion plainly depends upon historical hypothesis, not any textual testimony.[39]

What ends were served by such exegesis? Demetrius's agenda surely had Jewish ends in view. That he was himself a Jew can hardly be questioned. Gentiles with an interest in the minutiae of biblical chronology or a concern about the disproportionate share meted out by Joseph to Benjamin would be rare birds indeed. But it is hard to detect any apologetic purposes here. The narrative is sober, dry, and colorless. No hint of polemic exists in Demetrius's austere renditions, no embellishments of character, no syncretistic transformation of biblical personages into figures of universal significance. The exercise has a starkly academic quality. Demetrius may well have imbibed the exacting principles of Alexandrian scholarship and put the techniques of Greek learning to the service of Jewish hermeneutics. Yet the extant fragments breathe hardly a hint of texts or traditions outside the Septuagint. Demetrius's narrative appears to be a rigorously internal one.

It does not follow that Demetrius provided exegesis for its own sake. His readership plainly consisted of Jews; why rewrite a historical narrative for those already familiar with it? In fact, Demetrius, as even the scanty fragments show, avoided a mere reproduction of Scripture. He abbreviated, streamlined, and modified the text—to the detriment of vividness and drama. He had other objectives. For Jews who read and spoke Greek, especially those attracted by Hellenic rationalism and critical inquiry, the Bible presented some vexing questions: inconsistencies, chronological disparities, and historical perplexities. Demetrius took up the tangles, reduced narrative to bare bones, assembled chronological data, straightened out genealogies, and supplied explanations for peculiar deeds and events. His work or works, therefore, offered reassurance on the reliability of the Scriptures. Demetrius engaged in ratiocination, not apologia. Nor did he offer an alternative to the biblical narrative. The authority of that narrative was taken for granted by the historian for whom it was the sole source of his reconstruction. He appealed to a sophisticated Jewish readership that posed tough questions but also sought edification. Demetrius's rewriting may have come at the cost of aesthetic quality and dramatic power. But it reinforced confidence in the tradition. Demetrius adapted the mode of Hellenic historiography to corroborate the record of his nation's past.

A more venturesome effort came from the pen of another Jewish historical writer, Eupolemus, who in the second century B.C.E. also composed a work entitled *On the Kings in Judaea*. Its scope extended beyond the limits suggested by the title, because even the scanty fragments include comments on Moses. The principal focus, however, evidently rested upon the era of the monarchy, at least to the inception of the Exile.[40]

Eupolemus took some interesting liberties in his narrative of David and Solomon. He records, for instance, a surprising string of military successes for King David. In his compressed account, David subdues Syrians dwelling along the Euphrates and the area of Commagene, Assyrians in Galadene, and Phoenicians; he further campaigns against Idumaeans, Ammonites, Moabites, Ituraeans, Nabataeans, and Nabdaeans. He then takes up arms once more against Souron the king of Tyre and Phoenicia, makes the people tributary to the Jews, and frames a pact of friendship with Vaphres, the ruler of Egypt.[41] Questions arise about virtually every name in the text—not to mention a glaring omission: David's renowned conquest of the Philistines. Eupolemus departs drastically from the biblical narrative. The king's exploits in 2 Samuel include only a small portion of these victories. The Hellenistic historian extends David's territorial advance well beyond the scriptural testimony.[42] His conquests extend to the Taurus range in the north, the Euphrates in the east, and the Gulf of Aqaba in the south. Eupolemus takes a marked departure also in his treatment of Solomon. An exchange of correspondence between Solomon and Vaphres of Egypt appears in the text—a sheer invention. Solomon requests that Vaphres supply men to assist in the completion of his new temple, and the pharaoh responds with deference. He addresses Solomon as "great king," reports his joy at Solomon's accession, and expresses readiness to send workers from various parts of his realm.[43] The mutual messages are polite and cordial, drawing upon the Hellenistic conventions of royal correspondence. But, although Eupolemus takes care to affirm the independence and pride of the pharaoh, Solomon's ascendancy is clear and unequivocal.

Eupolemus's vision pierced beyond partisan politics and current events. The exaltation of Solomon through an ascendant relationship to pharaonic Egypt had wider significance. Vaphres not only acknowledges Solomon's superiority but even pays homage to the Israelite god.[44] The historian unhesitatingly "improved upon" the biblical account, depicting the ancient kingdom, at the time in which its sacred shrine was created, exercising widespread authority accepted even by the ruler of Egypt. Eupolemus may not have expected his Jewish readers to take the account literally, but it gave them the sense of a grand heritage, of a nation whose impressive history both reflected divine favor and earned the approbation of the great powers. For the Jews of Palestine and the Diaspora, that pride in their past buoyed the spirit and uplifted perceptions of national identity.

The fragment of Eupolemus on Solomon concludes in remarkable fashion. After the completion of the Temple, the king magnanimously restores the Egyptian and Phoenician craftsmen to their native lands with enormous severance pay, dispatches lavish gifts to Vaphres, and to Souron of Phoenicia he sends a golden column, set up at Tyre in the temple of Zeus.[45] Here once more Eupolemus supplies details for which no scriptural authority exists, employing the occasion to embellish the wealth, power, and generosity of Solomon. The final item, however, deserves special notice. Would the devout Solomon, having just completed the most monumental act of piety, actually send a pillar of gold to stand in a pagan temple? No need for tortured explanations here. The Bible itself records Solomon's penchant for foreign wives and for foreign gods. Among the divinities whom he honored was Astarte, the goddess of the Sidonians.[46] Eupolemus simply pursued the point a step further: Solomon enabled the Phoenician king to honor Zeus with a handsome offering. The implications of this notice deserve emphasis. Eupolemus saw no inconsistency in presenting Solomon both as a dedicated devotee of the Lord and as a patron of foreign princes who honored alien cults. This is not "syncretism," as some have characterized it. Rather, it

highlights Jewish superiority in the spiritual and material spheres. Solomon req-
uisitioned the manpower of other kingdoms to erect his magnificent structure
to the supreme deity; he could in turn take responsibility for subsidizing the
worship of his compliant neighbors.[47] That theme supplies a leitmotif for Jewish
depiction of ancestral achievements that extended even to the enhancement of
foreign cultures. The Jews had successfully enlisted the craft of historiography to
augment the accomplishments of their past.

Another form of Greek learning comes in for modification and manipulation
by a very different Jewish text. The *Letter of Aristeas,* composed probably in the
second century B.C.E., may be the most famous surviving product of Hellenistic
Judaism apart from the Septuagint—its fame due in no small part to the fact
that it recounts the creation of the Septuagint itself. The text describes the decision of Ptolemy II to have the Hebrew Bible rendered into Greek and added to
the shelves of the library in Alexandria, the negotiations with the high priest in
Jerusalem to send the most learned sages to Egypt to produce the translation,
their collaborative work, and the end product that was so warmly received by
Ptolemy and the Alexandrian Jews.[48] The tale, of course, should not be confused
with history. It is hardly likely that Ptolemy II marshaled the resources, commissioned the scholars, and financed the elaborate translation of the Books of
Moses just to add some volumes to the royal library. That Hellenistic Alexandria
was the site for a rendition of the Torah in Greek we may well believe. As late as
the time of Philo, in the first century C.E., Egyptian Jews still celebrated an annual festival on the island of Pharos to mark the completion of that task.[49] The
needs of Greek-speaking Jews who had lost command of or even contact with
Hebrew surely motivated the project to provide a Greek version for liturgical or
instructional purposes or even for private worship. But little else in the *Letter of
Aristeas* commands confidence as history. The yarn spun by its author is largely
creative fiction.

The story of the translation, however, though central to the narrative, actually
forms only a small part of it. For our purposes, another portion of the text, indeed a healthy chunk of it, holds special interest. When the Jewish elders, selected for their profound learning in both Hebrew and Greek literature, arrive in
Alexandria, Ptolemy orders an elaborate welcome: an extended symposium,
seven full days of formal banquets—all served with kosher food. In the course of
this drawn-out entertainment, the king puts a different question to each of his
guests, most of the questions concerning how best to govern a kingdom and to
conduct one's life. Each of the sages responds promptly, includes a reference to
God as principal ingredient in the answer, and receives warm compliments from
Ptolemy, who is awestruck by their acumen.[50]

What is one to make of this? Ptolemy II, as portrayed by "Aristeas," is in control throughout: his power and authority go unquestioned. He issues the orders to write to the high priest and get the project under way.[51] It is his decision to have the Hebrew Scriptures translated into Greek, that he might add them to his library.[52] He even orders the kosher meal for his guests and partakes of it as well, a gesture of his good nature, but also of his authority, the entire banquet orchestrated at his behest.[53] The dependence of the Jews upon royal power is unequivocally acknowledged. This is not a subversive document.

The Letter of Aristeas is thoroughly Hellenic in character, a fact of which the reader is repeatedly reminded. Greek men of learning and culture make an appearance or are referred to in the treatise. Even the Jewish high priest is described in terms that evoke a cultivated Hellenic aristocrat.[54] The scholars whom he sends to Alexandria not only command Greek as well as Jewish learning but express the noblest Hellenic ideal of striving for the "middle way."[55] The symposium in which the Jerusalemite sages are interrogated, of course, constitutes a fully Greek setting. And most of the sages respond with answers familiar from Greek philosophy or political theory—for example, they speak of the duty of the king to exercise restraint and honor justice; the definition of philosophy as reasoning well for every contingency, resisting impulses, and controlling the passions; and the designation of injustice as the greatest evil.[56] "Aristeas" has the high priest himself speak like a Greek philosopher.[57] The treatise plainly portrays Jews as comfortable in a Hellenic setting, attuned to Greek customs and modes of thought, and content under the protection of a Hellenistic monarch.

But to leave it at that is to miss the main message. The table talk of the symposium has a clear and unmistakable point: the superior wisdom of the Jews. Their representatives answer every question unhesitatingly, exhibiting their mastery of precepts familiar to the Greeks but incorporating in each response a reference to God as ultimate authority. The replies offer little that is distinctively Jewish—or even very specific. The sages never mention Moses, the Law, the Scriptures, or any practices peculiarly linked to Judaism. Indeed, God often appears in mechanical, even irrelevant fashion. The intellectual context is strictly philosophical, not at all theological—and rather superficial philosophy at that.[58] What matters is that the Jewish elders impress the king, over and over again. He commends every statement made, never moving from one interlocutor to the next without complimenting the speaker. The point of the episode, of course, is that the biblical scholars display an insight eclipsing anything that could be mustered by Greek philosophers. Ptolemy acknowledges it explicitly: the Jewish elders stand out in virtue and discernment, because the foundation of their reasoning lies in God.[59] More tellingly, the Greek philosophers themselves admit that they cannot equal the Jews' sagacity. The whole presentation has more than a touch of tongue-in-cheek. The narrator concludes his account of the seven banquets with a final dig at the Hellenic philosophers. In his own voice he observes that the scholars from Jerusalem were obviously worthy of the highest admiration from him, from those present, and especially from the philosophers.[60] That was no innocent remark.

The treatise of "Aristeas" is a complex, multilayered, and occasionally entertaining piece of work. No single purpose drove its composition. The idea, prevalent in modern scholarship, that it promoted a synthesis between Judaism and Hellenism is inadequate. The narrative implies that Jews are fully at home in the world of Hellenic culture. The use of a fictive Greek as narrator and admirer of Judaism carries that implication clearly enough. But the message has a sharper point: not only have Jews digested Hellenic culture but they have also surmounted it. Just as other Jewish writers displayed mastery of the tragic or epic art form, of romantic fiction, and of historiography, employing those Hellenic genres to embellish Israelite exploits, so the author of *The Letter* exhibits his familiarity with philosophic precepts and conventions while concocting a scenario in which all the advantage goes to the Jews.

Whether the texts discussed above typify Jewish attitudes cannot be said with certainty. But they (and other instances that could readily be cited) do represent a significant segment thereof. And the message rings loud and clear. The notion of a barrier that had to be overcome between Jewish and Hellenistic cultures casts precisely the wrong image. The Jewish intellectuals who sought to rewrite their past and redefine their traditions grew up in Diaspora or even Palestinian communities suffused with Hellenism. For them it *was* their culture. Their ideas and concepts expressed themselves quite naturally in Greek forms. But this in no way compromised, diminished, or undermined their sense of Jewish identity. On the contrary. Jewish thinkers and writers showed little interest in the Trojan War, the house of Atreus, the labors of Heracles, the customs of the Scythians, or the love of Cupid and Psyche. They mobilized the Hellenic crafts of epic, tragedy, philosophy, romance, and historiography to reproduce the record of their own people, to convey their conventions, and to enhance their achievements.

THE JEWISH CONSTRUCTION
OF GREEK CULTURE AND ETHNICITY

The embrace of Hellenic culture, as we have seen, served to reinforce rather than to dilute a sense of Jewish identity. But the broader the embrace, the more urgent it became to foreground those characteristics that distinguished Jews from the gentiles in whose lands they lived and with whose world they needed to come to terms. The Jews, in short, needed to establish their own secure place within a Hellenistic framework and to make it clear that they were not swallowed up by that prevailing cultural environment. The construct of Jewish identity, an ongoing, complex, and shifting process, was tightly bound up with the construct of Greek ethnicity—that is, the character, values, and beliefs of the Greek *ethnos* in Jewish eyes.

That these were constructs is inescapable. Although Jewish intellectuals could draw distinctions among Greek peoples, communities, and conventions, they frequently lapsed into broad characterizations and stereotypes. The reasons are obvious enough. They had a definite agenda. In some form or other, Jews had to confront—or to formulate—those Hellenic traits from which they wished to disassociate themselves and, at the same time, to account for those characteristics that they had themselves adopted.

Greeks regularly reckoned other people, including Jews, as *barbaroi* (barbarians): they did not speak Greek and hence were unintelligible. But the Jews could turn the tables. The author of the Second Book of Maccabees was a Hellenized Jew of the late second century B.C.E., a writer thoroughly steeped in the traditions of Greek historiography, who composed his work in Greek.[61] His topic, however, was the background, circumstances, and consequences of the brutal persecution of Jews by the Hellenistic monarch Antiochus IV Epiphanes. The Jews resisted and retaliated under Judas Maccabaeus. According to 2 Maccabees, they fought nobly on behalf of Judaism and, though few in number, ravaged the entire land and drove out the "barbarian hordes."[62] So the author, well versed in the conventions of the genre, employed the standard Hellenic designation for the alien—but applied it to the Hellenes themselves. And it was not the only such occasion.[63]

A whole range of texts discloses the drive of Hellenistic Jews to brand the Greeks as villainous or ignorant aliens, thus to distinguish more dramatically the advantages of being a Jew. Apocalyptic literature served this purpose. The visions of Daniel, which received their current shape in the very era of the persecutions, speak in cryptic but unmistakable tones of the catastrophic evils brought by the rule of the Hellenic kingdom. The terrifying dream that paraded four huge beasts in succession represented the sequence of empires, the fourth the most fearsome of all, a dreadful monster with iron teeth and bronze claws that devoured and trampled all in its path. That portent signified the coming of the Greeks. The forecasts given to Daniel, however, promised a happy ending: triumph over the wicked, a divine intervention to sweep aside the brutal Hellenic empire and bring about an eternal kingdom under the sovereignty of the

Most High.[64] The Greeks here embody the mightiest of empires—and the one destined for the mightiest fall.

That theme is picked up in the prophecies of the Third Sibylline Oracle. The Sibyl had venerable roots in pagan antiquity, but the surviving collection of pronouncements stems from Jewish and Christian compilers who recast them for their own ends. The contents represent the earliest portion, which is almost entirely the product of Jewish invention, and some parts of which at least date to the era of the Maccabees.[65] The text repeats in varied form the sequence of empires: representing the Greeks as impious and arrogant; forecasting internal rot; condemning the Greeks for overbearing behavior, the fostering of tyrannies, and moral failings; and predicting that Hellenic cities all over the Mediterranean would be crushed by a terrible divine wrath.[66]

The portrait is hardly less severe in the First Book of Maccabees. That work, extant now only in Greek, appeared first in Hebrew, the product of a strong supporter of the Hasmonaean dynasty; it was composed probably in the late second century B.C.E.[67] The book opens with a harsh assessment of Alexander the Great, an arrogant conqueror whose campaigns brought slaughter and devastation in their wake, and whose successors over the years delivered multiple miseries upon the earth.[68]

The stark contrast between Jew and Greek receives dramatic elaboration in the martyrologies recorded in 2 Maccabees. Under Antiochus Epiphanes, the elderly sage Eleazer resists to the death any compromise of Jewish practice, calmly accepting his agonizing torture. The same courage is exhibited by the devout mother who witnessed proudly the savage execution of her seven sons and joins them herself in death—memorable testimony to Jewish faith and Hellenic barbarity.[69] The stories were retold many generations later, in a text preserved in some manuscripts of the Septuagint under the title of 4 Maccabees, but at a time when the fierce emotions of the Maccabean era were a distant memory. The torments inflicted upon Eleazer and the unnamed mother with her seven sons were described in exquisite detail. The work was composed in Greek, probably in the first century C.E., by a Jew trained not in history but in Greek philosophy. He employed the martyrologies to illustrate Stoic doctrines of the command of reason over the passions. The author, therefore, ironically appropriated the Hellenic medium to express commitment to the Torah by contrast with the irrationality and atrocities of the Greeks themselves.[70] The schema that pits Jews against Greeks, the latter standing outside the bounds of morality and humane behavior, persists in all these texts.

A comparably sharp contrast surfaces in a most unexpected place. The *Letter of Aristeas* generally exudes harmony and common objectives between the cultures. Yet all is not sweetness and light even here. Eleazer the High Priest, when he responds to queries by Greeks about the peculiar habits of the Jews, affirms in no uncertain terms that those who worship many gods engage in foolishness and self-deception. Eleazer declares that Moses, in his wisdom, fenced the Jews off with unbreakable barriers and iron walls to prevent any mingling with other nations, to keep them pure in body and soul, and to rid them of empty beliefs.[71] So, even the veritable document of intercultural concord, the *Letter of Aristeas,* contains a pivotal pronouncement by the chief spokesman for Judaism, who sets his creed decisively apart from the ignorant and misguided beliefs of the Greeks.

The contrast is elaborated at some length by Josephus. The Jewish historian of the late first century C.E. distinguishes unequivocally between the steadfastness of Jews and the inferiority of Hellenic practices and institutions. He records repeated interference by Greeks with the ancestral practices of the Jews and outright atrocities in Cyrenaica, Asia Minor, Alexandria, Damascus, Caesarea, and other cities of Palestine.[72] Josephus pulls no punches: the disposition of the Greeks is labeled "inhumanity."[73]

Elsewhere Josephus conceives the contrast on a broader front. He singles out Moses as the most venerable of lawgivers and speaks with scorn of Greeks who take pride in such comparable figures as Lycurgus, Solon, and Zaleucus. He disparages Hellenic philosophy and education: the philosophers directed their precepts only to the elite, whereas Moses' teaching encompassed all. The study of Jewish traditions exposes the deficiencies and one-sidedness that inhere in both the Spartan and Athenian systems.[74] More important, he places particular weight upon the Jews' faithful and consistent adherence to their own laws. To the Greeks, such unswerving fidelity can hardly be imagined. Their history is riddled with inversions and deviations. Greek authors heap praise on the longevity of the Spartan system; for Josephus, that is preposterous. The endurance of that system was a mere trifle, not comparable to the 2,000 years that had elapsed since the time of Moses.[75] Josephus exploits Hellenic writings themselves to make a point about the foolishness and absurdity of their religious beliefs. The myths multiply deities without number, portray them in a variety of human forms, and have them engage in every type of licentiousness, misdemeanor, folly, and internecine warfare with one another. And, as if that were not enough, the Greeks grow weary of their traditional divinities and import foreign gods by the score, stimulating poets and painters to invent new and even more bizarre images of worship.[76] There could be no stronger contrast with the tenacity and constancy of Jewish practice.

The celebrated lines of the apostle Paul allude directly to the antithesis between the peoples: "there is neither Jew nor Greek, slave nor free, male nor fe-

male, for you are all one in Jesus Christ."⁷⁷ The string of antinomies makes it
clear that the two nations represented conventionally opposite poles. The distinction held firm in Jewish circles.

The evidence to this point seems clear and consistent. Jewish compositions
constructed the Hellenes as foils, as aliens, as "the Other," the better to set off
the virtues and qualities of their own *ethnos*. But those constructs do not tell the
whole story. The Jews' perceptions (or at least expressed perceptions) of the
Greeks were more complex, varied, and subtle. In other texts, Greek character
and culture acquire a more positive aspect, because they are conceived as owing
those qualities to the Jews themselves.

Aristobulus, a second-century-B.C.E. Jew of philosophic education and pretensions, played with what became a favored Jewish fiction: that Hellenic ideas
derived from Hebraic roots. A mere handful of fragments survive, and the identification of Aristobulus himself is disputed. But the emphasis on Jewish priority
in concepts later conveyed by Greeks is plain enough.⁷⁸

In Aristobulus's imaginative construct, Moses provided a stimulus for Hellenic philosophers and poets. The Torah inspired the loftiest achievements of
the Greek intellectuals. Aristobulus asserts that Plato's ideas followed the path
laid out by the legislation of Moses, indeed that he was assiduous in working
through every particular contained in it. And he cites an earlier case still, an
equally distinguished name, the sixth-century philosopher Pythagoras, who also
found much in the Hebrew teachings that he could adapt for his own doc-
trines.⁷⁹ For any discerning reader, those pronouncements create some serious
chronological problems. How would the Greek sages have had access to the Hebrew Scriptures generations or centuries before the Septuagint? Aristobulus has
no qualms about fabricating one fiction to save another. He reassures potential
skeptics by maintaining that translations of the Israelite escape from Egypt, conquest and settlement of the new land, and all the details of the law code were
available long before the composition of the Septuagint.⁸⁰ Aristobulus com-
pounds his creative fabrications.

That accomplished, Aristobulus proceeds with flights of fancy. He includes
Socrates with Pythagoras and Plato among those whose reference to a divine
voice in contemplating the creation of the cosmos derives from the words of
Moses. And he goes well beyond. Aristobulus offers a broadly embracing doctrine that sweeps all of Greek philosophy within the Jewish orbit. He affirms
universal agreement among the philosophers that only pious opinions must be
held about God. And, since that view is embedded in Mosaic law, it follows that
Jewish conceptualizing supplied the wellspring for Hellenic philosophizing.⁸¹

If Jewish inspiration could be claimed for Greek philosophy, why not for poetry? Aristobulus and others had no hesitation in extending the Jewish reach

into that realm. References to the number seven in Greek poetry were seized upon as evidence that the institution of the Sabbath had seeped into Hellenic consciousness. Aristobulus goes back to the beginning. He summons up the verses of Greece's premier epic poets, Homer and Hesiod, to affirm that they endorsed the biblical sanctification of the holy day. This requires some fancy footwork. Aristobulus or his Jewish source exercise special liberties in twisting the texts to his will. Hesiod's reference to a seventh day of the month becomes the seventh day of the week, and a Homeric allusion to the "fourth day" is transformed through emendation to the "seventh day." Other lines quoted by Aristobulus but not attested in the extant texts of Homer and Hesiod may also have been tampered with or simply invented.[82] The subtle—or not so subtle—reworking had Homer and Hesiod acknowledge the consecration of the Sabbath. From the vantage point of Aristobulus, it is all for a good cause: to demonstrate the dependence of Greece's most ancient bards upon the teachings of the Torah. Observance of the Sabbath, in this conception, is no mere idiosyncrasy of an alien and self-segregated sect but a principle cherished in Hellenic song. Aristobulus thereby harnessed some of the most celebrated Greek thinkers and artists, real or legendary, to the antique traditions of the Jews.

In this venture Aristobulus was by no means alone. Jewish intellectuals ransacked the texts of Greek drama, chasing after verses that might suggest Hellenic borrowings from Hebraic ideas. And when they did not find appropriate lines, they simply manufactured them. Concepts with Jewish resonance were ascribed to the great fifth-century-B.C.E. tragedians Aeschylus, Sophocles, and Euripides, and to the comic poets Menander, Philemon, and Diphilus.[83]

Thunderous verses allegedly composed by Aeschylus exalt the authority of God. The eminent tragedian warns mortals to acknowledge his splendor and to recognize his presence in every manifestation of nature, an omnipotence that can shake the earth, the mountains, and the depths of the sea: "The glory of the highest god is all-powerful."[84] Such sentiments, whether authentic Aeschylus or not, would certainly play into Jewish hands. Sophocles too was exploited, for similar purposes. He trumpeted the unity and uniqueness of the Lord, rebuking mortals who installed graven images of bronze, stone, gold, or ivory.[85] He even supplied an eschatological text that forecast the destruction of the universe in an all-consuming flame to issue in the salvation of the righteous.[86] Euripides also served to advance the cause. A passage attributed to him asserts that no dwelling fashioned by mortal hands can contain the spirit of God, and another characterizes God as one who sees all but who is himself invisible.[87] These concocted lines—and doubtless many others no longer extant—conscripted the Attic tragedians in the service of Hellenistic Judaism.

A similar process enlisted Greek comic poets. Passages ascribed to one or another of them disclose the objectives of those who preserved (or forged) them. They include admonitions to the wicked, assertions that God punishes the unjust, insistence that upright conduct is more important than sacrificial offerings, and exhortation to honor the one God who is Father for all time, the Inventor and Creator of every good.[88]

Hellenistic Jews were evidently tireless in rummaging through the Greek classics to find opinions and sentiments that evoked scriptural teachings. The assiduous efforts gave forceful reminders to their countrymen of Jewish priority in the thinking of great thoughts. More striking still, they imply that the Hellenic achievement, far from alien to the Hebraic, simply restated its principles.

A famous story, but not one usually cited in this connection, underscores the point. Paul's celebrated visit to Athens in the mid-first century c.e. can exemplify this form of appropriation. The tale is told in the Acts of the Apostles.[89] Paul proselytizes among the Jews and "God-fearers" in the synagogue—and with any person who passes by in the *agora* (central market place). This upsets certain Stoics and Epicureans, who haul him before the high tribunal of the Areopagus and question him about the new doctrine. Paul is quick to turn the situation to his own advantage—and in a most interesting way. He remarks to the Athenians that they are an uncommonly religious people. He has wandered through many of their shrines and has found one altar inscribed to an "unknown god." Of course, he is there to tell them precisely who that "unknown god" happens to be. Paul then speaks of the sole Divinity, Creator of the world and all that is in it, a God who dwells in no temples and can be captured in no images.[90] The description plainly applies to the God of the Hebrew Bible, with no Christian admixture. Paul, like other inventive Jews, quotes Greek poetry to underpin his claims. So, he remarks to the Athenians, "as some of your own poets have said, 'We too are His [God's] children.' "[91] The poet in question is, in fact, Aratus of Soli, no Athenian. But that detail can be comfortably ignored. The parallels with other texts cited above are quite striking. Paul deploys Greek poetic utterances as certification for Jewish precepts, and he cites a Greek dedicatory inscription as evidence for Hellenic worship of the right deity—even if the Greeks themselves do not know who he is.

This heartening construct of Hellenic dependence on Jewish precedents appears notably, and perhaps surprisingly, even in the work of Josephus. As we have seen, he took pains to underscore differences between the Jews and the Greeks, to stress the stability of Jewish institutions and the durability of faith as against the multiple inadequacies of Hellenic practices. Yet Josephus also follows the line that many Greeks have embraced Jewish laws—though some have been more consistent in maintaining them than others. Indeed, he acknowledges,

Jews are more divided from Greeks by geography than by institutions.[92] Like Aristobulus and others, he finds Greek philosophers hewing closely to the concept of God that they obtained from acquaintance with the Books of Moses—noting in particular Pythagoras, Anaxagoras, Plato, and the Stoics.[93] And he makes still larger claims. Greek philosophers were only the first of those drawn to the laws of the Torah, adopting similar views about God, teaching abstinence from extravagance, and harmony with one another. The masses followed suit. Their zeal for Jewish religious piety has now spread around the world so that there is hardly a single community, whether Greek or barbarian, unaffected by observance of the Sabbath, various Jewish practices, and even dietary restrictions. Indeed, they labor to emulate the concord, philanthropy, industry, and undeviating steadfastness characteristic of the Jews.[94] The hyperbole is obviously excessive. But Josephus's insistence on the Greek quest to duplicate Jewish ethics, religion, institutions, and customs is noteworthy—and quite different from his drive elsewhere to underscore the distance that separated Jew from Greek.

An ostensible tension thus exists in Jewish perspectives on Hellas. A strong strain emphasized the differences in culture and behavior between the peoples, categorized the Greeks as aliens, inferiors, even savage antagonists. Other voices, however, embraced and absorbed Hellenic teachings, reinterpreting them as shaped by acquaintance with the Hebraic tradition and as offshoots of the Torah. From that vantage point, the Hellenic character becomes, through emulation and imitation, molded to the model.

Is there an explanation for these discordant voices? The discrepancies that we discern or construct may not have had comparable significance in antiquity. It is especially striking that the supposedly different voices coexist in the same texts. The matter is obviously complex and involved.

The author of 2 Maccabees, as we have seen, writing in Greek and in the genre of Hellenistic historiography, reversed convention and labeled the Greeks themselves as *barbaroi*. That was ironic and pointed—but it did not set a style. Other Jewish writers adopted the very antithesis long current in the classical world, contrasting Greek with barbarian. It can be found, for instance, in the philosopher Philo of Alexandria, who boasts of the widespread attraction of Jewish customs, embraced in various parts of the world by both Greeks and barbarians.[95] Josephus employs the contrast regularly as a means of dividing the non-Jewish world.[96] It appears also in Paul, who proclaims his message to "Greeks and Barbarians, the wise and the ignorant"—no pagan could have said it better.[97] Philo, in fact, can even adopt the Hellenic perspective wholesale and count the Jews among the *barbaroi*![98] Here is inversion indeed. Contrast between the nations need not betoken irreconcilability.

Nor, however, do the texts that signal cultural conjunction negate the force of pronouncements that differentiate the peoples. In various formulations, Greek poetic inspiration came from a Hebrew bard; Hellenic philosophers, dramatists, and poets who recognized the sole divinity, expressed lofty ethical precepts and honored the Sabbath took their cue from the Torah; and even the Athenians unwittingly paid homage to the god of the Scriptures. These fictive inventions hardly dissolved the distinctions between Hebrews and Hellenes. Instead, they elevated the best in Hellenism by providing it with Hebrew precedents. The rest, by definition, fell short.

The Jews' reconception of the Hellenic achievement turned it to their own benefit. They simultaneously differentiated their nation from that of the Greeks and justified their own immersion in a world of Hellenic civilization.

INVENTIVE TALES FOR POPULACE AND ELITE

A critical question must now be addressed, a troubling but inescapable complication. To what degree do the Jewish texts that survive from this era give access only to a small, elite segment of society? Do they seal us off from anything that might be considered "popular culture"?

A difficult matter. Indeed, it raises further and even more formidable questions: how are these texts to be understood, to whom were they directed, by whom were they composed, and what were their objectives?

The limitations under which we labor have to be acknowledged at once. We normally do not know the author, the date, the place of composition, or the historical context of these works—let alone the motivations or intentions of the composer. Much scholarly energy has been devoted to reconstructing (or, better, to conjecturing and speculating about) when, where, and under what circumstances a text was produced. Much of it is an exercise in futility. More important, however, the very questions of who, what, when, and why are not only often unanswerable but are probably the wrong questions. It is crucial to remember that we are dealing with texts that, for the most part, have gone through many versions, revisions, recasting, and redaction, and have passed through many hands, indeed perhaps circulated orally over an extended period of time before reaching the stage in which we finally possess them. Hence, to puzzle out the historical circumstances of the original composition, the Ur-text, the audience to which it was directed, and the society it reflects, even if we could do so, might not be very helpful.

The texts as we have them are the ones with which we must grapple. If they appear to have different layers of meaning and more than one level of understanding, that should not surprise us. Indeed, it makes them all the more valuable—especially for the complex issue of elite vs. popular culture. That dichotomy itself misleads and deceives. The texts can work on several planes, and they appeal to a diverse readership. The same stories ostensibly designed for "popular" consumption, such as folktales, romances, and fantasies, and plainly enjoyed on that level, can also carry deeper meaning and greater nuance directed to a sophisticated audience.

Joseph and Aseneth serves as an example. The entertainment value of the novel is high. The dramatic transformation of the two chief figures from bristling antagonists to a loving couple certainly has that quality. So does the adventure story that has the "good" brothers of Joseph prevail over the wicked sons of Leah and the nefarious plots of Pharaoh's son. The work can happily be read for diversion and amusement, and in that sense it is attractive to what is customarily considered a "popular" constituency.

But more serious, complex, and even baffling elements lurk within. As we have seen, the text raises pointed issues about Jewish/gentile relations in the circumstances of the Diaspora. Recurrent tension, animosity, and open conflict have as counterpoint union and harmony, reconciliation and communal concord. The meaning is not easy to ferret out. Further, the balance between royal authority and Joseph's extraordinary powers possesses political implications not readily explicable to readers content with the surface narrative.

Still more difficult matters confront interpreters of the text. Aseneth's adoption of Joseph's faith (nowhere identified as "Judaism" in the narrative) has stirred widespread discussion of what "conversion" might mean, whether the tract encourages missionary activity, what message is delivered about mixed marriages, and how gentile converts were viewed from a Jewish perspective.[99] All of this may be a red herring. An author engaged in missionary efforts would not likely feature a story in which the impulse to conversion came from sexual passion! But the ambiguities at least prompt deeper probing.

Even better examples occur in the Greek additions to the Book of Daniel. The author or authors, probably in the late second century B.C.E., fiddled freely with the received text, inserting folktales of independent provenance and applying some acid drollery to refashion the Jewish image. These include two quite amusing pieces of folklore: "Bel and the Dragon" and "Susanna."

"Bel and the Dragon" actually consists of two tales cobbled together and placed at the conclusion of what became the canonical text of Daniel. The first features Cyrus, king of Persia, as a devoted disciple of the Babylonian god Bel, on whom is lavished vast quantities of sheep, flour, and wine every day. Cyrus wonders why his chief adviser Daniel does not share his enthusiasm for this divinity.

Daniel retorts that he worships only the God who created heaven and earth, not some fabricated idol, and offers to prove that Bel is the invention of conniving Babylonian priests. He devises a clever scheme whereby ashes are scattered around the floor of the sealed temple one night, after offerings are made to the idol. Telltale footprints the next morning showed that the priests and their families used a trapdoor to steal off with the provisions themselves. The somewhat dull-witted Cyrus now sees the light, orders the execution of the priests and their families, and turns the statue of Bel over to Daniel, who promptly destroys it and its temple.[100]

The narrator proceeds directly to the next legend, that of the dragon or the snake. Here the king, still looking for a tangible deity to revere, points to the large snake that the Babylonians worship and bids Daniel to pay it homage as well. The Jewish counselor, of course, remains faithful to his own God, and he offers to expose the snake's impotence by killing it without recourse to a weapon. Cyrus grants permission. Daniel then mixes a concoction of pitch, fat, and hair and feeds it to the snake, which bursts open on the spot, allowing Daniel to crow, "Now look at your object of worship!" The Babylonians strike back, pressuring the king to turn Daniel over to them and cast him into the lions' den. But Daniel is undeterred. The prophet Habbakuk, sent flying through the air by an angel who tugs him by the hair, brings food to Daniel that sustains him in the pit. And when the king finds him miraculously unharmed after seven days among the beasts, he heaps praise upon Daniel's god, rescues his counselor, and tosses his enemies to the lions.[101]

These tales amuse and instruct. Most readers would delight in the triumph of virtue over evil, of monotheism over the practitioners of idol worship, a dominant theme in biblical and post-biblical literature, an easy and obvious moral to grasp. But that does not exhaust the implications of the fables. In fact, theology hardly gets much emphasis in the narrative. Daniel makes only passing references to his God and says nothing about his beliefs. The emphasis throughout rests not on divine intervention but on Daniel's own sagacity and resourcefulness.

Different undercurrents would appeal to those, whether elite or common, who read more closely. Cyrus holds a high place in Jewish memory as the monarch responsible for the return of the Jews from the Babylonian Exile. But in these tales, the king, far from being a magnanimous benefactor of the humble Jews, is represented as something of a dullard, manipulated and even mocked by those around him—including the shrewd Jew. Daniel more than once laughs at Cyrus's folly. The Persian ruler is as gullible about the snake as about the idol, is brow-beaten and intimidated by his Babylonian subjects, and has little influence on the course of events. The narrator misses no chance to expose his naiveté and deride his vacillation. There is subtle irony here, not mere playfulness. If this is the ruler under whom the Jews returned to their homeland, one must infer that a Jew pulled the strings on this hapless puppet. The story has deeper meaning for a Diaspora existence. Daniel's people may have to live under the rule of alien kings, but the rewritten fables reassure them of how far they surpass those kings in mental agility and insight. The irony reflects a shared perspective of author and reader, a joint scorning of the inadequacies of the political authority. That element takes the stories out of the realm of mere diversion.

More revealing still is the celebrated tale of Susanna and the elders in the Greek text of Daniel. Is it "highbrow" or "lowbrow" literature? Is it a pleasant yarn conceived to amuse or does it have a deeper structure to provoke reflection upon Jewish conditions in the Diaspora? Is it aimed at a select group of intellectuals or the "common man"? Is it imaginative fiction or an authentic evocation of Jewish experience? In fact, one can argue, it is all of the above.

According to the narrative, Susanna, the beautiful and devout wife of a prominent Jew in Babylon, is lusted after by two elders of the people. They hide in the garden, spy upon her in the bath, and confront her with an intimidating proposition: either have intercourse with them or face (fraudulent) charges of adultery with a young man. Susanna, coerced into an unwelcome decision, chooses the latter. The lecherous elders then deliver their indictment before a gathering of the people and persuade the congregation to condemn Susanna to death. Young Daniel, however, emerges as God's answer to Susanna's prayer, roundly rebukes the people, and denounces them for exercising peremptory judgment even without interrogating the elders. He denies the validity of their statements and offers to grill them himself. Daniel wisely takes the precaution of separating the two men and questioning each independently. In this fashion, he brings to light discrepancies in their claims, exposes their perjury, and draws cheers from the congregation. The elders are executed, the virtuous Susanna is vindicated, and Daniel gains great esteem among the people from that day on.[102]

To what audience would such a work be addressed? It contains obvious folktale elements. The story of the wise youth outsmarting the wicked elders has many parallels. So does the motif of the innocent woman as victim but vindicated in the end. Analogous tales can be found in the *Arabian Nights,* Grimm's fairy tales, and a variety of Eastern and Near Eastern literary texts.[103] It has been widely popular across the ages and was doubtless popular in antiquity. The engaging character of the tale guarantees that. Daniel's outwitting of the two bungling, dirty old men and the confirmation of the matron's virtue would have wide appeal. For many readers or auditors, no more was needed: good yarn, happy ending, virtue rewarded, villains punished. It was also reassuring to have flawed leaders exposed and flawed procedures denounced. Such might be a "popular" reading—and a perfectly legitimate and meaningful one.

It need not, however, be the only one. The tale takes place in Babylon; the Jews are presumably in exile or, at least, in an alien land. But they are represented as an autonomous community, with its own leaders, its own process of governance. The malefactors are Jews, not gentiles. And not only does the text depict the elders as corrupt and immoral, but it portrays the populace that rendered judgment as compliant, easily swayed—and not very bright. It requires a noble youth to bring them to their senses and rescue the maligned but blameless Susanna. Indeed, the noble youth himself is far from flawless. Daniel succeeds not as a devout adherent of the faith but as a crafty prosecuting attorney. He convicts the elders even before questioning them, and he declares the first to be a lascivious perjurer although his story has yet to be contradicted.[104] The lawyerly techniques hardly embody exemplary justice. A clear strain of Jewish self-criticism exists in this text. It offers a subtle reminder that Jews need to look to their own shortcomings, especially in a Diaspora setting. The legend, in short, carried import at more than one level and could have resonance with more than one stratum of society.

Does this narrative actually describe life in the Jewish community of Babylon at a particular point of history? That is more than dubious. The text mentions Babylon at the beginning to supply an ostensible context, but the remainder of the work gives no concrete details about location. The story could take place anywhere; the setting is imaginary, and the events, of course, are fictitious. But the message is meaningful, more than mere entertainment. The exposure of arrogance in the leadership and gullibility in the rank and file delivered a pointed lesson to the nation. It recalled to mind basic principles of justice and morality that needed to be observed—especially in Jewish communities that governed their own activities but whose internal divisions could make them vulnerable to greater powers. The message did not apply to a particular geographic locale or to a specific time period. Indeed, the significance of the story is precisely that it transcends time and place. Nor does it speak only to an elite or only at a popular level. It holds a place in the cultural legacy for Jews across the generations, across geographical boundaries, and across intellectual strata.

An altogether different text can offer comparable conclusions. In 2 Maccabees one finds a peculiar and puzzling work that continues to intrigue scholars and students. It is a work of history, but one punctuated by miracles, marvels, and martyrologies. It celebrates the deliverance of Jerusalem, its Temple, and its inhabitants from the terrors wrought by a Hellenistic king, but it was composed, at least in its fuller form, by a Hellenized Diaspora Jew from Cyrene. It bears notice here for certain arresting stories that it preserves and that certainly cater to what is conventionally categorized as popular taste.

An engaging tale occurs near the beginning of the main narrative. Heliodorus, the agent of the Seleucid king, arrives in Jerusalem to check on reports that the Temple treasury possesses incalculable riches. When told by the high priest that there are indeed deposits held in trust for widows and orphans as well as the savings of a prominent and wealthy Jewish leader, Heliodorus insists that the monies belong to the king and should be handed over to him. He heads for the Temple to make an inventory, alarming the priests and people. Heliodorus, however, presses on. He is about to enter the Temple with his bodyguards when a fearsome rider on a mighty horse, splendidly attired, attacks him. Two strapping youths, magnificent in beauty and strength, then appear and pummel him further. The minister is carried off in a litter, now obliged to acknowledge the sovereignty of God. Indeed it looks as if he will not recover. But the merciful high priest Onias III sacrifices to God for Heliodorus's recovery, and he is spared. He goes back to the king and extols the power and majesty of the Jewish God.[105]

The popular appeal of such a story is obvious. The greedy minister of the king gets his comeuppance, the sacred Temple is spared, and divine intervention saves the day. But subtle thrusts exist in this text that go beyond the surface reading. The author has a wry sense of humor that seems aimed at a discriminating reader. One might note, for instance, the prayer uttered by the priests and the people when Heliodorus is about to violate the Temple treasury. It was not a plea to God to protect the sanctity of his house; rather, it calls upon the Lord Almighty to keep the deposits safe and secure for those who have placed their cash there![106] The author composed this with a wink and a nod. And Heliodorus receives no conventional punishment. He gets a double dose. It is not enough that a horse charges him and kicks him. There are also two powerful young men who beat him to a pulp.[107] That seems a bit of overkill—and another example of some whimsy on the author's part. The penchant for irony can hardly be missed in the finale of this episode. Heliodorus, though practically breathing his last, is spared by the high priest and returned to Antioch. When asked by his king who should next be sent to Jerusalem in order to recover the money, Heliodorus replies, in effect, "If you want to send somebody, send your worst enemy; he will get thoroughly thrashed." And still another concealed barb can be discerned. Heliodorus remarks, "If you have an enemy or a plotter against the government, send him to Jerusalem."[108] As it happens, it was Heliodorus himself, not long thereafter, who plotted against the king and was responsible for his death. The anticipated audience here had to know its contemporary history—and to appreciate the irony.

In a different mode, it is instructive to look at the treatment in 2 Maccabees of the villainous Antiochus IV. The scene of his agonizing death is justly famous. The gory details, including the worms swarming about him and flesh rotting off, can be paralleled by various Greek texts. It appears to be a motif for the deaths of cruel tyrants. But the author of 2 Maccabees added an extra touch of his own when he had the persecutor repent in the end, declare Jerusalem a free city, grant prerogatives to the Jews, and promise to adorn the temple with lavish gifts and finance all its sacrifices.[109] The characterization of one of these promises is especially noteworthy. Antiochus vows that he will give privileges to the Jews equal to those enjoyed by the citizens of Athens. This would seem to be an allusion to the golden age of democratic Athens. Such an age, however, had long since passed— contemporary Athens was hardly a model of autonomy and privilege. The insertion here is yet another instance of the author's sardonic streak. Only a few select readers would detect that allusion.

The Book of Judith, composed perhaps in the early first century B.C.E., provides an edifying and uplifting tale. One need not have intellectual credentials to appreciate it. The setting (wholly imaginary) is a putative military campaign ordered by Nebuchadnezzar, here identified as an Assyrian monarch, against various peoples of the Near East, including those dwelling in Judaea and Samaria. The military man Holofernes is appointed commander-in-chief of the armies that sweep through the lands, looting, sacking, and destroying sacred shrines. When the forces threaten Judaea, the Israelites, their high priest, and their officials are terrified, block the mountain passes, put on sackcloth and ashes, and pray to the Lord for rescue. The Ammonite chieftain Achior, whose people have already surrendered to the invaders, warn Holofernes that the Israelites are invincible if their God favors them, but vulnerable if they have sinned against Him. Holofernes scorns the advice, mocks Achior, and delivers him to the Israelites themselves. The army then undertakes the siege of the (unlocatable) Israelite town of Bethulia. Its inhabitants swiftly become desperate, the people pressing their leaders to surrender before they are annihilated. The city's most prominent figure, Uzziah, proposes a five-day wait, in hopes that God might intervene, but promises surrender if there is no sign of such intervention.[110]

At this point Judith enters the scene. A respected and wealthy widow, renowned for her piety and wisdom, Judith denounces the city's elders for giving a deadline to God and promises that she will take action to deliver Israel with the aid of the Lord. Uzziah and the magistrates give her free rein. Judith first prays to God, then takes matters into her own hands. A beautiful as well as wise woman, she bedecks herself alluringly and, with a single maidservant, goes straight to the camp of Holofernes. Judith dazzles the general not only with her beauty but also with beguiling and manipulative language, leading him to believe that, with her aid, he can subdue the Israelites without difficulty. A few days later comes the inevitable invitation to spend the night in Holofernes' tent. Judith arouses his desire, then plies him with wine. When the intoxicated Holofernes passes out, Judith, armed with prayer and a sword, lops off his head. She slips from the camp with the head in a sack and has the elders display it proudly on the battlements. The people are in awe of the deed, and Achior the Ammonite faints dead away. Upon recovery he praises Judith to the skies, has himself circumcised, and converts to the Israelite religion. The Assyrians, stunned and crestfallen, are easy prey for the Israelites. The city is saved, the enemy routed and despoiled. Judith, much lauded not only by the citizenry of Bethulia but also by the high priest and his council in Jerusalem, retires to her own estate, emancipates her loyal attendant, declines all offers of marriage, and lives out her days in serenity, dying at the age of 105.[111]

As a tale of Jewish success against heavy odds, this narrative has immense appeal. It was often retold over the ages and has been represented many times in European art. The image of Judith holding Holofernes' head can be found in museums throughout the world. Its hold on popular imagination is clear and readily comprehensible.

But, here again, currents of a less distinct and more subterranean character come into play. The tale upsets expectations, inverts the norm, and invites thoughtful interpretation.

Judith herself is an ambivalent, often surprising figure. Her story can be correspondingly perplexing. She is an adherent of law and ritual but has no hesitation in practicing deceit. She roundly rebukes Uzziah and the elders, but, far from feeling aggrieved, they give her full authority. She exhibits greater devoutness than the males in her society but also exercises greater ruthlessness. She uses sexual wiles on Holofernes but remains a chaste widow to the end of her days. She plays the most central public role, and then retreats to an innocuous private life. She utters repeated prayers to the Lord but, in fact, accomplishes all through her own wits and guile.

Holofernes is a no less surprising, indeed implausible character. He rampages through most of the Near East and is then content with a long and leisurely siege of a small Judaean town. He swallows wholesale Judith's line about the Israelites and their God, although he has just rejected the same line when uttered by Achior. He waits patiently for four days before trying to seduce Judith—and then falls into a stupor when the opportunity arrives.

Minor personalities also behave in peculiar ways. Achior, gentile though he be, has a clearer vision of Jewish principles than Uzziah, the Judaean magistrate. Achior, warrior though he be, keels over at the sight of a severed head. And

Uzziah, chief magistrate though he be, allows Judith to proceed with her plan—despite the fact that he has no idea what it is.

Reversals and surprises abound. Just what they signify cannot be determined with any certainty. But they subvert a simplistic reading. The text plays with chronology and geography, turns history into fantasy, casts doubt upon Jewish leaders' grasp of their own precepts and traditions, both asserts and questions religious values, and confuses gender roles. The Book of Judith blurs boundaries throughout. The straightforward triumph of pious Jews over gentile aggressors, exemplified by the image of Judith brandishing the head of Holofernes, dissolves upon closer scrutiny. Reception of the tale for its entertaining quality constitutes but one mode of understanding. Like all the works discussed here, the Book of Judith operates at several levels. Therein lies its strength and its enticement.

As is clear, these texts undermine any lowbrow/highbrow dichotomy. The idea that creations of this sort could only be appreciated either by a "popular" mentality or by a sophisticated elite breaks down upon examination. Such a boundary eludes sharp definition. Folktales and romances are regularly transformed through retelling over time, with a range of readers or auditors. Populace and intelligentsia alike could take pleasure both in their narrative charm and in their subversive character. The richness of the texts signals a multitude of voices and the complex process of reshaping wrought by the interests and concerns of many generations.

WOMEN IN FICTION AND FACT

The tale of Judith draws attention to yet another complication: the constructs of gender. Narrative texts that engaged Jews with gentiles or probed Jewish self-perception in a broader culture frequently centered upon the demeanor, actions, and place of women. The frequency of such constructs by (presumably) male authors betrays a need to confront the tensions produced in gender roles by the pressures of a wider society.

The subordinate position of Jewish women in this period (as in most others) is marked and clear. Hellenistic writers make no bones about it. A purveyor of proverbs, hymns, and doctrinal advice called Ben Sira, writing in the early second century B.C.E., deemed the birth of a daughter to be a major burden for her father, who would have to supervise her behavior and protect her chastity. Daughters are a constant source of anxiety, prone to be wayward, keeping fathers awake with concern lest they be unmarried or childless or, worse, unwed mothers. Given the slightest chance, they will leap into the embrace of strangers. Without surveillance, they are liable to humiliate their parents, bring disgrace on their families, and make their fathers a laughingstock to their foes and a disgrace in public. Not that wives are any better. Ben Sira claims that he would rather share a house with a lion or a snake than an evil woman. Husbands can expect nagging, tantrums, and misery. Indeed, he goes so far as to assert that a man's wickedness is preferable to a woman's goodness![112] Comparable statements can be found in other Jewish-Hellenistic texts.[113] The expressions are rhetorical and extreme. Ben Sira acknowledges that a virtuous woman can bring benefits. But the characterization of that virtue is still more revealing: a man can count himself happy in having a sensible and devoted wife.[114] That translates into a wife who is chaste and beautiful, honors her husband—and keeps quiet.[115]

Ben Sira's attitude corresponds, in no small measure, to the position of women in Second Temple society. They were expected to maintain a chaste and modest demeanor, remain for the most part at home, stay out of the sight of strangers, and hold as first priority the reputation of the household. Marriages, at least among the middle and upper classes, were arranged by parents. And wedlock was far from an equal partnership. Men had the option of polygamy; women did not. Adultery was punishable as a crime, but only for women; men were exempt—unless they dallied with a married woman. A man could initiate a divorce at any time; a woman had no comparable privilege. Women were not even qualified to serve as witnesses in a legal proceeding. They could inherit, own, and bequeath property, but the instances of such activity are few in the era of the Second Temple. Insofar as they engaged in occupations and professions, these were largely confined to supporting their husbands and grew out of household tasks or areas appropriate to women such as weaving, spinning, cooking, baking, and midwifery.[116] In such circumstances, women could hardly expect to exercise leadership or achieve positions of authority.

Literature, however, seems to tell a different story. Women are conspicuous, active, and pivotal in the narratives. Memorable heroines stand out: Judith, Esther, Susanna, Aseneth. Did this represent a critique of gender hierarchy, a subversive treatment of societal norms? A closer reading of the texts may suggest more conformity than censure.

Judith is unquestionably the most potent female figure in Jewish-Hellenistic literature. She rescues a nation driven to despair and on the point of catastrophe. She rallies sagging spirits, seizes initiative from a languid leadership, devises a bold plan, and executes it remorselessly. Her resolute actions destroy the enemy and restore her nation to its glory. No male had been up to the task.

Yet even this dramatic narrative, with all its role reversal, does not challenge conventional social expectations. The dynamic and resourceful character of Judith serves primarily as a means to discredit the timid leaders of the community at a moment of crisis. The fact that Holofernes has to be dispatched by a woman, underscored more than once in the text, has less to do with female emancipation than with the acute humiliation of the men whose trust in the Lord has eroded.[117] Judith's rebuke of the elders is pointed and piercing.[118] Her own successes, even when achieved through guile and audacity, are always accompanied by prayers to Yahweh and humble obeisance to His presumed will, which is ultimately responsible for the outcome. Judith's piety is her most conspicuous characteristic.[119] And the outcome of her exploit is to restore an order and stability to the realm that allow it to settle back into its conformist mode. Appropriate gifts are offered to Yahweh, not only the customary sacrifices but also all the spoils from the camp of Holofernes. The Jews withdraw, each to his own inherited property, signifying the return of routine existence. Judith herself repairs to her estate, her public appearance brief and now concluded for good. She retired to private life and widowhood, a status she maintained throughout the many decades that remained to her. Fittingly enough, she chose to be buried with her husband. Her spectacular deed has saved the nation. But, lest there be any anxiety over a reversal of social and gender hierarchy, Judith's withdrawal to quiet piety puts it to rest.[120]

The figure of Esther also upsets certain expectations—but reinforces most.[121] Her famous tale opens at the court of Ahasuerus, master of the Persian Empire, whose domain reaches from India to Ethiopia. The king hosts a lavish banquet for all the officialdom of the realm, thus to put his great wealth on display. The festivities are to be culminated by a visit from the ravishing Queen Vashti, summoned by the ruler to exhibit her beauty for his guests. Vashti, however, refuses to parade herself before the assemblage. Ahasuerus swiftly consults his counselors and then banishes Vashti from his presence forever. He subsequently warns all women in his kingdom to be deferential to their husbands.

Ahasuerus decrees a competition—a beauty contest for the realm's young virgins—to find a new queen. Among those who answer the call is the beautiful Jewess Esther, an orphan raised by her cousin Mordekhai. After each of the maidens has undergone elaborate cosmetic treatments and spent a night with Ahasuerus, he selects Esther as his favorite (she had concealed her Jewish identity, on Mordekhai's advice) and sets the regal crown on her head. The event is celebrated by yet another extravagant banquet.

Ahasuerus's principal vizier is the ambitious Haman, promoted and honored by the king but ever grasping for more. The minister's demand for obeisance has been flouted by Mordekhai, who declined to bend a knee, thus prompting Haman to seek revenge on Mordekhai and the entire Jewish people. The compliant Ahasuerus authorizes the slaughter of Jews everywhere, man, woman, and child.

Mordekhai greets the news with sackcloth and ashes. But he also communicates with Esther, reminding her of her origins, and prodding her to intervene with the king. Esther overcomes her initial reluctance and takes the grave risk of an unsummoned appearance before Ahasuerus. Fortunately for Esther and for the Jews, he is still smitten with his young consort, promising her anything, up to half his kingdom. Esther plays her cards carefully, inviting the king and Haman to dinner on two consecutive evenings, piquing the interest of the former and deftly misleading the latter.

Ahasuerus, in the meantime, learns that Mordekhai had once saved his life by warning him of an assassination plot. He therefore plans to honor the Jewish courtier. Haman, assuming at first that such favor will be his, learns with dismay of Mordekhai's elevation. The humiliations multiply. Not only must Haman humble himself before Mordekhai; he has to hear from his own wife that he cannot succeed against the Jew.

Esther's plan can now come to fruition. She unveils her request at last: a plea that she and her people be spared destruction. And she dramatically points to Haman as the villain who had plotted the genocide. Ahasuerus directs that his minister be hanged on the very gibbet he had prepared for Mordekhai.

The king's about-face is complete. He awards Haman's estate to Esther and gives carte blanche to Mordekhai and Esther to compose a decree that will be sent to every province of the empire, not only rescinding Haman's instructions but also authorizing the Jews to take up arms against their enemies, kill them all, and confiscate their property. The Jews implement those orders unhesitatingly and ruthlessly. Mordekhai took his place as the most trusted and powerful of the king's ministers as well as chief advocate for the welfare of Jews throughout the realm.

What implications does this story possess for the expectations and aspirations of women? The opening scene sets the conventions within which society operates. Vashti defies her husband and is banished. An imperial edict demands that wives respect the authority of their husbands and that men be masters in their own homes.[122] The setting, of course, is Persian, not Jewish, and the satiric quality of the account is transparent, but the restrictions on female behavior would not be altogether unfamiliar to a Jewish readership.

Esther is a complex and changing character, but she does not stray far beyond the boundaries. Mordekhai pushes her into the contest; Esther meekly complies. She continues to obey Mordekhai, who checks up on her daily.[123] When he learns of the palace plot to assassinate Ahasuerus, he directs Esther to disclose it, and she does.[124] When Mordekhai dons the garb of mourning, Esther, concerned but clueless, sends him some new clothes.[125] He has to instruct her on how to dissuade the king from the slaughter of the Jews. And his suggestion that she might have been made queen precisely to rescue her people gives her courage.[126]

Esther matures swiftly and suddenly. From this point on she acts with resolution and resourcefulness. She will face Ahasuerus no matter what the risk. Now it is she who gives Mordekhai instructions—which he obeys. She appears before the king, ensnares Haman, and persuades Ahasuerus to reverse his homicidal decree.[127]

Has Esther been transformed from obedient ward to formidable potentate, a model for subordinate Jewish women aspiring to burst the bonds of convention? Not exactly. Ahasuerus may be putty in her hands, but the lines of authority are not breached. The king awards Haman's estate to Esther, appropriately enough, for women could own property in the Persian system. Esther, however, immediately turns it over to Mordekhai. A magnanimous gesture by a queen? Perhaps. But more likely a dutiful gesture by a foster-daughter. This restores the proper gender relationship. Ahasuerus notably gives his signet ring—and with it the authority to issue decrees in the king's name—to Mordekhai. Esther gets her way, but only by falling at the feet of Ahasuerus, bursting into tears, and pleading with him to avert the calamity that Haman had planned for the Jewish people.[128] It is Mordekhai who, clad in royal purple and sporting a golden crown, wields power in the palace and directs the celebration of the festival of Purim.[129] The Book of Esther concludes with a reference to the royal chronicles, in which were inscribed the authority of the king and next to him, as second in command, his grand vizier Mordekhai, most powerful of the Jews and spokesman for their welfare. No mention of Esther.[130]

As in the Book of Judith, the traditional order, in the end, is reinforced. Esther, demure and docile at the outset, placed in the palace through Mordekhai's machinations, spurred into action by his instructions, evolves into a clever and designing woman, even a vindictive one—but never usurps the role occupied by ascendant males.

The date of composition for the canonical Book of Esther cannot be fixed with precision. In all probability it came sometime in the late Persian or early Hellenistic period (between the mid-fifth and mid-third centuries B.C.E.). But supplements were added in Greek, which must be Hellenistic in date, and these include a striking revision of the character of Esther.

Additions C and D, so labeled by scholars, were inserted in the story right after Mordekhai's appeal to Esther to intercede with Ahasuerus. The first invented prayers by both Mordekhai and Esther; the second supplied the actual encounter between Esther and the king. Esther's plea in Addition C is unlike anything in the Hebrew text. She strips off her splendid garments, covers herself with ashes and dung, and makes herself as unattractive as before she had been comely. She concedes that she slept with the uncircumcised king—but she hated every minute of it. Yes, she wears a crown, but only in public and only because she must. She twice proclaims her loathing of the crown and compares it to a polluted rag. She insists even that she never took food at Haman's table, thus to declare her adherence to dietary laws—though the canonical account betrays no concern on the matter.[131] The queen protests too much. The author of the addition, by stressing her strained denials, calls attention to her weaknesses.

Addition D buttresses this conclusion. It describes the audience of Esther before the king. Unlike the Hebrew text, she is here depicted as terrified. She has dressed herself once more in resplendent robes, she has summoned her God and savior, and she glows at the peak of her beauty, but inside she is racked with fear. When she sees the king, magnificent and awesome on his throne and flashing an angry glance at her, she passes out on the spot, not once but twice.[132] This is hardly the stuff of a heroine. The interpolator evidently augmented the tale at Esther's expense. Lest anyone think that Esther comes off too well in the Hebrew version, the Hellenistic Jewish author decided to fix that.

As for the striking figure of Aseneth: the chaste and haughty virgin who defies her parents and heaps scorn upon the noble Joseph, only to shift suddenly into reverse, shattering idols and abasing herself, cuts a memorable figure. With what meaning? One cannot argue that her saga, set in the milieu of the Egyptian elite in the legendary era of Jacob and Joseph, reflects in any significant way the ordinary lives of Hellenistic Jews. But it may well resonate with ideological presuppositions about women's appropriate role in Jewish society.[133]

Aseneth's arrogance, disdain, disobedience of her parents, and virginal superiority represent all that Jews (and not they alone) found threatening and repugnant in women. She even boasts of a bed in which she sleeps alone and which has never been sat upon by man or woman.[134] The fiery Aseneth breaches every convention, and her actions, for the author of the text, naturally go hand in hand with ignorance of the true God and reckless idolatry. Aseneth has few redeeming features.

With the arrival of Joseph, however, Aseneth's hard exterior, cockiness, and contemptuousness vanish. Once the embodiment of all that is undesirable in a woman, she is now submissive, subservient, and self-abasing. And her rescuer from the abyss of despair is, appropriately, a male, the angelic figure whose ministrations restore her former beauty and make her a fitting bride—though only after she has made a fool of herself yet again.[135] Aseneth humbly and gratefully welcomes her marriage, accepting her role as handmaiden to her bridegroom and insisting on washing his feet.[136] Her gratitude, expressed in a prayer to the

Lord, consists of further self-denigration, confession of sins and offenses, and a declaration that her previous arrogance has been recast as humility.[137] Her former assertiveness could only be undone by degradation. *Joseph and Aseneth* reaffirms the suitable demeanor of women: deference to parents and submissiveness to husbands. Aseneth, who violates all the norms at the outset, spends much of the remainder of the tale reproaching herself, *ad nauseam.*

The story of Susanna sustains the theme. No need for remorse or transformation here: Susanna is virtue itself from the outset. The prim, modest, faithful matron was brought up properly by her parents: they instructed her in the Law of Moses. And she has been wed to a pillar of the Jewish community. Susanna epitomizes the figure of the pious and demure wife.[138] Her very innocence, however, renders her vulnerable to the wicked elders who present her with a grievous choice. The unhappy woman chooses the lesser evil: an unfair trial rather than the loss of her virtue. But her decision only underscores her helplessness. This is not so much steadfastness as resignation.

Susanna suffers further humiliation at the hearing: she is stripped naked (so the Septuagint version indicates), a prejudgment of her crime and public mortification. She does not utter a word in self-defense; only after being condemned does she release a plaintive wail, asking the Lord why an innocent victim must perish.[139] She is, of course, rescued and vindicated, but not through any actions of her own. Daniel materializes, as God's agent, to foil the elders' scheme.

The heroine of this tale, in short, is hardly heroic—an admirable, but a purely passive, figure. Susanna lacks the weight to resist the mighty and lets her fate be decided by others. At the conclusion, her reputation restored, she returns meekly to the household of her husband—who, so far as we can tell, had not even been present at her trial. The public credit for this success goes to Daniel.[140]

Women, in sum, figure prominently in the fictional compositions of Hellenistic Jews. But these creations do not serve to challenge the conventions of society; they manage, in fact, to reinforce and confirm them. The uppity Aseneth becomes a penitent, and arrogance is turned into abject submissiveness. Esther's position gives her access to power and a means to save her people, but she needs to be prodded, gives way to stereotypically female faintheartedness, and defers to male authority. The innocent and docile Susanna, the ideal wife, is helpless in the face of injustice but is rescued by a male hero and restored to the bosom of her presumed protectors. Even Judith, the respected widow, who bursts from her privacy to eclipse inept male leadership, reverts to private life and public invisibility. The inventive constructs of fertile writers largely reasserted the values of their society and the place of women within it.

DIASPORA AND HOMELAND

A firm sense of Jewish identity required more than the definition of a relationship with other cultures and peoples. A matter internal to the nation demanded repeated reappraisal: the issue of Diaspora and the homeland.

The destruction of the Second Temple in 70 C.E. constitutes, in most analyses, a watershed event for the Jews of antiquity. The elimination of the center, source of spiritual nourishment and preeminent symbol of the nation's identity, compelled Jews to reinvent themselves, to find other means of religious sustenance, and to adjust their lives to an indefinite period of displacement. That trauma has pervasive and enduring resonance. But it tends to obscure a striking fact. Jews faced a still more puzzling and problematic situation *prior* to the loss of the Temple. Diaspora did not await the fall of Jerusalem. Very large numbers of Jews dwelt outside Palestine in the roughly four centuries from the time of Alexander the Great to that of Titus.[141] The era of the Second Temple in fact brought the issue into sharp focus, inescapably so. The Temple still stood, a reminder of the hallowed past, and a Jewish regime had authority in Palestine. Yet the Jews of the Diaspora, from Italy to Iran, far outnumbered those in the homeland. Although Jerusalem loomed large in their self-perception as a nation, only a few of them had seen it, and few were likely to. How then did Diaspora Jews conceive their association with Jerusalem, the emblem of ancient tradition?

A dark picture prevails. Diaspora appears as something to be *overcome.* Thunderous biblical pronouncements present it as the terrible penalty exacted by God for the sins of the Israelites. They will be scattered among the nations and pursued by divine wrath. Spread among the lands, they will worship false gods and idols and enjoy no repose from the anger of the Lord. If the children of Israel abandon the ancestral precepts, they will have to enter the servitude of foreign lords in foreign parts. They will be dispersed among peoples unknown to them or to their fathers and will suffer God's vengeance until their destruction.[142] Through much of the Scriptures, only a single goal keeps flickering hopes alive: the expectation, however distant, of returning from exile and regaining a place in the Promised Land. Obedience to the Lord and repentance for past errors will induce Him to regather the lost souls spread across the world and restore them to the land of their fathers. He will raise a banner among the nations and assemble the people of Judah from the four corners of the earth.[143] It should be no surprise that a negative verdict on Diaspora life and a correspondingly gloomy attitude are conventionally ascribed to the Jews of the Second Temple period.[144]

Yet that convention ignores a grave implausibility. It is not easy to imagine that millions of Jews in the Diaspora were obsessed with a longing for Jerusalem that had little chance of fulfillment. It seems only logical that they sought means whereby to legitimize the existence that most of them inherited from their parents and would bequeath to their descendants.[145] Large and thriving Jewish communities existed in numerous areas of the Mediterranean, with opportunities for economic advancement, social status, and even political responsibilities.[146] Did their members, as some have claimed, take recourse in the thesis that the nation is defined by its texts rather than by its location?[147]

The dualism is deceptive. The Jews of antiquity, in fact, never developed a systematic theory or philosophy of Diaspora. The whole idea of valuing homeland over Diaspora or Diaspora over homeland may be off the mark. Second Temple Jews need not have faced so stark a choice.

The characterization of Diaspora as exile occurs with some frequency in the works of Hellenistic Jewish writers. But close scrutiny discloses an important and neglected fact. The majority of these grim pronouncements refer to the *biblical* misfortunes of the Israelites: expulsion by Assyrians, the destruction of the Temple, and the Babylonian captivity. Were they all metaphors for the Hellenistic Diaspora? The inference would be hasty, and it begs the question.

Ben Sira, for instance, laments the sins of his forefathers and records the fierce retaliation of the Lord that uprooted them from their land and dispersed them into every other land.[148] The reference, however, is to the era of Elijah and Elisha, to the ills of the Northern Kingdom, and to the Assyrian conquest that scattered the Israelites. It may have carried a warning to Ben Sira's contemporaries, whose shortcomings paralleled those of his ancestors—but it did not condemn the current Diaspora. The Book of Tobit tells a tale that ostensibly transpires in the Assyrian captivity as well. Tobit bewails his own fate, prompted by the sins of his forefathers, and the fate of his countrymen, an object of scorn and a vulnerable prey to those in the nations whence they have been dispersed.[149] But Tobit also forecasts the recovery of the Temple and portrays the outcome as the culmination of Israelite dreams, a happy ending to endure indefinitely.[150] This hardly suggests that the Hellenistic Diaspora is a vale of tears.

One text, to be sure, with explicit reference to Hellenistic Jews, does suggest that they were in dire straits in the Diaspora. The inventive tale of 3 Maccabees, composed probably in the second or first century B.C.E., places the Jews of Egypt in the gravest peril. Thrice they are almost annihilated by the wicked schemes of the mad monarch Ptolemy IV. The fantasy implies a precarious existence at the mercy of their enemies. They are to perish unjustly, a foreign people in a foreign land.[151] But the dire foreboding does not come to pass. The Jews triumph, their enemies are thwarted, and their apostates are punished. More significantly, the victory will be celebrated by an annual festival—in Egypt.[152] The Diaspora existence can go on indefinitely and contentedly.

Satisfactory circumstances in the Diaspora, however, did not diminish the sanctity and centrality of Jerusalem. Its aura retained a hold on the consciousness of Hellenistic Jews, wherever they happened to reside. Jerusalem is referred to on several occasions as "the holy city." The Jews' devotion to their sacred "acropolis" is observed even by the pagan geographer Strabo.[153] Numerous other texts characterize Palestine as the "holy land." The designation appears in works as different as 2 Maccabees, the Wisdom of Solomon, the Testament of Job, the Sibylline Oracles, and Philo.[154] Most, if not all, of these texts stem from the Diaspora. They underscore the reverence with which Jews around the Mediterranean continued to regard Jerusalem and the land of their fathers. But the authors who speak of reverence do not demand the "Return."

How compelling was the notion of a "homeland" to Jews dwelling in Mediterranean communities? In principle, the concept held firm. Loyalty to one's native land was a deep commitment in the rhetoric of the Hellenistic world.[155] Philo more than once endorses the idea that adherence to one's *patris* has singular power. He speaks of the charms of kinsmen and homeland; trips abroad are good for widening one's horizons, but nothing better than coming home. Failure to worship God is put on a level with neglecting to honor parents, benefactors, and patris. Defending one's country is a prime virtue. And, as Philo has Agrippa say to Caligula, love of one's native land and compliance with its precepts is deeply ingrained in all men.[156] It does not follow, however, that Diaspora Jews set their hearts upon a return to the fatherland. Broad pronouncements about love of one's country accord with general Hellenistic attitudes and expressions. They do not require that those native environs be reinhabited for life to be complete.

Did Jewish settlement abroad carry a stigma? Jews in fact formed stable communities in the Diaspora, entered into the social, economic, and political life of the nations they joined, and aspired to and obtained civic privileges in the cities of the Hellenistic world. Josephus maintains that Jews have every right to call themselves Alexandrians, Antiochenes, or Ephesians. And Philo refers to his home as "our Alexandria."[157] That form of identification surfaces more poignantly in the petition of an Alexandrian Jew threatened with the loss of his privileges. He labels himself an "Alexandrian" at the head of the document, alluding to his father, also an Alexandrian, and the proper education he had received, and expresses his fear of being deprived of his patris.[158] Whatever legal meaning this terminology might have carried, it signals the petitioner's clear affirmation of his roots in the community. A comparable sentiment might be

inferred from an inscription of the Phrygian city of Acmonia, alluding to fulfillment of a vow made to the "whole patris." A Jew or a group of Jews must have
commissioned it, because a menorah appears beneath the text. Here again the
"native city" is honored, presumably through a gift for civic purposes. The donor
pronounces his local loyalty in a conspicuous public manner.[159] Philo confirms
the sentiment in striking fashion: Jews consider the holy city as their "metropolis," but the states in which they were born and raised and which they acquired
from their fathers, grandfathers, and distant forefathers they adjudge their *pa-
trides*.[160] That fervent expression eradicates any idea of the "doctrine of return."
Diaspora Jews, in Philo's formulation at least, held a fierce attachment to the
adopted lands of their ancestors.

Commitment to one's local and regional community in no way diminished
one's devotion to Jerusalem. That the two were mutually exclusive alternatives is
plainly false. Reverence for Jerusalem was indeed publicly and conspicuously
demonstrated every year by the payment of a tithe to the Temple by Jews all over
the Mediterranean.[161] The ritualistic offering carried deep significance as a bond-
ing device.

In the mid-sixties B.C.E., economic circumstances in Rome and abroad
prompted a series of decrees forbidding the export of gold. In accord with this
policy, the Roman governor of Asia, L. Valerius Flaccus, banned the sending of
gold by the Jews of Asia Minor to Jerusalem. The action not only provoked resentment in Flaccus's province but also stirred a hornet's nest of opposition in
Rome itself. Cicero, who conducted Flaccus's defense at his trial for extortion
in 59, comments bitterly about the horde of Jews crowding around the tribunal,
exercising undue pressure upon the proceedings, and passionately exhibiting
their "barbaric superstition."[162] The account, of course, is partisan, rhetorical,
and exaggerated—but Cicero conveys some precious information. First, he indicates the Jews' earnest commitment to provide funds annually to the Temple
from Italy and from all the provinces of the Roman empire. Next, his record of
Flaccus's activities indicates that Jewish communities collected the tribute, city
by city, wherever they possessed sufficient numbers in Asia Minor. And, most revealing, his speech, however embellished and overblown, shows that the plight
of the Asian Jews who were prevented from making their contributions stirred
the passions of their compatriots far off in Rome and generated impressively
noisy demonstrations on their behalf.

References to the importance of the tithe abound. Josephus proudly observes
that the donations came from Jews all over Asia and Europe, indeed from everywhere in the world, for countless years. And when local authorities interfered
with that activity, the Jews would send up a howl to Rome.[163] The emperor Au-

gustus himself, and Roman officials acting in his name, intervened to ensure the untroubled exercise of Jewish practices in the province of Asia and elsewhere.[164] And the Jews in areas beyond the reach of Roman power also tithed with rigor and consistency. Communities in Babylon and other satrapies under Parthian dominion sent representatives every year over difficult terrain and dangerous highways to deposit their contributions in the Temple.[165] The issue of paying homage to Jerusalem was paramount. Indeed the Romans, even after they destroyed the Temple, did not destroy that institution—an ironic acknowledgment of its power. They simply altered its recipient. The tithe would no longer go to the demolished shrine; it would metamorphose into a Roman tax. The money would now subsidize the cult of Jupiter Capitolinus.[166]

The stark symbolism of the tithe had a potent hold upon Jewish sentiment. That annual act of obeisance was a repeated reminder, or rather display, of affection and allegiance, visible evidence of the unbroken attachment of the Diaspora to the center. How to interpret its implications? Did the remittance imply that the Diaspora was only a temporary exile?

In fact, the reverse conclusion holds. The yearly contribution proclaimed that the Diaspora could endure indefinitely and quite satisfactorily. The communities abroad were entrenched and successful, even mainstays of the center. Diaspora Jews did not and would not turn their backs on Jerusalem, which remained the principal emblem of their faith. Their fierce commitment to the tithe delivered that message unequivocally. But the gesture did not signify a desire for the "Return." It rendered the Return unnecessary.

A comparable phenomenon reinforces that proposition: the pilgrimage of Diaspora Jews to Jerusalem. Major festivals could attract them with some frequency and in quantity. According to Philo, myriads came from countless cities for every feast, over land and sea, from all points of the compass, to enjoy the Temple as a serene refuge from the hurly-burly of everyday life abroad.[167] The most celebrated occasion occurred after the death of Jesus. The feast of Pentecost brought throngs of people into the city from far-flung and diverse locations: from Parthia, Media, and Elam, from Mesopotamia and Cappadocia, from Pontus and Asia, from Phrygia and Pamphylia, from Egypt and Cyrene, from Crete and Arabia, and, indeed, even from Rome, all witness to the miracle of the disciples speaking in tongues.[168] The women's court at the Temple was large enough to accommodate those who resided in the land and those who came from abroad—a clear sign that female pilgrims in some numbers were expected visitors.[169]

The holy city was a forceful magnet, but the demonstration of devotion did not entail a desire for migration. Pilgrimage, in fact, by its very nature, signified a temporary payment of respect. Jerusalem had an irresistible and undiminished claim on the emotions of Diaspora Jews; it was indeed a critical piece of their identity. But home was elsewhere.

The self-perception of Second Temple Jews projected a tight solidarity between Center and Diaspora. Images of exile and separation did not haunt them. What affected the dwellers in Jerusalem affected Jews everywhere. The theme of intertwined experience and identity is reiterated with impressive frequency and variety.

The Letter of Aristeas, for instance, makes an unequivocal connection between Jerusalemites and other Jews. King Ptolemy's letter to the high priest in Judaea asserts that his motive in having the Hebrew Bible rendered into Greek is to benefit not only the Jews of Egypt but all Jews throughout the world—even those not yet born. And it is fitting that, when the scholars from Jerusalem complete their translation and it is read out to the Jews of Egypt, the large assemblage burst into applause, a dramatic expression of the unity of purpose.[170]

The narrative of 3 Maccabees depends on that same unity of purpose. It presupposes and never questions the proposition that the actions of Jerusalemites represent the sentiments of Jews anywhere in the Diaspora. When Ptolemy IV is thwarted in his design to enter the Holy of Holies in Jerusalem, he resolves to punish the Jews of Egypt. The king is determined to bring public shame upon the *ethnos* of the Jews generally. Egyptian Jews are "fellow-tribesmen" of those who dwelled in Judaea.[171]

The affiliations emerge most dramatically and drastically in the grave crises that marked the reign of the emperor Caligula (37–41 C.E.). Harsh conflict erupted in Alexandria, bringing dislocation, persecution, and death upon the Jewish community. And a still worse menace loomed over Jerusalem when the erratic emperor proposed to have a statue of himself installed in the Temple. When Alexandrian Jews were attacked, says Philo, the word spread like wildfire. As the synagogues were destroyed in Alexandria, reports swept not only through all the districts of Egypt but from there to the nations of the east and from the borders of Libya to the lands of the west. Jews had settled all over Europe and Asia, and the news of a pogrom anywhere would race through the entire network.[172] Philo's claim of such speedy communications may stretch a point, but the concept of tight interrelationships among Jews of the Diaspora is plain and potent.

Philo himself headed the delegation to the emperor that would plead the cause of the Alexandrian Jews. Their objective, however, was swiftly eclipsed by word of Caligula's decision to install his statue in the Temple at Jerusalem. Philo's words are arresting: the most grievous calamity fell unexpectedly and brought peril not to one part of the Jewish people but to the entire nation at once.[173] The letter of Agrippa I, a friend of the emperor and recently awarded a kingdom among the Jews, urgently alerted Caligula to the gravity of the situation. Agrippa maintained that an affront to Jerusalem would have vast repercussions: the holy city was not merely metropolis of Judaea but of most nations in the world since Jewish colonies thrived all over the Near East, Asia Minor, Greece, Macedon, Africa, and the lands beyond the Euphrates.[174] The image of Jerusalem as binding together Jews everywhere in the world held a prominent place in the self-perception of the Diaspora.

A moving passage elsewhere in Philo encapsulates this theme. Although he thrived in the Diaspora, enjoyed its advantages, and broadcast its virtues, Philo nevertheless found even deeper meaning in the land of Israel. He interprets the Shavuot festival as a celebration of the Jews' possession of their own land, a heritage now of long standing, and a means whereby they could cease their wandering.[175] Philo saw no inconsistency or contradiction. Diaspora Jews might find fulfillment and reward in their communities abroad, but they honored Judaea as a refuge for those who were once displaced and unsettled—and the prime legacy of all.

Josephus makes the point in a quite different context but with equal force. In his rewriting of Numbers, he places a sweeping prognostication in the mouth of the Midianite priest Balaam. The priest projects a glorious future for the Israelites: they will not only occupy and hold forever the land of Canaan, a chief signal of God's favor, but their multitudes will fill all the world, islands and continents, outnumbering even the stars in the heavens.[176] That is a notable declaration. Palestine, as ever, merits a special place. But the Diaspora, far from being a source of shame to be overcome, represents a resplendent achievement.

The respect and awe one paid to the Holy Land stood in full harmony with a commitment to the local community and allegiance to gentile governance. Diaspora Jews did not bewail their fate and pine away for the homeland. Nor, by contrast, did they shrug off the homeland and reckon the Book as surrogate for the Temple. The postulated alternatives are reductive and simplistic. Palestine mattered, and it mattered in a territorial sense—but not as a required residence. A gift to the temple and a pilgrimage to Jerusalem announced simultaneously one's devotion to the symbolic heart of Judaism and a singular pride in the accomplishments of the Diaspora.

The Jews forever refashioned their identity and adjusted their self-perception with an eye to the cultural milieu in which they found themselves. The age when Hellenic culture held sway in the Near East was no exception. Jews adopted a range of strategies that allowed them to negotiate their presence within that milieu. I have endeavored in this chapter to break down the usual dichotomies and question the customary boundaries. The image of confrontation, tension, and antagonism between Judaism and Hellenism needs to be reassessed. This was no zero-sum game in which every move toward Hellenism meant a loss for Jewish tradition. A complex process of adjustment took place whereby Jews found expression for their own heritage in the language and conventions of the larger community. The process, to be sure, sometimes involved struggle, dissension, and occasional catastrophe, but it did not reduce itself to mere conflict between the cultures.

Jewish perspectives on the Greeks (or gentiles generally) in this era show variety, overlapping, and nuance, rather than the simplistic alternatives of sharp differentiation or a striving for accommodation. The internal boundaries were as fluid as the external ones. The divide between elite and popular Jewish culture is elided by the nature of our texts and their history. The process of transmission and rewriting over the course of many generations produced cultural artifacts that spoke in a variety of voices and at several levels of meaning across conventional social and intellectual barriers. Women were reconceived by Jewish fiction as figures of prominence and high visibility, in ostensible contradistinction to the realities of social life. Yet fiction and fact had more convergence than divergence: the imaginative tales largely endorsed the gender hierarchy. And even the familiar duality of homeland and exile requires reconsideration. Jews thoroughly embraced the Diaspora communities in which they could lead full and rewarding lives—without compromising their allegiance to the symbol of their faith in Jerusalem. They successfully negotiated their own place within the world of Greco-Roman society: they were appropriationists rather than assimilationists. And they shunned the melting pot.

NOTES

1. 1 Maccabees 15:22–23.

2. Strabo, in Josephus, *Ant.*, 14:115.

3. See, e.g., V. Tcherikover, *Hellenistic Civilization and the Jews* (New York, 1970), 90–116.

4. The surviving fragments of the play were preserved by the first-century-B.C.E. pagan writer Alexander Polyhistor and transmitted by the Church fathers Clement and Eusebius. Ezekiel wrote a number of tragedies on Jewish themes, as we know from Clement, *Stromata* 1.155.1. One may conveniently consult the fragments in the fine studies by H. Jacobson, *The Exagoge of Ezekiel* (Cambridge, Engl., 1983), 50–67, and C. Holladay, *Fragments from Hellenistic Jewish Authors: Vol. II: The Poets* (Atlanta, Ga., 1989), 344–405. The date and prove-

nance of the work can be determined only within broad limits. Ezekiel employed the Septuagint version of the Pentateuch, as his language makes clear, and he must precede Alexander Polyhistor—thus sometime between the later third and early first centuries. The subject matter of the *Exagoge* does not suffice to fix the place of composition in Alexandria or elsewhere in Egypt. On these issues, see Holladay, *Fragments*, 2: 308–13, with references to earlier literature.

5. Ezekiel, in Eusebius, *Praeparatio Evangelica* [hereafter *PE*], 9.29.4–6.

6. Numbers 12:6–8.

7. The text is contained in Euseb. *PE*, 9.22.1–11. It can be conveniently consulted in A.-M. Denis, *Fragmenta Pseudepigraphorum Quae Supersunt Graeca* (Leiden, 1970), 204–7; H. Lloyd-Jones and P. Parsons, *Supplementum Hellenisticum* (Berlin, 1983), 360–65; and Holladay, *Fragments*, 2:106–27, with translation. Theodotus's date and provenance remain uncertain. For a survey of modern opinions, see Holladay, *Fragments*, 2:68–72, with notes.

8. Genesis 33:18–34:31, 49:5–7.

9. Euseb. *PE*, 9.22.1–11.

10. Ibid. 9.22.1.

11. Ibid. 9.22.8.

12. Gen. 33:18–20; Euseb. *PE*, 9.22.4.

13. Gen. 34:18–23; Euseb. *PE*, 9.22.5, 8.

14. Text in Denis, *Fragmenta*, 203–4; Lloyd-Jones and Parsons, *Supplementum Hellenisticum*, 328–31; and Holladay, *Fragments*, 2: 234–45. A single reference survives to one other Jewish presumed practitioner of epic poetry: a certain Sosates described as the "Jewish Homer in Alexandria" (C. Frick, *Chronica Minora* [Leipzig, 1892], 278).

15. The most valuable treatments of Philo may be found in Y. Gutman, "Philo the Epic Poet," *Scripta Hierosolymitana* 1 (1954): 36–63, and the exhaustive notes of Holladay, *Fragments*, 2: 205–99.

16. Euseb. *PE*, 9.20.1.

17. Ibid., 9.24.1.

18. Gen. 41:45, 50–52, 46:20.

19. On *Joseph and Aseneth* as a Hellenistic romance, see M. Philonenko, *Joseph et Aséneth* (Leiden, 1968), 43–47; S. West, "Joseph and Aseneth: A Neglected Greek Romance" (1974): 71–77; and C. Burchard, "*Joseph et Aséneth: Questions actuelles*," in W.C. van Unnik, ed., *La littérature juive entre Tenach et Mischna* (Leiden, 1974), 84–96. For parallels with Jewish fiction, see C. Burchard, *Untersuchungen zur Joseph und Aseneth* (Tübingen, 1965), 106–7. See also L. M. Wills, *The Jewish Novel in the Ancient World* (Ithaca, N.Y., 1995), 170–84.

20. *Joseph and Aseneth*, 1–8.

21. Ibid., 9–21.

22. Ibid., 22–29.

23. See the thorough and analytic review of the scholarship by R. D. Chesnutt, *From Death to Life: Conversion in Joseph and Aseneth* (Sheffield, Engl., 1995), 20–93.

24. *Joseph and Aseneth*, 1:4.

25. Ibid., 3:1–6, 4:8; cf. 20:7.

26. Ibid., 5:4–10.

27. Ibid., 6:2; cf. 5:6.

28. Ibid., 13:11, 18:1–2, 21:21.

29. Ibid., 20:6–21:5.

30. Ibid., 29:10–11.

31. Ibid., 7:1; Gen. 43:32.

32. *Joseph and Aseneth*, 21:4.

33. Ibid., 23:3; cf. 24:7.

34. Ibid., 29:5–7.

35. The most fundamental and thorough study of Demetrius is in J. Freudenthal, *Alexander Polyhistor* (Breslau, 1875), 35–82. The fragments can be usefully consulted in C. R. Holladay, *Fragments from Hellenistic Jewish Authors: Vol. I: Historians* (Chico, Calif., 1983), 51–91, with Holladay's valuable introduction and notes. More recently, see the discussion by G. E. Sterling, *Historiography and Self-Definition: Josephos, Luke-Acts, and Apologetic Historiography* (Leiden, 1992), 153–67, with excellent bibliography.

36. Euseb. *PE*, 9.21.3–5.

37. Ibid., 9.21.14–15; Gen. 43:34, 45:22.

38. Euseb. *PE*, 9.21.1–3.

39. Ibid., 9.29.16; cf. Exodus 13:18.

40. Among recent treatments of Eupolemus, see B. Z. Wacholder, *Eupolemus: A Study of Judaeo-Greek Literature* (Cincinnati, 1974); Holladay, *Fragments*, 1: 93–156; Sterling, *Historiography and Self-Definition*, 207–22.

41. Euseb. *PE*, 9.30.3–4.

42. The narratives of David's victories and annexations appear in 2 Samuel 5:17–25. 8:1–14, 10:6–19. Souron the king of Tyre, represented as a victim of David, is obviously equivalent to the biblical Hiram with whom David enjoyed a positive and productive association (2 Sam. 5:11). The Egyptian Vaphres has a place in the pharaonic royal genealogy but long after any putative date for David.

43. Euseb. *PE*, 9.31.1, 9.32.1.

44. Ibid., 9.32.1.

45. Ibid., 9.34.18.

46. 1 Kings 11:1–6.

47. A similar posture was taken later by King Herod, both rebuilder of the Temple and subsidizer of pagan shrines.

48. Among the more useful editions or commentaries, see R. Tramontano, *La Lettera di Aristea a Filocrate* (Naples, 1931); M. Hadas, *Aristeas to Philocrates* (New York, 1951); A. Pelletier, *Lettre d'Aristée à Philocrate* (Paris, 1962); and N. Meisner, *Jüdische Schriften aus hellenistisch-römischer Zeit*, vol. 2 (Gütersloh, Germany, 1973), 1, 35–87. A general bibliogra-

phy is in E. Schürer, *The History of the Jewish People in the Age of Jesus Christ*, rev. ed. by G. Vermes, F. Millar, and M. Goodman (Edinburgh, 1986), vol. 3.1, 685–87.

49. Philo, *Moses*, 2:41.

50. *Letter of Aristeas*, 187–294.

51. Ibid., 11.

52. Ibid., 38.

53. Ibid., 181.

54. Ibid., 3.

55. Ibid., 122.

56. Ibid., 209, 211, 222–23, 256, 292.

57. Ibid., 128–70.

58. On the banquet and the dialogue, see O. Murray, "Aristeas and Ptolemaic Kingship," *Journal of Theological Studies* 18 (1967): 344–61. Cf. P. M. Fraser, *Ptolemaic Alexandria* (Oxford, 1972), 701–3, and F. Parente, "La lettera di Aristea come Fonte per la storia del Giudaismo Alessandrino durante la prima metà del I secolo a. C.," *Annali della Scuola Normale Superiore di Pisa*, 2, no. 2 (1972): 546–63.

59. *Letter of Aristeas*, 200.

60. Ibid., 200–201, 235, 296.

61. The work itself is an epitome of the now lost five-volume history of the Maccabees by Jason of Cyrene, plainly also a Hellenized Jew (2 Macc. 2:19–31). For a recent register of scholarship on 2 Maccabees, see Schürer, *History of the Jewish People*, vol. 3.1, 536–37.

62. 2 Macc. 2:21.

63. 2 Macc. 10:4; cf. 5:22.

64. Daniel 2:31–45, 7:1–27, 8:1–26, 11:21–45, 12:1–3.

65. The chronology is complex and contested. A valuable recent treatment may be found in J. M. G. Barclay, *The Jews in the Mediterranean Diaspora* (Edinburgh, 1996), 216–25.

66. 3 Sibylline 166–90, 202–4, 341–49, 381–400, 545–55, 638–45.

67. On the date, see Schürer, *History of the Jewish People*, vol. 3.1, 181, and J. Sievers, *The Hasmoneans and Their Supporters* (Atlanta, Ga., 1990), 3.

68. 1 Macc. 1:1–4, 9, 43–44.

69. 2 Macc. 6:18–7:41.

70. 4 Macc. 4–18. For recent discussions of the text, with bibliography, see H. Anderson, "4 Maccabees," in J. Charlesworth, ed., *The Old Testament Pseudepigrapha*, vol. 2 (Garden City, N.Y., 1985), 531–43, and Schürer, *History of the Jewish People*, vol. 3.1, 588–93.

71. *Letter of Aristeas*, 134–39.

72. See, e.g., Josephus, *Ant.*, 16:160–61, 18:257–60, 19:300–312, 20:173–84.

73. Ibid. 16:161.

74. Josephus, *C. Apionem*, 2:154–56, 168–74.

75. Ibid., 2:220–31, 279.

76. Ibid., 2:239–54.

77. Galatians 3:28; cf. 1 Corinthians 12:13.

78. An up-to-date edition of the fragments, with translation, thorough notes, and comprehensive bibliography has been produced by C. Holladay, *Fragments from Hellenistic Jewish Authors: Vol. III: Aristobulus* (Atlanta, Ga., 1995).

79. Aristobulus, in Euseb. *PE*, 13.12.1; Clement, *Strom.* 1.22.150.1–3.

80. Aristobulus, in Euseb. *PE*, 13.12.1; Clement, *Strom.* 1.22.150.2.

81. Aristobulus, in Euseb. *PE*, 13.12.3–4, 8; Clement, *Strom.* 5.14.99.3.

82. Aristobulus, in Euseb. *PE*, 13.12.13–15; Clement, *Strom.* 5.14.107.1–3. See the careful discussion in N. Walter, *Der Thoraausleger Aristobulos* (Berlin, 1964), 150–58, with reference to the relevant Homeric and Hesiodic lines; cf. Y. Gutman, *ha-Siprut ha-Yehudit-ha-Helenistit*, vol. 1 (Jerusalem, 1958) 210–12, and Holladay, *Fragments*, 3:234–37.

83. The fragments can be found in A.-M. Denis, *Fragmenta*, 161–74. A translation by H. Attridge is in J. Charlesworth, ed., *Old Testament Pseudepigrapha*, 2: 824–30. And see the valuable treatment by M. Goodman in Schürer, *History of the Jewish People*, vol. 3.1, 656–61, 667–71, with bibliographies.

84. The lines appear in Pseudo-Justin, *De Monarchia* 2; Clement, *Strom.* 5.14.131.2–3; Euseb. *PE*, 13.13.60.

85. Ps. Justin, *De Monarch.* 2; Clement, *Strom.* 5.14.113.2; Euseb. *PE*, 13.13.40.

86. Ps. Justin, *De Monarch.* 3; Clement, *Strom.* 5.14.121.4–122.1; Euseb. *PE*, 13.13.48.

87. Clement, *Strom.* 5.11.75.1; *Protrepticus* 6.68.3; cf. Ps. Justin, *De Monarch.* 2.

88. Clement, *Strom.* 5.14.119.2, 5.14.121.1–3, 5.14.133.3; Euseb. *PE*, 13.13.45–47, 13.13.62, 13.36.2; Ps. Justin, *De Monarch.* 2–5.

89. Acts of the Apostles 17:16–33.

90. Acts 17:24–26.

91. Acts 17:28.

92. Josephus, *C. Apionem*, 2:121–23.

93. Ibid., 2:168; cf. 1:162.

94. Ibid., 2:280–84.

95. Philo, *Moses* 2:18–20.

96. See, e.g., Josephus, *BJ*, 5:17; *Ant.*, 4:12; *C. Apionem*, 2:282.

97. Romans 1:14.

98. Philo, *Moses* 2:27; *Quod Omnis Probus Liber Sit*, 73–75.

99. For a sampling of divergent views, see Philonenko, *Joseph et Aséneth*, 53–61; Chesnutt, *From Death to Life*, 153–84; and Barclay, *Jews in the Mediterranean Diaspora*, 204–16.

100. Daniel 14:1–22. On the texts that convey this tale, see C. A. Moore, *Daniel, Esther, and Jeremiah: The Additions* (Garden City, N.Y., 1977), 23–34. The date of composition, perhaps later second century B.C.E., remains uncertain; cf. M. J. Steussy, *Gardens in Babylon: Narrative and Faith in the Greek Legends of Daniel* (Atlanta, Ga., 1993), 28–32.

101. Dan. 14:23–42.

102. Dan. 13:1–64.

103. Cf. Moore, *Daniel, Esther, and Jeremiah,* 88–89, and L. M. Wills, *The Jew in the Court of the Foreign King: Ancient Jewish Court Legends* (Minneapolis, 1990), 76–79.

104. Dan. 13:49, 54–55.

105. 2 Macc. 3:1–40.

106. Ibid. 3:15, 22.

107. Ibid. 3:25–27.

108. Ibid. 3:37–38.

109. Ibid. 9:13–16.

110. Judith 1–7. See the valuable editions and commentaries in M. S. Enslin, *The Book of Judith* (Leiden, 1972), and C. A. Moore, *Judith* (Garden City, N.Y., 1985).

111. Jth. 8–16.

112. Ben Sira 7:24, 22:3–5, 25:16–26, 26:6–12, 42:9–14. A useful translation and full commentary may be found in P. W. Skehan, *The Wisdom of Ben Sira* (New York, 1987).

113. See, e.g., Testament of Reuben, 5:1–3, and Josephus, *Ant.,* 5:294.

114. Ben Sira 25:8, 40:19.

115. Ibid. 26:13–26, 36:27–29.

116. On all this, see the fine study of T. Ilan, *Jewish Women in Greco-Roman Palestine* (Tübingen, 1995), esp. 79–88, 122–47, 163–72, 184–90.

117. See Jth. 13:15, 14:18, 16:5.

118. Jth. 8:12–15.

119. Jth. 8:6–8, 25, 9:1–14, 10:9, 12:8, 13:4–7, 14–16, 16:1–5, 13–17, 19.

120. Jth. 16:18–25. See the cogent comments of A. -J. Levine "Sacrifice and Salvation: Otherness and Domestication in the Book of Judith," in J. C. VanderKam, ed., *"No One Spoke Ill of Her": Essays on Judith* (Atlanta, Ga., 1992), 17–30.

121. Valuable analyses of the narrative may be found in S. B. Berg, *The Book of Esther: Motifs, Themes, and Structures* (Missoula, Mt., 1979); M. V. Fox, *Character and Ideology in the Book of Esther* (Columbia, S.C., 1991); and J. Levenson, *Esther* (Louisville, Ky., 1997).

122. Esther 1:12–22.

123. Ibid. 2:5–20.

124. Ibid. 2:21–22.

125. Ibid. 4:1–4.

126. Ibid. 4:5–16.

127. Ibid. 4:17–5:8, 7:1–10.

128. Ibid. 8:1–6.

129. Ibid. 8:15 9:3–4, 20–23, 29–32.

130. Ibid. 10:2–3.

131. Ibid., Addition C, 12–13, 26–28.

132. Ibid., Addition D, 1–15.

133. See the provocative suggestions in R. S. Kraemer, *When Aseneth Met Joseph* (Oxford, 1998), 191–221.

134. *Joseph and Aseneth,* 2:8–9.

135. Ibid., 14–17; see, esp., 17:7–10.

136. Ibid., 19:4–5, 20:4–5.

137. Ibid., 21:11–21.

138. Dan. 13:1–4.

139. Dan. 13:32–35, 41–43.

140. Dan. 13:63–64; cf. 13:30.

141. For population estimates, see *Encyclopaedia Judaica,* 13: 866–903, and L. H. Feldman, *Jew and Gentile in the Ancient World* (Princeton, 1993), 23, 468–69, 555–56.

142. Leviticus 26:33; Deuteronomy 4:26–28, 28:63–65; Jeremiah 5:19, 9:15.

143. Deut. 30:2–5; Isaiah 11:12.

144. See, e.g., Y. F. Baer, *Galut* (New York, 1947), 9–13, and A. Eisen, *Galut* (Bloomington, Ind., 1986), 3–34. The most sweeping argument on melancholy Jewish attitudes toward the Diaspora in the Second Temple era is made in W. C. van Unnik, *Das Selbstverständnis der jüdischen Diaspora in der hellenistisch-römischen Zeit* (Leiden, 1993), *passim.* See also the very useful survey by W. D. Davies, *The Territorial Dimension of Judaism* (Berkeley, 1981), 28–34, 61–100.

145. See I. M. Gafni, *Land, Center, and Diaspora* (Sheffield, Engl., 1997), 19–40.

146. The classic study is J. Juster, *Les juifs dans l'empire romain,* 2 vols. (Paris, 1914). Among recent treatments, see Schürer, *History of the Jewish People,* vol. 3.1, 1–176; Barclay, *Jews in the Mediterranean Diaspora,* 19–81, 231–319; and I. Levinskaya, *The Book of Acts in Its Diaspora Setting* (Grand Rapids, Mich., 1996), 127–93.

147. See, esp., G. Steiner, "Our Homeland, The Text," *Salmagundi* 66 (1985): 4–25. On the ambivalence of exile and homecoming in recent Jewish conceptions, see the comments of S. D. Ezrahi, "Our Homeland, the Text . . . Our Text, the Homeland: Exile and Homecoming in the Modern Jewish Imagination," *Michigan Quarterly Review* 31 (1992): 463–97.

148. Ben Sira 48:15.

149. Tobit 3:3–4, 13:3–6, 14:4.

150. Tob. 13:10–11, 14:5–6.

151. 2 Macc. 6:3; cf. 6:10.

152. 3 Macc. 6:36, 7:15, 19.

153. 2 Macc. 1:12; Philo, *Legatio ad Gaium* 225, 281, 288, 299, 346; Strabo, 16.2.37.

154. 2 Macc. 1:7; Wisdom of Solomon 12:3; Testament of Job 33:5; 3 Sib. 267, 732–35; 5 Sib. 281; Philo, *Heres* 293; *In Flaccum* 46; *Leg.* 202, 205, 330. Cf. Zechariah 2:16.

155. Cf. Polybius 1.14.4.

156. Philo, *De Abrahamo* 63, 65, 197; *Mos.* 2:198; *De Mutatione Nominum* 40; *De Cherubim* 15; *Leg.* 277, 328.

157. Josephus, *C. Apionem,* 2:38–39; Philo, *Leg.* 150.

158. *Corpus Papyrorum Iudaicarum,* II, #151.

159. *Corpus Inscriptionum Iudaicarum,* #771.

160. Philo, *Flacc.* 46.

161. See the useful summary of testimony and the discussion in S. Safrai and M. Stern, *The Jewish People in the First Century* (Philadelphia, 1974), 1:186–91.

162. Cicero, *Pro Flacco,* 66–68.

163. Josephus, *Ant.,* 14:110, 16:28, 45–50; cf. 18:312–13; *BJ,* 7:45.

164. Philo, *Leg.* 291, 312; Josephus, *Ant.,* 16:163, 166–71.

165. Philo, *Leg.* 216.

166. Josephus, *BJ,* 7:218; Dio Cassius, 66.7.2.

167. Philo, *Spec. Leg.* 1:69; cf. Safrai and Stern, *Jewish People,* 1:191–94.

168. Acts 2:1–11; cf. 6:9.

169. Josephus, *BJ,* 5:199.

170. *Letter of Aristeas,* 38, 307–11.

171. 3 Macc. 2:21–27, 3:21.

172. Philo, *Flacc.* 45–46.

173. Philo, *Leg.* 184; cf. 178, 351, 373.

174. Philo, *Leg.* 277–83; cf. 330.

175. Philo, *Spec. Leg.* 2:168.

176. Josephus, *Ant.,* 4:115–16. Josephus departs here quite substantially from the corresponding text in Numbers 23:6–10. Cf. also Josephus, *Ant.,* 1:282, 2:213.

SELECTED BIBLIOGRAPHY

Barclay, J. M. G. *The Jews in the Mediterranean Diaspora.* Edinburgh, 1996.

Bickermann, E. *The Jews in the Greek Age.* Cambridge, Mass., 1988.

Braun, M. *History and Romance in Graeco-Oriental Literature.* Oxford, 1938.

Brenner, A. *A Feminist Companion to Esther, Judith, and Susanna.* Sheffield, Engl., 1995.

Charlesworth, J., ed. *The Old Testament Pseudepigraphy.* Vol. 2. Garden City, N.Y., 1985.

Cohen, S. J. D. *The Beginnings of Jewishness.* Berkeley, 1999.

———. *From the Maccabees to Mishnah.* Philadelphia, 1987.

Collins, J. J. *Between Athens and Jerusalem.* 2d ed. Grand Rapids, Mich., 2000.

Feldman, L. H. *Jew and Gentile in the Ancient World.* Princeton, 1993.

Gafni, I. M. *Land, Center, and Diaspora.* Sheffield, Engl., 1997.

Grabbe, L. L. *Judaism from Cyrus to Hadrian.* 2 vols. Minneapolis, 1992.

Gruen, E. S. *Heritage and Hellenism: The Reinvention of Jewish Tradition.* Berkeley, 1998.

———. *Diaspora: Jews amidst Greeks and Romans.* Cambridge, Mass., 2002.

Hayes, J. H., and S. R. Mandell. *The Jewish People in Classical Antiquity.* Louisville, Ky., 1998.

Hengel, M. *Judaism and Hellenism.* 2 vols. London, 1974.

Ilan, T. *Jewish Women in Greco-Roman Palestine.* Tübingen, 1995.

Levine, L. I. *Judaism and Hellenism in Antiquity.* Seattle, 1998.

Modrzejewski, J. *The Jews of Egypt.* Princeton, 1995.

Momigliano, A. *Alien Wisdom: The Limits of Hellenization.* Cambridge, Engl., 1975.

Nickelsburg, G. *Jewish Literature Between the Bible and Mishnah.* Philadelphia, 1981.

Safrai, S., and M. Stern. *The Jewish People in the First Century.* 2 vols. Philadelphia, 1974.

Schürer, E. *The History of the Jewish People in the Age of Jesus Christ.* Vol. 3.1. Rev. ed. by G. Vermes, F. Millar, and M. Goodman. Edinburgh, 1986.

Sterling, G. E. *Historiography and Self-Definition: Josephos, Luke-Acts, and Apologetic Historiography.* Leiden, 1992.

Tcherikover, V. *Hellenistic Civilization and the Jews.* New York, 1970.

VanderKam, J. *An Introduction to Early Judaism.* Grand Rapids, Mich., 2001.

Wills, L. M. *The Jewish Novel in the Ancient World.* Ithaca, N.Y., 1995.

Ancient synagogue at Khirbet Shema', near Meiron, looking southwest.
The building dates to the third and fourth centuries C.E. and is the only broadhouse
synagogue with internal columnation in ancient Palestine.
(Courtesy Eric Meyers)

JEWISH CULTURE IN GRECO-ROMAN PALESTINE

ERIC M. MEYERS

In the early third century C.E., the Mishnah (the first edited body of rabbinic writings) tells the following story about Gamaliel, the *nasi*, or patriarch, of the Palestinian Jewish community in the previous century:

> Proklus the son of Philosophus asked Rabban Gamaliel who was bathing in Acco in the Bath of Aphrodite. He said to him: "It is written in your Torah, 'And nothing of the devoted (forbidden) thing should cling to your hand' (Deuteronomy 13:17). Why are you bathing in the Bath of Aphrodite?" He answered him: 'One ought not respond in a bath." When he came out he [Rabban Gamaliel] said to him: "I did not come into her borders, she came into mine! People do not say, 'Let us make a bath for Aphrodite,' but rather, 'Let us make Aphrodite an ornament for the bath.' Moreover, even if they would give you a large sum of money, you would not approach your idol naked and suffering pollutions, and urinate before it; yet, this goddess stands at the mouth of a gutter and all the people urinate before her. [Lastly] it is written 'Their gods' (12:3), that which they refer to as a god is forbidden and that which is not referred to as a god is permitted."[1]

The Greek philosopher accuses Gamaliel of hypocrisy: how can he bathe in a bathhouse dedicated to Aphrodite when the Torah clearly forbids benefiting from idolatry? Gamaliel responds by denying that the statue of Aphrodite, especially one placed above the public urinal, is anything more than ornamentation. Bathing is not worship and statues are not necessarily idols! Yet, by going to the public bath in the first place, Gamaliel, the titular leader of the rabbinical caste, engaged in behavior that clearly reflects the influence of Greco-Roman culture. For Gamaliel, though, the bath is not a foreign institution: "I did not come into her borders, she came into mine!" The very exchange between the rabbi and the Greek philosopher, fictional though it may have been, also attests to the sense the Jews had of participation in the discourses of the wider culture.

In this pregnant text, we find precious evidence of the complex cultural interchange between the Jews and the Greeks and Romans in whose empires they lived. They absorbed many elements of Greco-Roman culture but at the same time transformed them into something indigenous. Yet they were equally preoccupied with maintaining firmly the boundaries between their own identity and religion and that of their non-Jewish neighbors. The ancient biblical struggle against Canaanite idolatry took new forms as the Jews confronted the religions of the Greeks and Romans. As we shall see, these complex processes took place in Jewish Palestine on a variety of levels and in a variety of genres: from the elite, rabbinic culture represented by Rabban Gamaliel to the popular, material culture of cities like Sepphoris in the lower Galilee, from literary texts to engravings on sarcophagi. I will argue that it was Hellenism, as both a challenge and an inspiration, that produced the most creative expressions of Jewish culture in Palestine, expressions that greatly enriched the Jewish tradition without sacrificing its own indigenous, semitic core.

The period of this chapter—from the return from the Babylonian Exile in the sixth and fifth centuries B.C.E. to roughly the third century C.E.—was a time when the Jews of Palestine lived under great world empires: the Persian Empire established by Cyrus the Great, the Hellenistic empires that came after the conquests of Alexander the Great, and the Roman Empire. Although the biblical kingdoms of Israel and Judah were occasionally dominated by imperial powers—Assyria and Babylonia—the Second Temple state (and its immediate successor) was primarily a vassal of the great world empires. This political fact had major cultural consequences, especially when the Jews confronted, for the first time, a world culture, Hellenism. In many ways, the manner in which the Jews accommodated to living in such a world culture, or were acculturated to it, became the paradigm for future accommodation to other major world civilizations, such as Rome, Byzantium, Islam, and Christianity.

As a result of this confrontation with a world culture, the Jews developed new identities that were also to become paradigms for Jewish identity in the coming millennia. During the First Temple period, the ethnic group referred to typically by others as "Hebrews" called itself the "Children of Israel," thus designating its descent from the founder Israel, or Jacob. But those who went into exile in Babylonia were known to others, as to themselves, as "Judaeans," for they came from the southern kingdom of Judah. With the early Persian period, "Judaeans" took the place of "Israelites." But what was a Judaean? Clearly it meant someone descended from an ethnic group connected to a particular geographical location, Judaea or Palestine (to use the later Latin terms) or *Yehud* (Judah—as it is known from archaeological inscriptions). But it also came to designate a fol-lower of a particular religion that was not geographically or even ethnically limited. As we shall see, when the Hasmonaean kings conquered other ethnic groups, such as the Edomites, and forced them to convert to Judaism, they broadened the definition of a Judaean beyond an ethnic category: this was one stage in the transformation of "Judaeans" to "Jews." These Jews followed a religion that a few Greek texts came to call "Judaism," a term that was, nonetheless, relatively rare in antiquity. By the time of the Mishnah, the rabbis had evolved a legal procedure for conversion from other religions to Judaism: one could become a Jew, even if one were not born one.[2] This was a revolutionary development, with implications not only for Judaism but for other ancient identities as well.

THE PERSIAN PERIOD

When the Judaeans or Jews returned from the Babylonian Exile, these events would still lie far in the future. Indeed, if the text with which we began from the end of our period attests to broad cultural interchange between rabbis and Greeks, the period opens with a far more xenophobic expression: the ban on intermarriage by Ezra the Scribe in the middle of the fifth century B.C.E. Defining his people as *zera kodesh* (a holy seed), Ezra sought to erect high walls between the returnees and the "people of the land," who may have been a mixture of remnants of the indigenous Canaanites and of Judaeans and Israelites who had not gone into exile. Ezra represents the opposite pole to the figure of Gamaliel in our opening story: the voice of ethnic and religious segregation in the face of outer pressures for accommodation and acculturation. Indeed, throughout our period, these two poles, the forces of separation and assimilation, struggled with each other in ways that are more complex than is commonly believed.

The response of the Judaeans in exile to the Persian offer to return to Palestine was underwhelming at first, and even after the Second Temple was rededicated (515 B.C.E.) the number of returnees to Yehud was very small. Such a modest return perhaps meant that Jews in the Diaspora, mainly Egypt and Babylonia, were so successful and assimilated that they viewed Zion more as their ancestral homeland than as a place to which they and their extended families would return. The extent of assimilation of the Egyptian-Jewish community situated at Elephantine is well documented, especially in the onomasticon of the papyri from there; a similar case may be made for some of the Jewish communities in Babylonia. When Ezra reestablished the Torah in Israel in the second half of the fifth century B.C.E., there were 18,000–20,000 Jews in all of Yehud—the majority of Jews remained in the Diaspora. By about 400 B.C.E., the reforms of Ezra and

Reconstruction of the Second Temple after L. Ritmeyer.
(Israel Exploration Society)

Nehemiah were in place as Yehud became a theocracy based on the Hebrew Bible and run primarily by priests. In addition to the priests, there were probably also nonpriestly "elders" who shared in the governance of the province (the Mishnah refers to the "men of the Great Assembly," a body whose historicity cannot be definitively established). Nehemiah, the Persian-appointed governor (*peḥah*), took the place of the earlier kings and foreshadowed the later role of the patriarch. This political system may have survived into the Greek period.

That the Jewish community survived both Persian and early Greek rule was a direct result of their flexible attitude, which would justify a Judaean leadership without a king but with a governor. The reestablishment of the Jewish community in Palestine and the rebuilding of the Temple in Jerusalem ensured a certain measure of continuity between the First and Second Temple periods. The Temple priesthood and its hierarchy would assume an even greater role in society than before. They would even take on a new role in explaining biblical law to the people, a development that would presage the era of the sages.[3]

Said the Book of Haggai:

> Seek a ruling from the priests, as follows: If a man is carrying sacrificial flesh in
> a fold of his garment and with that fold touches bread, stew, wine, oil, or any
> other food, will any of these become sanctified? In reply, the priests said, "No."[4]

Although the priestly leadership no doubt took a major role in editing and promulgating the earliest forms of the Bible, the Pentateuch (*Ḥumash*) and the books of the Prophets, other individuals, perhaps wisdom teachers as well as some teaching priests, and a new cadre of translators or interpreters (Nehemiah 8) assumed an entirely new role in communicating the interpreted word of God's scriptures. This is quite clear from the report of Ezra's reading the law at the Feast of Tabernacles when Nehemiah was governor. Ezra, who was both priest and scribe, read from a wooden platform or *bema* as in the later synagogue with the help of many others: "They read from the scroll of the Teaching of God, translating it and giving the sense; so they understood the reading."[5]

It was thus during the Persian and early Greek periods that the process of organizing, editing, and promulgating large portions of the Hebrew Bible took place. These portions probably included the Pentateuch, the historical writings (Judges, Joshua, Samuel, and Kings), the major and minor Prophets, and some of the Writings, such as the Psalms and Proverbs. The impulse toward this first stage of canonization may have been partly the result of similar efforts initiated by the Persians in Egypt, Babylonia, and other satrapies.[6] If this was the case, then the Hebrew Bible, the literary record in which the Jews asserted their singularity, was, ironically, in part the product of an international process. But it was also during this period that other books of the Bible were actually composed. These included the postexilic prophets Haggai, Zechariah, and Malachi, the book of Daniel, the books of Ezra and Nehemiah, and the books of Chronicles, in addition to certain priestly writings that were incorporated into the Pentateuch.

Scholars have also speculated that some of the so-called Wisdom literature—as well as other less easily categorized literature, such as Job, Ecclesiastes, and perhaps Jonah and Ruth—was written during this period. Although it is difficult to speculate about the settings in which these books were written, we can identify some common themes that suggest the cultural mentality of the age. As opposed to pre-exilic biblical books, God does not speak directly and unproblematically to human beings. In Job, for instance, God's silence is the central concern of the book and God's speech out of the whirlwind at the end is less a prophetic message than a show of divine power. In Job, we find a new sensibility about God's justice, quite different from the earlier prophetic idea of divine punishment for sin; here, God's ways are mysterious and the righteous suffer despite their virtues.

In Ecclesiastes, God is equally mysterious. Whether or not it was influenced by Greek philosophy, as some have claimed, Ecclesiastes confronts an intellectual world at odds with biblical religion and betrays a sense of cynicism and frustration: "Utter futility!—said Kohelet—Utter futility! All is futile! What real value is there for a man in all the gains he makes beneath the sun? One generation goes, another comes, but the earth remains the same forever."[7]

The word "futility" *(hebel)* appears 38 times in the work and is applied to all manner of human activity and pursuits. The futility of life or even the pursuit of wisdom in this age evokes the memorable statement: "For in much wisdom is much vexation, and those who increase knowledge increase sorrow."[8] And at the end: "The making of many books is without limit and much study is wearying of the flesh."[9] If this is wisdom literature, it is wisdom turned against itself! Is it possible that, in denouncing the writing of books, the author may be reflecting a struggle within the culture over the editing and canonization of the Book of Books? Or, alternatively, might this comment reflect the proliferation of many books composed in this era and competing to enter the developing canon? If so, then we are in possession of only a small fragment of what must have been a large and vibrant literature.

Many of these works seem deliberately archaic—that is, they are set in earlier, even mythological periods of Israel's history: Job in the time of the biblical patriarchs, Ecclesiastes in the time of Solomon, Jonah rather vaguely in the period of the Assyrian Empire, and Ruth in the period of the Judges. In the persistent tendency of this literature to situate itself in the distant past, we sense a nostalgia for a golden age that has irrevocably disappeared. With the substance of God's revelation a thing of the past, it was a time of small men and small deeds. Perhaps this is the reason also for the fact that, after Ezra and Nehemiah, we cannot identify any author by name—until Ben Sira at the end of the third century B.C.E. Not without reason have some labeled the late Persian and early Hellenistic period, the 200-year period from the end of the fifth century, an "age of silence."

EARLY PALESTINIAN HELLENISM

Alexander the Great conquered the Near East at the end of the fourth century B.C.E., but, as opposed to what many have assumed, Hellenistic culture did not follow suit in quite as rapid a way. The process was more complex. Archaeology teaches us that the influence of the Greeks predated even Alexander. Already in the fifth century B.C.E., the first clear signs of the appeal of Greek culture began to appear in Yehud: the adoption of coinage as a medium of exchange along with the use as the standard of the Attic tetradrachm with Greek symbols, such as the Athenian owl; the establishment of Greek trading emporia along the coastal plain; the importation of Attic black-glazed ceramic wares as luxury items; and the opening of new trade routes connecting the Persian Gulf with the Aegean as well as others that would bring Egypt in closer touch with both the Levant and the Aegean. Numerous Palestinian sites both on the coast and inland, moreover, have yielded statues of Greek figures. All of these developments occurred when Persia held sway in the region.

After Alexander's death, his generals established two successor Hellenistic empires in the east: the Seleucids in Syria and the Ptolemies in Egypt. Now Greek culture became more prominent in Yehud: in the orthogonal plan adopted in some cities, the layout of some walls, the introduction of round towers for additional protection, forms of dress, and some types of ceramic fineware. The coins of the Judaean capital, minted in Jerusalem, show a strong continuity with the Persian era. The few coins of the Ptolemaic era that we do have date to Ptolemy I (301–282 B.C.E.) and depict Ptolemy, his wife Berenice, and the Ptolemaic eagle. These coins lack the identification of the "secular" Jewish authority, *peḥah,* and hence seem to suggest a shift in authority to the high priesthood, signaling a major trend that was to influence the course of events, namely, the increasing involvement of the Temple officers and establishment in the affairs of state. The Yehud coins of this era with their secondary Hebrew inscriptions were of very small denominations, ⅛ to¹⁄₉₆ of a tetradrachm, and reflect the limited means of the constituency being served. That the Ptolemies allowed the Jews to mint coins, albeit in standards adopted from them, shows how they intended to control and exploit the local constituency at least until the time of Ptolemy II (282–246 B.C.E.), but such limited privileges by no means indicated autonomy for the Jewish community.

But Hellenistic culture encroached only gradually and unevenly in Palestine. The archaeological record from monumental remains suggests strong Greek influence at coastal sites such as Dor, where a Greek-style fortification was introduced in the time of Ptolemy II. Dor has also produced the earliest examples of indigenous pottery stamped with Greek letters. But we should not infer from Dor too much about Palestine as a whole, since many of the towns and villages were completely unaffected by Hellenism. Especially in the Judaean heartland, with Jerusalem at its center, there is little evidence for the encroachment of Greek culture, while just 40 kilometers to the southwest a Sidonian colony was established by the Ptolemies at Marissa in a purely Greek layout. Ptolemaic and Greek influence tended to be focused around the cities that had military or strategic importance or cities or sites that were important economically but had only small Jewish minority communities.

There is another small corpus of stamped jar handles from Yehud that should be mentioned in this connection; both are dated to the mid-third century B.C.E. and shed light on the administrative structure that operated in Palestine before the Maccabean uprising. Many of them are stamped with YHD in paleo-Hebrew letters and bear a variety of symbols that appear to be a government seal. Another large group bears the letters YRŠLM (Jerusalem) between the axes of a five-pointed star, the symbol of the high priest. These jar handles point to a very traditional repertoire of symbols in a time when many scholars assumed Hellenism to be making great inroads. This relatively small group of stamps with a limited symbolic vocabulary demonstrates quite clearly that Hellenistic culture had not yet affected the heart of Judaean culture. That these stamps point to a centralized system of taxation, however, cannot be doubted.[10] The corpus of stamped jar handles testifies to the rather complex system of taxation that was introduced by the priests. It is quite clear too from this evidence that not all of the priesthood shared in the new wealth; it was the Jerusalem priesthood and establishment that benefited the most.

The economic upgrading of the Levant as a result of Ptolemaic rule and its mercantile practices had an enormous effect on Judaean life. The emergence of a Jewish middle class, merchants and bureaucrats, transformed society. While the Greek ethnic population remained in the strong military bases among the coastal cities, some settled in Idumea to the southeast and Samaria to the north, thus promoting increased mercantile activity. As a result of this new international commerce, there emerged in Ammon (or Transjordan) one of the most prominent Jewish families, probably descended from the Tobiads mentioned in the prophets Isaiah and Zechariah. Although they were well established before the Ptolemies, they became involved with the new Ptolemaic infrastructure for tax collection. By the end of the third century or beginning of the second century B.C.E., the Tobiads had built a huge administrative center and trading emporium just south of Amman at Arak el-Emir.

In short, during the Ptolemaic era Palestine underwent enormous change, albeit at an uneven pace. The culture of Palestinian Jewry slowly began to be transformed by new political and social circumstances, but not all segments of society were pleased by these developments. In addition to the effect of the new economy on social stratification, the new intellectual world appeared to be at odds with biblical religion and nascent Judaism. Among the most serious philosophical challenges that came from the Greeks was the Orphic view that the individual is dualistic in nature and that the "soul" is immaterial, encased in a physical body. The dominant semitic view, however, was that the human being is a unitary entity and the "soul," or *nefesh*, is the totality of all the physical parts along with the deeds and accomplishments of the individual. A name or reputation would symbolize the "corporate" personality of the individual, and mortal or physical remains had to be buried and cared for in very special ways. (Biblical and rabbinic law forbid both cremation and embalming, such laws arising out of the biblical view of the unitary nature of the individual.)

In another important area, too, the world of Greek philosophy began to make its influence felt—that is, the world of critical or empirical thinking. The preexilic Israelite religion challenged the Near Eastern myths in which divinity and nature were often seen as synonymous. The Israelites articulated a new idea of God, removed from nature and history, yet able to control the world from beside or above it. Here was the origin of the idea of "the will of God." In serving God, human beings could help the divine will prevail in history. Such a conception was at odds not only with Near Eastern mythology but also with Greek philosophy, which viewed the world as an entity made intelligible by the use of reason. Just how much Greek philosophy penetrated the intellectual world of Yehud remains a mystery. Even though Greek material and political culture was having an increasing influence, it seems less likely to be true of more rarefied ideas. Yet it is possible that the Book of Ben Sira, written between 198 and 175 B.C.E., may reflect explicit knowledge of and rejection of philosophical Hellenism. A wisdom teacher who brought the fundamentals of Jewish life to the communities he visited, Ben Sira describes Wisdom in strictly biblical terms: "All this [Wisdom] is in the book of the covenant of the most High God, the law which Moses commanded us as an inheritance for the congregation of Jacob" (24:23).

Ben Sira wrote in Hebrew but his words were translated into Greek by his grandson for the Egyptian Jewish community. Some have seen in the work echoes of Stoic thought, but, even if one can trace some Hellenistic influences, it is clear that Ben Sira wanted his audience to find Wisdom in the biblical tradition and not in the works of the Greek philosophers.

THE HASMONAEAN ERA

At the beginning of the second century B.C.E., the Seleucid Empire in Syria succeeded the Ptolemies as the landlords of Palestine. In the 160s, a bitter revolt, led by the Maccabee family of the clan of Hashman (Hasmonaeans), broke out against the Seleucids, ultimately resulting in a period of Jewish sovereignty in the Land of Israel from 142 to 63 B.C.E., when the Romans entered the scene. The Maccabean Revolt is usually associated with the struggle against Hellenization of Jewish culture and with the will to fight foreign intervention. Both of these considerations figure into the reasons for the bitter war between the Judaeans and the Seleucids, but the story, as we shall see, was more complex. A new class of well-to-do Jewish citizens emerged in the Ptolemaic era, many of them attached to or even related to the influential priestly families. It is not difficult to imagine how such circles became easily enamored with the new Greek lifestyle that embraced clothing, language, education, and a willingness to cooperate with foreign rule, first the Ptolemies and subsequently the Seleucids. This new constituency may be described as pro-Hellenizing, although it has been argued that their main interest was not Hellenistic culture but rather the political and economic benefits that might be obtained by converting Jerusalem into a Greek *polis* (city-state). In an effort to secure these benefits, they turned the office of the high priest into a political pawn to be bought or sold. The attempt to transform Jerusalem into a polis challenged the traditional political order, since the Jews were no longer governed according to "the traditions of their fathers." The resistance to this new state of affairs may have involved less rejection of Hellenism per se, than class rivalry over control of the city. Cultural factors may have played a smaller role than later Hasmonaean propaganda claimed, for, as we shall see, the Maccabees themselves were not immune to Hellenistic influences.

Considerable debate continues among historians about the sequence of events that precipitated the revolt: whether the ban by Antiochus IV on the Sabbath, circumcision, and other rituals of traditional Judaism were the cause or, perhaps, constituted some kind of punishment for a prior civil war within Jewish society. But in addition to banning Judaism, Antiochus, or his soldiers, erected "an abomination of desolation upon the altar of burnt offerings" in the Temple.[11] This "abomination" seems to have been a statue of the Syrian Baal, which was probably identified with the Greek god Zeus. Other deities worshiped there included Dionysus and Anath, the consort of Baal, who is associated with prostitution in the Temple.[12] This evidence suggests that, although the biblical Canaanites had long disappeared from the scene, elements of their religion remained and were now combined syncretistically with Greek religion.

Resistance to the Seleucids came from several sources. Those who remained committed to the more conservative way of life were called "pious ones," or *Hasidim*. But, as is often the case with conservatives, this faction may have itself represented something new. The Book of Maccabees claims that these pietists would not fight on the Sabbath, a prohibition unknown in the Bible. The awakening of resistance to the Greeks may have thus created new forms of piety. Indeed, the Hasidim's resistance to change and suspicion of the foreigner foreshadow the more xenophobic monastics of the Dead Sea community at Qumran.

The main resistance was led by the Hasmonaean family, of whom Judah "the Maccabee," or "hammer," was the leading figure. The Hasmonaeans were rural priests, and their role in the revolt may have had something to do with rejection of the more cosmopolitan urban priesthood of Jerusalem. The Hasmonaean Revolt was, in some measure, an uprising of the countryside against the city. The highly partisan accounts in 1 and 2 Maccabees emphasize the popular resistance and the courage of the martyrs, but it is likely that only a small minority chose resistance, at least initially. Nevertheless, from 167 to 164 B.C.E., the resistance movement led by Judah and his brothers Jonathan and Simon achieved remarkable success in a brief time. And on 25 Kislev (December 164 B.C.E.), Judah re-took the Temple, which was purified and rededicated to the worship of Yahweh, the sole God of the Jewish people:

> At the very season and on the very day that the gentiles had profaned [the altar], it was dedicated with songs and harps and lutes and cymbals. All the people fell on their faces and worshiped and blessed Heaven, who had prospered them. So they celebrated the dedication of the altar for eight days and offered burnt offerings with gladness; they offered a sacrifice of deliverance and praise.[13]

The festival of rededication was based on the festival of Tabernacles, which the Maccabees claimed they had not been able to celebrate since the Temple had been desecrated. Like Tabernacles and Passover, it lasted eight days (1 Maccabees 4:36–61; 2 Maccabees 10:1–8). But the festival, which soon became known as Hanukkah ("Dedication"), was intended to be a new holiday to celebrate the Maccabees' victory, and it was, in fact, the only festival, with the exception of Qumran, added to Jewish practice in the Second Temple period that is not mentioned in the canonical Bible. In creating a new holiday commemorating the restoration of traditional Judaism, the Maccabeans departed from Jewish practice and imitated their Hellenistic enemies.

The Hasmonaean family subsequently provided the accepted leadership of Judaea, and during the next 20 years or so they successfully repulsed Seleucid political interference, exploiting weaknesses in their empire. Jonathan was the first Hasmonaean to become high priest of the Jewish people, in 152 B.C.E. By 142, his brother Simon declared independence; he too was recognized as high priest, in 140 B.C.E. By declaring himself *hegemenos* (leader), *strategos* (general), and high priest (1 Maccabees 14:41–47), Simon revolutionized the priestly state and signaled his clear intention to restore Judaea to the glories of the past kingdoms of David and Solomon. It was not until Aristobulus I (r. 104–3 B.C.E.) and Alexander Jannaeus (r. 103–76 B.C.E.), however, that the Hasmonaeans took the title of "king" to be used alongside that of high priest. Although the Hasmonaeans did not claim to be descendants of King David, a number of their actions, such as adopting the paleo-Hebrew script on coins and seals, were designed to give their regimes a sense of antiquity and legitimacy. At the same time, as the above titles make clear, their political vocabulary was drawn from the Hellenistic world and their rule resembled that of other Near Eastern states in this period. They took Greek names and adopted foreign symbols such as the sun, anchor, caduceus, and cornucopia in imitation of other regimes, seeking to combine the old with the new, the religious with the political. Despite their ideology of ethnic and religious nationalism, the Hasmonaeans had no qualms about conforming to the conventions of the Hellenistic world.

It was the assumption of the office of the high priesthood by the Hasmonaean family that occasioned the most opposition from among those who had so successfully fought beside them to oppose the Syrians. The high priesthood by ancient custom was the ancestral inheritance of the family of Zadok; the Hasmonaeans, however, did not descend from Zadok. The usurpation of this office, more than that of the royal crown, occasioned open hostility, resentment, and ultimately sectarian opposition that would not go away. Thus, less than a century after the Maccabean wars began, a permanent rift between the leaders of the revolt and their sometime followers and comrades had opened. No more inauspicious way could have been conceived for the reestablishment of Judaean independence and religious freedom. In the hundred years or so of Hasmonaean control, this egregious affront to biblical tradition, the combining of royal and priestly powers, could not be overcome, leading ultimately to enervating divisiveness. Yet it does not appear that the Hellenistic elements of Hasmonaean rule were a major cause of dissension. There is enormous irony in the fact that the reestablishment of Judaean independence and religious freedom by the Hasmonaeans became the setting in which new sectarian opposition would emerge from the very ranks of individuals who years before had been their chief supporters.

The Hasmonaean kings enlarged the orbit of Jewish culture by forcibly converting inhabitants of the biblical lands of Ammon and Edom, east of the Jordan. Some of these areas—Ammon, with its tradition of the Tobiads, and large parts of Peraea—were successfully absorbed into the new kingdom and remained Jewish at least until the Great Revolt (66–70 C.E.). In Galilee, mainly depopulated since the Assyrian conquest in the eighth century B.C.E., excavations and surveys indicate that there were a significant number of new settlements by the time of Jannaeus, whose coins appear nearly everywhere. At Sepphoris, in the lower Galilee, an *ostrakon* (a pottery shard bearing an inscription) from about 100 B.C.E. suggests the complicated relationship that emerged between the Hasmonaean state and Hellenistic culture. The letters are Hebrew but the language is Greek: *epimeles* (or *epimeletes*), the designation for an official of the Jewish community or perhaps a quartermaster in the Hasmonaean army. In establishing political independence from a Hellenistic empire, the Hasmonaeans became the new sponsors of Hellenistic culture.

HEROD THE GREAT TO THE FIRST CENTURY C.E.

Hasmonaean rule and full Jewish sovereignty in the Land of Israel came to an abrupt end with Pompey's annexation in 63 B.C.E. With two descendants of the Hasmonaeans engaged in civil war over the dynastic succession, some Jews welcomed Rome as an alternative to the excesses and divisions perpetrated by the Hasmonaeans, their erstwhile liberators. For others, however, Roman rule quickly became as odious as anything they had endured earlier. An apocryphal Psalm of Solomon alludes to Pompey's invasion and prophesies the coming of the Davidic messiah who would reverse the status of Judah as a client kingdom to Rome and reestablish the Davidic kingdom. Pompey's annexation signaled politically the end of the Hellenistic age in Jewish history and the beginning of the Roman period, but because the dominant culture in the Eastern Mediterranean (and, indeed, to some degree, in Rome itself) remained Greek, the Roman period is aptly designated "Greco-Roman."

The Romans preferred to rule their empire through local authorities, and, failing to find a reliable agent from within the Jewish elite, they elevated Herod (37–4 B.C.E.), whose grandfather was an Edomite converted by the Hasmonaeans and whose father, Antipater, was already a high official under Roman rule. Herod the Great is one of the most controversial figures in Jewish history, a tyrant who massacred members of his own family, a calculating ally of Rome, and a builder on a monumental scale. Herod's shrewd and prescient shift to support Mark Anthony along with Octavian and Lepidus in the Second Triumvirate was a major factor in his rise, as he had come to power with the assistance of Roman soldiers.[14] His strategy, to serve Rome's larger interests in the region through cooperation, was not that different from earlier attempts in the Second Temple period to assuage the dominant superpower. Herod exercised control over the Judaean state and over his enemies by maintaining a first-rate army of Edomites and Jews. He was free to indulge himself at home as long as Rome was happy. That meant paying tribute, keeping the borders of the state free of unwanted foreign intrusions such as the Nabataeans or Parthians, maintaining order and peace within his own territory, and being ready to serve Rome's larger military needs at a moment's notice.

Herod's most important cultural legacy was the magnificent architectural monuments he left behind: the rebuilt Temple with its magisterial scale and classical style; his theaters; his resorts and refuges at Masada and Herodium; and his glorious harbor at Caesarea. Jerusalem and its environs were alive with artists and architects from abroad, and the harbor at Caesarea teemed with boats brim-

Caesarea Maritima: Theater from the time of Herod the Great
(Courtesy Eric Meyers)

ming over with new supplies and wares from the Mediterranean Basin. Herod's remodeled Jerusalem Temple came to be considered one of the wonders of the Roman world and attracted tourists, both Jewish and non-Jewish, from far and wide.

In all these activities, Herod was meticulous in not offending Jewish sensibilities. His palaces in places like Jericho contain numerous ritual baths, which suggests that he was meticulous in making the Jewish purity laws available to his staff and family. He was also careful to build institutions of Hellenistic culture primarily in areas not dominated by Jews. Only in Acco/Ptolemais, or Tripolis, or in Damascus, for example, did Herod venture to build a *gymnasion,* where youths were educated in Greek language and culture. Only in Caesarea Maritima did he organize the quinquennial games. And in Samaria/Sebastia he built a new city for gentiles. Near Jerusalem, possibly outside the city, Herod added a few items of Greco-Roman culture that could have aroused the concerns of some of the Jewish population: a theater, amphitheater, and hippodrome, probably because (like his Roman sponsors) he enjoyed sports and spectacles. Thus, he attempted to shrewdly solve the inherent conflict between Jewish and Hellenistic culture by a policy of geographical separation between predominantly Jewish and non-Jewish areas.

In so doing, Herod demonstrated that he was acutely cognizant of one of the persistent features of Palestine throughout our period: the Jews' sharing of the land with other peoples, including Greek descendants of Alexander's armies, Syrians, and other Near Eastern ethnic groups. Jewish culture could never remain pure and traditional in such a multiethnic and multicultural atmosphere. Whereas the Hasmonaeans had sought, at least in some areas, to create or impose ethnic and religious homogeneity by converting other groups to Judaism, Herod's tactic was less coercive. But this mixture of populations, starting with biblical times and continuing long after our period (indeed, even to the present day), remained a central and unsolvable political and cultural issue for the Land of Israel.

A CULTURE OF SECTARIANISM

Herod's rule was despotic, and he destroyed many members of his family as well as other potential challengers from the Judaean elite. When he died in 4 B.C.E., he left a political vacuum, soon to be filled by Roman procurators. Jewish self-government in the first century C.E. was severely weakened, and a variety of groups competed for political power and cultural and religious authority. Some of these groups originated in Herod's time and perhaps even earlier, during the Hasmonaean period, reflecting the tensions and divisiveness of these regimes. These were the Sadducees, Pharisees, and Essenes as well as the revolutionary Zealots. The Sadducees, the party of priests, enjoyed particular power and enhanced status in Herod's remodeled Temple. In order to undermine the Hasmonaean priests and co-opt the priesthood for his regime, Herod brought in priestly families from Egypt and Babylonia.[15] The Sadducean party was therefore, at least in part, a foreign import.

The Pharisees, the forerunners of the rabbis, evidently suffered from persecution from the Herodians, but it was in this period that some of their "founding fathers" flourished: Shemaiah and Abtalion, Hillel and Shammai. Their alienation from the government is captured in a saying from the Mishnah, which, though compiled 200 years later, may reflect the atmosphere of the Herodian period and its immediate aftermath: "Shemaiah and Abtalion who received the tradition from Simeon ben Shetach and Judah ben Tabbai. Shemaiah said: 'Love labor and hate the government, and seek not intimacy with the ruling powers.' "[16]

The Qumran Sect reached its height during the Herodian period, although it continued to the Great Revolt. This monastic community by the Dead Sea reflected the separatism of certain pietists, called Essenes, perhaps spiritual descendants of the Hasidim of the Hasmonaean age. Some of these Essenes were located in cities such as Jerusalem, while others, such as the "covenanters" of Qumran, left society for the desert. It is probable that the term "Essene," used by

Josephus in his histories written at the end of the first century C.E., refers not to one specific group but to a wide variety of pietistic rebel sects. Indeed, Josephus cast his description of the various Jewish parties, including the Essenes, as philo-sophical schools to make them comprehensible to his Roman audience. But who they really were and how they related to each other may have been considerably different from Josephus's overly stylized portrait.

With the discovery of the Dead Sea Scrolls and the excavations of Qumran, where the library of the scrolls was located, it is possible to obtain a window onto Second Temple sectarian culture independent of Josephus. Many members of the Dead Sea community were men of priestly descent who rejected the prac-tices of the Jerusalem priesthood; their story therefore belongs to the internal history of the priesthood. It is possible that they opted out of Jerusalem society as a result of the Hasmonaean usurpation of the office of high priest. Although the Essenes as described by Josephus were not all necessarily priests, I believe that the Qumran covenanters belong to this general category of pietists.

On the basis of coins and pottery, we can say that the community at the Dead Sea was established around the time of Simon Maccabee, circa 140 B.C.E., plus or minus a decade. Paleographic evidence for some of the scrolls recovered from the nearby caves predates this by more than a century, meaning that sectarian

Aerial view of Khirbet Qumran, ruin of the Dead Sea sect.
(Courtesy Richard Cleave, Pictorial Archive)

ideas did not originate wholly after or as a result of the Maccabean rebellion. Also, many of the earlier scrolls are not sectarian but merely noncanonical. The *floruit*, or heyday, of the community at Qumran thus occurred during the years of Alexander Jannaeus and Herod the Great, though there may have been a short hiatus in connection with a violent destruction around 9–8 B.C.E. The resettlement of the community, after a very brief abandonment, survived until the first Roman War.

The Dead Sea community's separatism was expressed in the sense of their election as the "True Israel" and their apocalyptic mentality, the idea that they were living in the "end time." They were the first group to explicitly deny that other Jews were true Jews and, in their messianic doctrine of a "New Covenant," paved the way for later Christian supersessionism, the belief that the Church was the true Israel. Although such exclusivism may be traced back to Ezra the Scribe, who, we recall, called the returnees from Babylonia the "holy seed" and banned intermarriage, it is by no means certain whether those Ezra opposed were in fact Jews or foreigners. The Qumran sectarians, however, labeled the Jerusalem establishment the "children of darkness," in part because of their violation of the sect's ideas of purity and in part because of their alliance with the Romans (referred to in some of the scrolls as *Kitti'im*). The sect believed that Roman rule presaged a final apocalyptic war and that those on the side of the imperial authorities would be destroyed along with them. The "holy ones" were the forces of light in whom the gifts of the holy spirit were manifest. Those contradictory forces would face each other in a final end-of-time battle that is described in the famous War Scroll. Not only did the Essenes adopt an apocalyptic view of the end of time, but they also believed that God had predetermined everything.

In light of their belief in predetermination, the Dead Sea community's calendar was of great importance. They followed a 364-day solar calendar at Qumran that was at variance with the 354-day lunar-solar calendar of the Jerusalem community. At Qumran the day was reckoned from sunrise to sunrise. In Jerusalem the day was reckoned from sundown to sundown. Holidays could never be celebrated together. In fact, the Habakkuk Scroll relates that the "Wicked Priest" (possibly a Hasmonaean or Herodian high priest?) attacked the sect on Yom Kippur, the Day of Atonement, when a high priest (not to speak of any other Jew) would be fasting and sacrificing in the Temple. The calendar dispute was understandably a central bone of contention between the communities. The Jerusalem Temple establishment was therefore deemed to be corrupt and, because it was perpetually in violation of the calendar, thoroughly impure.

Because time was conceived to be at the edge of a momentous event about to happen, the Dead Sea Sect applied certain biblical laws with much greater severity than was the case for the priestly establishment. For example, in wartime the laws of ritual purity operated in a very strict way, especially as they related to sexual activity, which was prohibited. The so-called Temple Scroll prescribes much stricter standards of purity not just for the Temple but for the city of Jerusalem as a whole. The sectarians thus lived as if they were at the time of that final battle, in a state of ritual purity. They held all goods in common, practiced ritual immersion regularly, would not eliminate bodily fluids or wastes within the camp, studied and worshiped much of the day, and believed in two messiahs, one priestly and one Davidic.

In their material culture, though, the sectarians were quite normal in respect to purity laws, utilizing stone vessels for hand-washing just as did the pious in Jerusalem or Sepphoris. Although some of their pottery exhibits new shapes, especially the jars containing their scrolls, most of the pottery and glass reflect the early Roman-period culture of Palestine at large. The architecture at the Dead Sea community is familiar as well, though the communitarian aspect of the sect is reflected in the organization of the tiny hamlet, large enough for only around 120 souls. The number of ritual baths discovered suggests the special emphasis on purity.

COMMON JUDAISM

The sectarian nature of the Dead Sea community should not, however, mislead us. Despite the tensions and conflicts between Sadducees, Essenes, Pharisees, and other groups, this period of factionalism was also a period in which what might be called "common Judaism" began to emerge. Indeed, a true portrait of the Jewish culture of the period needs to emphasize not only the culture of sectarianism but also the way in which certain common ideas and practices, based on biblical sources, pointed ahead toward later rabbinic Judaism.

The historian Josephus is our primary ancient source for Jewish sectarianism in the prerabbinic period. In both the *Jewish Antiquities* and the *Jewish Wars*, he describes the various sects, which he calls, in Greek, *philosophiai* or *haireseis*. These passages not only cover Pharisees, Sadducees, and "Essenes" but also include the controversial discussions of Jesus, James the brother of Jesus, and John the Baptist and his followers. It is remarkable, therefore, that in another book, his *Contra Apionem*, Josephus describes the Jews in the following terms:

> To this cause above all we owe our remarkable harmony. Unity and identity of religious belief, perfect uniformity in habits and customs, produce a very beautiful concord in human character. Among us alone will be heard no contradic-

tory statements about God, such as are common among other nations, not only on the lips of ordinary individuals under the impulse of some passing mood, but even boldly propounded by philosophers; some putting forward crushing arguments against the very existence of God, others depriving Him of His providential care for mankind. Among us alone will be seen no difference in the conduct of our lives. With us all act alike, all profess the same doctrine about God, one which is in harmony with our Law and affirms that all things are under His eye.[17]

This statement stands in seeming contradiction to Josephus's careful accounts of Judaism as divided into three "philosophiai" or "haireseis." Unless we assume that, in our text, Josephus is simply obfuscating for the purposes of apologetics, we must conclude that he did not perceive the "haireseis" of his time as equivalent to its later meaning of "heresy" or *minut*, its Hebrew equivalent.[18] These schools in no way disturbed the essential religious and communal unity of the Jewish people, certainly no more than did the divisions among the Greeks between Cynics, Epicureans, and Pythagoreans. Indeed, for Josephus, the differences between these Greek sects or philosophies was much more fundamental than that between Pharisees, Sadducees, and Essenes, who, for all their divisions, were still committed to observance of God's Torah around questions of Sabbath, *kashrut*, circumcision, and confession of the Shema. In short, the "sectarianism" of the Second Temple period did not preclude inclusiveness or a sense of a "pluralistic" Israel.

The discoveries at Qumran can shed light not only on sectarian differences but also on commonalities. From texts such as the Temple Scroll and the MMT Scroll ("Some of the Works of the Torah"), a letter probably intended for the priests in Jerusalem delineating the differences between the two groups, we can observe the development of later rabbinic law at an early stage. In the MMT Scroll, in particular, it becomes evident that the sect's *halakhah* (law) shared certain key ideas with what must have been Pharisaic legal arguments of the time. The complex biblical hermeneutics utilized by the sectarians, including their extensive use of biblical intertextuality, also suggest real similarities to the methods used by the later rabbis.

The vast library at Qumran also sheds light on literary activity in the last few centuries of the Second Temple period. Eleven caves in the immediate vicinity of Qumran produced fragments of nearly 800 manuscripts. A number of them have been dated paleographically to the third or early second centuries B.C.E., before the establishment of the Qumran settlement. These scrolls were almost certainly brought from elsewhere, though this does not mean that all other scrolls were brought to Qumran from elsewhere, as a small group of scholars still maintains. The sectarian documents all date to the period of settlement at Qumran and no doubt relate to the unique history and ideology of the community that made its home in the monastery located below the caves.

Many of the scrolls contain books or fragments of books of the Hebrew Bible. It is no surprise that the Pentateuch is so well represented in the corpus. The Book of Deuteronomy is first among the five, found in 29 manuscripts; only Psalms is found more frequently, in 36 manuscripts. The third most attested book in the Qumran library is the Book of Isaiah, which is found in 21 manuscripts. Not unexpected is the fact that the only other books represented in double digits are those in the rest of the Pentateuch, namely Genesis, Exodus, Leviticus, and Numbers. In all, 202 copies or fragments of biblical books are represented, or around 25 percent of the total trove. Although the statistics surely inform us about the importance of biblical books in the lives of the people who lived in Qumran, the sum total of all the manuscripts demonstrate the richness of literature that was available, mainly in Hebrew and Aramaic, outside of what was to become the Hebrew canon of Scripture in the later centuries c.e. In this connection, the absence of any copies or fragments of the Book of Esther is noteworthy. Though it may be the result of happenstance, Esther is the only book in the Hebrew Bible that does not mention the name of God; nor does it mention the city of Jerusalem, the festivals, and many Jewish laws and practices. The feast of Purim that is associated with the book, likewise, is never mentioned in any Qumran text. Although its absence could be due to sheer chance, perhaps it was its lack of piety or its celebration of a victory of the Diaspora Jews that caused the Essenes to reject it.

Among the remainder of the manuscripts are many of the apocrypha and a new corpus of Jewish pseudepigrapha, and the rewritten Torah. Other texts deal with the cycle of Jewish worship and holidays, especially the Sabbath, within the framework of the distinctive solar calendar of the sect. All of these materials testify to the centrality of biblical texts and biblical figures in the Jewish literature of the turn of the common era, to the rich variety of genres found in the sectarian library, and to the belletristic character of the entire corpus, both sectarian and nonsectarian. All of this compositional activity occurred well in advance of the finalization of the Jewish canon of Scripture in the first centuries c.e. Moreover, the great variety of types of writing reflected in the Qumran corpus shows that the sectarians as well as most other Jewish groups were more or less in accord about the Pentateuch and Prophets, although the Kethubim or Writings were still in a state of some flux in the first centuries c.e. The copious use of quotations from the Hebrew Bible in the New Testament (especially the Gospel of

Matthew) further confirms that even sectarian groups like the early Christians relied on the same scriptures as the elite establishment. The common Judaism that was emerging at this time was based on what was developing into a commonly held library of texts, but the sense that Scripture was still unfulfilled and incomplete, in both a canonical sense and an eschatological sense, allowed openings to apocalyptic groups such as the Qumran community and the early Christians to base their visions of the future on the biblical text.

The figure of Hillel, elevated to leader *(nasi)* of the Pharisaic legislative body around 30 B.C.E., affords a helpful example of the similarities among the early Jewish sects. Whereas our sources for Hillel stem from several centuries later, many of the sayings attributed to him resonate with other sources that are demonstrably from his time. His use of intertextuality or midrash exegesis, or citing Scripture to support his views, was not unlike the Essene hermeneutic or the exegesis attributed to Jesus; this method doubtless developed long before in Palestine and can even be found in the Bible itself.

Hillel's preoccupation with social concerns echoed the prophets and demonstrated the persistence of these subjects at the turn of the era. His successful campaign for banking reform and the adoption of the *prosbul* placed him clearly on the side of the poor.[19] The prosbul was a legal device for securing the repayment of loans in the sabbatical year. Without this legal enactment, moneylenders were hesitant to make loans in the sixth year of the seven-year cycle, because debts could not be collected in the seventh year. That the prosbul was practiced is clear from a text found in the Judaean desert and dated to the second year of Nero (Oct. 55–Oct. 56 C.E.), in which a borrower promises to repay a loan plus interest of one-fifth "even if it is a year of rest."[20] In his defense of the poor, Hillel's teachings bear a striking resemblance to those of the Jesus of the Gospels. Most famous of all is his summary of the whole of the Torah "while standing on one foot": "What is hateful to you do not do to your neighbor—this is the Torah; the rest is commentary."[21] But his advocacy of love and humility as the core teachings of Torah can be found equally in the sectarian literature of the time, as well, of course, as in the Christian Gospels.[22] Like Qumran and the early Christians, the Pharisees formed "table fellowships," pietistic circles who ate together, preserving a special sense of their own purity. Unlike the sects, however, the Pharisees appear to have sought reforms within society. In the words attributed to Hillel: "Do not separate yourself from the community."[23]

Another unifying element was the Temple. All the competing groups of the Second Temple period recognized the Temple as the central institution of the Jewish religion. Although the Dead Sea community was at war with the contemporary custodians of the Temple, their vision of an eschatological future included a purified Temple. The early Christians, too, although they later came to reject Temple sacrifices, at least initially made the Temple their place of regular prayer and the breaking of bread.[24] And Jesus himself was reported to have prophesied that, following the destruction of the Temple, a new Temple would take its place, but not one built by human hands.[25] Finally, all these groups appear to have believed in the coming of a messianic age, even if they differed on the details. Apocalyptic groups, like the Dead Sea community, the Zealots, and the early Christian Church, were all radical offshoots of a common belief.

All these common principles—the Bible and its interpretation, the Temple, and the Messiah—compensated for the differences between Sadducees, Pharisees, Essenes, Zealots, and early Christians. In fact, close examination often reveals surprising similarities. According to Josephus as well as later Jewish tradition, the Sadducees rejected the Oral Law and belief in the afterlife, whereas the Pharisees affirmed these two principles as core beliefs.[26] Yet the Sadducees did have their own "oral" traditions, especially, as one might expect from priests, related to ways of performing sacrifices, purity laws, criminal law, and aspects of civil law as well. At times, their interpretations of these issues were more remote from the literal meaning of the Bible than those of the Pharisees.[27]

Similar blurring of boundaries becomes evident over the question of resurrection of the dead. Here, one of the most vexed questions in Palestinian archaeology may shed some light: the custom of *ossilegium* (collecting the bones of the deceased around a year after death and reburying them in a container in a subterranean tomb chamber or catacomb). Ossuary reburial is not prescribed in the Pentateuch and clearly puts at risk of defilement the person involved in the act of reburial. By the time of the Mishnah, it had become a well-established custom, because the Mishnah regards the reburial of a parent as a paramount obligation that overrides all else, "for on that day (the day of reburial), it is an occasion for rejoicing."[28] It seems likely that expending considerable effort on a second burial would signify some sort of belief in postmortem existence, which would, in turn, justify incurring the ritual impurity associated with corpses. For this reason, both ancient sources and modern interpreters have identified the custom with the Pharisees. But there is considerable evidence that the practice extended beyond the Pharisees to include Jews from different strata of society.

Where did this practice come from? There is substantial evidence that it was very ancient, even if it seems to contradict biblical custom. We know from archaeological finds that there was a 3,000-year history in Palestine of what is called "secondary burial," in which the disarticulated remains are transported to a charnel house or family chamber without housing them in a container.[29] The Romans, however, buried incinerated remains in ossuaries or urns. The wealthy classes in our period may have borrowed the practice of reburial into ossuaries from the Romans, but I believe that the custom was taken over from the Parthians, who practiced decarnation by vultures and subsequent reburial into ossuaries called *astodans;* such a practice was only reinforced by Roman custom. Whatever the case, we have here an interesting amalgamation of an old Palestinian custom—Jewish and non-Jewish—of secondary reburial with a custom imported from abroad of reburial in a receptacle.

The recent discovery in Jerusalem of the tomb and ossuary of Caiaphas, the high priest who presided over the trial of Jesus, reinforces the view that a common Jewish burial practice undergirded many and diverse forms of Jewish life and culture in the first century C.E.[30] A coin of Herod Agrippa I, dated to 42–43 C.E., was found in the skull, a Greek custom (also found in a Jericho tomb) signifying payment to the Greek deity Charon for carrying the deceased's spirit across the river Styx. However, the remains of Caiaphas were deposited in an ossuary in a very traditional Jewish loculus tomb located south of the Hinnom Valley and Abu Tor, well beyond the city limits and away from the busy pathways of shoppers, pilgrims, and other visitors. Once again, we are witness to cultural syncretism in burial practices in which Greek, Jewish, and possibly Roman or Parthian customs all played a role. Moreover, because Caiaphas was unquestionably a Sadducee, his reburial strongly suggests that even the Sadducees may have held some belief in what Josephus calls "renewed existence."[31] This fact urges us to be cautious in taking the Sadducean belief system too literally, especially on the matter of life after death. Actual cultural practices, as revealed by the archaeologist's spade, once again complicate the neat ideological divisions of the literary texts. And we must be equally cautious in assuming that the Sadducees knew nothing of the Oral Law, later codified in the Mishnah.

The belief that one was released from judgment at a second burial also left an echo in the New Testament, in Matthew 8:21–22 and Luke 9:59–60. When a would-be disciple expresses his readiness to follow Jesus after he has (re)buried his father, Jesus refuses to accept the delay: "Let the dead bury their own dead," he responds.[32] The passage is often taken to refer to Jesus' demand for an absolute commitment to leave family ties behind and follow him. Assuming the common practice of secondary burial, we may conclude that the disciple is asking for time to fulfill his familial obligation. In their burial practices, as in so much else, the early Christians were as much a part of the larger Jewish culture as the Pharisees and Sadducees.

PRIVATE LIFE AND POPULAR CULTURE

Most of the literary texts of our period were products either of elite groups, like the Qumran sect or the historian Josephus, or of the later rabbinic elite. Although archaeology can help illuminate private life, we are fortunate in possessing another body of literature that offers us a unique window onto the culture of the folk in the first century C.E.: the library of the early Christians. The historicity of the Gospel documents remains hotly contested, but regardless of whether or not Jesus actually said and did the things attributed to him, the New Testament texts can be used for another purpose altogether: to gain some insight into the rural culture of first-century Palestine.

Whereas the early Church was primarily an urban movement, the Jesus movement itself came from the countryside of Galilee. Jesus was from Nazareth, in the lower Galilee, and although the New Testament does not mention his having set foot in nearby Sepphoris, which was the major urban center in Galilee at the time, he could hardly have avoided going there on occasion. As we shall see, by the late second and early third centuries C.E., Sepphoris was to become a highly Hellenized city, but we do not have evidence that this was the case in the time of Jesus. So, despite efforts by some to see in Jesus a preacher of a popular form of Greek Cynic philosophy, there is little evidence that he could read Greek philosophy, although he probably knew enough Greek to get along in the marketplace. His language was Galilean Aramaic, and he probably also knew some Hebrew. In short, it is doubtful that Jesus was exposed to the kind of urban Hellenistic culture that might be found in Jerusalem or Caesarea.

Each of the three villages near the Sea of Galilee mentioned in the New Testament—Bethsaida, Capernaum, and Chorazin—probably consisted of fewer than 2,000 souls and was agricultural in character. This kind of settlement was the focal point of Jesus' ministry. But he did not avoid all cities, because he was, in fact, active in some where there were Jewish minorities and audiences of gentiles to address. His visit to Caesarea Philippi (Baneas), where there was an active shrine to Pan, included the "villages" that were part of the municipal territory of the city.[33] In places with mixed populations like Tyre or Bet Shean (Scythopolis), Jesus might have found a more tolerant audience than in Sepphoris, where the population was overwhelmingly Jewish and the Jewish authorities dominated.

The synoptic Gospels are filled with parables based on agricultural metaphors, as one might expect from a primarily agrarian society: "The kingdom of heaven is like a landowner going out at daybreak to hire workers for his vineyard."[34] The parable goes on to ground its message—"the last will be first and the first, last"—in what must have been a common wage dispute between itinerant field hands and their employer. Or, the eschatological teaching might be based on the experience of farmers whose fields were vulnerable to sabotage by their enemies: "The kingdom of heaven may be compared to a man who sowed good seed in his field. While everybody was asleep his enemy came and sowed darnel all among the wheat."[35]

The Jesus of the Gospels is also heavily engaged in faith healing and exorcism, magical practices that must have been crucial to his rural society. The Talmud contains stories of charismatic magicians, such as Honi the Circle Maker, who were also active around the same time in the Galilee.[36] Men like Jesus and Honi were not, however, the only magicians at work in popular culture. The Talmud also regularly associates women with magic, some of which it pejoratively labels "witchcraft."[37] Amulets from the later rabbinic period show that both men and women engaged in various forms of magic. The use of amulets was so widespread that we must question whether the rabbis, who generally condemned such magic when practiced by those outside their own caste, really controlled this aspect of popular culture.

Much of Jesus' preaching took place in Galilean synagogues.[38] Although there are presently only architectural remains of few synagogues from first-century Palestine—Masada, Herodium, Qiryat Sefer, and Gamala—there can be no doubt that the synagogue was already well established in Second Temple times as a site for local religion. The Temple remained the primary cultic destination on the major pilgrimage holidays, but everyday worship and teaching of the Torah took place in the synagogue. In addition to these ritual and study functions, synagogues might serve as hostels for pilgrims, as the Theodotus inscription from Jerusalem makes clear:

> Theodotus, son of Vettenos the priest and archisynagogos [synagogue leader], son of an archisynagogos and grandson of an archisynagogos, built the synagogue for reading the Law and studying the commandments, and as a hostel with chambers and water installations to provide for the needs of itinerants from abroad, which his fathers, the elders and Simonides founded.[39]

Three generations of priests were involved in building and maintaining this particular Jerusalem synagogue, whose existence near the Temple suggests that many of the functions the synagogue would fulfill after the Temple's destruction in 70 C.E. were already in place while the Temple still stood.

Surprisingly enough, the title "archisynagogos" was not limited only to men. On a marble plaque from Smyrna (Izmir), we find the following: "Rufina, a Jewess, head of synagogue, built this tomb for her freed slaves and the slaves raised in her house. No one else has the right to bury anyone here."[40] Inscriptions found in Diaspora synagogues contain the names of women who evidently served in similar roles. Moreover, it appears that women and men may have sat together in the synagogue, because excavations of synagogues from both the Diaspora and Palestine do not seem to include separate women's galleries. Contemporary practices from Qumran and later rabbinic strictures against women's participation in worship may not reflect the most common customs of the earlier period. Although women were excluded from the Inner Court of the Temple, they were not as segregated from men in public worship elsewhere, nor were they excluded from the study of Torah to the extent that at least some rabbinic authorities desired. The fact that women were active in the Jesus movement and in the early Church may have been more a reflection of contemporary Jewish popular culture than a radical departure from it.

Similarly, the layout of private houses, as revealed by archaeological excavations, challenges the assumption, derived from rabbinic texts, that men and women were regularly separated at home for moral, purity, or legal reasons.[41] Women had their own defined sphere, to be sure: following common practice in the ancient Mediterranean, spinning and weaving were ritualized occupations for them.[42] But in both their private and their public roles, women were less excluded and segregated than is commonly believed.

If life in the Galilean countryside remained largely insulated from Hellenistic influence during the first century C.E., the same cannot be said for a major urban center like Jerusalem or, perhaps to a lesser extent, Judaea as a whole. The homes that have been uncovered in Jerusalem illustrate a lifestyle and degree of wealth previously thought unlikely. The homes are huge in size and functional within. Excavations reveal mosaics, decorated stucco or frescoes in houses, expensive glassware, imported eastern *terra sigillata,* impressed fineware typically from North Africa, amphorae from Italy, and jars of wine from Rhodes. The upper classes, especially the priestly families, were able to purchase such items and decorate their houses with them. The Jerusalem elite was tied into the global material culture of the time, and their everyday life reflects a largely Hellenistic lifestyle.

In addition to Hellenistic material comforts, the residents of Jerusalem seem to have been quite familiar with the Greek language. Greek inscriptions number about one-third of all known inscriptions from the city, and 37 percent of Jewish ossuaries bear Greek inscriptions. In the Bar Kokhba letters from the 130's C.E., which were discovered in caves overlooking the Dead Sea, the rebels against Rome wrote not only in Hebrew and Aramaic but also in Greek. (The Greek documents appear to be primarily related to business matters.) The culture of Judaea appears therefore to have been trilingual—Hebrew, Aramaic, and Greek—and we shall have occasion to see how this linguistic fact would find echoes in later rabbinic culture.

Many, if not most, of the Jerusalem houses had internal ritual baths. Individual families would go to great lengths to install these *mikva'ot*, for the common Judaism of the day made purity of the body a central element of everyday life, especially for priests. It took great ingenuity and considerable technology to accommodate the law for ritual immersion. A fresh water source had to be brought from a considerable distance via aqueducts and underground channels. In Jerusalem, at least part of the year, rainwater could be saved on the roof and then used for ritual purposes. However it was stored, it had to be transported to the bath in such a way that there was always a proper mixture of pure or running water and stored or standing water. The dramatic remains of these installations provide striking, visual corroboration of the halakhic orientation of Judaism as practiced at the highest level of government and in private life. It also reinforces the thesis that the leadership saw no inherent contradiction between a Hellenized lifestyle and Jewish practice.

The poor of the city enjoyed the material benefits of Hellenistic culture far less than the wealthy, but we are hard pressed to say a great deal about their lives. That harmony scarcely reigned between the upper and lower classes becomes evident from a talmudic text that sounds very much like an authentic popular chant against the families of high priests:

> Woe is me because of the House of Boethus, woe is me because of their denunciations.
>
> Woe is me because of the House of Elisha, woe is me because of their fist.
>
> Woe is me because of the House of Ishmael ben Phiabi who are high priests and their sons-in-law are trustees and their servants come and beat us with sticks.[43]

Despite the violence to which this text bears witness, it is notable that popular discontent is not focused on the Hellenized lifestyle of the priests. While it may be difficult to speculate from silence, it appears that the inner social tensions that were to burst forth in revolt against the Romans in 66 C.E. had little to do with the influence in Jerusalem of Greco-Roman culture as such. Whatever the political and religious causes of the Great Revolt, it was not primarily an attempt to eradicate the culture that had struck such deep roots in Judaea since Alexander the Great, if not earlier.

THE EMERGENCE OF "RABBINIC JUDAISM"

Whether the Great Revolt of 66–70 C.E. was the product of sectarian forces, such as the Zealots, or reflected a common resistance to Roman oppression remains a hotly debated issue among historians. Josephus, whose history is our main source, is clearly biased, because he was a general in the early stages of the revolt and subsequently switched sides. It was in Josephus's interest to portray the first part of the revolt as united and the later period as riven by extreme factions. Similarly biased are the later talmudic accounts, which portray Yoḥanan ben Zakkai, the subsequent rabbinical patriarch, as an opponent of the revolt who was smuggled out of the besieged Jerusalem in a coffin. By the time these texts were written—possibly hundreds of years later—the rabbis, like Josephus, had an interest in distancing themselves from rebellion against the Roman Empire.

The trauma of defeat and the sacking of Jerusalem meant tremendous dislocation for the great masses of people in Judaea, many of whom sought to resettle in the Galilee, which had remained largely Jewish during the first century. This process of depopulation of Judaea and shift of the center to the Galilee was to accelerate dramatically after the Bar Kokhba Revolt in 132–35 C.E. Still others left for faraway places in the Diaspora where they knew Jews were living or welcome. The Essenes and Qumran covenanters were swept away into the dustbin of history, the apocalypse of the Roman War having produced the wrong outcome, although some have argued that their ideology was an important component of the nascent Jesus movements. There is increasing evidence that groups of priests continued to function as organized bodies and leaders for quite a few centuries in Palestine, even perhaps retaining sufficient vitality to enable a recovery of leadership with the demise of the patriarchate in the early Byzantine period. Sadduceeism, however, as a separate religious identity, seems to have receded gradually during the early centuries of the Christian era in the face of increasing rabbinic dominance. The more extremist elements of Judaism, the Zealots and their followers, either went underground or changed their views on war as a vehicle for bringing about change. The first Christians, the earliest Jewish Christian community in Judaea, in part fled perhaps to Transjordan, to Pella, and in part fled to the north with their fellow Jews. In both these regions they sank their roots, while their gentile counterpart was absorbed in the West and Asia Minor and Greece.

The destruction of the Temple necessarily had cataclysmic political and religious consequences. Because the Temple had functioned as a political as well as cultic center, its loss left a vacuum into which the rabbis would move, eventually becoming, with the confirmation of the Romans, the primary legal and governmental authorities. According to talmudic legends appropriated as history by many historians, following Yoḥanan ben Zakkai, Gamaliel II, whom legend claims to have been descended from Hillel, established the patriarchate as the Jewish self-government and received the imprimatur of the Romans. Other scholars, reading the talmudic record more critically, assume that the narratives of both Yoḥanan's and Gamaliel's patriarchates are virtual foundation legends of the house of Rabbi Judah the Prince, the first named patriarch, appointed by the Romans in the late second century c.e. to govern the Jews in a manner that would be productive for the *Pax Romana*. By the late second century, in any case, the patriarch had become a quasi-prince, with mercenary guards and significant powers bestowed by the Romans. The political history of this period demonstrates real tensions between the patriarchs, descendants of the House of Gamaliel, and the first group of rabbis, the early *tanna'im*, who were formed primarily of the disciples (and *their* disciples) of Rabbi Yoḥanan ben Zakkai.[44] It was, however, the power of the patriarch, as well as his relative closeness to the various groups of scribes and Pharisees remaining vibrant after the two revolts, that enabled the rabbinic movement to consolidate itself out of the joining of these various groups and the gradually successful imposition of their religious views as a virtual orthodoxy on the Jews of Palestine, Babylonia, and eventually—after several centuries—the Diaspora as well.[45]

The loss of the Jerusalem Temple also meant that the Jewish religion had to transform itself from a Temple-based, sacrificial cult to a culture rooted in domestic and local practices: prayer; celebration of the annual cycle of agriculturally based holidays; and transferal of the purity laws to the home and to the house of study. This work of transformation was undertaken in the years after 70 c.e. by Yoḥanan ben Zakkai and his successors. Although the stories about the court at Yavneh, which Yoḥanan established either during or immediately after the war, may have been fictions projected back into history by later generations of rabbis, there can be little doubt that he and his disciples began the process of turning priestly Judaism into the rabbinic culture that developed in subsequent years. The house of study *(bet midrash)* and the synagogue, both of which were institutions long in existence during the late Second Temple period, now became primary; indeed, most of the synagogue sites excavated in Palestine stem from the third century and later. The synagogue liturgy developed beyond its Second Temple origins and became the basis for all Jewish liturgy in subsequent centuries. The rabbis were not, however, to control the synagogue institution and its traditional religious forms for centuries.[46]

The transformation of Pharisaism from a sect into a hegemonic orthodoxy took place over the course of the second and third centuries, during which time it dropped the name Pharisee (which means "Separatist" and ran, therefore, counter to the new ideology of a common, catholic Judaism). The statement attributed to Gamaliel III (mid-third century; Avot 2:4), "Do not 'separate' from the public," is a reflection of the new status of the erstwhile sect of the Pharisees.[47] To the extent that we know anything about them—a very limited extent indeed—it would seem that the leaders at Yavneh had fairly modest and limited aims: it fell to the next generation of tanna'im to expand the purview of rabbinic law and practices. Some scholars have held that the canon of Scripture was established at Yavneh, but this view has been largely discredited in recent scholarship.[48] Some have held that events at Yavneh precipitated the final split between Judaism and Christianity,[49] the so-called parting of the ways, but this view is even more discredited than the previous one.[50] The following example apparently exemplifies the very limited scope of any Yavnean adjustment in Jewish law. Before the destruction of the Temple, when a New Year fell on the Sabbath, the shofar would only be sounded in Jerusalem. The amended law allows for the shofar to be blown wherever the Jewish court or Sanhedrin would sit (Mishnah Rosh Hashana 4:1). In such a revision, the sages declared their courts the lawful successor to the priestly court of Jerusalem. Their preoccupation with such matters was not unlike that of the exiles in Babylonia in the sixth century B.C.E., who sought ways for the community to stay together without a Temple and in a foreign land.

Just as the Primary History, consisting of the Pentateuch and Former Prophets, most noticeably influenced by Deuteronomic theology, had interpreted the destruction of the First Temple as having been occasioned by sin and idolatry or covenant disobedience, so too did some of the contemporaries of Yavneh see the destruction in 70 as arising out of sin—God acted righteously in punishing Israel (2 Baruch 10:6–7, 9–15, 17–18)—though, with repentance, redemption would ultimately come about (44:12–15). In the end the Temple will be reinstituted along with its sacrificial system, God will redeem humankind, and the Messiah will come to transform the world.

The tanna'im, however, took a more cautious position on messianism. According to later tradition, Yohanan ben Zakkai taught that, if one is engaged in planting a vineyard and someone announces the coming of the Messiah, then one should finish planting.[51] However, other traditions claim that significant members of a later generation of rabbis, especially the great Rabbi Akiva, supported the Bar Kokhba Revolt and considered its leader, Simon Bar Kokhba, to have been the Messiah. The fact that many rabbis were martyred by the Romans for their support of this revolt seems to corroborate this tradition. It is somewhat hard to believe that the disciples of Yohanan's school would have taken such a strong eschatological stance less than 60 years after their teacher had eschewed messianism. It is more likely that the Yohanan tradition was created by a later generation of post–Bar Kokhba rabbis who drew the lesson from that disastrous revolt that messianism exacted too high a price. Their compromise was to preserve the messianic idea but to relegate it to the future.

Although Rome remained their historic enemy, some of the rabbis made pragmatic accommodation with the empire their guiding principle:

> Our [ancient] Rabbis have taught: When Rabbi Yose the son of Kisma became ill, Rabbi Hanina the son of Teradion went to visit him. He said to him: "Hanina, my brother, don't you know that this nation was set to rule over us by Heaven, and it has destroyed His house, and burned His temple, and killed His saints, and destroyed His goodly things, and still it exists, and I have heard that you gather crowds together in public, with a Scroll of the Torah in your lap, and you sit and teach!" He [Hanina] said to him, "From Heaven they will have mercy." He [Yose] said to him, "I say logical things to you, and you answer me: 'From Heaven they will have mercy!' I will be surprised if they do not burn you and the Scroll of the Torah with you."[52]

Rabbi Hanina is one of the prototypical martyrs in the talmudic literature.[53] This text thus eloquently reflects the critique that much of post–Bar Kokhba rabbinic culture produced against any open resistance to Roman rule, arguing instead that Jewish law and the study of Torah should be maintained in private, while, in public, attempts would be made to accommodate to the empire. Any open resistance, according to the position attributed to Rabbi Yose, will result in Hanina's needless death.

An exchange attributed to two other rabbis of the post–Bar Kokhba era captures the duality of the rabbis' view of Rome. Rabbi Judah ben Ilai is quoted as saying: "How beautiful are the deeds of that nation [the Romans]. They set up marketplaces, build bridges, construct baths." Rabbi Simon bar Yohai is said to have retorted: "Everything they do for their own good. They set up marketplaces to place their harlots there, baths for their pleasures, bridges to levy tolls."[54] But, as the story with which we began this chapter—of Gamaliel in the Roman bath—makes clear, the Jews themselves, including the rabbis, took advantage of the many benefits of the empire.

Following the devastating defeat of the Second Revolt under Bar Kokhba in 135, the Jews virtually abandoned Judaea, and the Galilee became the center of Jewish life and culture for the next 400 or 500 years. This shift to the north coincided with Rome's general policy of urbanization of the eastern part of the empire, which resulted in an even greater concentration of wealthy landowners in Sepphoris and Tiberias. The localization of such considerable wealth in cities no doubt led to the increase in civic building projects that included colonnaded streets, market buildings, shops, and public buildings, which in turn led to a greater acceptance of a Hellenistic lifestyle, at least from an external point of view.

The reconfiguration of Jewish life took place in several locations in the north. Judging from the amount of new settlements in the Upper Galilee, considerable numbers of Jews chose the rugged and isolated mountain terrain of the Meiron Massif over the gentle rolling hills of the Lower Galilee. The Upper Galilee had remained more or less untouched by the massive urbanization policies of the Romans, who administered this region through a small confederation of four medium-sized villages. The culture of Tetracomia, or "Four Villages," was distinctive in significant ways: it was purely rural; its dominant language was Aramaic, with almost no Greek; and it lacked almost totally high Hellenistic art or architecture. Yet, numismatic evidence demonstrates that the Upper Galilee engaged in active trade with the city of Tyre, providing it with workmen, agricultural goods, and ceramics. While this remote region was therefore economically tied into city life, it remained culturally isolated.

Adjacent to and east of the Upper Galilee, in the high, elevated plateau of Transjordan, is the Golan Heights, ancient Gaulanitis. In many ways the Golan resembles the culture of the Upper Galilee, though the farther north one goes in the Golan the closer one comes to the cities of Damascus or Baneas (Caesarea Philippi). Toward the southern end of the plateau, one approaches the city of Gadara. The relative isolation of the Golan, however, and its contiguity with a large portion of Galilee, suggest that many Jews of Roman Palestine sought isolation from the mainstream out of fear or choice, and they chose a rather conservative cultural lifestyle over one more intensely involved with Roman culture and Greek language and mores. Yet Roman-style baths are known in the Golan (at Hamath Gadera) as well as other aspects of Greco-Roman culture, so the area was not completely immune to outside influence. But, in general, the villages of this large region correspond more to the Upper Galilee than to the more urban and Hellenized Lower Galilee.

It was, however, in the Lower Galilee that the bulk of the Jewish population settled, and there, from a cultural point of view, the greatest creativity was manifested. In the cities of Usha, Tiberias, and Sepphoris, the Sanhedrin, transplanted from Yavneh, flourished. In these cities the tanna'im and their successors, the amora'im, compiled their great literary and legal works. As we shall see, rabbinic culture took form precisely in those areas in which Hellenism was most prominent, rather than in the more conservative Upper Galilee.

Before turning to the Hellenistic context in which the rabbis operated, I will describe briefly the major features of the nascent culture of the tanna'im. As we have seen, traditions of legal exegesis reached back into the Second Temple period and included many Jewish groups, including the Qumran sect and the

Sadducees as well as the Pharisees. There was undoubtedly a fund of popular religious practice as well. With the rabbis now establishing themselves as the sole legal authorities, they sought to ground their traditions, which they called the "Oral Law," in Divine Authority. In sharp contrast to earlier groups, however, such as the Qumran covenanters and authors of the Book of Jubilees, the rabbis did not seek to add to Scripture itself. Although there is reason to believe that the canon of Scripture had essentially been established and closed before the end of the Second Temple period, later talmudic tradition insists that it was at Yavneh and later that these decisions were taken. The sacred status of certain books of the Bible, including the Song of Songs, Ecclesiastes, Esther, Ezekiel, and Proverbs, is represented to have been debated at Yavneh.[55] The possibility that certain books might not be included in the canon and the institution of a category of "external books" (sefarim hitzonim) were the product of the rabbinic belief that prophecy had ceased with the destruction of the Temple. Taken together, these rabbinic legends constitute a powerful technique for the transfer of power from traditional modes of authority, whether prophetic or popular, to the newly constituted institution, the House of Study, and its denizens, the rabbis themselves.

God no longer revealed Himself to His followers, so the Palestinian rabbis could not rely on direct revelation as their source of legitimacy. Instead, in a development closely related to the Hellenistic philosophical schools that traced their lineage back to Plato himself, they created a "chain of tradition" that stretched back to Moses.[56] According to this chain, the process of ordination of rabbis by their teachers had started with Moses. The earliest such chain of tradition appears in a Mishnaic book, the "Sayings of the Fathers" (Pirkei Avot).[57] Here the rabbis trace the lineage of their authority back through the Prophets and elders who had inherited the chain of ordination from Joshua and Moses. In an innovation roughly parallel in time to the second-century invention of the "apostolic succession" among Catholic Christians (and indeed among some of their opponents as well), this chain became transformed from the succession list of a particular school of rabbinic thought and practice, that of Yohanan ben Zakkai, to the guarantor of the sole legitimacy of the "universal" rabbinic leadership. It also served as a foundation myth for the political leadership of the patriarch.

Astonishingly, this fictitious political history leaves out the kings and priests who, of course, were the primary authorities in the First and Second Temple states. Moses is called "our rabbi" (Moshe rabenu), thus turning him into the source of rabbinic legitimacy. In addition to a chain of authority, the rabbis also claimed that their legislation was not new but was, rather, an "Oral Law" revealed to Moses at Sinai. In a kind of circular argument, they held that possession of this Oral Law was proof of their divine appointment: the chain of tradition and the Oral Law mutually reinforced each other's antiquity and authenticity.

By claiming that revelation and prophecy had ceased, the rabbis implicitly banished God from the stage of history and arrogated to themselves exclusive power to interpret the revealed law. An extraordinary talmudic legend summarizes this theory of rabbinic autonomy. A majority of rabbis take a certain position and are opposed by Rabbi Eliezer, who calls upon a series of divine miracles to prove that God Himself is on his side. The majority rejects this procedure out of hand: "It [the Torah] is not in the heavens" and "We do not pay attention to a heavenly voice *[bat kol]*." The story ends with God laughing and exclaiming: "My sons have defeated Me, my sons have defeated Me."[58] Here, then, is a legend that paradoxically invokes a heavenly voice at the end for the rejection of heavenly voices. And it is no accident that it is God's "sons" who have defeated Him, for the rabbinic consolidation of all religious authority in their own hands involved displacement of women's religious traditions, which, as we have seen, had left traces of their vitality in the synagogue and elsewhere. Women were sometimes thought to have charismatic authority, so the rabbis were clearly interested in rejecting such prophetic activity.

This legend also highlights the singular culture of disputation that we find in rabbinic literature. The rabbis grounded their laws in the Bible by hermeneutic or exegetical arguments, but they never promulgated one authoritative or dogmatic procedure. Thus, different schools, such as that of Rabbi Ishmael versus that of Rabbi Akiva, disagreed not only over substantive legal matters but also over the correct exegetical methods to derive these laws. And the proof that neither substance nor method ever became dogmatic is that minority opinions, such as that of Rabbi Eliezer, are preserved in the later edited texts. The definition, however, of who constituted a legitimate voice within the chorus of dissent was sharply constrained. Indeed, it could be argued that the very possibility of a multivocal, elastic understanding of the truth of Oral Torah was contingent on the rabbis legitimating themselves as the sole and unchallenged arbiters of Jewish life. As opposed to orthodox Christianity, as it began to develop by the end of the second century C.E., rabbinic Judaism never developed a set of dogmas, but neither was it quite as open as it seems or as some have claimed it to be. Those whom the rabbis included within their circles were allowed extraordinary freedom of expression and interpretation. Those who were excluded were suppressed, notably the groups called *minim* ("kinds" or "sects"), those Jews who did not accept universal rabbinic hegemony.

Many of the minim or heretics appear to have been Jewish Christians, and there are echoes in tannaitic literature of actual discussions or debates that were carried on between these Christians and the rabbis. These early Palestinian Christians may have been much closer to the rabbis than the later tradition wishes us to remember. They had their own halakhic interpretations that were of interest to certain rabbis. Indeed, the same Rabbi Eliezer is said to have listened favorably to a piece of law from the mouth of a min—which was perhaps one reason that he himself was suspected of heresy.[59] In fact, the story of Eliezer, as well as other rabbinic stories of dealings with Jewish Christians, demonstrate that the split between Judaism and Christianity did not occur as early and as definitively as is often believed. Christians continued to frequent synagogues throughout the second century (and undoubtedly much later as well). The "curse on the minim," which appears in the Palestinian liturgy, probably comes from the late second century, rather than from the first, as has often been assumed, as both rabbis and Church fathers tried to disentangle the two traditions.

The existence of active groups of Jewish Christians throughout the tannaitic period suggests that the Palestinian Jewish community was by no means monolithic in the generations following the destruction of the Temple. The sects of the Second Temple period were no longer on the scene, to be sure, but the fact that political power came to be concentrated in the hands of the patriarchate and the rabbis did not mean that all Jews followed their traditions. Rabbinic literature from the period testifies to many practices, including magic and astrology, with which the rabbis disagreed but which were nevertheless common among the folk.

The Jewish Christians are proof that identity was not entirely stable. We also know of groups of pagans—referred to as "fearers of heaven"—who followed certain aspects of Jewish law or worshiped the Jewish God, without converting fully to Judaism. In many of the cities of second-century Palestine, such as Caesarea, Bet She'an (Scythopolis), Acco (Ptolemais), Samaria (Sebaste), Neapolis, and Tyre, Jews lived in close proximity with non-Jews. At the beginning of the Great Revolt, tensions between Jews and non-Jews in some of these places broke out into full-fledged warfare, which was one of the causes of the Jewish rebellion against the Roman occupiers. But there was another side to these mixed cities, and that was the more positive cultural and religious discourse between the Jews and their neighbors. It is no surprise, therefore, that some of these pagans might find aspects of Judaism attractive, just as the Jews would incorporate features of pagan culture into their own.

HOW MUCH GREEK IN JEWISH PALESTINE?

We now return to the subject with which this chapter began: the degree to which the Jews adopted Greco-Roman culture in the century or two after the destruction of the Second Temple. Was Rabban Gamaliel's willingness to enter a bath boasting a statue of Aphrodite a flagrant violation of Judaism or perhaps a symptom of a much more complex relationship between Jewish and Hellenistic culture? The answer to this question is itself complicated. For instance, the rabbis were acutely aware of the idolatrous rituals of their pagan neighbors; the tractate Avodah Zara of the Talmud catalogues these practices in minute detail. One has the sense that in order to build high fences against pagan cults, it became necessary to do extensive anthropological fieldwork to describe them. Yet the general rabbinic attitude toward the pagans themselves was, on the whole, quite tolerant.

Greco-Roman culture often glorified the body, and sports such as wrestling were a prominent part of everyday life.[60] The rabbis rejected sports as an occupation and even criticized someone who acted during ritual immersion as if he were engaged in water-sports.[61] However, they did not forbid physical exercise outright, as long as it did not contradict the law. The gymnasium had evidently become far less threatening than it was prior to the Maccabean Revolt, when those opposed to Hellenism regarded as a flagrant provocation the sight of Jewish men concealing their circumcisions to participate naked in sports. Moreover, the case of Gamaliel in the bath demonstrates that care of the body, beyond the requirements of ritual purity, was acceptable to the rabbis, as long as the ritual bath (mikveh) was not confused with the Roman bath.

The Greek language became the lingua franca of many urban Jews by the second century. An educated person was expected to know Greek, and even the lower classes knew some as well. Rabbi Simon, the son of Gamaliel, claimed, "There were a thousand young men in my father's house, five hundred of whom studied the Law, while the other five hundred studied Greek wisdom."[62] His son, Rabbi Judah the Prince (the editor of the Mishnah), reinforced this view: "Why speak Syriac [Aramaic] in Palestine? Talk either Hebrew or Greek."[63] Rabbinic literature from this period contains thousands of Greek words, testifying to the prevalence of the Greek language at all levels of the culture, from the legal and political to mundane matters of the marketplace and even to prostitutes and criminals. Rather than seeing these as "loan words," it would be more useful to think of the presence of so much Greek as the sign of a new amalgam or fusion language, containing Hebrew, Aramaic, and Greek. The culture was indeed trilingual but was also in the process of forging a new language out of all three.

The influence of Greek culture can be seen in many spheres of Jewish life. The rabbinic school of Rabbi Ishmael is said to have used 13 methods of legal exegesis. It has been shown that these methods as well as other related forms of talmudic literature have their precise parallels in Greek legal hermeneutics.[64] Similarly, the Jews took over Greek artistic forms. As the Jerusalem Talmud relates about the synagogues of the third and fourth centuries: "In the days of R. Yoḥanan [third century C.E.], they began depicting [figural representations] on walls, and he did not protest; in the days of R. Abun [fourth century c.e.], they began depicting [such figures] on mosaic floors, and he did not protest."[65]

The fact that the text considers it noteworthy that the rabbis did not protest such decoration, of course, suggests that a significant change had occurred. The coins of the Hasmonaean and Herodian periods lack figural representations, which may mean that such art was considered to violate the Second Commandment prohibiting graven images. But, by the middle-late Roman period, this understanding of the commandment, if that is what it was, no longer pertained. Virtually every archaeological site from this period contains some representational art, whether it is a figurine, a statue, or something else. Zodiac themes on mosaics only appear from the fourth century on, but earlier mosaics and decorated architectural fragments often bear such figures as an eagle (Gush Halav), a sheep, or a rabbit (Nabratein).

The decorated sarcophagi from the Roman-period catacombs at Bet She'arim provide the most stunning and irrefutable evidence that the rabbis were at home with pagan art and its mythological scenes, such as Leda and the Swan. At Bet She'arim some of the most important rabbis of the time, including Judah the Prince, chose to be buried. Some scholars have suggested that pagan scenes appear because the artisans were gentile or that they are merely ornamental, without intrinsic meaning. But whatever the reason for it, the presence of mythological Greek images on the sarcophagi of the sages suggests that burial in such containers did not contradict rabbinical Judaism.

Let us conclude this discussion of the synthesis between Greek and rabbinic culture by examining one city of Lower Galilee, Sepphoris, which was the seat of the patriarchate under Judah the Prince. It was here that the Mishnah was codified in the early third century. What did this city, the seat of what we might anachronistically today call "orthodox Judaism," look like when Rabbi Judah held court there? Sepphoris dates back to the Hasmonaean period, from which time, we recall, an ostrakon with a Greek word written in Hebrew characters was found. Herod Antipas, the son of Herod the Great, had ambitious plans in the early first century for converting Sepphoris into a great oriental city, "the ornament of all Galilee," but he was not able in his lifetime to complete those objectives. The main north-south roadway of the Lower City, the cardo, may well be attributed to his activities, but the main buildings alongside the cardo come from a slightly later period, probably the second century. When Jesus was active in the Galilee, Sepphoris was probably one of the major urban centers, but, as we have observed, Jesus is not mentioned in any literary sources as having been there, though no doubt he may have visited from time to time. Moreover, the evidence for spoken Greek at Sepphoris at so early a time is almost nonexistent.

It was not until the late first or early second century that Sepphoris began to expand and become what Antipas had wished it to be. The great theater, with its 4,500 seats, though thought at one time to be from the period of Antipas, most likely dates from this period. Indeed, it is possible to suggest that the urban expansion of Sepphoris is attributable to its unique position vis-à-vis Rome during the Great Revolt. Though it was fortified and Roman troops were even stationed there for a while, sometime in the year 67 or 68 C.E. the city decided to adopt a pro-Roman stance and not be part of the larger Jewish war effort.

As a consequence of these actions, Emperor Nero granted Sepphoris the unusual privilege of minting its own coins. These coins, struck in 68 C.E., bear the legend "Irenopolis" or "City of Peace." (Apparently an influential group of Sepphoreans had been so inclined when a delegation of them welcomed Vespasian and his army into the country.) The coins also bear the legend "Neronias," in honor of the emperor Nero, but it is significant to note that they bear no image or any pagan elements that might offend more traditional elements of the city. By the time of Trajan, however (98–117 C.E.), the Sepphoris coins do in fact bear the image of the bust of the emperor, and the city is renamed "Diocaesarea." On the other side, however, are Jewish or neutral symbols: two ears of barleycorn. The coins also record the special privilege given the boulē, or council, of Sepphoris to mint them. A medallion with a bust of Caracalla is on the obverse of one, and a very special inscription on its reverse reads: "Diocaesarea the Holy City of Shelter, Autonomous. / Loyal [a treaty of] Friendship and Alliance with the Romans." This alliance between Sepphoris and the Roman government lends some credibility to the later talmudic legends that say Rabbi Judah had a special relationship with the emperor.

It is no wonder that the city blossomed as an urban center with an overwhelmingly Jewish majority after 68 C.E. The multiethnic character of much of the site during the Byzantine period has been confirmed by extensive analysis of animal remains. The areas presumed to be Jewish have yielded no pig bones whatsoever, and more public areas from later periods have produced only 18–20 percent pig bones, a percentage that would be quite a bit higher for one of the mixed cities.[66] All the houses had immersion pools that were most probably ritual baths, so it is reasonable to infer that they were Jewish. The Jewish demographic dominance at Sepphoris culminated when Judah moved the Sanhedrin there and undertook to edit and redact the Mishnah with the other sages who assisted in this task at the beginning of the third century C.E.

Given the heavily Jewish population of the city and the presence of Judah and his court, it is particularly striking how Hellenistic the material culture of Sepphoris was. The Dionysos mansion near the theater stems from the period of Rabbi Judah's life. This building, which was probably an inn or guesthouse for distinguished visitors, contains 15 scenes from the legends of the god Dionysos, with explanatory labels in Greek. Of all the gentile gods, Dionysos was perhaps the most popular, due no doubt to his association with wine, revelry, the theater, and the afterlife.[67] His popularity at such a nearby city as Bet She'an may have influenced the decision to depict him in the mansion in a drinking contest with Heracles.

Panel of so-called Mona Lisa from the Dionysos mosaic at Sepphoris.
The level of artistry in the mosaic is unparalleled in the ancient Near East.
(Courtesy Joint Sepphoris Project)

It is therefore clear that the rabbinic leadership saw no conflict between the Greco-Roman culture of the day and their own. Judging from Sepphoris and Bet She'arim, most of the leadership viewed that culture and its art, including mythological scenes, as a means of participating in a larger cultural identity. An inscription or menorah might identify such individuals as Jewish, and they often appeared alongside a pagan symbol. The urban environment that produced so great and productive a mixture as that which emerged in third century Sepphoris, when the Mishnah was published or promulgated, was certainly a fertile setting for a constructive symbiosis between Jewish and Hellenistic cultures. If the whole history we have discussed of Palestine under Persians, Greeks, and Romans bears witness to an extended experiment in negotiating between Jewish identity and cosmopolitan cultures, it was the tannaitic rabbis who seem to have found the most stable resolution of this dilemma. Far from attempting to preserve some archaic "biblical" culture in the face of foreign temptations, they forged a new culture out of old traditions, their own innovations, and the language, art, and law of the Greco-Roman world of which they were an active and integral part.

NOTES

1. M. Avodah Zara 3.4.

2. See Shaye J. D. Cohen, *The Beginnings of Jewishness: Boundaries, Varieties, Uncertainties* (Berkeley, 1999), 25–69.

3. See C. L. Meyers and E. M. Meyers, *Haggai, Zechariah 1–8. Anchor Bible 25B* (Garden City, N.Y., 1987), 76–82, where Haggai's priestly ruling on a very complicated matter of biblical law concerning purity is discussed. The prophet mediates the discussion between the priests and God and utilizes the answer to make his own points about the priests and biblical law. The language is very stylized and suggests a kind of proto-rabbinic discourse.

4. Haggai 2:11–12.

5. Nehemiah 8:8; see further vv. 4, 7.

6. See J. Cook, *The Persian Empire* (New York, 1983).

7. Ecclesiastes 1:2–4.

8. Ibid. 1:18.

9. Ibid. 12:12.

10. Paul Lapp argued that the two groups of stamped handles pointed to a division of power between the civil and religious authorities, a separation he argues that went back to the Persian era in the pattern of a dyarchy, governor and high priest. But there is no evidence other than this small corpus, and the Yehud coins to make a compelling case that Judaea was autonomous in the time when the Ptolemies were in charge of taxation. Indeed,

the testimony of the Zenon Papyri shows how very intimately the Ptolemies were—the papyri are from Ptolemy II Philadelphus (261–229 B.C.E.)—involved in tax collecting. Judaea was administered in the same way as Egypt, which was a royal estate, to the degree that the local population cooperated with their Ptolemaic/Egyptian administrators. There is no recognition among the papyri that deal with Egypt and Palestine that Judaea had a governor. See Paul Lapp, "Ptolemaic Stamped Handles from Judah," *Bulletin of the American Schools of Oriental Research* 172 (1963): 22–35, and R. Harrison, "Hellenization in Syria-Palestine: The Case of Judea in the Third Century B.C.E.," *The Biblical Archaeologist* 57 (1994): 98–108.

11. 1 Maccabees 1:54. See also Daniel 11:31, 12:11, and 2 Maccabees 6:2.

12. See 2 Macc. 6:4, 7.

13. 1 Macc. 4:54–56. See also 2 Macc. 10:1–8.

14. Herod's political savvy is central to understanding his life's accomplishments at home and abroad. Peter Richardson's biography, *Herod: King of the Jews and Friend of the Romans* (Columbia, S.C., 1996), examines and expands on this theme in a most compelling way.

15. Hananel was a Babylonian of "high priestly" ancestry (Ant. 15:40–41), but in m. Parah 3.5a one Hanamel *(sic)* is referred to as an Egyptian. For a full discussion of this problem, see Richardson, *Herod,* 242–44.

16. M. Avot 1:10.

17. Josephus, *Contra Apionem,* 2:179–81. Compare *Antiquities,* 18:11–24. The term "common Judaism" is based on E. P. Sanders' use in *Judaism: Practice and Belief, 63 B.C.E.–66 C.E.* (Philadelphia and London, 1992), 47–303.

18. See Martin Goodman, "The Function of Minim in Early Rabbinic Judaism," in H. Cancik, H. Lichtenberger, and P. Schäfer, eds., *Geschichte—Tradition—Reflexion: Festschrift für Martin Hengel zom 70. Geburtstag* (Tübingen, 1996) 1: 501–10.

19. The prosbul is attributed to Hillel in Sifre Deut. 113 (cf. Shebiith 10:3–4).

20. See P. Benoit, J. T. Milik, and R. de Vaux, eds., *Discoveries in the Judaean Desert II: Les grottes de Murabba'at* (Oxford, 1961), 100–104, no. 18.

21. BT Shabbat 31a.

22. For Qumran, see 1 QS 10:17–21; see also the Testament of Benjamin 4:2–34 and Matthew 5:43–44.

23. M. Avot 2:4.

24. Acts 2:42.

25. Mark 14:58, Matt. 26:61.

26. See M. Sanhedrin 11:1.

27. See Lawrence Schiffman, *Reclaiming the Dead Sea Scrolls* (Philadelphia, 1991), 73–75.

28. Moed Qatan 1:5.

29. I have discussed this topic at length in my book, *Jewish Ossuaries: Reburial and Rebirth* (Rome, 1971). My views are opposed to those of L. I. Levine in *Judaism and Hellenism in Antiquity: Conflict or Confluence?* (Seattle, 1998), 65–71.

30. See D. Flusser, *Jesus* (Jerusalem, 1997), esp. 195–206.

31. Josephus, *Contra Apionem* 2:218 (cf. fn. 17 where Josephus text is *Contra Apionem*).

32. See B. McCane, "Let the Dead Bury Their Own Dead: Secondary Burial and Mt. 8:21–22," *Harvard Theological Review* 83 (1990): 31–43.

33. Mark 8:27. Jesus appears in some places to reject overtures from non-Jews, but the geographical evidence from the New Testament suggests that he must have had gentile audiences.

34. Matthew 20:1–16.

35. Ibid. 13:24–25.

36. M. Ta'anit 3.8. for a discussion of Jewish charismatics in relation to Jesus, see G. Vermes, *Jesus the Jew* (London, 1973), 58–82.

37. Y. Sanh. 7, 19, 25d. On this subject, see M. Aubin, "Gendering Magic in Late Antique Judaism" (Ph.D. diss., Duke University, 1998).

38. See, e.g., Luke 4:15–30, 33, 38, 44.

39. This translation is taken from L. I. Levine, ed., *The Synagogue in Late Antiquity* (Philadelphia; 1987), 17. Levine has an excellent discussion of the evidence of the synagogue in the Second Temple period in his new book, *The Ancient Synagogue* (New Haven, Conn., 2000), 42–73.

40. See Bernadette Brooten, *Women Leaders in the Ancient Synagogue* (Chico, Calif., 1982), 35 (for quote), 103–35 (for discussion about a women's gallery).

41. See Cynthia Baker, "Bodies, Boundaries, and Domestic Politics in a Late Ancient Marketplace," *Journal of Medieval and Early Modern Studies* 26 (1996): 391–418, and her "Rebuilding the House of Israel: Gendered Bodies and Domestic Politics in Roman Jewish Galilee c. 135–300 C.E." (Ph.D. diss., Duke University, 1997).

42. Miriam Peskowitz, *Spinning Fantasies: Rabbis, Gender, and History* (Berkeley, 1997), offers a new perspective on rabbinic Judaism by examining everyday tasks and artifacts. She demonstrates how issues of gender were inextricably tied up with the emergence of post-Temple Judaism.

43. T. Menahot 13.20, BT Gittin 55b–56a, and B. Shabbat 119b.

44. Albert I. Baumgarten, "The Akivan Opposition," *Hebrew Union College Annual* 50 (1979): 179–97.

45. Jacob Neusner, "The Formation of Rabbinic Judaism: Yavneh (Jamnia) from A.D. 70 to 100," in Wolfgang Haase, ed., *Principat: Religion (Judentum)* (Berlin, 1979), 3–42; Daniel Boyarin, "The *Diadoche* of the Rabbis; or Tractate Avot and the Patriarchal Presumption" (forthcoming).

46. Cynthia Baker, "Neighbor at the Door or Enemy at the Gate? Notes Toward a Rabbinic Topography of Self and Other" (paper presented at the American Academy of Religion, New Orleans, 1996). But see also Levine, *The Ancient Synagogue,* 501–60.

47. Boyarin, "The *Diadoche* of the Rabbis."

48. David Aune, "On the Origins of the 'Council of Yavneh' Myth," *Journal of Biblical*

Literature 110, no. 3 (1991): 18–33; Günther Stemberger, "Die sogennante 'Synode von Jabne' und das frühe Christentum," *Kairos* 19 (1977): 14–21.

49. W. D. Davies, *The Setting of the Sermon on the Mount* (Cambridge, Engl., 1966), 256–351.

50. Reuven Kimelman, "Birkat Ha-Minim and the Lack of Evidence for an Anti-Christian Jewish Prayer in Late Antiquity," in E. P. Sanders, A. I. Baumgarten, and A. Mendelson, eds., *Aspects of Judaism in the Greco-Roman Period* (Philadelphia, 1981), 226–44; 391–403.

51. Aboth d.R. Nathan B XXXI. N. N. Glatzer translates the text in *The Judaic Tradition* (Boston, 1969), 239: "Rabban Jochanan ben Zakkai used to say: If there be a plant in your hand when they say to you: Behold the Messiah!—Go and plant the plant, and afterward go out to greet him."

52. BT Avodah Zara 18b.

53. See Daniel Boyarin, "Martyrdom and the Making of Christianity and Judaism," *Journal of Early Christian Studies* 6, no. 4 (1998): 577–627.

54. BT Shabbat 33b.

55. BT Shabbat 13b, 30b, and Hagigah 13a. See also J. T. Barrera, *The Jewish Bible and the Christian Bible: An Introduction to the History of the Bible* (Grand Rapids, Mich., 1998), 165–67, and S. Leiman, *The Canonization of Hebrew Scripture: The Talmudic and Midrashic Evidence* (Hamden, Conn. 1976). Aboth d'Rabbi Nathan A. ch. 1 reports: "Originally it is said, Proverbs, Song of Songs, and Kohelet were suppressed: for since they were held to be mere parables and not part of the Holy Writings (the religious authorities) arose and suppressed them."

56. On the Hellenistic schools, see John Glucker, *Antiochus and the Late Academy* (Göttingen, 1978). On the rabbinic chain of tradition, see Elias Bickerman, "La chaine de la tradition pharisienne," *Revue biblique* 59, no. 1 (1952): 44–54, and Boyarin, "The *Diadoche* of the Rabbis."

57. M. Avot 1:1.

58. BT Baba Metzia 59b.

59. T. Hullin 2:24.

60. For a general discussion of games and athletics in Palestine in Roman times, see Z. Weiss, "Buildings for Entertainment," in D. Sperber, *The City in Roman Palestine* (New York, 1998), 77–91.

61. See Saul Lieberman, *Greek in Jewish Palestine* (New York, 1942), 92–93.

62. BT Sotah 49b.

63. Ibid.

64. D. Daube, "Alexandrian Methods of Interpretation and the Rabbis," in *Festschrift Hans Lewald* (Basel, 1953), 27–44. See also the essays in H. Fischel, ed., *Essays in Greco-Roman and Related Talmudic Literature* (New York, 1977).

65. JT Avodah Zara 3.3 42d.

66. See Billy J. Grantham, "A Zooarchaeological Model for the Study of Ethnic Complexity at Sepphoris" (Ph.D. diss., Northwestern University, 1996).

67. See M. Smith, "On the Wine God in Palestine (Gen 18, Jn 2, and Achilles Tatius)," in *Salo W. Baron Jubilee*, vol. 2 (Jerusalem, 1975), 815–29.

SELECTED BIBLIOGRAPHY

Aubin, M. "Gendering Magic in Late Antique Judaism." Ph.D. diss., Duke University, 1998.

Aune, D. "On the Origins of the 'Council to Yavneh' Myth." *Journal of Biblical Literature* 110, no. 3 (1991): 18–33.

Baker, C. M. "Bodies, Boundaries, and Domestic Politics in a Late Ancient Marketplace." *Journal of Medieval and Early Modern Studies* 26 (1996): 319–418.

————. "Neighbor at the Door or Enemy at the Gate? Notes Toward a Rabbinic Topography of Self and Other." Paper presented at the American Academy of Religion, New Orleans, 1996.

————. "Rebuilding the House of Israel: Gendered Bodies and Domestic Politics in Roman Jewish Galilee c. 135–300 C.E." Ph.D. diss., Duke University, 1997.

Barrera, J. T. *The Jewish Bible and the Christian Bible: An Introduction to the History of the Bible.* Grand Rapids, Mich., 1998.

Baumgarten, A. I. "The Akivan Opposition." *Hebrew Union College Annual* 50 (1979): 179–97.

Bickerman, E. "La chaine de la tradition pharisienne." *Revue biblique* 59 (1953): 44–54.

Boyarin, D. "The *Diadoche* of the Rabbis; or Tractate Avot and the Patriarchal Presumption." Forthcoming.

————. "Martyrdom and the Making of Christianity and Judaism." *Journal of Early Christian Studies* 6, no. 4 (1998): 577–627.

Brooten, B. *Women Leaders in the Ancient Synagogue.* Chico, Calif., 1982.

Chancey, M., and E. M. Meyers. "How Jewish Was Sepphoris in Jesus' Time?" *Biblical Archaeological Review* 26 (2000): 18–33.

Cohen, S. J. D. *The Beginnings of Jewishness: Boundaries, Varieties, Uncertainties.* Berkeley, 1999.

Cook, J. *The Persian Empire.* New York, 1983.

Daube, D. "Alexandrian Methods of Interpretation and the Rabbis." In *Festschrift Hans Lewald.* Basel, 1953.

Davies, W. D. *The Setting of the Sermon on the Mount.* Cambridge, Engl., 1966.

Fischel, H., ed. *Essays in Greco-Roman and Related Talmudic Literature.* New York, 1977.

Flusser, D. *Jesus.* Jerusalem, 1997.

Glucker, J. *Antiochus and the Late Academy.* Göttingen, 1978.

Grantham, B. J. "A Zooarchaeological Model for the Study of Ethnic Complexity at Sepphoris." Ph.D. diss., Northwestern University, 1996.

Kimelman, R. "Birkat Ha-Minim and the Lack of Evidence for an Anti-Christian Jewish Prayer in Late Antiquity." In E. P. Sanders, A. I. Baumgarten, and A. Mendelson, eds., *Aspects of Judaism in the Greco-Roman Period*. Philadelphia, 1981.

Levine, L. I. *Judaism and Hellenism in Antiquity: Conflict or Confluence?* Seattle, 1998.

———. *The Ancient Synagogue: The First Thousand Years*. New Haven, Conn., 2000.

———, ed. *The Synagogue in Late Antiquity*. Philadelphia, 1987.

Lieberman, S. *Greek in Jewish Palestine*. New York, 1942.

McCane, B. "Jews, Christians, and Burial in Roman Palestine." Ph.D. diss., Duke University, 1992.

———. "Let the Dead Bury Their Own Dead: Secondary Burial and Mt. 8:21–22." *Harvard Theological Review* 83 (1990): 31–43.

Meyers, C. L., and E. M. Meyers. *Haggai, Zechariah 1–8. Anchor Bible 25B*. Garden City, N.Y., 1987.

Meyers, E. M. "Jesus and His Galilean Context." In D. R. Edwards and C. T. McCullough, eds., *Archaeology and Contexts in the Greco-Roman and Byzantine Periods*. Atlanta, Ga., 1997.

———. *Jewish Ossuaries: Reburial and Rebirth*. Rome, 1971.

———. "The Pools of Sepphoris: Ritual Baths or Bathtubs?" *Biblical Archaeology Review* 26 (2000): 46–48, 60–61.

———, ed. *Galilee Through the Centuries: Confluence of Cultures*. Winona Lake, Ind., 1999.

Neusner, J. "The Formation of Rabbinic Judaism: Yavneh (Jamnia) from A.D. 70 to 100." In W. Haase, ed., *Principat: Religion (Judentum)*. Berlin, 1979.

Peskowitz, M. *Spinning Fantasies: Rabbis, Gender, and History*. Berkeley, 1997.

Sanders, E. P. *Judaism: Practice and Belief, 63 B.C.E.–66 C.E.* Philadelphia and London, 1992.

Schiffman, L. *Reclaiming the Dead Sea Scrolls*. Philadelphia, 1991.

Sperber, D., *The City in Roman Palestine*. New York, 1998.

Weiss, Z. "Buildings for Entertainment." In Sperber, ed., *The City in Roman Palestine*, 77–91.

The figure of Helios (Sol Invictus) on the floor of the Hammath-Tiberias synagogue. (Israel Antiquities Authority, Jerusalem)

FIVE

CONFRONTING
A CHRISTIAN EMPIRE:

Jewish Culture in the World of Byzantium

ODED IRSHAI

On an early spring morning in the fourth century C.E., the Palestinian sage Hanina attended the service in the new and small but elaborately decorated synagogue of Hammat Tiberias. On his way out he was intercepted by a certain Pinehas, a wood merchant from the nearby village of Kifrah, who asked Rabbi Hanina how he could have set foot in a House of God whose floor was adorned with a figure clad like an emperor, holding a scepter and a bronze globe, with seven rays coming out of his head. Hanina was not entirely surprised by this query, for he had been perplexed when he discovered, some months earlier, this iconographical ornament. Now he replied to Pinehas that, in his judgment, the figure, though resembling the usual representation of the pagan sun god Helios, might be interpreted simply as a personification of the sun. On second thought, Hanina added, the imperial figure could be read as the personification of the Messiah, whom the liturgical poets of the day described as the "Light of Israel," "the Eternal Sun." And, he went on, he had heard that some of the Jews' most bitter opponents, the Christian preachers, faced the same dilemma concerning the adoration of the sun among their own flocks—and had come up with similar interpretations.

This dialogue (which I have invented) expresses the sentiments of the Jews who encountered this and similar icons on the floors of some half-dozen synagogues in Byzantine Palestine. It reflects both the internal cultural concerns of a society living with growing apocalyptic anxieties and the cultural encounters and tensions between that society and the surrounding pagan and Christian world of Late Antiquity.[1]

The period between the fourth and seventh centuries C.E. was one of momentous change for the inhabitants of Palestine. Gradually, Palestine ceased to be predominantly Jewish. Most of the Jews were still concentrated in the Galilee (though not all of it) and the Golan, but much of the country's non-Jewish

population had been won over by Christianity, which ruled the land under the
aegis of the Roman emperors. The Jews had lost their central leadership, the institution of the patriarchate; their copious literary legacy was redacted and completed; and the centers of their spiritual creativity, the academies *(yeshivot)*, were
in decline. A strong trend to decentralization augmented the status of the local
communities whose public life centered on the synagogues, in which liturgical
poets, preachers, and interpreters from Hebrew into Aramaic were active. In the
words of the midrash, "A small city, that is a synagogue, and the few people
there—that is a community" (Ecclesiastes Rabbah 9:21). In short, the cultural
center of gravity shifted over time from the intellectual elite of the academy to
the "masses" in the synagogues. The void created among Diaspora Jews, who had
previously been under the sway of the Palestinian patriarchate,[2] was increasingly
filled by the leadership in Babylon, which by the early days of the Muslim conquest established itself as the dominant cultural and political center of Jewry.
But the saga of Palestine and its Jewish inhabitants in this period is of utmost
relevance to our understanding of the transformation of Jewish life, institutions,
and culture from the nascent rabbinic period during the early centuries of the
Common Era to the Middle Ages.[3]

For the most part, these alterations occurred as a result not of internal Jewish
needs or pressures but of the strife caused by the growing presence and power of
Christianity in Palestine. From the fourth century on, Palestine became a focus
of interest for Christians who, with the help of the emperors and other powerful figures, transformed their utopian religious vision into reality.[4] The barren
country's historical sites became holy places and shrines, and the idea of *Terra
Sancta* (the Holy Land) was thus formed. This annexation of the local collective
(though primarily Jewish) memory and topography had a major impact on the
Jews' sense of identity. The encounter with victorious Christianity and some of
its most zealous representatives was aptly recorded by a contemporary liturgical
poet: "We do not have the splendid attire of the *kohen* [priest], and the wearers
of sackcloth [monks] rule over us."[5]

Apart from this and a few other scanty references in fragmentary collections
of rabbinic legal rulings, midrashic texts, liturgical poetry, and apocalyptic treatises, our main source of information on the life and culture of the Jews of this
period is Christian: the writings of the Church fathers and Church historians,
plus travel guides, pilgrims' itineraries, and polemical disputations.

THE THIRD-CENTURY "CRISIS"
AND THE TRANSFORMATION OF THE EMPIRE

From the early fourth century, the Roman Empire, under the rule of the enig-matic Constantine the Great,[6] was transformed into a Christian society. What exactly precipitated the "crisis" that led to this political and cultural transition is still debated, but there is hardly any doubt that its early stages were already visi-ble during the third century, when Rome witnessed immense internal political instability—an eclipse of the Senate and a corresponding rise in the influence and power of the army—exacerbated by economic hardships (debased currency, agricultural failure) and mounting military pressures from barbarian tribes to the north and west and the assertive Persian-Sassanian kingdom in the East.[7]

The repeated and devastating Persian invasions during the middle of the cen-tury must have had some impact on the Jews residing on either side of the Eu-phrates in Mesopotamia and Syria, and in Palestine. Roman rule in the East was frail, and though some of the soldier-emperors managed to negotiate settle-ments with the mighty Persian emperor Shapur I, the region was far from se-cure. In some intellectual circles (among which we find the rabbis), the political situation and the attendant anxiety were seen as signs that the ailing Roman Em-pire was on its last legs. However, when Rome was rescued (during the 260s) from a Persian military victory and humiliation by its client princedom Palmyra in the Syrian desert, sentiments of deep disappointment were voiced. In both in-stances rabbinic utterances disclose a sense of what could be easily regarded as apocalyptic frustration.[8]

A dialogue of the period, recorded in the rabbinic commentary on Genesis, illustrates the Jews' intense expectation that Rome would fall:

> A *hegemon* [Roman military officer] asked a man of the House of Silani [a re-spected Jewish family in Tiberias]: "Who will seize [power] after us?" He [of the House of Silani] brought a piece of paper, took a quill, and wrote on it: "Then his brother emerged, holding onto the heel of Esau; they said: See old things from a new old man." (Genesis Rabbah 63:9)

Toward the end of the century, it seemed that conditions had ripened for Rome's complete collapse. When a Dalmatian cavalry officer named Diocletian seized power in 284 under somewhat suspicious circumstances,[9] people thought that he, like his predecessors, would not last long. In a Palestinian midrash, he is por-trayed as the "one heralding the last king of Edom."[10]

However, much to the chagrin of the sages, this emperor succeeded in holding onto his throne for some two decades, finally relinquishing it of his own free will. Diocletian demanded that his subjects receive him with rituals of quasi-divine adoration, but he set the empire on a new path by presenting a model of orderly, planned succession that would give the empire political, defensive, and economic stability. In the Roman Orient, he redivided some of the provinces, among them the Provincia Palestina, to which he annexed territories from Arabia. This made Palestine the largest and most important of the provinces that bordered on Sassanian territory.[11]

Far more significant for our discussion here were Diocletian's religious reforms. He created a unifying religio-political mechanism through which he led the entire empire toward a monarchy under the exclusive aegis of Jupiter and Hercules, whom the Romans also venerated as a god. At the core of this new imperial theology was a system of divine cooperation with the temporal monarch, which in essence resembled Christian theological constructs.[12] These far-reaching steps, taken by Diocletian with the objective of stabilizing the government and renewing the ancient Hellenistic ideal of a monarch who represents a god, prepared the ground for the revolutionary measures of the first Christian emperor, Constantine the Great, who joined the imperial leadership cadre in 306, at the height of the great persecutions of the Church and its believers. The growing affinity of ideas between pagans and Christians exacerbated the tension, for the closer the two religious camps came to each other, the greater was the pagans' need to create effective symbols of political allegiance to the empire and the emperor.[13]

Animosity toward the Christians broke out in full force throughout the empire when decrees were issued between 303 and 312 that imposed public cultic sacrifice on all. Eusebius, bishop of Caesarea, recorded at length (in a volume called *Martyrs of Palestine*) the lives, and especially the trials, of Christians who were executed, banished, or sentenced to hard labor. This Christian ordeal, which according to Eusebius surpassed any similar event elsewhere in the empire, can be said with hindsight to have been a kind of sacrificial altar on which the land was presented to the Christians.[14] For the Jews, the internal tension that accompanied the persecutions may have added another dimension to the wobbly image of the state and to their sense of its approaching end, but they were to be disappointed. Rome did not collapse; it merely changed its appearance. Constantine, who during the years of the "Great Persecutions" was ruler of the western regions of the empire, quite dramatically issued an edict of toleration of the Christians under his control following the end of the persecutions (in 313).[15]

The embracing of Christianity by Constantine, who would 10 years later become the sole, unchallenged ruler of the empire, was to have a decisive influence on the political and religious character and culture of Palestine. The local rabbis, whose explicit reactions to this great transformation have not come down to us,[16] found some consolation in the change, and the form of their expectations of the approaching salvation adjusted to the new reality. The support of an official as important as Constantine foreshadowed the Christianization of the whole empire. Deep down, this was the historical and theological dilemma with which the rabbis contended: as Rome converted from paganism to Christianity, should they consider the Christian Empire a new entity, or simply a mutation of the old? If the latter, faithful to their own contention that redemption would come once the "empire shall fall into heresy" (Mishnah, Sotah 9, 15), then salvation was around the corner.[17] Therefore, this item in the description of the eschatological scheme of the "End of Days" was reformulated by a contemporary sage: "Rabbi Isaac said: Until the whole Empire is converted to the heresy" (BT Sanhedrin, 97a). By this textual emendation, not only was the estimated time of the End of Days postponed but, paradoxically, the Jews joined with the Christians in seeking to hasten the transformation, though from opposing motives. After all, prominent Church fathers (such as the Caesarean Origen) also believed that salvation would come about only as a consequence of the spread of the Christian faith among all the nations of the world.[18]

The Christianization of the empire presented Constantine with an extraordinary opportunity to harness the imperial system, which had already undergone some changes, in the service of a universal religion possessing a heritage, authority, and a well-established missionary apparatus. In the eyes of the Jews, this radical change apparently symbolized the transition of Rome from a nation and a rule that, though it placed a heavy yoke on the Jews, nevertheless tolerated them as a nation, to one that was the utterly polar opposite to Judaism.[19] The new situation also altered the dimensions and fundamental assumptions of contemporary Christian apologetics and polemics. For instance, Bishop Eusebius went to great lengths, utilizing much theological ingenuity, to define the Church's attitude toward the Jewish nation.[20] The rabbis must have seen the hostile relations between Caesarea (the seat of the Roman governor and thus a symbol of Rome itself) and Jerusalem as beyond reconciliation. They described both centers as though they could not endure under one roof: "That Caesarea is laid waste and Jerusalem flourishing, or that Jerusalem is laid waste and Caesarea flourishing, believe it" (BT Megillah, 6a).

A quick deliverance from the yoke of Christian Rome was, as we have seen from Rabbi Isaac's saying, an aspiration for the future. A similar sentiment was voiced by the renowned fourth-century Babylonian sage Rava, who adopted the terminology of the biblical laws concerning leprosy and applied it, metaphorically and suggestively, to the current state of affairs: "That is the meaning of the verse, He has turned all white" (Leviticus 13:13; BT Sanhedrin, 97a). Rava compared heresy to leprosy this way: just as when leprosy has completed its spread throughout the body, then—quite paradoxically—it is healed and is ready to be purified, so too when heresy (i.e., Christianity) has completed its takeover of the empire, then the time of Redemption will finally come.

It was apparently no coincidence that this simile was used in another rabbinical tradition. Famous among the stories that sprouted up around the figure of Constantine, this one described the legendary circumstances of his conversion: While the Christians were being hounded to death and Sylvester, Bishop of Rome, had gone into exile, Constantine became severely afflicted with leprosy. His physicians and other savants having failed to find a cure for his illness, priests of the Capitoline temple in Rome proposed that he come to them and immerse his body in the blood of infants. Constantine, horrified by this notion, stopped his chariot on the way to the temple and addressed the masses, resolutely declaring that it was unfitting for a warrior such as himself to be healed by such means. He immediately commanded that the babies that had already been brought to the temple be returned to their mothers. That very night the patron saints of Rome, Peter and Paul, appeared to Constantine in his dream and promised him salvation and healing by means of the immersion (i.e., baptism) that the exiled Sylvester would conduct for him; and so it happened. Cured of leprosy, Constantine tied his destiny to that of the Church and promulgated decrees for its benefit.[21] The following midrash seems to allude to the same story:

> For this reason it was said, When a person has on the skin of his body a swelling, a rash, or a discoloration, and it develops into a scaly infection on the skin of his body; and so forth (Leviticus 13:2). The text speaks of [four] kingdoms. A swelling is Babylon . . . a rash is the kingdom of the Medes . . . a discoloration is the kingdom of Greece . . . a scaly infection is the kingdom of evil, Edom [Rome], that the Holy One Blessed Be He afflicts with leprosy, and likewise its prince [the emperor]. (Midrash Tanhuma, Tazri'a, 11)

Shortly after Constantine gained control over the whole empire in 324, he began to put into practice his plan to appropriate Palestine for the Christians. From that time on, relations between the Jews and Christian Rome and its official Church were much determined by their opposing eschatologies. This was nowhere more apparent than in Palestine, the land that harbored their mutual collective memories of their formative history, and yet was to be the venue of their contradictory scenarios of the "End of Days."

GALILEE AND JUDAEA: CENTER AND PERIPHERY

By the 320s, when Constantine began to implement his plan to make the "Holy Land" Christian, the Galilee was densely inhabited by those Jews who rejected the Gospel. Eusebius and his contemporaries, who were the driving force behind the changes taking place in Palestine, were probably quite disappointed that they were, so to speak, "effectively expelled from the Galilee, the homeland of their Lord."[22] By the late third century, the Galilee had been well established as the "new Judaea," and its inhabitants began to form what seems to have been a regional Jewish identity. By weaving expressions concerning place and time into an extensive fabric, the Galilean Jews created their own local, mythic-historic past, importing many biblical narrative traditions from other parts of the land. For instance, they identified the spot where the Children of Israel crossed the Jordan not near Jericho but in a place not far from the Lake of Genesereth, and they transferred the tomb of Joshua from the region of Samaria to a location in the Lower Galilee. Through such transferals of personages, tombs, and events, the Galilean Jews sought to challenge the new, unwelcome inheritors of the land.[23] Hence it is not surprising that those who molded the sacred traditions of Christianity transferred narratives connected to Jesus from the Galilee to the terrain of Judaea and Jerusalem and downplayed the importance of other Galilean sites. Nor is it surprising that in some Jewish polemics of the same period we find the Passion of Jesus set not in Jerusalem but in Tiberias,[24] or that in Jewish apocalyptic literature we are told that the early signs and initial activities of the coming messiah will also take place in the Galilee.[25] The Christians who successfully appropriated Judaea and other areas still found it difficult, through most of the Byzantine era, to penetrate the region that had been the site of their Savior's initial success. Each side, in drawing a sort of demarcation line between them, essentially sought to claim that its own share of the land represented the whole—*pars pro toto*.

This kind of historical revisionism tells us much about the psychological framework in which Palestinian Jewish culture evolved between the fourth and seventh centuries. But this evolution did not occur in an environment dominated solely by the Christian-Jewish encounter. Rather, it bears the marks of a wider interaction with late Hellenistic culture. As Eric Meyers shows in the preceding chapter, the elaborate mosaics discovered in Sepphoris—one showing Dionysus[26] and another depicting the pagan Nile festival—are significant signs of this interaction, although the houses in which these mosaics were found have not been identified as having belonged to Jews. Other evidence is even more de-

finitive of cross-cultural influence between Hellenistic and Jewish culture. Archaeologists have found the portrait of Siren tempting Odysseus in the house of
a Jew named Leontius who lived in Scythopolis (Bet She'an). And the representation of the sun god Helios that we encountered at the beginning of this chapter, in the central panel of a Tiberias synagogue, shows that such influences were
not limited to the private sphere. The meaning and significance of these mosaics
have been evaluated in several ways[27] as evidence of an internalization of influences with various degrees of compromise, or as a sign of a diffused "realm of
culture."[28] But in either case, Jews, like Christians of the time, were part of a
wider Greco-Roman culture.

The Galilean cultural matrix was exceptional only in its intensity and duration, for there were similar encounters between Jews and other religious and
ethnic groups elsewhere in Palestine in towns such as Lydda (Diospolis), as well
as in the metropolis of Caesarea. In these centers the Jews were considerably outnumbered, though the surrounding areas were studded with small and medium-
sized Jewish communities.[29] In Caesarea, the city with the most mixed population
in Palestine, Samaritans, pagans, Christians, and an ever-increasing number of
Jews lived side by side in relations that fluctuated between reserved neighborliness and frequent friction. The city's cosmopolitan character had been shaped
by its position as an administrative and military center of Roman (and, later,
Byzantine) rule and as an important international port.[30] It was in Caesarea that
an almost unique social and religious fabric of life was woven among the different religions. Thus, in fourth-century Caesarea one could hear Jews—possibly
immigrants from the Diaspora—recite the *Shema* in Greek.[31] (This astonished
the sages; nevertheless, they accepted it.) And there one might come upon a Jew
who was a stagehand and maintenance man in the local theater.

The Christian intellectual elite of Palestine had established itself in Caesarea,
led by the Church father, preacher, and exegete Origen (d. ca. 253) and his successor Eusebius (d. 339), the most prominent bishop of his day. Rabbi Abbahu of
Caesarea (d. ca. 300), who was acquainted with the Greek culture and language
(and may even have been fluent in it), provided his daughters with a Greek education, and was a constant visitor to the home of the Roman governor, was extremely well suited to serve as the main Jewish spokesman in the developing
conflict between Judaism and Christianity. Like Origen, Abbahu understood
that at the heart of the conflict lay what was also the most important element
linking the two camps: the Bible. Abbahu declared to the *minim* (heretics; that
is, Judeo-Christians or gentile Christians) of his city that their neighbors, the
Jews, had the responsibility of studying the Bible in order to respond to their
arguments—just as, a few decades earlier, Origen had advised a friend to study

the Bible diligently so that he would be able to combat Jewish claims and interpretations.[32] Caesarea thus became an important outpost on the frontline of the
Jewish-Christian encounter.

Although the importance of Caesarea in Roman Palestine cannot be exaggerated, the fourth century saw a diminution of its status when the province was
subdivided into several smaller regions, each with its own administrative center.
Nonetheless, Caesarea continued to have an influential status in Palestine, and it
strove forcefully to preserve its primacy in Church administration against the
rising power of the bishopric of Jerusalem, which in the first half of the fifth century was declared a Christian patriarchate.[33]

Although Caesarea and Diospolis were outstanding centers of Torah study in
their own right, the threads of spiritual creativity woven in them were drawn to
and from the Galilee, where most of the religious literature—Talmud, midrash,
and apparently the wealth of early liturgical poetry too—took their final shape.
These works, most of which were compilations of earlier material (though some
were composed in this period) tell us nothing about their authors, and only
careful reading between the lines teaches us something about the circumstances
of their creation. Thus, without ignoring the important contribution of Caesarea and Diospolis, one can state that the Galilean intellectual elite was the driving force shaping Jewish culture in this period.

THE SON OF DAVID AND THE SONS OF AARON:
A TRANSITION IN LEADERSHIP

An important ingredient in the cultural identity of the Palestinian Jews was the
hereditary office of the patriarch. Perceived by Christians and, to a certain extent, by the Jews as something like a client king, he nevertheless was a respected
political figure with substantial communal functions and power, his authority
having been ratified in fourth-century imperial legislation.[34] We possess reports
that the patriarch was involved in administrative appointments made by the
secular authorities, and that he intervened in the affairs of the Diaspora communities. For a while his political influence was so great that at least once,
toward the end of the fourth century, a conflict between a patriarch named
Gamaliel VI and a senior Roman official led to the latter's execution.[35]

The patriarchs also served as religious and cultural figures, as is apparent
from the wide-ranging correspondence between Gamaliel V and the famous
fourth-century Antiochean orator Libanius.[36] However, by this period we witness signs of decline in the patriarchate.[37] At the beginning of the third century,
Rabbi Judah the Prince had been the uncontested leader of the laity as well as

of the intellectual elite (the sages), but during the fourth century the emperor himself had to forbid public displays of contempt of the patriarch.[38] The third-century patriarchs are known to us by their names and their deeds (which were not always approved of by some of the contemporary sages), but with those of the fourth century we are much less familiar. In fact, much of our information about them emanates from Christian sources that tended to denigrate them. But it has been suggested that the later patriarchs lacked the spiritual stature and the level of learning of their forerunners and gradually became alienated from the community, which they treated aloofly and haughtily.[39] As early as the beginning of the fourth century, matters had reached such a point that a prominent sage, Rabbi Jeremiah, sent a letter to the patriarch containing an especially insulting phrase: "To hate those who love you and to love those who hate you" (JT Megillah, 3:2b). Lurking in the background of this local contest of authority and prestige was another, between the head of the Babylonian Jewish center, the *Rosh Gola*, and the Palestinian patriarchate. As Isaiah Gafni argues in the next chapter, in the second half of the third century the rising center of Judaism in the East was claiming superiority over the Land of Israel in more than one sense. The Babylonian community's antique roots and its long and stable history—only a small portion of which has been preserved in the records—became a source of deep cultural "local patriotism." And when its leadership, too, claimed a Davidic pedigree, this thriving cultural and spiritual center asserted itself vigorously as an alternative to the one in Palestine.[40]

However, the more immediate interests of the patriarchate, especially during the fourth and early fifth centuries, concerned the Jews and their Christian opponents. The patriarch did serve his people as a sort of perpetual symbol of Jewish "sovereignty," especially in the Diaspora communities,[41] but this image, based on the notion that the patriarch was a descendant of the House of David, irritated Christians who could not tolerate another claimant to Christ's royal, messianic pedigree. A long stream of polemical statements defamed the image of the patriarchs and the patriarchal family, a wave of criticism that intensified during the fourth century.

Here is a story that illustrates this dispute and the methods adopted by the Christians to win it. About the year 375, the fanatical Church father Epiphanius of Salamis (in Cyprus), who had been raised in the vicinity of Eleutheropolis (Beth Govrin, in the southwestern area of Judaea), recorded a testimony that he had heard some two decades earlier from a Jew named Joseph, a confidant of the Jewish patriarch. Joseph, who subsequently converted to Christianity and became close with Emperor Constantine, was actually relating the story of his own life and the circumstances of his conversion, but he spun his tale around his intimate acquaintance with the patriarch. Among other things, he recounted the ailing patriarch's concealed conversion to Christianity, when he supposedly had secretly received the sign of Jesus (i.e., baptism) from the bishop of Tiberias. As if this were not enough, Joseph supplied Epiphanius with tales about the decadent lifestyle in the household of the patriarch, elaborating on the wretchedness of his sons "who acted like reckless good-for-nothings."[42] Epiphanius emphasized the patriarch's role in the leadership of the Jewish community (corroborated by other Christian and pagan writers), which only made more poignant his underlying message that those who accepted this tarnished leadership really deserved a new patron, the Church.

Although it is doubtful whether any of the Jews actively wanted to do away with the patriarchate, it is difficult to overlook the simultaneous eruption of criticism from within the community and the attack from without. Even given the meager historical value of the tales recounted by Epiphanius,[43] his "message" must have played a role in the battle of disinformation that was an attempt to abolish the institution. The portrayal of the patriarch's sons as unworthy to inherit the office, and the attempt by some other Church fathers to disprove the family's genealogical claim to it,[44] made a fitting backdrop to Joseph's libelous tale of the patriarch's alleged conversion.

However, from a literary point of view, the episode narrated by Epiphanius can be seen as a cultural duel, full of symbolism, between the "doomed" Jewish nation and the victorious Christian power.[45] Against the "inheritance of the flesh" that passed from father to son in the patriarchal family, the Christians proposed an "inheritance of the spirit."[46] The patriarchs symbolized the leadership of the vanishing past, and the Church symbolized that of the felicitous present and future. Not everyone, however, shared these polemical sentiments, because they led to a conflict of interest between the Church and the imperial authorities who desired to preserve the power and dignity of the patriarchate in order to monitor and control their relations with the Jewish community. But, though official policy lagged behind the wishes of the Church, it was not by much. The mounting pressure of venomous Christian propaganda, coupled with what the authorities deemed unlawful behavior by Patriarch Gamaliel VI, led in the autumn of 415 to the stripping of his honor and the curbing of his power.[47] (Ironically and perhaps as a sign of collapse of patriarchal power, this was the very Gamaliel who only a few years earlier had been able to orchestrate the execution of a Roman official.) By 429, the Roman authorities were alluding to the patriarchate as a thing of the past.

Nothing is known of the methods, composition, and character of the new leadership. However, if we may judge from contemporary inscriptions and later evidence, some vestige of the patriarchate was preserved, especially in matters having to do with the ties between the community in Palestine and those in the Diaspora. For example, the funerary inscription of the daughter of a sixth-century Jewish municipal leader in Venosa in southern Italy mentions the presence and eulogies of two emissaries and two sages ("Apostoles and Rebbites") from the Land of Israel.[48] As in the days of the patriarchs, these emissaries may have been sent to collect contributions (despite the legal limitations imposed by the authorities on fundraising at the end of the fourth century), but their primary objective was probably to guide the Diaspora communities in spiritual matters.

The demise of the patriarchate occurred around the time when Jewish literary activity in Palestine was in decline. The Jerusalem Talmud and the classical *Midrashei aggadah* (a compendium of exegetical and homiletic material on the Bible that also incorporated other legendary and folkloristic tales) were being redacted. Indeed, most of the canon of Jewish lore was completed at this time,[49] a development that led to a loss of status and prestige for the Palestinian centers of learning and their leaders. Thus, by the mid-fifth century, the historical role of the two leading elements of Jewish cultural and political life in Palestine seems to have come to an end. The creation of halakhic works did not entirely cease, but the format changed to compendia of rabbinical dicta such as the treatise known as *Sefer ha-Ma'asim* (The Book of Rulings).[50] This compilation, extensive sections of which have survived in the Cairo Genizah, reflects everyday life in Palestine during the sixth and seventh centuries. The tone of these dicta, which may have originated in the registers of the rabbinic court in Tiberias, is that of late Hellenistic culture, and they are suffused with the legal and economic terminology of their surroundings.

What we learn about the lives of women is especially fascinating; for example, "And it is forbidden for a woman to adorn her daughter and take her out to the marketplace because she is risking her life, and a woman who has perfumed herself and goes to [houses] of idol worship is to be flogged and her hair shaved off."[51] The rabbis' objective, the preservation of female modesty, was compatible with the demands Church leaders made of the Christians.[52] The Jews sought to adopt some of the practices of the surrounding society, because they were fearful of the social proximity between the groups. Indeed, questions that emerged in the wake of instances of conversion make up much of this collection of rabbinical rulings. It is tempting to envisage the compilation of this practical compendium and the earlier redaction of the Talmud as being something of a rabbinical equivalent of the codification of Church canonical and Byzantine imperial laws that was achieved during the fifth and sixth centuries.[53]

Thus, by the middle of the fifth century, the Jewish cultural elite was facing a substantial transformation. There are strong grounds to assume that the vacuum created by the decline of the patriarchal dynasty, and in some sense also of the rabbinical leadership, was being filled by another element that claimed an aristocratic lineage: the priestly caste. Although the priests' status had diminished since (and because of) the destruction of the Temple, they nonetheless represented the most significant era of the Jewish past, its cultic age, which every Jew prayed would return. As early as the Yavneh generation (ca. 100 C.E.) and for hundreds of years afterward, the priests sought to maintain their special status and influential position, at times in conflict with the sages, but more often with their homologous leaders, the patriarchs as well as with the Babylonian exilarchs. When the Palestinian patriarchate no longer existed, they were, it seems, presented with an opportunity to reenter the public sphere. Explicit hints of this major change have been preserved, surprisingly enough, in Christian writings. Time and again, fifth- and sixth-century Christian authors supply information about the leading priests in Tiberias. Thus, we learn that a man named Pinhas (a priestly appellation) from that city participated in a Christian assembly that convened in Alexandria in 552, as an expert on the calendar.[54] Elsewhere we read that priests sent by the Jewish authorities in Tiberias were involved in agitation against the Christians by the Judaizing Himyarite kingdom in southern Arabia (which will be discussed later in this chapter).[55] However, the most significant attestation comes from a series of anecdotes in a treatise composed in Carthage (ca. 634) by two Jewish converts to Christianity. The two, Jacob and Justin, who lived in Acare and Sycamina (near Haifa) and converted during the days of the Byzantine emperor Heraclius, describe priests as leading communal figures in places like Tiberias and Acco.[56] It is unlikely that such recent converts made faulty use of the term "priests" or were anachronistically reviving a concept from the biblical or post-biblical past. What sort of leadership did this priestly caste represent? Was it perceived by the community as a substitute for the patriarchate? Most probably not; however, our sources do not provide a clear answer.

PRIESTS, PREACHERS, AND SAGES: THE SYNAGOGUE VS. THE HOUSE OF STUDY

Although the reemergence of the priests was probably facilitated by the leadership void, it was more an effect of the relocation of the public center of gravity from the house of learning to the synagogue. The priests stood at the core of this transformation of Jewish communal life. With the disintegration of the traditional leadership, the synagogue remained the last element that could still serve

the Jews as a focus of attraction. A set of three imperial laws promulgated between the years 415 and 438 prohibited them from building or establishing new
synagogues. But a short while later, around 442, in Constantinople, the imperial
center of Christian rule, the Jewish community procured permission from the
local governor to build a synagogue in the copper market, not far from Hagia
Sophia. And though this building was confiscated a few years later by Pulcheria,
the sister of Emperor Theodosius II, who dedicated the edifice to Mary, this instance demonstrates just how strictly the law was obeyed.[57] However, archaeological research has revealed that, at least in Palestine, and especially in the
Galilee, these laws were defied and the construction of new synagogues actually
increased.[58]

In a flourishing synagogue culture, the priests played a major role, especially
in the formulation of the liturgy. It is in this period that a list of "priestly courses"
was drawn up which included the names of the various watches (divisions) that
had served in rotation in the Temple, and their places of residence (mostly in the
Galilee). Though historicity of this document is subject to doubt, its importance
is more symbolic than historical. The many early liturgical poems *(piyyutim)*
dealing with the list, the references to it in synagogue inscriptions in Palestine
and the Diaspora (in Yemen), and the custom of publicly recalling the watches
and their service every Sabbath in the synagogues reinforced the prestige of the
contemporary priests' lineage and antiquity.[59] The priests understood that, in
order to sustain the Jewish community and its spiritual assets in a hostile world,
they must mold that community's identity and foster it by forging a link to the
synagogue. They revived the saga of the priestly lineage of the Hasmonaean
kings. Synagogue ritual and liturgy reflected increasing messianic themes in
prayers that envisioned the approach of a new age in which the Temple would be
rebuilt and its cult reinstated.[60] Only the priests, who were historically the custodians of this cult, could lead this new liturgical synagogue ritual.

The description "A small city, that is a synagogue" (Ecclesiastes Rabbah 9:14)
signifies precisely the social and cultural atmosphere of this period. Synagogue
inscriptions that include the terms *kehillah* (community) and *kehillah* or *karta
kadishah* (holy community or village) illustrate this dictum.[61] In this new
context, the influence of the communal leaders, the congregational leaders
(archisynagogoi), the attendants (here called *ḥazanim*), and the priests increased
greatly, whereas the status of the sages, traditionally connected with halakhic
teachings and rulings, somewhat declined.[62] How did this transformation come
about?

Earlier we described the decline of the regional centers of learning and national institutions, and the decentralization of Jewish cultural and public life

that shifted the center of gravity from the cities (Tiberias, Sepphoris, Caesarea, and others) to the smaller towns and the rural areas.[63] The decentralization of communal life has registered, however faintly, in one of the most central elements of congregational life: the yearly calendar. In some communities, the local calendar was at variance with the one supervised by the rabbis.[64]

The flowering of the local communities centered on the synagogues. Despite the imperial ban mentioned earlier, the Jews were able to build and embellish their synagogues and make them centers of communal and cultural activity as well as worship.[65] For example, on the floor of the Ein Gedi synagogue (western shore of the Dead Sea), an Aramaic inscription cautioned the congregants against dissension and slanderous speech, and above all against the revelation of communal secrets to the gentiles.[66] Although synagogue premises were also used as houses of learning, they were, for the most part, not a locus of this traditional function of the rabbinical class. Christian sources describing synagogue activity do not mention the rabbis, and no rabbi known to us from the literary corpus is mentioned in any of the numerous synagogue inscriptions.[67] On the contrary, some rabbis seem to have disapproved of synagogue practices, and others stated

A votive inscription commemorating a certain R. Isi, a priest, for donating a mosaic floor for the Hurvat-Susiya (south of Hebron) synagogue.
(From *Qadmoniot*, Vol. 5, 1972, Israel Exploration Society, Jerusalem)

openly that they held the academy in higher regard. Thus, in the social and cultural matrix of Late Antiquity, the academy and the synagogue seem to have been distinct, even contradictory institutions, serving different social strata.[68] The vast repertory of synagogue inscriptions in the everyday languages of the people—Hebrew, Greek, and most frequently Aramaic—reflects a social world that is quite diverse and stratified, with great involvement of the prosperous and the influential. In one inscription we encounter Severianos Ephros, the highly praised archisynagogos of Tyre who settled in Sepphoris. In another, among the worshipers at the famous synagogue at Sardis in Asia Minor we find city councilors and procurators. Still other inscriptions disclose the trades and professions of members of the congregation—wood merchants in Gaza, *scholastikoi* (lawyers) in Sepphoris—and their financial means, revealed by their contributions to the synagogues.[69] As Eric Meyers has suggested in his chapter, there is even evidence in the inscriptions that women served as leaders of the synagogues. Scholars are still debating whether they held true leadership functions or were merely wealthy benefactors; it is also doubtful whether such women had any liturgical functions.

However, the growth of the synagogues may well have further weakened the social cohesion and solidarity between the different communities, especially those of the Babylonians, Alexandrians, Tyrians, and others who had returned to Palestine with a sense of common origin, established their own synagogues, and made little effort to integrate with the larger community.[70] It is possible that rudeness and arrogance directed at these immigrants (for example, the harsh statements of the rabbis concerning the Babylonians) contributed to their alienation.[71]

Communal worship in Palestine (particularly in the Galilee and its periphery) inspired great intellectual and spiritual works—the piyyutim (a term derived from the Greek word for poetry) and the homilies. Whatever the origin of the piyyut, or the historical circumstances surrounding the birth of this novel facet of Jewish spiritual culture,[72] these liturgical hymns were composed to accompany sections of the service and the order of reading the Pentateuch and accompanying chapters from the prophets,[73] and they shaped the nature of the synagogue ritual for generations to come.

Among the *paytanim* (liturgical poets) were quite a few priests, such as Yose ben Yose (perhaps the earliest of them all, though whether he actually was a priest has been questioned), Simeon ha-Kohen be-Rabi Megas, Yohanan ha-Kohen, and Pinhas ha-Kohen son of Jacob from Kifra (a suburb of Tiberias), nearly all of them Galileans.

The return of the priests to the cultural arena revived an old, esoteric, but la-

A Cairo Genizah fragment of a Jewish Palestinian Mahzor (a festival prayer book)
from c. early tenth century C.E. This particular text is a liturgical poem lamenting
the contemporary status of the priesthood due to the ruination of the Temple.
(Bodleian Library, University of Oxford; MS Heb. d.41 fol. 1-42714/1)

tent trend in Jewish thought: the mystical speculations expressed in the Hekhalot literature.[74] This priestly mystical literature has strong echoes of the Dead
Sea scrolls from nearly half a millennium earlier.[75] The paytanim lamented that
the status of the priesthood was lowly because the Temple was still in ruins, and
they expressed profound yearning for its reconstruction. Long works were com-

posed on the high priest's rite in the Temple on Yom Kippur. Indeed, the poet-s'interest in such subjects did not derive only from their need to remind the public of the prestige of the priesthood. Rather, it seems that they intended to arouse and express intense messianic expectations that were reinforced by the increase in apocalyptic predictions among their contemporaries, most notably from the fifth century on.

Preoccupation with the oppressive subjugation of the Christian world and concern with the approaching redemption were not limited to a few individuals. The poets expressed the deepest, most existential aspirations of the entire community of worshipers; moreover, the rise of Jewish liturgical poetry and the significant role of salvationist themes within it were paralleled in time, and perhaps even in content, by a similar process among Christians. From the second half of the fourth century, major transformations were wrought in the Christian religious rites, changes in which the Jerusalem Church played a decisive role. During the fifth century, especially in its latter years, anxious Christians aroused by millennial anxiety were also awaiting the approaching Salvation. There are signs that these phenomena, occurring within both the Jewish and the Christian folds, were connected in some way, inspiring mutual agitation; however, such a conclusion necessitates further study.[76]

The fact that piyyutim were accepted and integrated into the established liturgy with little opposition indicates that we are dealing with works suitable for all. These works were certainly complex, embracing various cultural tastes, but apparently they were also accessible to the general public's level of knowledge and understanding. However, this body of work, composed in a variety of languages (Hebrew for liturgical purposes, Aramaic for joyous occasions and eulogies, with touches of Greek), doubtless reflected to some extent the gap between the lofty style of the elite and the more common taste and proficiency of the populace.[77]

The liturgical poets had important partners in the process of transforming the synagogue into a central institution of Jewish society in Palestine as well as in the Diaspora. These were the translators (from Hebrew to Aramaic) and the preachers. Both accompanied the three-year cycle of readings from the Torah. (Some scholars contend that a one-year cycle also existed in Palestine, and consider it to be a more ancient one that for some reason has become fixed in people's minds as a Babylonian custom.) Translations into the Aramaic vernacular, which was first used in services during the Second Temple period (as is demonstrated in both the New Testament and rabbinic writings),[78] accompanied the public readings from the Torah, a verse or two or three at a time, and provided explanation and clarification by incorporating midrashic material as well as popular lore and customs.[79] The rabbis established the manner in which the translator was to carry out his task, seeking to prevent his art from overshadowing the reading itself; but he became part of the regular, paid staff of the synagogue. The narrator mediated between the biblical text and its "consumers," the congregants, who came from many social strata.

However, the full integration of the biblical text with the public celebration of the holidays (Sabbaths, festivals, days of atonement and mourning) was achieved by means of the public sermon. This custom, too, was an ancient one, going back to the Second Temple period.[80] At the end of the third century, there was an about-face in the sages' attitude toward synagogue sermons and those who prepared and delivered them. It is difficult to know what caused this turnabout and whether or not it was connected to the decline in creativity in the academy. According to at least one tradition, the growing stature of the sermon was an outcome of the unique, social needs of the public as it experienced increasing distress. Thus, for example, Rabbi Isaac said: "Formerly, when a man possessed a *prutah* [small coin], he yearned to hear passages from the Mishnah and the Talmud, and now when he does not have a prutah, and especially when we are sick of [being oppressed by] the government, a man longs to hear words from the Bible and the Aggadah."[81] However, we must distinguish between scholarly sermons and addresses whose place was in the house of study[82] and the homilies that were delivered in the synagogue in the presence of tanners, filigree makers, women, and infants, a distinction that has some bearing on the dissimilarity we have described between the synagogue and the House of Study *(bet midrash)*.[83] Scholars have recently concluded that, though many anecdotes are scattered through the Talmud and the aggadic literature concerning the delivery of sermons in public (that is, to the community), these sermons were in fact expounded to students in the houses of study.[84] They were learned and elitist in content and vocabulary, and were generally not understood by the ordinary public, although there is some evidence that at times members of the multitude did also flock to the houses of study.[85] It stands to reason, however, that the sages fostered an exalted image of the lessons taught in the bet midrash while they disparaged the synagogue preachers for being able to attract a larger audience. The popular sermons were delivered in the synagogue as an exposition of and elaboration upon the cycle of biblical recitations (along with their rendering into Aramaic) as part of the liturgical rite. The topics discussed in the sermons addressed the immediate issues that weighed upon the community, and, as in the liturgical poems, the vocabulary was adapted to suit the hearers. When matters of Jewish law were part of the sermons, they were presented clearly so as not to mislead the listeners.[86]

Enjoyment of the sermon and adherence to its message depended on the preacher's merits, the content of his address, and the manner in which it was delivered. His strength lay in his ability to fascinate his audience and give it not only a moral lesson but entertainment and aesthetic pleasure as well. Allegories, tales, expositions, and narratives done up in a wealth of rhetorical devices imbued his talk with beauty and helped to draw the public's attention, to the point that the rabbis compared these sermons to the Roman theater or circus, praising the Jews who attended the former and avoided the latter.[87] These rhetorical devices did fall short of the perfected art of classical civilization, and it is doubtful whether even those aggadic scholars who were exposed to Greek culture were familiar with the rhetorical manuals compiled by Menander of Laodicea or Quintilianus.[88] However, the public sermon served to bind and sustain the community and was a tool of the first order for persuasion, or illustrating a point. If we are to judge by the sarcastic comments of the Church Father Jerome, the preachers did their work well, since "they succeed through theatrical means in causing their listeners to believe in the fictions that they invent."[89]

The third element in the public liturgical framework was the work of the artists who decorated the synagogues with wall paintings or mosaics. These decorative elements first appeared in synagogues during the third and fourth centuries and, as Eric Meyers has shown in his chapter, even enjoyed the sanction of the sages, or at least a tacit approval that may have stemmed from a growing acceptance of the importance of such ornamentation as a liturgical tool. Synagogue architecture also changed at this time, especially in the Galilee, where some of the later edifices (fifth to seventh centuries)—such as Beit Alpha and Sepphoris and others noted for their elaborate internal decorations—showed the influence of the Byzantine basilica style.[90] Forerunners of the embellished interior were also to be found in Diaspora communities, such as in the third-century synagogue in Dura Europos, on the Euphrates.

The decoration of the synagogue was intended to be a visual narration of the biblical stories and at times to represent the thoughts and allusions of the preachers. A comment by the Church Father Gregory of Nyssa (second half of the fourth century) can well be applied to synagogue floor mosaics. Referring to the Church of Theodore the Martyr, Gregory wrote: "The hues of the ornamentation in the church are veritably like a book that speaks, for painting even if silent knows how to speak from the wall."[91] The biblical scenes, the complex symbols, and their interrelationship required from the observer a considerable intellectual effort, though here too we are dealing not with an elitist work but with one that, like the piyyut and the sermon, was adapted to the taste and ability of the observer.

Indeed, a great deal of effort went into the decoration of the synagogues. The stunning mosaic floors offered an abundance of decorations and symbols, some of them clearly Jewish (candelabra, shovels for incense burning, the four species of plants shown on Sukkot to represent the harvest in the Land of Israel, and the ram's horn) and biblical (especially the Binding of Isaac), and others distinctly non-Jewish (the zodiac, Helios, and representations of the four seasons). Scholars may differ on the nature and interpretation of this amalgamation of motifs; nonetheless, the synagogue was a faithful reflection of the cultural world in which it stood. It is no wonder that, in an atmosphere so redolent of syncretism, the Jews did not hesitate to adopt, for instance, the symbol of Helios, nor to turn toward it in prayer, as we see in the fourth-century *Sefer ha-Razim* (The Book of Secrets, a treatise on magic).[92]

The mosaic floor recently discovered at Sepphoris contains a wealth of biblical scenes and symbols, some unknown heretofore. Analysis of the individual panels and of the mosaic as a whole suggests that the unifying motif is God's promise to Abraham (in the Binding of Isaac) and the expected Redemption. This connection was made clear to those frequenting the synagogue by depicting the consecration of Aaron the Priest and the daily sacrificial offerings, the latter symbolizing the continuity of the ritual even in a time when actual sacrifices could not be carried out. Many sermons and piyyutim were heard in that synagogue on those very topics. By integrating what was heard and what was seen, the expectation of Redemption was instilled in those who entered the synagogue to pray.[93]

Salvation was linked, no doubt, to another motif: that of undisguised hostility toward the Sons of Esau, that is, Edom, the Empire of Heresy (i.e., Christianity) that ruled over the Jews. In the world of the sages, the polemic with the Church was conducted on an intellectual plane in a cultured manner, but in the emotionally charged atmosphere of the synagogue the dispute became rancorous. The poets set the tone, filling their work with expressions of scorn toward the Christian Savior, as in the words of the paytan Yannai: "Those who praise the *kilai sho'a*" ("generous miser"; also a play on the Hebrew name for Jesus and on the word for "salvation," *yeshu'a*). And they demanded of God, "Uproot the Empire of Dumah" (*Piyyutey Yannai* 11; again a play on words: Dumah = Edom, and perhaps also an allusion to Roma = Rome). (A Byzantine melody called "On Earthquakes and Fires," written by one Romanos, who lived in Constantinople, may have been a Christian reply to those aspirations. It mocked the ruins of the Temple of Solomon by contrasting them with the splendor of the Church of Hagia Sophia, which had also been damaged by Heaven with fire and earthquake, followed by local political upheaval known as the Nika ("victory")

revolt in 532 C.E., but had immediately been reconstructed.)[94] Despite these in-
sults, the synagogues, especially during the festivals, seem to have attracted not
only Jews but also Christians with Judaizing tendencies. In the late fourth century, the Church Father John Chrysostom bitterly attacked members of his congregation who attended synagogue services on Sabbath and other festivals.[95]

The similarities between the Jewish and Christian cultures in Palestine
extended even further. As the focal point of Jewish life shifted from the scholarly
elitism of the academy to the public arena of the synagogue, a parallel development occurred among the Christians, albeit in a different manner. Hesi-
tantly, and despite the open hostility of the zealots, the Christians adorned their
churches with handsome mosaic floors and frescoed walls.[96] By the fourth century, the churches echoed to orderly, well-executed liturgical ceremonies that
were based on selected readings from Holy Scripture and accompanied by sermons. Christian liturgy attained a significant level of refinement and was shaped
by the hallowed space in which the services were held, both inside the edifice and
outside it (in nearby holy sites). The Church authorities attempted to create a
nexus and harmony between the two kinds of space and to make the worshiper-
pilgrim feel as close as possible to the event being celebrated. Indeed, the Christian world was engaged increasingly in the sanctification of space,[97] a concept
made especially tangible in the Jerusalem liturgy that was developed in this pe-

A fresco from sixth-century Caesarea, depicting three Christian holy men
in a posture of prayer. (Israel Antiquities Authority, Jerusalem; no. 2000-803)

riod and was to influence decisively the liturgies of other Christian centers such as Antioch and Constantinople.[98]

While there was considerable innovation in ritual and ornamentation in the churches, when it came to sermons the Christian preachers had recourse to the traditional world of classical rhetoric. Although they would never admit it, their writings demonstrate that they internalized the devices but avoided the pomposity, because the public welfare required that the sermon suit the audience. Origen, the famous third-century presbyter of Caesarea, saw the high priest's service in the Temple—slaughtering the sacrificial animal, flaying it, separating its organs, and sacrificing them—as a kind of paradigm of the task of the preacher, who stripped the text of its attire and divided it into its several meanings (from the plain and simple to the allegorical).[99] If the preachers took care to follow this procedure, the worshippers who heard his sermon would be able to savor the scriptural texts. Fourth-century Church fathers such as Jerome and John Chrysostom repeatedly advised the preachers to take into account the narrow minds and shallow knowledge of their listeners, and to deliver their sermons calmly and logically, not loudly or hastily.[100]

The centrality of the rules of rhetoric to Christian public discourse was clearly expressed in pictorial art, both in choice of subject matter and in the location of works of art within the church space. In this place of public assembly, it was especially important to combine all the components of the discourse described above into a unified setting. Thus, in Christian society too the house of worship became the religious center of attention,[101] part of a remarkable trend toward the democratization of public and religious life. John Chrysostom asked: "Did you know of such a burning desire to hear sermons among our Christian contemporaries?"[102]—one more indication of the increasing involvement of the simple masses in shaping the spiritual environment. In church, Christian men and women absorbed the principles of their faith and fostered and refined their emotional world. But they were also exposed in sermons and prayers to propaganda and vicious attacks on the enemies of the Church, among whom the Jews occupied a special place.

Thus, the Church and the Synagogue faced one another, each struggling to preserve its identity, each rejecting the other. From the early fourth century the Church had enjoyed the advantage of imperial sponsorship, and by the middle of the sixth century the authorities were intervening harshly in synagogue affairs. In 553 Emperor Justinian issued a decree that was intended to redirect the contents of study and ritual activity. Study of the Mishnah (*Deuterosis*) was forbidden, and readers of the Bible in Greek were specifically obliged to use the Septuagint or the Aquila translation. This was part of the emperor's campaign to bring the Jews "to the prophecies contained in [the Holy Books] through which they will announce the great God and the Savior of the human race, Jesus the Christ."[103] If further proof were needed of the vitality of the synagogue and its centrality to Jewish culture in this period, this blunt attack on the institution would convince us. The monitoring of the synagogues is emblematic of the disintegration of the Jewish community, whose other traditional institutions and authority systems were, as we have seen, in decline. The end of the Palestinian hegemony approached while the Babylonian center arose that was to govern Jewish society for centuries to come.[104]

The author of an early-ninth-century pamphlet known as "The Epistle of Pirkoi ben Baboi" describes from a Babylonian perspective the cultural and spiritual bankruptcy of the Palestinian Jewish community in the period under Christian rule:

> Thus, said Mar Yehudai [one of the most important of the early *geonim*] of blessed memory: religious persecution was decreed upon the Jews of the Land of Israel—that they should not recite the *Shema* and should not pray, because the practice of renouncing religion is what evil Edom [Rome, Byzantium] decreed, religious persecution against the Land of Israel that they should not read the Torah, and they hid away all the Torah scrolls because they would burn them and when the Ishmaelites [Muslims] came they had no Torah scrolls and they had no scribes [to copy scrolls] who knew the pertinent laws for doing [this]. . . and up till now they carry on like this. . . . But in Babylon Torah [study] has not ceased among Israel . . . and the Evil Empire [i.e. Rome] did not rule over Babylon . . . and two *yeshivot* have not forgotten the Oral Law nor the law to be practiced from ages ago until now.[105]

Was Pirkoi referring, among other things, to Justinian's draconian law? We cannot know. However, if what he wrote had any basis in reality, it reflected a very grim picture of Torah study or the forms of halakhic decision making in Palestine, and more so of the faulty customs surrounding the liturgy and prayer in its synagogues. Pirkoi's categorical assertions regarding the wretched spiritual condition of the Palestinian Jews were part of the long-standing rejection of the ancient center of Jewish culture in the Land of Israel by the young, proud Babylonian center. Pirkoi's readers were highly receptive to such remarks, which signify the transition from one cultural center to another and the passage into a new age in the history of the nation.

BABYLON'S ASCENDANCE TO DOMINANCE, AND OTHER COMMUNITIES OF THE DIASPORA

As Gafni discusses in the next chapter, everything that the Jews of Palestine wished for was already enjoyed by their brethren in Babylon: benevolent treatment, on the whole, by the Sassanian state; a recognized leadership, centralized and vigorous, in the form of the exilarchate; a diverse and creative world of Torah study; and economic security. All they lacked was a unique status and prestige in the network of Jewish centers in the Diaspora. The Babylonian was the earliest of the Diaspora centers and had long existed in a truly stable manner. But this did not suffice as long as the center in Palestine survived.

The Babylonian Jews' struggle to achieve political and cultural ascendancy constituted only one part of the Jewish cultural scene of this period. While the Babylonians were promoting their own interests and image, the influence of the Palestinian center was still strong in other Mediterranean communities such as Antioch, Constantinople, and those in Egypt (mainly the one in Alexandria) and Rome.

The level of cultural and religious contact between Egypt and Palestine is indicated by a marriage contract from Antonopolis dated 417, in Aramaic and Greek (written in Hebrew letters and according to the Palestinian marriage ordinances), and by a series of questions posed to the Palestinian center by the Alexandrian Jews. The appearance of Hebrew on other papyri of this period is surprising; however, it does not mean that a full-scale retreat from the Greek language and culture in favor of Hebrew was under way. It is safer to postulate the existence of a lively cultural diversity among the Egyptian communities.

The Christian onslaught on the pagans (toward the end of the fourth century) left the Jews as the only strong oppositional minority in Alexandria. The tension between Jews and Christians reached its peak during the riots of 414–15, in the course of which the synagogues were destroyed and the Jews were, for a limited time, expelled from the city, which was followed by a wave of conversions. The ongoing animosity led to the compilation of a set of treatises, *Contra Judeos*, formatted as dialogues between representatives of the two faiths. Although it is difficult to know to what extent these dialogues represent "face-to-face" confrontations, they do on the whole reflect contemporary notions and anxieties in both camps. Notwithstanding the tense atmosphere in Alexandria, in general the Jews of Egypt maintained social and cultural contacts with their surroundings.[106] Indeed, such inter-religious and communal relations, together with the links with the Palestinian center, determined the culture of most of the Jewish communities of the Mediterranean basin.

The extent to which the Palestinian center influenced the Italian Jews is unknown, though evocative funerary and synagogue inscriptions have been found
in several locations. Few and scattered though they are, apart from attesting to
the strict observation of the Jewish calendar and the occasional visit of "apos-
toloi" (emissaries from Palestine), these inscriptions "tend to confirm the importance of the study of the Law, the gradual revival of Hebrew, and the coming
into currency of the term 'rabbi.' "[107] Yet the Jews of Rome, like those of Alexandria, exhibit a clear pattern of interaction with non-Jews. In the remnants of artifacts and catacombs from third- to fifth-century Rome, we see ornamentation
and iconography that display a shared workshop identity with the local pagan
and Christian cultures as well as distinct, unmistakable expressions of Jewish
identity. Indeed, the *Collatio Legum Moisacarum et Romanarum*, a systematic
comparison of Mosaic and Roman law probably produced by a Roman Jew
toward the end of the fourth century, has the same characteristics. Its author intended it "to stress the great age of the Mosaic Law and emphasize its essential
conformity to the legal system of other, non-Jewish peoples."[108]

During the early Middle Ages, Italian Jews remained on the receiving end of
the spiritual and cultural heritage of the Palestinian Jewish center. The surviving
works of the gaonic period indicate that this influence was most apparent in the
areas of liturgical poetry and synagogue ritual. But the Italian link with Palestine
was not exclusive, for ties with the Babylonian center were formed as well.[109]

AN AGE OF TRANSITION: EMPIRES IN CONFLICT

In the year when the King-Messiah is revealed, all the kings of the
nations of the world will challenge each other.
—PESIKTA RABBATI, QUMI ORI, 36

Although the splendor of the Land of Israel had faded somewhat for the Jews,
the gentiles now turned their attention to it. The sixth and early seventh centuries were a stormy period for the Jews of Palestine, an age imbued with apocalyptic expectations, when ruling empires changed position and the people heard
tidings of Redemption.

Did the Jews take advantage of this volatile situation? They seem to have been
quite proactive, taking part in bloody skirmishes with the Byzantine authorities
that had been initiated by the Samaritans, and getting involved in or perhaps (as
some Christian sources would have us believe) themselves initiating a political-
religious conflict far from the borders of Palestine, in the land of the Himyarites
in the southern Arabian peninsula. Were these actions merely the attempts of an

oppressed people to avenge itself against the ruling power, or was there more to them? Let us look more closely at the events in Himyar.

Although the focus of the conflict was Himyar, its reverberations were felt far away, in the capitals of Persia and Byzantium. At that time, in the 520s, the influence of the Jewish presence around the southern shores of the Red Sea and along its important trade routes was felt—according to Christian sources—in the conversion to Judaism of the Himyarite king, Joseph Dhū Nuwās. Contemporary documents ascribe to emissaries of the priests of Tiberias a significant role in the affair. Were it not for the important location of Himyar, on the southern shores of the Red Sea very near the trade routes to the kingdom of Axum (Abyssinia, which had only recently been Christianized), and if Dhū Nuwās had not begun to persecute the Christian communities in his kingdom and in the area to the north, in the city of Najran, it is doubtful whether this episode would have attracted so much attention. One Christian author even claimed that Joseph's pretext in instigating this persecution against the local Christians was to alleviate the empire's pressure on its Jews. But the conflict in Himyar ended with the defeat of King Joseph by a unified Byzantine camp consisting of the joint forces of Justin I and the Axumite king.[110] According to a later, perhaps legendary tale, at this very time a sage from Babylon named Mar Zutra was appointed head of the local academy in Palestine. This Mar Zutra was the only son of the exilarch, also named Mar Zutra, who had been executed by the Persians toward the end of the fifth century, after an uprising that reached its climax with the creation of an autonomous Jewish territory.[111] Did the appearance of a new scion of the House of David in Palestine infuse the events in Babylon and Himyar with messianic overtones? Did the Jews of Palestine seek to restore past glory by replanting an offshoot of the stock of Jesse in their midst? At first sight this seems very doubtful, until we recall the cultural climate in the synagogues of Palestine, an atmosphere of mounting enmity toward Rome and Christianity. Political unrest and other signs of the empire's coming collapse fanned messianic hopes among the Jews. These lines by Yannai, a poet whom we have already encountered, are a sample of the vigor with which this "public campaign" was conducted:

May it be reported of Edom [Rome] as it was reported of Egypt
The vision of Dumah like the vision of Egypt
Receiving retribution from Pathros [Upper Egypt], at the end of a tenth plague
And a tenth horn shall utterly settle accounts with Edom.[112]

Apocalyptic expectations, which would later emerge in a form of "End of Days" literature, were thus to color much of the Jewish culture of this region until the Arab conquest in the seventh century.

The death of Emperor Justinian in 565 foretold the approaching end of Byzantine rule in Palestine. The ticking of the apocalyptic clock became much louder. Growing tensions between the Sassanian kingdom and Byzantium gave new meaning to the rabbinic saying that Rome would be brought down by the hands of the Persians, because it was the Persians who initiated the building of the Second Temple, which the Romans had destroyed.[113] This ancient belief was to be realized in the early decades of the seventh century.

Messianic fervor intensifies in times of political, social, and religious instability, of which violence is an important ingredient. One of the characteristics of this age was increasing violence, in which the Jews had a share. Jewish people enjoyed going to the theater and to gladiatorial fights, circuses, and chariot races, activities that were criticized by both the rabbis and the Church fathers. The races inspired riotous factional rivalries between the charioteers' ardent partisans, *iuvenes* (youngsters) with "Hunnic" hairstyles, beards, mustaches, and special garments. This tumultuous atmosphere did not deter the Jews. In Alexandria, Antioch, and Constantinople, they not only attended the spectacles but on many occasions also joined the melee. The riots had religious and political overtones, and more than once they resulted in the looting and the burning down of a synagogue or the destruction of a church.[114] At the turn of the sixth century, factional rivalry was an important factor in the strife that swept the East and contributed to the downfall of two successive Byzantine emperors, Maurice and Phocas, and to the accession of a third, Heraclius. We may plausibly tie some of this spell of violence to the growing apocalyptic fervor among the Jews.

A converted Jew named Jacob attested to these hopes. While describing an encounter in Acre that he witnessed in his youth during the reign of Emperor Maurice (582–602), Jacob told of "a priest from Tiberias" who had a vision that the Messiah, King of Israel, would come at the end of eight years.[115] If the Tiberian indeed saw this vision toward the end of Maurice's reign, then its "fulfillment" would have begun in 611 with the conquest of Antioch by the Sassanian army. We may assume from this story that messianic fervor had not waned among the Galilean Jews, who played an important role during the Persian invasion of Palestine. According to Christian sources, the Jews joined forces with the Persians who invaded the country through eastern Galilee. The line of advance passed through lower Galilee to Caesarea and Jerusalem, where the Persians slaughtered many Christians, apparently with the Jews' help. The taking of Jerusalem, the crowning achievement of the campaign, was viewed by the Jews in redemptionist terms. The many apocalyptic treatises compiled at this time reflected, no doubt, contemporary anxieties and widely held expectations.[116] This literature had much to do with the writings known as the Hekhalot and Merkavah, which describe mystical journeys to the heavenly palaces and give esoteric explanations of the divine chariot in the biblical Book of Ezekiel, and which some scholars maintain was contemporaneous.[117] The author of the apocalyptic Book of Zerubbabel wrote: "All the children of Israel will see the Lord like a man of war with a helmet of salvation on His head. . . . He will do battle against the forces of Armilus [an epithet for the king of Rome, the Antichrist] and they will all fall dead in the Valley of Arbael."[118] Here again we see the array of mythic traditions that the Galileans had formed about their region.

The reconquest of Palestine by the Byzantine emperor Heraclius in 630, a conquest that had messianic connotations for the Christians (restoration of the True Cross to Jerusalem from its Persian captivity, and a campaign of persecution against the Jews), intensified the Jews' sense of the approach of the End of Days. And when the Muslims appeared in Palestine four years later, a liturgical poet recalled the apocalyptic vision of Zerubbabel:

[The kings from the land of] Edom will be no more
And the people of Antioch will rebel and make peace
And Ma'uziya [Tiberias] and Samaria will be consoled
And Acre and the Galilee will be shown mercy
Edomites and Ishmael will fight in the Valley of Acre.[119]

The Arab conquest, which at first was deemed by the Jews to be a stage in the divinely determined redemption, soon appeared to be yet another yoke.[120] In these dismaying circumstances, the words of this anonymous poet may have been of some comfort: "The Messiah will emerge in dignity like the sun rising in strength." In this light, when a worshiper entered a synagogue and encountered the seemingly pagan image of *Sol Invictus* (the Sun Triumphant), exemplifying the figure of the Redeemer, it must have served as the ultimate consolation and promise for the victory of the Jews over their opponents.

NOTES

1. One ought obviously to place some limitations on the interpretation of Jewish art from that period. On the considerations involved in this process, see the most comprehensive study yet of the Jewish synagogue: Lee I. Levine, *The Ancient Synagogue: The First Thousand Years* (New Haven, Conn., 2000), 569–79.

2. The patriarch's influence and control was apparent mostly among the Diaspora Jews; see S. Shwartz, "The Patriarchs and the Diaspora," *Journal of Jewish Studies* 50 (1999): 208–22.

3. For a comprehensive survey on the history of the Jews in Palestine during the period under discussion, see M. Avi-Yonah, *The Jews of Palestine: A Political History from the Bar Kokhba War to the Arab Conquest* (Oxford, 1976). However, see also G. Stemberger, *Jews and Christians in the Holy Land: Palestine in the Fourth Century* (Edinburgh, 2000). Stemberger's study, though covering only the initial part of the period, offers many new insights.

4. See Robert L. Wilken, *The Land Called Holy: Palestine in Christian History and Thought* (New Haven, Conn., 1992).

5. Cairo Genizah fragment, *Cambridge, Taylor-Schechter,* H 6.38.

6. A recent treatment of Constantine's political policies and cultural endeavors has been offered by H. A. Drake, *Constantine and the Bishops: The Politics of Intolerance* (Baltimore, Md., 2000).

7. On the third-century "crisis" and its different dimensions, see David S. Potter, *Prophecy and History in the Crisis of the Roman Empire: A Historical Commentary on the Thirteenth Book of the Sibylline Oracle* (Oxford, 1990), 3–69. For a more toned-down view, see A. Watson, *Aurelian and the Third Century* (London, 1999), 1–38.

8. See O. Irshai, "Dating the Eschaton: Jewish and Christian Apocalyptic Calculations in Late Antiquity," in Albert I. Baumgarten, ed., *Apocalyptic Time* (Leiden, 2000), 113 ff., esp. 135–39.

9. See *Historia Augusta, Carus, Carinus and Numerian,* 13 ff.

10. *Genesis Rabbah* 83:4: "A vision appeared to R. Ammi in a dream. Today Magdiel has become king, said he [R. Ammi]: Yet one more king is required for Edom [i.e., Rome]." On this midrash, see D. Sperber's attractive interpretation, "Aluf Magdiel: Diocletian," in his *Magic and Folklore in Rabbinic Literature* (Ramat Gan, 1994), 127–30. Compare this to a contradictory, extremely confident mood concerning Diocletian's achievements reflected in a Latin dedicatory inscription from Heliopolis in Syria, describing him as "the liberator of the Roman World, the bravest and most dutiful and most unconquered," *Inscriptions grecques et latines de La Syrie* 6, no. 2771.

11. See T. D. Barnes, *The New Empire of Diocletian and Constantine* (Cambridge, Mass., 1982), 213–15.

12. See J. H. W. G. Liebeschuetz, *Continuity and Change in Roman Religion* (Oxford, 1979), 242–44, and G. Fowden, *Empire to Commonwealth: Consequences of Monotheism in Late Antiquity* (Princeton, N.J., 1993), 53–54.

13. In recent years, scholars have made it quite clear that the path leading to the success of Christianity in the fourth century was laid by third-century Roman emperors who reformed state religion, unified it, and granted it a "monotheistic" aura. Such was the case in Aurelian's cult of Sol, the Sun, a decade prior to Diocletian's accession, and was most probably the case already in Decius's day, when persecution of the Christians was conducted under the notion that Roman religion was evolving into a universal organism; thus, compliance with decrees relating to it was a declaration of membership in the Roman Empire and adherence to the imperial religion. See, e.g., J. B. Rives, "The Decree of Decius and the Reli-

gion of Empire," *Journal of Roman Studies* 89 (1999): 135–54. If accepted, this reconstruction alters significantly the prevailing theory dating the cultural change to Constantine's day and attributing it much to his own efforts. According to the new evaluation, Christianity's triumph had begun as early as circa 250 C.E. See, e.g., T. D. Barnes, "Constantine and Christianity: Ancient Evidence and Modern Interpretations," *Zeitschrift für Antike und Christentum* 2 (1998): 274–94.

14. The driving force behind the creation of the matrix of sacred space in the new Christian world was the developing cult of saints and martyrs. For one exemplary instance describing the path between martyrdom and cultic reverence, see Eusebius, *Martyrs of Palestine*, 11, 28. Cf. R. A. Markus, "How on Earth Could Places Become Holy," *Journal of Early Christian Studies* 2 (1994): 257–71. For a more comprehensive and up-to-date view of this aspect of Christian culture, see B. Caseau, "Sacred Landscape," in G. Bowersock, P. Brown, and O. Grabar, eds., *Late Antiquity: A Guide to the Postclassical World* (Cambridge, Mass., 1999), 21–59.

15. For Constantine's portrayal by the contemporary historian and the emperor's panegyrist, the above-mentioned Eusebius of Caesarea, see A. Cameron and Stuart G. Hall, eds. and trans., *Eusebius: Life of Constantine* (Oxford, 1999).

16. This in itself is quite puzzling. However, in light of T. D. Barnes's recent contention (see n. 13 above), it is not entirely surprising. Another view arguing that the rabbis simply ignored the transformation that took place in the empire has been recently put forward by M. Goodman, "Palestinian Rabbis and the Conversion of Constantine," in P. Schaefer and C. Hezer, eds., *The Talmud Yezushalmi and Graeco-Roman Culture*, vol. 2 (Tübingen, 2000), pp. 1–9.

17. The Christian thinkers who basically accepted the biblical eschatological blueprint were faced with similar dilemmas. When Christianity arose under pagan Roman rule, they had to come to terms with the prospects of salvation under this rule, a matter most probably referred to by Paul in his Second Epistle to the Thessalonians, 2:7: "For the power of wickedness is at work, secretly for the present until the Restrainer disappears from the scene." Cf. Tertullian's explanation in his *De resurrectione mortuorum*, 24. However, once Rome became Christian, the question became even knottier: were conditions ripe for the Second Coming of Jesus?

18. On the opposing views of historical destination and eschatological redemption in both camps as they evolved in the fourth and fifth centuries, see Irshai, "Dating the Eschaton," 139–53.

19. It must be emphasized that recent studies have convincingly demonstrated that the fourth century presents a watershed in the relations between Christianity and Judaism from without as well as toward the heretical sects (Arians, Neo-Arians, and others) within. On this, see D. Boyarin, *Dying for God: Martyrdom and the Making of Christianity and Judaism* (Stanford, 1999), 18.

20. This runs in many of Eusebius's works, though it is most apparent in his apologetic

treatise *The Proof of the Gospel,* especially in books 2 and 3. On Eusebius's theological attitude toward Jews and Judaism, see J. Ulrich, *Euseb von Caesarea und die Juden: Studien zur
Rolle der Juden in der Theologie des Eusebius von Caesarea* (Berlin, 1999).

21. This legend appeared in the *Actus beati Silvestri,* and though its earliest attested written form dates from the sixth century, most probably oral versions circulated as early as the
latter part of the fourth century. On that stage of the legend and its impact on Christian-
polytheist relations, see G. Foweden, "The Last Days of Constantine: Oppositional Versions
and Their Influence," *Journal of Roman Studies* 84 (1994): 146–70. On the Jewish angle of this
tradition, see Israel J. Yuval, "Jews and Christians in the Middle Ages: Shared Myths, Common Language. Donatio Constantini and Donatio Vespasiani," in R. S. Wistrich, ed., *Demonizing the "Other": Anti-Semitism, Racism and Xenophobia* (Amsterdam, 1999), 88–107.

22. See Eusebius, *Demonstratio Evangelica,* IX, 8, on the important role of the Galilee in
the initial dissemination of the Gospel. For more on Eusebius's complex attitude toward the
Galilee, see P. W. L. Walker, *Holy City, Holy Places? Christian Attitudes to Jerusalem and the
Holy Land in the Fourth Century* (Oxford, 1990), 133–70.

23. This phenomenon (which admittedly became full-fledged during the high Middle
Ages) and the process by which it evolved has been demonstrated in the most fascinating
manner by E. Reiner, "From Joshua to Jesus: The Transformation of a Biblical Story to a
Local Myth—A Chapter in the Religious Life of the Galilean Jew," in A. Kofsky and Guy G.
Stroumsa, eds., *Sharing the Sacred: Religious Contacts and Conflicts in the Holy Land—First
to Fifteenth Centuries c.e.* (Jerusalem, 1998), 223–71.

24. This tradition is found in various versions of the "Toldoth Yeshu" (The Life of Jesus)
that had circulated widely since its early formation, most probably during the later talmudic period. See S. Krauss, *Das Leben Jesu nach jüdischen Quellen* (Berlin, 1902), 43–45,
146–47, and W. Horbury, "The Trial of Jesus in Jewish Tradition," in E. Bammel, ed., *The
Trial of Jesus: Cambridge studies in honour of C.F.D. Moule* (London, 1970), 108–9.

25. See, e.g., in the Book of Zerubbabel, trans. M. Himmelfarb, in D. Stern and Mark J.
Mirsky, eds., *Rabbinic Fantasies: Imaginary Narratives from Classical Hebrew Literature*
(Philadelphia, 1990), 74, 77.

26. On the place of Dionysus in late antique culture, see G. W. Bowersock, *Hellenism in
Late Antiquity* (Ann Arbor, Mich., 1990), 41–53.

27. See, e.g., Lee I. Levine, *Judaism and Hellenism in Antiquity: Conflict or Confluence*
(Seattle, 1998), 3–32, 96–179 (discussing the earlier rabbinic period too).

28. Y. Tsafrir and G. Foerester, "From Scythopolis to Bysān: Changing Concepts of Ur-
banism," in G. R. D. King and A. Cameron, eds., *The Byzantine and Early Islamic Near East,*
vol. 2 (Princeton, 1994), 102.

29. For an up-to-date survey of archaeological findings in Byzantine Palestine, see
S. Thomas Parker, "An Empire's New Holy Land: The Byzantine Period," *Near Eastern Archaeology* 62, no. 3 (1999): 134–80 (with extensive bibliography).

30. See Lee I. Levine, *Caesarea Under Roman Rule* (Leiden, 1975). Since the publication of
Levine's important monograph, much more of Caesarea's architectural structure and, with

it, more of its unique cultural setup have been revealed, on which see the recent collection of studies, Kenneth G. Holum, ed., *Caesarea Maritima—Retrospective After Two Millennia* (Leiden, 1996).

31. JT *Sotah*, 7:1 (21b). S. Lieberman's classic studies concerning the knowledge and usage of Greek in rabbinic circles, *Greek in Jewish Palestine* (New York, 1942) and *Hellenism in Jewish Palestine* (New York, 1950), have so far not been surpassed. However, some of his basic premises and conclusions have been recently challenged by A. Wasserstein, begging for more caution in the examination of the sources and suggesting that the presence of a large number of Greek words in rabbinical traditions should be attributed to the apparent dependence of the rabbis on the Aramaic dialect in which many of the Greek loanwords had been absorbed earlier. See A. Wasserstein, "Non-Hellenized Jews in the Semi-Hellenized East," *Scripta Classica Israelica* 14 (1995): 111–37, esp. 119–30.

32. BT *Avodah Zara*, 4a. Compare Origen's *Epistle to Julius Africanus*, 5, and see also Mark G. Hirshman, *A Rivalry of Genius: Jewish and Christian Biblical Interpretation in Late Antiquity* (Albany, N.Y., 1996), and W. Horbury, "Jews and Christians on the Bible: Demarcation and Convergence," in his *Jews and Christians in Contact and Controversy* (Edinburgh, 1998), 200–25.

33. E. Honigmann, "Juvenal of Jerusalem" *Dumbarton Oaks Papers* 5 (1950): 212–16 (on the background leading to Juvenal's acclamation as the patriarch of Jerusalem). For an up-to-date survey of the struggle between the sees, see Z. Rubin, "The See of Caesarea in Conflict Against Jerusalem from Nicaea (325) to Chalcedon (451)," in Holum, ed., *Caesarea Maritima*, 559–74.

34. Theodosian Code, 16:8:8, 16:8:11. Over the past decade or so, much has been written about this institution. There are varied views concerning its origins and period of consolidation; see, e.g., D. Goodblatt, *The Monarchic Principle* (Tübingen, 1994) and M. Jacobs, *Die Institution des jüdischen Patriarchen* (Tübingen, 1995).

35. Jerome, *Epistle 57* (to Pammachius).

36. See M. Stern, *Greek and Latin Authors on Jews and Judaism*, vol. 2 (Jerusalem, 1980), fragments 496–504, pp. 589–99.

37. Lee I. Levine, "The Status of the Patriarch in the Third and Fourth Centuries: Sources and Methodology," *Journal of Jewish Studies* 47 (1996): 1–32.

38. Theodosian Code, 16:8:11. See Levine, "Status of the Patriarch, 2, n. 6.

39. The status of the patriarch in imperial law is somewhat enigmatic. The Theodosian Code acknowledges the preeminence of the institution for the first time as late as the days of Theodosius the First (392 C.E., though the patriarch is mentioned previously in an epistle of Julian the "apostate" from the spring of 363), and from there in a somewhat strange manner in a set of laws and decrees stretching to the year 415. Studied more closely, it seems that the constant changes for the worse in the imperial legislation toward the patriarchate might have come as a result of what was perceived by the authorities as the patriarch's misconduct, as well as a result of the mounting pressure within clerical circles to annul this institution.

40. For a detailed account of this most important transformation in late antique Jewish

history, see I. M. Gafni, *Land, Center and Diaspora: Jewish Constructs in Late Antiquity* (Sheffield, Engl., 1997), esp. 96–117.

41. See Schwartz, "The Patriarchs and the Diaspora."

42. Epiphanius, *Panarion,* 30, 4–12.

43. For instance, the mentioning of a Bishop of Tiberias, when in all probability the earliest period one could imagine the presence of a Christian bishop in that predominantly Jewish town was during the second half of the fifth century.

44. See Cyril of Jerusalem (ca. 350), *Catechetical Lectures,* 12, 17.

45. The Epiphanian story has been interpreted in this way only recently in a fascinating study by E. Reiner, "Joseph the Comes from Tiberias and the Jewish-Christian Dialogue in Fourth-century Galilee" (Hebrew), (forthcoming).

46. See, e.g., the new model of the monastic bishop advanced by the Cappadocian Church fathers: A. Sterk, "On Basil, Moses and the Model Bishop: The Cappadocian Legacy of Leadership," *Church History* 67 (1998): 227–53.

47. *Theodosian Code,* 16:8:22.

48. See D. Noy, *Jewish Inscriptions of Western Europe,* vol. 1 (Cambridge, Engl., 1993–95): 114–19. For more on the Jewish community of Venosa (southern Italy), see M. Williams, "The Jews of Early Byzantine Venusia: The Family of Faustinus," *Journal of Jewish Studies* 50 (1999): 38–52.

49. See G. Stemberger, *Introduction to the Talmud and Midrash,* 2d ed. (Edinburgh, 1996).

50. A critical edition of this most important register of halakhic rulings accompanied by a historical analysis is currently being prepared by Dr. Hillel Newman.

51. J. Mann, "Book of the Palestinian Halachic Practice" (Hebrew), *Tarbiz* 3 (1930): 12.

52. On women's lifestyle in that period and the ideals of domesticity and asceticism required of them, see G. Clark, *Women in Late Antiquity: Pagan and Christian Lifestyles* (Oxford, 1993), esp. 94–118.

53. Although this novel construct requires a more thorough exposition, see for now the interesting comparisons demonstrated by C. Hezser, "The Codification of Legal Knowledge in Late Antiquity: The Talmud Yerushalmi and the Roman Law Codes," in P. Schäfer, ed., *The Talmud Yerushalmi and the Graeco-Roman Culture* (Tübingen, 1998), 581–641.

54. The anecdote originating from a Christian tradition is cited by S. Lieberman, "Neglected Sources" (Hebrew), *Tarbiz* 42 (1973): 54.

55. On this episode as reflected in the contemporary Christian sources, see I. Shahid, *The Martyrs of Najran—New Documents* (Brussels, 1971), 11–117. For a more up-to-date historical survey on the princedom of Himyar, see Walter W. Müller, under "Himyar" in the *Reallexicon Für Antika und Christentum,* vol. 15 (Bonn, 1991), col. 303–31. (German).

56. The treatise was a polemical work addressed to their ex-brethren, the Jews. For a critical edition of this unique text, see G. Dagron and V. Déroche, eds., *Doctrina Jacobi nuper baptizati, Travaux et Mémoire* 11 (1991), pp. 17–43 (historical introduction), 47–219 (Greek text and French translation). The anecdotes on the priests appear in ibid., III, 12 (171–73); V, 6 (193).

57. Concerning the laws, see Theodosian Code, 16:8:22 (415 C.E.); 16:8:25 (423 C.E.); Theodosius II, Novella, 3 (438 C.E.). According to the legislation, existing synagogues were to remain intact and protected from Christian violence. On Pulcheria's action against the Jewish synagogue, see Theophanes, *The Chronicle of Theophanes Confessor: Byzantine and Near Eastern History*, A.D. 284–813, ed. and trans. C. Mango and R. Scott (Oxford, 1997), 159.

58. See R. Hachlili, ed., *Ancient Synagogues in Israel: Third–Seventh Century C.E.* (Oxford, 1989), 1–6, and, more recently, J. Magnes, "Synagogue Typology and Earthquake Chronology at Khirbet Shema, Israel," *Journal of Field Archaeology* 24 (1997): 211–20.

59. E. Reiner, *Mishmarot Ha-Kehunah: Mythos Byzanti Glili* (in preparation).

60. The Hasmonaean priests' saga, especially their zealous and heroic struggle with the Greeks, resurfaces in the liturgical poetry of the sixth century. See, e.g., J. Yahalom, *Poetry and Society in Jewish Galilee of Late Antiquity* (Tel Aviv, 1999), 113–14. It is interesting to note that this phenomenon had its parallel in the Christian Maccabean martyr's cult that evolved in Antioch during the second half of the fourth century, in part as a result of the strained relations between Christians and Jews in that city. See M. Vinson, "Gregory Nazianzen's Homily 15 and the Genesis of the Christian Cult of the Maccabean Martyrs," *Byzantion* 64 (1994): 166–92. As to the messianic tone in contemporary synagogue liturgy, see W. Horbury, "Suffering and Messianism in Yose ben Yose," in W. Horbury and B. McNeil, eds., *Suffering and Martyrdom in the New Testament: Studies Presented to G. M. Styler* (Cambridge, Engl., 1981), 143–82. Concerning synagogal ornament, see my opening paragraph concerning the presence of Helios, the sun god, on synagogue mosaics and its possible context and meaning.

61. On the synagogue as a communal center in Late Antiquity, see Levine, *Ancient Synagogue*, 357–86. Generally speaking, epigraphy as well as rabbinical sources have demonstrated that the synagogues were products of local communal enterprises. A similar phenomenon can be detected in Christian communities, where churches were being founded by the local residents rather than by central government; see L. Di Segni, "The Involvement of Local, Municipal and Provincial Authorities in Urban Building in Late Antiquity," *Journal of Roman Archaeology* 14 (1995): 317 ff. The centrality of the synagogue, at least (and this is not entirely surprising) in the institutional and cultural dimensions of Diaspora Jewry, is reflected in the great interest the Church fathers took in it; see Epiphanius, *Panarion*, 30:11.

62. On the *archisynagogos*, see T. Rajak and D. Noy, "*Archisynagogoi*: Office, Title and Social Status in the Greco-Jewish Synagogue," *Journal of Roman Studies* 83 (1993): 75–93. It seems that the rabbis changed their public function and increasingly assumed the role of deliverers of sermons. On Late Antiquity rabbis as homilists and public rhetoricians, see the anecdote on Rabbi Samuel the son of Yossi son of Bun (late fourth century), JT Horayot, 3:8 (48c).

63. The centers of learning were mostly concentrated in the cities. See H. Lapin, "Rabbis and Cities in Later Roman Palestine: The Literary Evidence," *Journal of Jewish Studies* 50 (1999): 187–207. It could have also been the case that the process described here occurred within the cities themselves, where their communal cohesion, led by a central or dominant

center or synagogue, simply disintegrated into smaller fractions of communities. Nonetheless, archaeological surveys of recent years, especially in the Galilee and on the Golan, have pointed out the great upsurge in synagogue as well as church building in rural areas.

64. This striking phenomenon seems to emerge from a set of dated funerary inscriptions found in the town of Zoar (south of the Dead Sea); see S. Stern, *Calendar and Community: A History of the Jewish Calendar Second Century* BCE–*Tenth Century* CE (Oxford, 2001), 87–98, 146–54.

65. On imperial restrictions and the significance of their ineffectiveness, see G. Stemberger, *Jews and Christians in the Holy Land,* 121–60. However, for a description of a much more relaxed interreligious atmosphere in Late Antiquity Palestine, consult G. W. Bowersock, "Polytheism and Monotheism in Arabia and the Three Palestines," *Dumbarton Oaks Papers* 50 (1997): 1–10.

66. See Levine, *Ancient Synagogue,* 362.

67. This assessment is based on the strange phenomenon that none of the rabbis mentioned in the epigraphical findings can be identified by our rabbinic literary sources; see S. J. D. Cohen, "Epigraphical Rabbis," *Jewish Quarterly Review* 72 (1981–82): 1–17.

68. See Levine, *Ancient Synagogue,* 440–51. For a different view on the matters discussed here, at least in regard to Palestine, see C. Hezser, *The Social Structure of the Rabbinic Movement in Roman Palestine* (Tübingen, 1997), 119–23, 214–25.

69. Several collections and surveys of synagogue inscriptions have been carried out in recent decades. See J. Naveh, *Al Pesefas ve-Even: ha-Ketovot ha-Aramiyot ve-ha-Ivriyot mi-Batei ha-Keneset ha-Atikim* (Jerusalem, 1978) (mainly on the Palestinian synagogues); L. Roth-Gerson, *The Greek Inscriptions from the Synagogues in Eretz-Israel* (Jerusalem, 1987); W. Horbury and D. Noy, *Jewish Inscriptions of Greco-Roman Egypt* (Cambridge, Engl., 1992) (covering the entire corpus of inscriptions, but mainly relating to an earlier period than the one discussed here); and D. Noy, *Jewish Inscriptions from Western Europe,* 2 vols. (Cambridge, Engl., 1993–95).

70. Although this phenomenon goes back to the decades preceding the destruction of the Second Temple, we encounter it later in, among other places, Tiberias, Sepphoris, and Lydda.

71. Rabbi Shimon son of Lakhish (late third century) once said to the Babylonian sage Rabbah bar Hannah that God hated them (the Babylonian Jews) for not returning to the Land of Israel as a whole during the days of Ezra (see BT *Yoma* 9b). In fact, the Babylonian Jews were blamed for the harsh fate of the entire nation (see Song of Songs Rabbah, 8, 9). In one case, immigrants in Sepphoris complained that the locals refrained even from greeting them (JT Sheviit, 9, 5). On this phenomenon, see S. Lieberman, " 'That Is How It Was and That Is How It Shall Be': The Jews of Eretz Israel and World Jewry During Mishnah and Talmudic Period" (Hebrew), *Cathedra* 17 (1981): 3–10.

72. Varying and at times contradictory views have been voiced concerning this rather difficult problem; see Levine's summary in *The Ancient Synagogue,* 552–53.

73. On the latter custom, see the early attestations found in the Gospels, Luke 4, 16–20.

74. The Hekhalot (literally, "halls" or "palaces") literature is a set of mystical speculations and visions centering around the heavenly halls through which the mystic travels in order to reach the divine throne. The term *hekhal* is based on the concept and modeled on the architecture of the halls in the earthly Jerusalem Temple. This and the Merkavah (literally, "chariot") literature—a complex of mystical speculations and visions about the *divine chariot* described in Ezekiel chap. 1—were most probably redacted and written during the period of the fifth to sixth centuries.

75. See R. Elior, "From Earthly Temple to Heavenly Shrines: Prayer and Sacred Song in the Hekhalot Literature and Its Relation to Temple Traditions," *Jewish Studies Quarterly* 4 (1997): 217–67.

76. On millennial calculations in Christian circles at that period, see R. Landes, "Lest the Millennium be Fulfilled: Apocalyptic Expectations and the Pattern of Western Chronography 100–800," in W. Verbeke et al., ed., *The Use and Abuse of Eschatology in the Middle Ages* (Leuven, Belgium, 1988), 137–211. On a possible correlation between Jewish and Christian calculations, see Irshai, "Dating the Eschaton," 139–53.

77. See Yahalom, *Poetry and Society*, 46–63.

78. See the anecdote in the Tosefta, Shabbat, 14, 2. The rabbis regarded the Targum as an oral form of the Bible; see JT, *Megillah*, 4, 1 (74a). On the links between the New Testament and the Targum, see B. D. Chilton, *Targumic Approaches to the Gospels: Essays in Mutual Definition of Judaism and Christianity* (Lanham, Md., 1986).

79. A. Shinan, "The Aramaic Targum as a Mirror of Galilean Jewry," in Lee I. Levine, ed., *The Galilee in Late Antiquity* (New York, 1992), 241–51.

80. Performed by Jesus, Luke 4:20–21, and described by Philo, *Hypothetica*, 7, 13; see Levine, *Ancient Synagogue*, 145–47.

81. Pesikta de-Rav Kahana, 12:3.

82. For the different views on this term and the reality reflected by it, see C. Hezser's summary, *The Social Structure of the Rabbinic Movement in Roman Palestine* (Tubingen, 1997), 195 to 214.

83. See Levine, *Ancient Synagogue*, 449–51. The assertion at hand also concerns the physical layout; that is, are we dealing with different locations altogether or with different spaces under the same roof?

84. J. Fraenkel, Darkhê ha-Aggadah we-ha-Midrash, vol. 1, *Giv'ataim* (1991), 17–26, and M. Hirshman, "The Preacher and His Public in Third-Century Palestine," *Journal of Jewish Studies* 42 (1991): 108–14.

85. See JT *Baba Mezia*, 2:11 (8d).

86. The formula, consisting of a homiletic midrash coupled with a halakhic poem, is best seen in the Midrash Tanhuma-Yelamdenu, on which see G. Stemberger's recent survey in *Introduction to the Talmud and Midrash*, 302–6.

87. See Lamentations Rabbah, Petichta, 17. In this context it is interesting to note the entirely opposite impression reported by the fifth-century Church historian Socrates

Scholastikos, who described the conduct of the Alexandrian Jews of his day thusly: "the Jews being disengaged from business on Sabbath, and spending their time not in hearing the Law, but in theatrical amusements" (*Church History*, 7, 13).

88. On rabbinic acquaintance with Greek lore, see notes 27; 31 above. Concerning rabbinical acquaintance with rhetoric, some scholars have recently insinuated that this might have well been the case; see J. Yahalom's interpretation of the Akedah (the sacrifice of Isaac) scene on the Sepphoris synagogue floor, *Et Ha'Daat* 3 (2000), Hebrew University, Jerusalem, 40–41.

89. Commentary on Ezekiel 34:3.

90. On the ongoing debate surrounding the architectural typology of Palestinian synagogues, see Levine, *Ancient Synagogues*, 296–302.

91. On this and other links between art and homiletic expression in early and late Byzantium, see H. Maguire, *Art and Eloquence in Byzantium* (Princeton, N.J., 1981), p. 9 ff.

92. The supplicant entreats "the adored Helios, the radiant leader" (*Sefer ha-Razim*, ed. M. Margalioth [Jerusalem, 1967], 99). On magic among the Jews in Late Antiquity, see, e.g., J. Naveh and S. Shaked, *Amulets and Magic Bowls: Aramaic Incantations of Late Antiquity* (Jerusalem, 1985). On magic and its function in the ancient world, see, e.g., the celebrated monograph of F. Graf, *Magic in the Ancient World*, trans. Philip Franklin (Cambridge, Mass., 1997).

93. See Z. Weiss and E. Netzer, *Promise and Redemption: The Synagogue Mosaic from Sepphoris* (Jerusalem, 1996).

94. Romanus Melodus, "On Earthquakes and Fires," 21; see R. J. Schork, trans. and ed., *Sacred Song: From the Byzantine Pulpit to Romanus the Melodist* (Gainesville, Fla., 1995), 193.

95. John Chrysostom, *Against Judaizing Christians*, 1.5, 8.4, 8.8; see also Robert L. Wilken, *John Chrysostom and the Jews: Rhetoric and Reality in the Late Fourth Century* (Berkeley, 1983), 73–79. On the Jewish community of Antioch in late antiquity, see Bernadette J. Brooten, "The Jews of Ancient Antioch," in Ch. Kondoleon, ed., *Antioch: The Lost Ancient City* (Princeton, 2000), 29–37.

96. For a succinct and well-presented description of the transformation of art and its links with religion in Late Antiquity, see J. Elsner, *Imperial Rome and Christian Triumph* (Oxford, 1998), 199–235.

97. See Caseau, "Sacred Landscape," esp. 38–45.

98. The earliest account of the institutionalized Jerusalem liturgy has been preserved in the late-fourth-century diary written by the pilgrim Egeria; see J. Wilkinson, *Egeria's Travels to the Holy Land*, rev. ed. (Warminster, Engl., 1981). On the underlying concepts of that local liturgical scheme, see Jonathan Z. Smith, *To Take Place: Toward Theory in Ritual* (Chicago, 1987), 74–95.

99. Origen, *Sermons on Leviticus*, 1:4.

100. See, e.g., Jerome, Epistle 52 (to Nepotianus). An unfriendly witness, the pagan histo-

rian Zosimos noted how John Chrysostom managed to control the masses during his sermons; see his *History*, 5, 23, 4. For more on the Christian styles and methods of preaching with a wide array of examples, see Mary B. Cunningham and P. Allen, eds., *Preacher and Audience: Studies in Early Christian and Byzantine Homiletics* (Leiden, 1998).

101. On different aspects of Church architecture, art, and liturgy as a center of spiritual guidance, as well as cultural and social cohesion in Byzantine society, see L. Safran, ed., *Heaven on Earth: Art and the Church in Byzantium* (University Park, Pa., 2000).

102. John Chrysostom, *On the Priesthood*, 5, 8.

103. Justinian, *Novellae*, no. 146.

104. One of the signs of the diminishing authoritarian power of the Palestinian center was the cessation (during the second half of the fifth century) of the "life line" of disciples traveling between Palestine and Babylon and transmitting to the latter the traditions and teachings of the Palestinian academies. See B. M. Levin, ed., *Iggeret Sherira Gaon* (Haifa, 1921), 61.

105. L. Ginzberg, *Ginze Schechter: Genizah Studies in Memory of Dr. Solomon Schecter*, vol. 2 (rpt., New York, 1969), 552, 561–62.

106. On Jews in Egypt in general, see Roger S. Bagnall, *Egypt in Late Antiquity* (Princeton, 1993), 275–78. For a more detailed account of the Jewish Alexandrian community of Late Antiquity, see Ch. Haas, *Alexandria in Late Antiquity: Topography and Social Conflict* (Baltimore, Md., 1997), 119–27 (with extensive bibliography).

107. See the careful survey of the evidence (which includes inscriptions from Spain and Asia Minor) by F. Millar, "The Jews of the Graeco-Roman Diaspora Between Paganism and Christianity, AD 312–438," in J. Lieu et al., eds., *The Jews Among Pagans and Christians in the Roman Empire* (London, 1992), 97–123, esp. 110–11.

108. On these issues, see the comprehensive study of Leonard V. Rutgers, *The Jews in Late Ancient Rome: Evidence of Cultural Interaction in the Roman Diaspora* (Leiden, 1995).

109. It has been postulated that, during the tenth and eleventh centuries, Palestinian traditions and lore were channeled via Italy to the newly forged German (Ashkenazic) community, which explains their strong presence in the local tradition. On Italy as a bastion of Palestinian Jewish traditions in the early medieval period, see A. Grossman, "The Yeshiva of Eretz Israel: Its Literary Output and Relationship with the Diaspora" (Hebrew), in J. Prawer and H. Ben-Shammai, eds., *The History of Jerusalem: The Early Moslem Period 638–1099* (Jerusalem, 1996), 243–56.

110. On this conflict, see M. Avi-Yona, *The Jews of Palestine: A Political History from the Bar Kokhba War to the Arab Conquest* (Oxford, 1976), 251–53; for more on this episode, see the studies cited above in n. 55. On the Byzantine campaign, see A. A. Vasiliev, *Justin the First* (Cambridge, Mass., 1950), 274–302, and I. Shahid, *The Martyrs of Najran* (Brussels, 1971).

111. *Seder Olam Zutah*; A. Neubauer, ed., *Medieval Jewish Chronicles, II* (Oxford, 1895), 72–73, 76. On the background of this tradition and its possible messianic connotations, see Irshai, "Dating the Eschaton," 152–53.

112. M. Zulai, ed., *Piyyutei Yannai* (Berlin, 1939), 90.

113. BT Yoma 10a.

114. See A. Cameron, *Circus Factions: Blues and Greens at Rome and Byzantium* (Oxford, 1976), 74–80, 149–52, 271–96.

115. Dagron and Déroche, eds., *Doctrina Jacobi nuper baptizati*, 5, 6, p. 193. Jacob reports at least two other similar episodes. Compare the apocalyptic visions reported by the contemporary Byzantine historian Theophylact Simocatta, in M. and M. Whitby, *The History of Theophylact Simocatta* (Oxford, 1986), 222–35.

116. Apart from the Book of Zerubbabel, we have the Book of Elijah and a few other smaller treatises; see Y. Even-Shmuel, *Midrashei Geulah* (Jerusalem, 1954), 15–64. *Sefer Zerubbabel* received a translation and commentary by M. Himmelfarb in Stern and Mirsky, eds., *Rabbinic Fantasies*, 67–90. It is important to note that earlier signs of Jewish-Sassanian collaboration against the Christian overlords had occurred in Southern Arabia already during the second half of the sixth century; see Ch. Robin, *L'Arabie antique de Karib'il à Mahomet* (Aix-en-Provence, 1993), 144–50.

117. See, e.g., J. D. Halperin, *The Merkabah in Rabbinic Literature* (Leiden, 1980), and P. Schaefer, *The Hidden and Manifested God: Some Major Themes in Early Jewish Mysticism* (Albany, N.Y., 1992). See also R. Eliot's study, n. 75 above.

118. Himmelfarb, *Sefer Zerbabel*, 78.

119. The text (in my own translation) is taken from the poem "In Those Days and In That Time"; see Even-Shmuel, *Midreshei Geula*, 114.

120. On the change of sentiment among the Jews, see J. Yahalom, "The Transition of Kingdoms in Eretz Israel as Conceived by Poets and Homelists" in *Shalem: Studies in the History of the Jews in Eretz Israel* 6 (Jerusalem, 1992), 1–22. It ought to be noted that the Arab conquest of the East posed a grave problem to the Christian concept of history as well, resulting in new waves of apocalyptic anxiety. For an overview of the Byzantine tick and chime of the eschatological clock, see P. Magdalino, "The History of the Future and Its Uses: Prophecy, Policy and Propaganda," in R. Beaton and Ch. Rouche, eds., *The Making of Byzantine History: Studies Dedicated to Donald M. Nicol on His Seventieth Birthday* (Aldershot, Engl., 1993), 3–34. One of the earliest and most influential attempts to address the historical transformation in apocalyptic terms was that known as the *Ps.-Methodius*, which was written in northern Syria circa 692 C.E. See G. J. Reinink, "Ps.-Methodius: A Concept of History in Response to the Rise of Islam," in A. Cameron and Lawrence I. Conrad, eds., *The Byzantine and Early Islamic Near East, Vol. 1: Problems in the Literary Source Material* (Princeton, 1992), 149–87.

SELECTED BIBLIOGRAPHY

Avi-Yona, M. *The Jews of Palestine: A Political History from the Bar Kokhba War to the Arab Conquest.* Oxford, 1976.

Cameron, A., and P. Garnsey, eds. *The Cambridge Ancient History.* Vol. XIII: *The Late Empire, AD 337–425.* Cambridge, Engl., 1997.

Cameron, A., B. Ward-Perkins, and M. Whitby, eds. *The Cambridge Ancient History.* Vol. XIV: *Late Antiquity: Empire and Successors, AD 425–600.* Cambridge, Engl., 2000. (Both volumes are the most comprehensive and up-to-date general introductions to a wide array of topics in the history of the Byzantine period.)

Elsner, J. *Oxford History of Art: Imperial Rome and Christian Triumph—The Art of the Roman Empire AD 100–450.* Oxford, 1998.

Levine, Lee I. *The Ancient Synagogue: The First Thousand Years.* New Haven, Conn., 2000.

Safran, L., ed., *Heaven on Earth: Art and the Church in Byzantium.* University Park, Pa., 2000.

Wilken, Robert L. *The Land Called Holy: Palestine in Christian History and Thought.* New Haven, Conn., 1992.

Two views of two incantation bowls.
(British Museum, London)

BABYLONIAN RABBINIC CULTURE

ISAIAH GAFNI

In the context of a lengthy discussion on the nature, merits, and handicaps associated with the ongoing scattering of the Jewish people, a dispersion for which no imminent conclusion was visible on the horizon, the Babylonian Talmud offers an ingenious observation on its own community's unique predicament. More than a millennium prior to the redaction of the Babylonian rabbinic corpus, vast numbers of Judaeans had been transplanted to lands east of the Euphrates River. The majority of these were captives, a consequence of the initial Babylonian capture of Jerusalem in 597 B.C.E. and the deportation to Babylonia[1] at that time of the Judaean king Yehoyakhin. Another wave of captives arrived shortly afterward, following the second conquest and final destruction of Jerusalem and its Temple by King Nebuchadnezzar in 586 B.C.E.[2] Why, the Talmud innocently asks, were the Israelites exiled to Babylonia rather than to any other land? Of course, the modern historian's response to such a question would simply be to point to precisely those events just cited. But in the context of rabbinic theodicy and an interpretation of history as the stage upon which a saga of providential causality was being played out, it made all the sense in the world to inquire as to the implications of a Babylonian setting for Jewish captivity and communal rebuilding. And thus the Talmud proceeds to explain why, in fact, it was Babylonia that was chosen: "Because He [God] sent them [back] to their mother's[3] house. To what might this be likened? To a man angered at his wife. To where does he send her—to her mother's house!" (BT Pesahim 87b).

The Jewish people, we are thus informed, were not merely removed to a random land of captivity but were benevolently transferred to what might be considered their original homeland, inasmuch as their patriarch, Abraham, had his roots in those very same lands east of the Euphrates. Implicit in this statement is not merely the theodicic observation that God did not randomly exile the nation for its sins, but also that they were granted haven in the one territory uniquely qualified to receive them in light of their ancient roots therein, thereby affording them, even while uprooted, a sense of comfort and familiarity rather than the expected alienation of captivity.

Familiarity with an ancient "homeland," however, need not presuppose an assimilatory process resulting from an identification with the local culture or civilization. Ironically, it would be precisely in this land of ancient roots, albeit imagined ones, that the Jewish community would evince the greatest degree of cultural autonomy, certainly when compared with parallel processes played out in communities west of the Euphrates, namely those situated within the political and cultural boundaries of the Hellenistic-Roman world. In time the sages of Babylonia would come to be recognized as the outstanding Jewish intellectuals of their day, vying with and ultimately surpassing their colleagues in Palestine. The achievements of this community would determine for almost a millennium central elements of a Jewish self-identity and religious expression, as well as the basic literary curriculum and legal code embraced by Jews throughout the world. If ever there were a communal success story in the annals of Jewish history, it was the meteoric ascendancy of the Babylonian rabbinic community in Late Antiquity and the early Middle Ages to a position of primacy within the Jewish world. It is to this story that the present chapter addresses itself.

A good place to begin our tale—and certainly one that the sages of Babylonia themselves would have recommended—is an event that took place some 800 years prior to the first appearance of a "rabbinic community" there. In the fourth year of the reign of the last king of Judah, Zedekiah (i.e., 594 B.C.E.), and just a few years before the final Babylonian onslaught and destruction of First-Temple Jerusalem, the prophet Jeremiah wrote a letter to those of his countrymen who had already been exiled to Babylon some years earlier.[4] In that letter, God, through the prophet, beseeches them:

> Build houses and settle down. Plant gardens and eat their produce. Marry and beget sons and daughters, in order that you may increase in number there rather than decrease. Seek the welfare of the country to which I have deported you, and pray on its behalf to God, for on its welfare your own depends. (Jeremiah 29:5–7)

One would be hard pressed to find another example in ancient Israelite history in which a community heeded the words of the prophet so scrupulously and in such detail. Not only were Jews destined to thrive demographically and economically in this new land of captivity,[5] but ultimately even the latter part of Jeremiah's exhortation, bearing a decidedly political significance, would achieve a fruition of sorts with the formulation by Samuel, a third-century Babylonian sage, of the well-known statement that "the law of the kingdom is law" (dina demalkhuta dina).[6] Although that principle appears in the Babylonian Talmud within a more narrowly defined legal context, recognizing the government's legitimate right to enforce the collection of taxes and customs and to determine legal frameworks for establishing land-ownership, the fact is that it ultimately attained a sweeping political significance for the totality of Jewish Diaspora life. In rabbinic eyes, however, past and present tend to coalesce, and thus in time the rabbinic community of Babylonia would point to those earliest biblical days of captivity as the first links in an unbroken chain of enhanced Jewish existence "by the rivers of Babylon," claiming that all the requisite trappings of a vital and self-sufficient community were transported from Jerusalem to Babylon even prior to the destruction of the First Temple.

And yet, if the great success story begins at that earliest of stages, one cannot ignore the fact that the very same story also represents one of the great riddles of Jewish history. To be sure, only a small portion of the Babylonian Jewish community participated in the "return to Zion" during the sixth and fifth centuries B.C.E., while the vast majority remained in the eastern Diaspora and ultimately grew to become second in size only to Palestinian Jewry among all the other concentrations of Jews throughout the world. But though they grew into a community of "countless myriads whose number cannot be ascertained,"[7] the Jews of Babylonia would at the same time recede into a shadowy background, with practically nothing to be heard from them for almost 750 years. Throughout the Second Temple period (516 B.C.E.–70 C.E.), and indeed for the entire tannaitic era of post-Temple Palestine as well (70–220 C.E.), this community provides us with no meaningful information on its inner development, nor do we possess any significant literary product from its midst. Inasmuch as Jewish historiography in Second Temple times focuses almost exclusively on the affairs of Jews situated within the Hellenistic-Roman spheres of influence (primarily in Judaea, but also in major Jewish centers such as Ptolemaic and Roman Egypt), allusions to Jews beyond the Euphrates are almost always linked to events in the west: thus, for example, we hear only fleetingly of the reception granted the captured high priest of Jerusalem, Hyrcanus II, by the Jews of Babylonia in the wake of the Parthian invasion of Judaea in 40 B.C.E.[8] Expressions of the commitment of Babylonian Jewry to the Temple of Jerusalem, exemplified by their annual monetary contributions as well as by their potential for armed intervention in the face of any perceived Roman tampering with the nature of the Jewish cultic center (as evinced in the days of Gaius Caligula), all find their way into the writings of Josephus and Philo, but even this information does not really shed any light on the communal structures and cultural character of the Babylonian community.

Nor does the appearance on the Judaean scene, beginning with the reign of King Herod (37–4 B.C.E.), of various Babylonian personalities such as Hillel the

Elder, really inform us about the nature of contemporaneous Babylonian Jewry, notwithstanding the claims of numerous Jewish historians of the nineteenth and twentieth centuries. The historical Hillel, it appears, is just one of the casualties of the vigorous controversy between liberal and traditional representatives of nineteenth-century Jewish *Wissenschaft*, many of whom frequently rendered ancient Jewish history a battleground for their own contemporary disputes. In the case of Babylonia, the paucity of any hard information from Second Temple times enabled liberal opponents of Jewish Orthodoxy to claim that the Babylonian Talmud—the ultimate legal authority in traditionalist eyes—was in fact conceived in a land at first devoid of ancient Jewish tradition and instead caught up in the "superstitions" of the Persian East.[9] Orthodox Jewish historiography would respond by projecting a "Torah-oriented" society among Babylonian Jews as far back as the earliest days of captivity.

In similar fashion, Hillel was cited by nineteenth-century writers as proof either of Babylonia's deep-rooted Torah orientation or of the total lack of Torah-knowledge in that land, which therefore required that Hillel "come up" to Palestine if he wished to engage in the study of Torah. In truth, nothing on the nature of Second Temple Babylonian Jewry can really be gleaned from the Hillel stories. It was precisely this lack of any real information that enabled both sides to play fast and loose with it. All this, then, tends to enhance the riddle. What were the objective political and social conditions that contributed to the fashioning of the Babylonian Jewish community, even as it remained out of close touch with the rest of world Jewry, and what were the factors that rendered the community so special in its own eyes, affording it a self-assuredness that determined its behavior toward surrounding cultures, on the one hand, and a distinct assertiveness in its relations with other Jewish communities—most notably that of Palestine—on the other?

In strictly political terms, the Jews of Babylonia were ruled over and influenced by a succession of kingdoms, each of which cultivated its own unique cultural environment. The Babylonian kingdom that originally transported the Judaean captives to their new surroundings was conquered shortly afterward by the Persian Achaemenid monarchy, under whose rule those Judaeans who so desired were allowed to return to the areas around Jerusalem and rebuild the Temple. We have, however, no substantial information on the nature of Jewish life under the Persians, and the same holds true for the subsequent period, when the bulk of Alexander the Great's eastern conquests came under Hellenistic-Seleucid rule (ca. 323–140 B.C.E.). What is noteworthy, however, is that this Seleucid rule over Babylonia marks the last chapter in ancient history during which the Jews of Palestine and their brethren east of the Euphrates were ruled by the same monarchy, a political reality to be reestablished only in the wake of the Islamic conquests of the East. The prolonged disintegration of the Seleucid Empire, beginning in the mid-second century B.C.E., would ultimately find the two Jewish centers separated again: Babylonian Jewry found itself under Parthian rule for over 300 years,[10] until the fall of the Parthian kingdom to the Sassanian rulers in the early third century C.E.—that is, precisely at the dawn of the Babylonian rabbinic era. The Jews of Palestine, meanwhile, would experience two generations of political independence under the Hasmonaean priests (141–63 B.C.E.), to be followed by the Roman conquest of the land and the establishment therein of successive regimes, all ultimately controlled by the Roman state.

It was arguably in this prolonged state of communal separation that much of the self-image of Babylonian Jewry may have been determined. The Parthian Empire differed both from its Achaemenid and Seleucid predecessors, and even more so from its Sassanian successor, in that it never constituted a unified empire under strong central rule. Instead it functioned as a weak confederation of vassal states whose loyalty to the Parthian sovereign was put to the test only during major confrontations with external threats, primarily in the form of Roman legions. But though usually successful in amassing great military force to thwart Roman designs, the Parthians evinced no zeal for the establishment of a unified social and political order, based on foundations that might have served to create a more homogeneous society. Particularly noteworthy is the lack of a formal state religion under the Parthians. While they did recognize Iranian deities and also fostered Zoroastrianism, this was never cultivated to the extent and with the dedication shown by their Sassanian successors. In fact, Hellenistic culture also served as a counter-influence in the Parthian court,[11] and although this may have been a superficial legacy from the Seleucid period, it nevertheless testifies to the lack of any predominant political or cultural enterprise on the part of the Parthian monarchy. What emerged was a loosely knit confederation with a decidedly feudal nature, and although this tended to weaken the kingdom as a whole, it also served as a unifying and strengthening factor for the individual ethnic groups within the empire, allowing them to cultivate a sort of tribal autonomy as long as the sovereignty of the Parthian ruler was officially recognized.[12]

Moreover, if the various ethnic communities managed to achieve a significant degree of political and military potency, they were in the advantageous position of being able to offer their services to the king should these be required for purposes of subduing rebellious elements within the empire. Josephus provides us with two stories relating to Jews or the Jewish community in first-century Parthia.[13] In both cases, the king was willing to grant elements within the community—be they renegade Jewish brothers who set up a short-lived pirate state, or recent converts to Judaism from among a local royal dynasty—an enhanced degree of regional autonomy in exchange for their support against all sorts of local satraps and strongmen who might be harboring mutinous aspirations. Although the novelistic and fictionalized elements in both narratives are apparent, they nevertheless represent an accurate picture of a decentralized environment, in which Jews were free to run their own lives unhindered by external political pressures and, even more important, were not engulfed by a pervasive, attractive, and assimilatory cultural presence so familiar to the Jews of the Hellenistic world. Given such an atmosphere, we can appreciate the concern expressed by representatives of the early rabbinic community with the fall of the Parthian kingdom and the ascendancy of the Sassanians. Upon the death of the last Parthian king, Artabanus V (ca. 224 c.e.), we are told that the renowned sage Rav proclaimed: "The bond is snapped" (BT Avodah Zara 10b).

RABBINIC BABYLONIA:
THE INTERSECTION OF PAST AND PRESENT

It was upon this extended period of communal autonomy that the rabbis of talmudic Babylonia would graft their own unique contribution to the social and cultural self-image of Babylonian Jewry. On the most basic level, Babylonian Jews even mildly conversant with biblical tradition would be aware that they dwelt not only in one of the ancient lands of the Bible but literally in the cradle of earliest biblical civilization. For instance, they were able to identify in their midst two of the four tributaries of the river that flowed out of Eden, namely the Tigris "which flows east of Assyria" (Genesis 2:14) and the Euphrates. It is hardly surprising that rabbis residing in the very setting of the opening chapters of Genesis identified sites mentioned in that book with Babylonian or Persian cities of their own day. Thus Genesis 10:11 tells us: "From that land [Bavel] he [Nimrod] went into Assyria [Ashur] and built Nineveh and Rehovoth-Ir and Kalah," and the Talmud records: "Rav Joseph taught: 'Ashur is Sileq [Seleucia]. . . . Nineveh is what it says, Rehovoth-Ir is Perat de-Meshan, Kalah is Perat de-Borsif' " (BT Yoma 10a).[14] Another example relates, " 'And the mainstays of his [Nimrod's] kingdom were Babylon, Erek, Akkad and Kalneh' (Genesis 10:10)—[they are] Edessa and Nisibis and Ktesiphon."[15]

In similar fashion, even though the giants Ahiman, Sheshai, and Talmai lived, according to Numbers 13:22, in the vicinity of Hebron, this did not prevent the sages in Babylonia from pointing to three islands in the Euphrates as having been built by them: "Ahiman built Anat, Sheshai built Alush, Talmai built Talbush" (BT Yoma 10a).[16]

The game of identifying ancient biblical cities with nearby and familiar sites thus transcended a simple form of geographical exegesis, because it effectively put the exegete himself—together with his audience—on the biblical map as well. But this was not just a process of biblical "immersion"; the intersecting of past and present took on a far greater significance when the past was not merely "biblical" but related to ancient Israelite (i.e., "Jewish") history as well. If, as we noted in the opening to this chapter, Abraham was perceived as being not just the first Hebrew but also a "Babylonian," how much more meaningful were those attempts at identifying sites connected with King Nimrod—inasmuch as rabbinic lore described how that ruler was responsible for the incarceration of "our patriarch" Abraham. A heightened sense of continuity with the biblical narrative, as well as an immediate link to the historical arena of that narrative, was the natural consequence. Nothing could now prevent the rabbis from identifying the very location of our patriarch's incarceration: "Rav said: 'Our father Abraham was imprisoned ten years, three in Kuta and seven in Kartu.' . . . Rav Hisda said: 'Ibra ze'ira [the small crossing] de Kuta—that is the Ur of the Chaldeans.' "[17]

Once these ancient biblical sites became "known" to the rabbis, this information could be introduced into their halakhic discourse as well: "Rav Hamnuna said: He who sees the lion's den or the furnace should say: Blessed is the one who performed miracles to our fathers on this spot" (BT Berakhot 57b).

Of course, the sages were well aware of the events that introduced the descendants of Abraham into the lands east of the Euphrates. Here, too, the attempt would be made to juxtapose past and present:

> R. Abba b. Kahana said: What is meant by "and the King of Assyria exiled Israel to Assyria and he settled them in Halah and along the Havor, and the River Gozan and the towns of Media" (2 Kings 18:11)? Halah is Helwan, Havor is Hadyab [Adiabene], the River Gozan is Ginzak, the towns of Media—this is Hamadan and its neighbors, and some say Nehavand and its neighbors. (BT Kiddushin 72a; BT Yevamot 16b–17a)

The focus of all this exegetical activity, if our analysis is correct, was not the Bible and a need for up-to-date knowledge of its geography but rather the self-image of the Jewish community of Babylonia in Late Antiquity. What we have seen up to now suggests yet another way for Jews to understand their position and status in a "foreign" land, where they are engulfed by an alien society and culture. Erich Gruen in his chapter in this volume has described the unique coming to terms of Hellenistic Judaism with the various strains of Greek culture. The nature of that environment, however, was totally different from what we have encountered in the East. The role of Hellenistic culture was so overpowering in countries such as Egypt that Jews—even if they were to preserve and perpetuate their culture—would have to do this through the media and the methods of that pervasive culture. A Jewish author in Egypt such as Artapanus (second century B.C.E.) would attempt to straddle both worlds—that of his Jewish roots along-side his Egyptian cultural environment—by evincing what the eminent classical historian Arnaldo Momigliano has referred to as "something like Egyptian pa-triotism."[18] Artapanus could thus recognize that the land of Egypt is the cradle of civilization but would claim that much of that culture was brought there by his Hebraic progenitors: Abraham taught astrology to the Egyptian king, Joseph introduced order into the country's economy, and Moses "the teacher of Or-pheus . . . invented boats and bricklaying machines, weapons for Egypt and tools for irrigation and war, philosophy, and also divided the land into thirty-six dis-tricts, assigning to each its own deity[!] . . . and thus Moses came to be loved by the masses and respected by the priests, and came to be known by the name of Hermes."[19]

The rabbis of Babylonia seem to have taken a different approach. For them, "belonging" did not so much require a cultural accommodation, and certainly this was not the legacy they received from the Parthian period and its decidedly amenable atmosphere of cultural and ethnic diversity. To be sure, that atmo-sphere would undergo definite changes during the Sassanian period, and we will address these shortly. But the first order of business seems to have been afford-ing the local Jewish community a sense of "home while abroad," and this was achieved at least in part by creating a sense of familiarity with the physical envi-ronment. Jews have roots there that go back to their ultimate patriarch, and pos-sess a literary tradition in which the surrounding geography plays a major role. In total contradistinction to the path taken by Hellenistic Judaism in Egypt, this sort of "belonging" does not require an accommodation with the surrounding culture or a meaningful social interaction, and it might even encourage a certain insularity. With such impeccable documentation of their inherent links to their surroundings, the urgency of evincing cutural ties toward that same end was sig-nificantly reduced.

ANTIQUITY AND CONTINUITY:
INTERCOMMUNAL RABBINIC IMPLICATIONS

Creating a sense of local antiquity for Babylonian Jews may have been only part of the rabbinic agenda, because the Babylonian rabbis were involved in a differ-ent confrontation with their contemporaries in Palestine. The stakes here were particularly high: of all the Diaspora communities in Late Antiquity, only the Babylonian one embraced the new (post-70 C.E.) Jewish devotion to Torah-study as a religious value and personal calling, a process frequently attributed to the sages at Yavneh following the destruction of the Second Temple and considered by some to be their singular greatest achievement. By the third century C.E., a parallel movement appears in Babylonia, probably drawing at first on the emigration of central rabbinic figures from Palestine but ultimately claiming to be on a par with their colleagues in the Holy Land. But that of course was precisely the problem: Babylonia was not "the Holy Land," and would that fact alone not automatically relegate its spiritual leadership to a secondary or subservient role within the rabbinic world?

It was precisely in this context that the Babylonian Jews' links with antiquity would come to play a second major role. To be sure, this process did not take place overnight, and the vigor with which the Babylonian rabbis asserted themselves vis-à-vis their Palestinian counterparts hinged to no small degree on political and religious developments over which the sages had no control whatsoever.

The earliest roots of the community, we have been told, were to be found not only in the patriarchal biblical narrative but, more immediately, in the mass removal of the Judaean population just prior to, and in the direct aftermath of, the destruction of the First Temple. These two waves of captives, we have already seen, were the recipients of Jeremiah's instructions regarding proper behavior while abroad, but just prior to the text of that communication the author of Jeremiah 29 actually spells out precisely the addressees of his letter: "To the *priests,* the *prophets,* the rest of the *elders* of the exile community, and to all the people whom Nebuchadnezzar had exiled from Jerusalem to Babylon—after *King Yekhoniah,* the queen mother, the eunuchs, the *officials* of Judah and Jerusalem, and the *craftsmen and the smiths* had left Jerusalem" (29:1–2). This, then, was no rabble or riffraff that set up shop in Babylonia but rather the most cultivated and esteemed strata of Judaean society. Centuries later, this fact was crucial, for it suggested that the captivity was the ancient repository of Judaean tradition as well. To the rabbinic ear, the term "elders" *(zekenim)* implied sagacity, and in similar fashion the "craftsmen and the smiths" of Jerusalem would be taken as an allusion to Torah scholars who were deported with providential care that a foundation for learning be established in Babylonia at the earliest stages of captivity.[20]

Indeed, this projection of the present into the past went even beyond the world of Torah and came to encompass all the communal institutions of Babylonian Jewry. The most prominent beneficiary of this process would be the Babylonian exilarch *(resh galuta).* Although we possess no hard evidence for the existence of this office prior to the late second or early third century C.E.,[21] the exilarchate could now claim that its Davidic pedigree went all the way back to the exiled House of Yehoyakhin (Yekhoniah). Even the synagogues of Babylonia would benefit from this bestowal of antiquity on communal institutions. Having established that the captives found solace in the fact that they were accompanied into exile by the *shekhinah* (divine spirit), the rabbis naturally inquired as to the precise location of God's presence: "Abaye said: In the synagogue of Huzal and in the synagogue of Shaf ve-Yatib in Nehardea" (BT Megillah 29a). By post-talmudic times, claims for such continuity were enhanced even more, and Rav Sherira Gaon (tenth century) informs us that the synagogue of Shaf ve-Yatib in Nehardea was actually built from the rubble of the destroyed First Temple, brought to Babylonia by the earliest wave of captives.[22]

It should be apparent, by now, how different the cultivation in Babylonia of this perception of "belonging" to the local environment was from that employed by the Jews of the Hellenistic world. But these same processes could be adapted by the rabbis of Babylonia in their contest over spiritual and legal authority with the sages of Palestine. The Babylonian position would be enhanced even more by claims to a purity of national pedigree that exceeded even that of Palestinian Jewry (the rest of world Jewry was of course a distant third).[23] The most blatant statement to this effect was the claim that Ezra rendered Babylonia "like pure sifted flour" by taking with him to the Land of Israel all the doubtful or not-quite-pure elements of the Jewish population.[24] It is for this reason, we are told, that "all countries are an admixture (with impure lineage) in comparison to Eretz Israel, and Eretz Israel is an admixture (in comparison) to Babylonia."[25] Indeed, to be sure one was marrying a "pure" Babylonian Jew, a person would have to make inquiries on the geographical background of a potential spouse, and this procedure actually led to the talmudic demarcation of boundaries for "Jewish Babylonia."[26] What ensued was an enhanced reverence for the physical "land" of Babylonia, a thinly disguised replication of the very attitude maintained by the Jews of Palestine toward their "Holy Land." Indeed, if burial in the Land of Israel had become by the third century yet another expression of devotion and religious piety,[27] can we be surprised at finding those who claim that even burial in Babylonia is equivalent to burial in the Land of Israel?[28]

What was being played out here was not only an exercise in ethnic and religious survival abroad but also a reimaging of the Babylonian community into something radically removed from any other communal context in the Jewish world. The ultimate conclusion—if not the original goal—of this exercise would be the Babylonian rabbinic statement, attributed already to a late-third-century sage, to the effect that "we have made ourselves in Babylonia the equivalent of Eretz Israel" (BT Gitin 6a; BT Bava Kamma 80a).

"IN THE SHADOW OF GOD":
JEWISH PROSPERITY IN A NON-ROMAN WORLD

We have yet to address the question of whether the reimaging of their community and its history for internal (i.e., local and inter-Jewish) purposes had a direct impact on the Babylonian rabbis' attitudes toward the political and cultural behavior of the gentile world in whose midst they also functioned.

Notwithstanding all the advantages of an unequaled communal antiquity, whether based on fact or fancy, the Jews of Babylonia were absolutely certain of one critical political and cultural reality: unlike their brethren in Palestine and the entire Hellenistic-Roman world, they were able to function beyond the political reach of the Roman state. For the sages, this was an object of considerable reflection: it touched directly not only on the degree of practical autonomy enjoyed by their community but, even more important, on the significance of Jewish removal beyond the all-embracing influence of Hellenistic culture. With the acceptance of Christianity by the Roman Empire in the fourth century, a major new component was added to this equation, because it now also placed the Jews of Babylonia and their spiritual leadership beyond the constant need to respond to theological confrontations with the Church, a new reality that would become increasingly apparent in the statements—to say nothing of the biblical exegesis—of the sages of Byzantine Palestine.

The following anecdote[29] expresses in no uncertain terms the Babylonian rabbis' awareness that their position was radically different from that of the Palestinians:

Rabbah bar bar Hanna was ill, and Rav Judah and the disciples entered to inquire about him. . . . meanwhile one of the *habarim* [Persian priests][30] came and took the candle from them. [Rabbah bar bar Hanna] said: "Merciful One [God]! [Let us live] either in your shade or the shade of the son of Esau [Rome]!" Does this imply that the Romans are preferable to the Persians? Did not R. Hiyya teach: "What is the inference of the scripture 'God understands the way to it, He knows its source' (Job 28:23)—God knew that Israel could not survive the decrees of the Romans and so he exiled them to Babylonia." This [seeming contradiction between the two rabbis] does not pose a difficulty: The [teaching of Rav Hiyya preferring Babylonia] was before the *habarim* came to Babylonia, the [statement of Rabbah bar bar Hanna]—after they came to Babylonia.[31]

All of the political acumen, as well as the doubts and fears, of the Babylonian rabbinic movement appear to be wrapped up in this anecdote. Indeed, we could not ask for a keener appreciation of the historical vicissitudes that transpired precisely as the leadership of that movement began to emerge and to compete for communal control with their counterparts in Roman Palestine.

Rabbi Hiyya's pronouncement seems to reflect the reality of his day (the late second and early third centuries c.e.). With the attractive possibilities for communal autonomy still available under a feudal Parthian regime, on the one hand, and, on the other, harsh memories of the aftermath of the Bar Kokhba rebellion and the ensuing religious persecution[32] still fresh in the mind, a preference for Parthian Babylonia was only to be expected. Moreover, Jews throughout the world could never forget that it was the Roman army that was responsible for the destruction of Jerusalem and its Temple. Although the political situation in late-second-century Palestine was about to undergo a temporary improvement, with the appearance on the scene of Judah the Patriarch and the improved relationship between Jews and the new Severan imperial dynasty, Hiyya (a Babylonian by birth who immigrated to Palestine) seems to reflect the established political wisdom born of decades of strained relations with Rome. The third decade of the third century, however, presented the Jews of Babylonia with a new and threatening political reality of their own: the Parthian Arsacid rulers had just been defeated by the armies of a family of Mazdean priests from the district of Fars in southeastern Persia. The new Sassanian dynasty that succeeded the Arsacids would be characterized by a more centralized political regime, imagining itself as the new coming of the ancient Achaemenids, and even more important by a new commitment to the old Zoroastrian religion.[33] This zeal manifested itself in the appearance of an assertive and revitalized state church, and the removal of a flame from among the rabbis in the talmudic anecdote is one of numerous allusions to the fire-priests (ḥabarim) who at first seem to pose a threat to the established freedoms of the local Jewish community.[34] These same priests are cited in the Babylonian Talmud as the reason that rabbis granted permission to move Hanukkah candles on the Sabbath; keeping the candles out of sight would, they hoped, preclude any hostile action by the fire-priests (BT Shabbat 45a).

The dilemma for the Babylonian sages was acute and somewhat ironic. If, indeed, their community had taken comfort in its relatively favorable political situation, compared to that of the Jews under Roman rule, now it too was confronted with a new situation that threatened to undermine those advantages. The fears related to political as well as religious winds of change. A frequently examined story in the Babylonian Talmud (Bava Kamma 117a) reports that Rav—

a Babylonian sage who spent part of his youth in Palestine but returned to Babylonia to witness the changing of the guard in his homeland—advised his disciple
Kahana to flee Babylonia after the latter had apparently taken the law into his
hands and executed a potential informer: "Until now [ruled] the Greeks [an
allusion to the Hellenistic influences manifest at the Parthian court][35] who
were not strict about bloodshed, now there are the Persians [a clear reference to
the neo-Persian self-image of the Sassanian dynasty][36] who are strict about
bloodshed—go up to the Land of Israel."

Ultimately these fears of forceful interference in the communal life of the Jews
would be proven exaggerated, and the modus vivendi formulated by Samuel—
the law of the kingdom is law—seems to be reflected in the amicable relationship between a number of Sassanian Kings and Jewish sages, at least according to
stories recorded in the Babylonian Talmud. Samuel is described in four talmudic
traditions as having maintained a decidedly courteous relationship with King
Shapur I.[37] Thus we are told that

> King Shapur once said to Samuel: "You [Jews] profess to be very clever; tell me
> what I shall see in my dream." He [Samuel] said to him: "You will see the Ro-
> mans coming and taking you captive, and making you grind date-stones in a
> golden mill." He [Shapur] thought about it all day, and in the night saw it in his
> dream.[38]

Another anecdote describes Samuel juggling eight glasses of wine before the
king.[39] A century later, we encounter a certain Ifra Hormiz,[40] mother of Shapur II
(309–79 C.E.) according to talmudic accounts, not only befriending some of
the sages but actually intervening on their behalf with her son. When a rabbi
(Rava) was suspected of having overstepped the bounds of recognized legal authority granted the Jews, she declared: "Have no dealings with [i.e., do not
punish] the Jews, for whatever they ask of their master He gives to them."[41] Another anecdote describes three fifth-century sages at the court of King Yazdagird I (399–420 C.E.) and again suggests a friendly context.[42] A number of factors
might have contributed to this atmosphere, not the least being the fact that Jews
under Persian rule would hardly be suspected of harboring loyalties toward the
mutually despised Roman Empire. With the embracing of Christianity by Rome
in the fourth century, any such suspicion would have been further alleviated; if
any elements of society were suspected of constituting a potential fifth column
in Sassanian Persia, these would more likely have been adherents of the Christian faith. The very fact that the Sassanian dynasty conjured up memories of a
"Persian" monarchy might have made it even easier for the sages to attach to

them the favorable memories of an earlier "Persia," and thus we encounter a uniquely rabbinic approach to the laws that govern the unfolding of historical processes:

> Rabbah bar bar Hanna, in the name of R. Yohanan, following a tradition from R. Yehuda b. Ilai, said: "Rome is destined to fall to Persia, kal va-homer [even more so]: If the First Temple, built by the sons of Shem [Israel] was destroyed by the Chaldeans [Babylonians], and the Chaldeans were defeated by the Persians, [and] the Persians built the Second Temple [through permission granted by Cyrus] [only to have it] destroyed by the Romans—is it not fitting that the Romans should fall to the Persians?"[43]

In another source, the Talmud actually appears to go out of its way to absolve the Persian king Shapur I of complicity, or at least of intentional malice, in the deaths of 12,000 Jews in Mazaca of Cappadocia during the wars of the mid-third century between the Sassanian Empire and Rome.[44] Nor do we hear of masses of Jews beyond the Euphrates rising up in support of the invading armies of Emperor Julian in the mid-fourth century, notwithstanding that ruler's promises regarding the rebuilding of the Jewish Temple. Politically, it would appear, the Jews of Babylonia did not suffer inordinately under the new Sassanian regime and probably fared significantly better under the new rulers than did their Christian contemporaries. In a total reversal of roles when compared to Palestine, it is striking to encounter the fourth-century Christian Father Aphraates, living in close proximity to the Jews of Ktesiphon, describe how the Jews mock the Christians in their midst for their lowly status and for the fact that God does not come to their aid![45]

Even more striking than the absence of any significant deterioration of the political status of Jews under the Sassanian monarchy was the lack of a systematic religious persecution at the hands of the new state church. Although the Talmud alludes to pressures felt as a result of action taken by the Zoroastrian clergy, a closer examination suggests that this was not a product of a coordinated persecution of Jews, nor even of any missionary zeal on the part of the local priests. Robert Brody has conclusively shown that, inasmuch as Zoroastrianism maintained a position of indifference toward conversion, there is no reason to believe that the actions described in the Babylonian Talmud, such as limiting certain Jewish practices, were the result of a concerted attempt at bringing over to the Persian religion—by force, if necessary—large numbers of Jews.[46] If, as we have seen, fire-priests intervened in Jewish life when they discovered the latter producing flames, this was a result of the clergy's wish to preserve the sanctity of fire, one of the central tenets of the Zoroastrian religion. Being Jewish or adhering to Jewish tradition was not the issue here; maintaining the purity of fire was. The same holds true for another Babylonian talmudic tradition that has been interpreted as referring to "persecution":

> They [the Zoroastrian clergy] decreed three because of three: they decreed concerning meat because of the [priestly] gifts, they decreed concerning bath-houses because of ritual immersion, they exhume the dead because of [Jewish] rejoicing on their [Zoroastrian] holidays. (BT Yevamot 63b)[47]

The source here appears to be saying that Jewish neglect of their religious ordinances (not granting the requisite portions of slaughtered animals to priests, laxity in the laws of purity and immersion, etc.) was the cause of their mistreatment at the hands of the Zoroastrian priesthood. The question is, does all this fall under the heading of religious persecution?

To be sure, the terminology—"they decreed" *(gazru)*—is the common talmudic allusion to religious persecution, more frequently found in the context of Roman Palestine. What we apparently have here, however, is a reference to those areas of daily Jewish life that might be affected by the more activist Zoroastrian clergy that appeared on the scene with the rise of the Sassanians. The source indeed alludes to three areas in which a uniquely Zoroastrian religious sensitivity would have caused new difficulties for ongoing Jewish behavior. Thus, for example, the exhuming of the dead by Zoroastrians is a clear consequence of that religion's unique concept of the earth's sanctity, which required that the dead be exposed rather than buried:[48] "Where then shall we carry the body of a dead man, where lay it down? Then said Ahuara Mazda: 'On the highest places, so that corpse-eating beasts and birds will most readily perceive it.' "[49] It is precisely in light of such beliefs that the following talmudic tale conforms so naturally with the surrounding religious environment:

> A *magus* used to exhume corpses. When he came to the [burial] cave of Rav Tuvi bar Matna, [the latter] seized him by his [the priest's] beard.[50] Abaye happened by and said to him [Rav Tuvi]: I beg you, release him. The following year he [the priest] returned. He [Rav Tuvi] seized him by his beard; Abaye came— but [Rav Tuvi] would not release him, until they brought scissors and cut off his beard. (BT Bava Bathra 58a)

In a similar manner, the immersion of menstruant women in waters deemed pure would be equally offensive to Zoroastrian believers.[51] And yet, all this

notwithstanding, one fails to sense an *ongoing* confrontation in rabbinic literature between Jews and representatives of the government or officials of the state
church. To be sure, gaonic chronicles such as Iggeret Rav Sherira Gaon describe
a series of anti-Jewish persecutions during the fifth century, beginning with
the reign of Yazdagird II (438–57 C.E.) and continuing under his son Peroz (459–
84 C.E.). Sabbath observance was forbidden, synagogues were closed, and Jewish
children were seized to become servants in fire-temples. All sorts of explanations
have been offered for this radical departure from the earlier atmosphere of relative tolerance; some point to the religious zeal evinced by Yazdagird II in his relations with Christians as well as Jews, whereas others have searched for factors that
may have weakened the central government and thereby enabled the more extreme elements within the church to consolidate their power through the use of
terror and persecution.[52] In truth, no single explanation has proven totally convincing, and the very need to provide some sort of rationale for an abrupt change
of policy points to the predominantly favorable relationship between the Jewish
and Iranian communities.

CROSSCURRENTS OF INFLUENCE:
CULTURAL CONTACTS BETWEEN JEWS AND PERSIANS

Charting the twisted and circular paths of cultural dissemination among communities of the ancient world is one of the more speculative undertakings of
historians. Attempts at uncovering ancient Iranian influences on the formative
stages of Judaism are no exception, and the question of the degree—and indeed
the very existence—of a significant Zoroastrian impact on Judaism dating back
hundreds of years prior to the rabbinic era finds scholars divided into diametri-
cally opposed camps: "One of these [camps] emphatically denies the actual existence or possibility of Persian cultural influence on Judaism as a factor affecting
Jewish thought. . . . [T]he other position is the one which would explain almost
everything in the development of post-biblical Judaism as stemming directly
from Iran."[53] To be sure, the Iranian and Jewish worlds of religious thought contain similar notions relating to a wide variety of themes. These include aspects of
dualism, angelology and demonology, the destiny of the world and the duration
of its existence, as well as various eschatological images and beliefs. What is
striking, however, is that almost none of these expressions can be found in any
extant pre-talmudic Babylonian Jewish literature, but instead they survived almost exclusively in the Palestinian Jewish writings of the Second Temple period.
Given the known policies of the Persian government in Achaemenid times, it
would be difficult to attribute such influences to a concerted effort on the part of

the Persian administrators of Palestine during the first centuries of the Second
Temple period. A more likely scenario would be to assume an initial Jewish exposure to Iranian ideas within the boundaries of Persia and Mesopotamia,
where Jews lived among a predominantly Persian population, and thus "the
most likely carriers of this new set of ideas may have been Jews from that Diaspora who had constant communication with their brethren in Palestine through
pilgrimage and immigration."[54]

Though addressing an earlier stage of Persian-Jewish contacts within Iran,
this proposal might nevertheless contribute to our understanding of the nature
and degree of cross-cultural influences in rabbinic Babylonia as well. To begin, it
is doubtful to what degree the feudalization within Iran, in Parthian as well as
Sassanian times, effected—as claimed by Salo Baron—a "mutual segregation of
all corporate groups, and particularly the ethnic-religious communities."[55] If
anything, the feudalization of the Persian Empire, which contributed toward the
maintenance of distinct tribal and ethnic identities, probably also produced a
sense of self-assuredness that would have allowed rabbis to loosen their reins
and enabled them to permit a significant degree of interaction with the surrounding society. If we nevertheless encounter numerous Babylonian talmudic
discussions that, in the context of attitudes toward idolatry, seek to erect barriers
between Jews and non-Jews by prohibiting access, among other things, to gentile
bread, wine, and other foods, we should note that almost all these "Babylonian"
discussions are based directly on the Palestinian Mishnah and the ensuing halakhic traditions that are also of Palestinian provenance. And so, just as certain
Persian concepts and attitudes might have been introduced into Palestinian Jewish society through the mediation of Jews traveling from Iran to western lands,
we may note in rabbinic times a reverse phenomenon: the rabbis of Babylonia
were almost certainly the recipients of certain religious and social attitudes
that were spawned in a decidedly Hellenistic-Roman and ultimately Christian
environment, one that demanded a heightened degree of caution in light of constant and even conscious efforts at cultural and religious assimilation. Morever,
even in certain spheres of "popular" cultural activity, such as magical incantations so frequently attributed to a Persian environment, we may in fact be confronted by behavior with decidedly Palestinian roots that found its way to
Babylonia through some sort of internal Jewish pipeline:

A comparison of the metal amulets from Palestine and surrounding countries
to the magic bowls from Mesopotamia shows in several cases clear Palestinian
influences and only rarely if ever can one detect influences in the other direction. . . . When formulae from the two geographical areas converge, it may be

invariably established that the origin of the theme is Palestinian, rather than
Babylonian.[56]

All this notwithstanding, the Jews of Babylonia lived in proximity to non-
Jewish centers of population and maintained ties on a daily basis with those
communities. Indeed, we find gentiles living in the same courtyards with Jews
(BT Eruvin 63b), and we even encounter a Jew and a gentile living in the same
house: "the Israelite in the upper story and the gentile in the lower" (BT Avodah
Zara 70a). Jews and non-Jews would greet one another in passing (BT Gitin 62a)
and would even offer a hand to the elderly of the other community (Kiddushin
33a). To be sure, our information on such matters is incidental and appears primarily within the context of some legal issue. Thus, for example, we find Samuel
in the house of a gentile on Shabbat, wondering whether he may make personal
use of a flame lit by the owner on the Sabbath—if the fire was not lit for
Samuel's benefit.[57]

We also encounter a reverse reality, in which gentiles can be found in the
houses of Jews on Jewish holidays (BT Bezah 21b). We even hear of Jews and gentiles exchanging gifts on the respective holidays of the two communities: a non-
Jew dedicated a candle to the synagogue of the third-century leader Rav Judah
(BT Arakhin 6b), and the same rabbi is supposed to have sent a gift to a gentile
on that person's holiday (BT Avodah Zara 64b–65a).[58] In fact, Rav Judah actually
permitted the sages to conduct business with gentiles on their holidays (BT Avodah Zara 11b). In sum, one senses, at least in this respect, a far more flexible and
cordial stance toward the surrounding community than the rigid and indeed at
times suspicious attitude evinced by the Palestinian rabbis. The same holds true
for a significant amount of commercial cooperation between the communities.[59]
Jews and gentiles worked the same fields and even took each other's place as
watchmen on the respective holidays of their partner (BT Avodah Zara 22a). We
find Jews and gentiles pressing grapes together in the city of Nehardea (BT Avodah Zara 56b) and a Jew renting his boat to a gentile for the purpose of shipping
wine (BT Avodah Zara 26b). What is striking is that the rabbis of Babylonia are
frequently named as maintaining a variety of business relations with gentiles;
they buy and sell fields from them, and one story even has Rav Ashi selling trees
to "a house of fire"—which to the Talmud sounds suspiciously close to indirectly lending a hand to some sort of idolatrous enterprise (BT Avodah Zara
62b). Clearly the segregation of ethnic communities is not the dominant reality
emerging from a wealth of talmudic anecdotes.

Even the most casual mingling of Jews and gentiles in Babylonia required a
common language of discourse, and such a tool most certainly existed. The daily

language of almost all the local Jews was undoubtedly Babylonian Aramaic, a dialect of eastern Aramaic[60] that served the Jewish community at least until the end of the gaonic period in the eleventh century. Rav Hai Gaon, head of the Pumbedita rabbinic academy at the beginning of the eleventh century, declares that "from long ago Babylonia was the locus for the Aramaic and Chaldean language, and until our time all [local] towns speak in the Aramaic and Chaldean tongue, both Jews and gentiles."[61] The Babylonian *geonim* (heads of the academies) refer to Aramaic as "our language," the one to be found "even in the mouths of women and youngsters."[62] By this statement the Babylonians did not wish to deny or ignore their obvious knowledge and literary use of the Hebrew language, but in all fairness it must be noted that, by talmudic times, Hebrew had reverted even in Palestine more into a literary vehicle within the Jewish community rather than a means of daily communication.[63]

Babylonian Jews were clearly aware that other languages were also in use in their immediate vicinity, most significantly the Parthian and Pahlavi dialects of what is commonly called "Middle Persian." Although the literary heritage of this dialect was preserved primarily in Zoroastrian writings rooted in the Sassanian period but surviving primarily in products of the ninth and tenth centuries,[64] it did serve as the vernacular of the Sassanians and would probably have been identified by the Babylonian rabbis as the language of the Iranian government and clergy. As such, the rabbis apparently attained some degree of familiarity with Middle Persian and even introduced it into their exegetical activity:

Rava said: "On what basis [i.e., what is the biblical analogy] do the Persians call a scribe *'debir'*? From this [scripture]: 'Now the name of [the city] *Devir* was originally Kiriath-*Sefer.*' " (BT Avodah Zara 24b)

The exegesis here is based on the Hebrew letters SPR, which can be read as either "book" *(sefer)* or "scribe" *(sofer)*. The fact that the biblical city of Kiriath-*SPR* was originally called "debir," which is also the Persian word for "scribe," facilitated the rabbinic etymological link—tenuous as it may be—of a familiar contemporary Persian word with a statement in biblical Hebrew.[65]

In the continuation of the same portion of the Babylonian Talmud, we find Rav Ashi explaining the Pahlavi word for menstrual blood—*dashtan*—on the basis of a contraction of Rachel's words in Genesis 31:35, "For the manner of women *[derekh nashim]* is upon me."

Such explicit allusions to "Persian," however, are sporadic at best and hardly represent an indication of the nature and extent of cultural ties or influence. The number of Persian loanwords found in the Babylonian Talmud, while considerable, is dramatically less than the thousands of Greek and Latin words found throughout the parallel rabbinic corpus of Palestine.[66] Moreover, the study or knowledge of "Persian" never assumed the ideological significance that accompanied a parallel pursuit of Greek in Palestine and that caused fathers to address rabbis with questions regarding the permissibility of teaching their sons (and daughters) Greek.[67] Nor were the qualities of the Persian language extolled in the manner that Palestinian sources refer to the Greek language, such as its being the only language into which the Torah might be accurately translated.[68] Indeed, the statement by Rav Joseph—"Why [speak] the Aramaic language in Babylonia, [better] either the Sacred Tongue [Hebrew] or the Persian language" (BT Sotah 49b)—can hardly be taken as a serious attempt at abandoning Aramaic in favor of a Persian dialect. The statement is no more than an artificial replication of a declaration attributed to the Palestinian patriarch Judah (180–220 C.E.): "Why speak Syriac [i.e., Aramaic] in Palestine? Talk either Hebrew or Greek" (BT Sotah 49b). Both statements recognize that Jews in Late Antiquity were interacting with three languages: the sacred Hebrew language of Scripture and synagogue liturgical activity; the vernacular (Aramaic); and the "official" language of the government and surrounding elements of the indigenous aristocracy or clergy. But the comparison ends here, and Persian among Babylonian Jews never assumed the position evinced by Greek among the Jewish populations of Palestine and the Roman Empire. The latter were surrounded by broad sections of a gentile society for whom the Greek language was not just a vehicle for daily discourse but the ultimate underpinning of an all-embracing culture. This was not the case in Babylonia; here no such equation between the "official" language of government and the vernacular of the cultured masses existed. Persian was far more limited to government and the Iranian church, whereas Aramaic served as the vernacular—both for Jews and for the indigenous non-Jewish population.

If, however, Middle Persian was perceived by the rabbis as primarily a language of the Iranian government and clergy,[69] the use—or at least passive knowledge—of words in that dialect by Babylonian Jews might nevertheless serve to indicate the areas of cultural interaction between the latter and certain representative elements of Iranian society. Sure enough, of those Persian words that found their way into the Babylonian Talmud, a significant number relate precisely to those spheres of public behavior where Jews and Persian officials came into actual contact. These include state administration, official titles of office, the administration of justice and forms of punishment, and military terms.[70]

Similarly, it is not at all surprising to find rabbinic allusions to the festivals of "the Persians." The main reference in the Babylonian Talmud (Avodah Zara 11b) lists four "Persian ones" alongside "four Babylonian ones," and this distinction—to say nothing of the actual names of the festivals cited for each group by the Talmud—is far from clear.[71] The parallel discussion in the Palestinian Talmud (Avodah Zara 1:1 39c) quotes Rav as saying that "three holidays are in Babylonia and three holidays are in Media." In both cases the names of the holidays were corrupted by copyists over the generations and thus prove nothing regarding the original familiarity of the talmudic rabbis with Iranian festivals.[72] But the vast scholarship on these lists[73] has succeeded at least in identifying two well-known Iranian holidays in both versions. They are "Noruz" ("Musardi" in manuscript versions of the BT; Noroz in the PT), which signified the coming of the spring or the summer,[74] and "Mihragan" ("Muharnekai" in the BT), which designated the onset of the rainy season. The halakhic context for the preservation of these lists was the Palestinian rabbinic prohibition on conducting business transactions with the heathen on their festivals (Mishnah Avodah Zara 1:1–2). Whereas the Mishnah proscribed such transactions "on the three days preceding the festivities," the Babylonian sage Samuel declared that "in the diaspora [Babylonia] it is only forbidden on the actual festival day" (BT Avodah Zara 11b), possibly hinting at a diminished fear in Babylonia that Jews might somehow become involved in local cultic worship.

The underlying assumption in all cases was that the Jew had sufficient knowledge of the surrounding calendar so that he might refrain from business on those days. It could be, however, that—as in the case of Iranian loanwords—here too the rabbis referred precisely to those days on the Persian calendar that directly affected their own lives. The two festivals noted above were apparently also days of tax collection in the Sassanian Empire, and indeed we hear elsewhere that Jews were accused of attempting to avoid payment of "the king's poll-tax" twice during the year, "a month in the summer and a month in the winter" (BT Bava Metzia 86a).[75] This would tend to dovetail with those sources cited already, relating to the interference of the Persian priests in the daily life of Jews, such as by the removal of fire from their midst. This sort of activity apparently also took place on specific days of the Persian calendar,[76] and so—as in the case of tax collection—rabbinic awareness of particular components of Iranian culture need not necessarily reflect an internalizing process of acculturation but instead might point at times to a more prosaic reality of Jewish life being affected by the proclivities of the surrounding—and ruling—local administration.

Yet when all is said and done, it would be impossible to deny some obvious similarities between certain Iranian and Babylonian rabbinic aspects of theology that manifest themselves not only in parallel terminology but also in actual expressions of popular belief and concomitant behavior. To be sure, not all "similarities" necessarily point to an Iranian influence upon Babylonian Jewry,[77] but the fact that we possess the literary product of two parallel rabbinic communities, those of Babylonia and Palestine, affords us with at least some degree of control. Consequently, when we encounter fairly obvious affinities of expression or behavior between Babylonian Jews and their Persian neighbors, with no parallel expression anywhere in Palestinian rabbinic literature, the likelihood of an internal Iranian process of acculturation is at least partially enhanced.

One seemingly obvious example of contact between popular Iranian culture and statements recorded in the Babylonian Talmud relates to the realm of demons and demonology.[78] To be sure, a belief in the existence of vast armies of demons and spirits existing alongside human beings and constantly interacting with them was shared by all the peoples of the Ancient Near East. Among the biblical sins of ancient Israel was their recurrent sacrificing to *shedim*, a Hebrew term translated in the Septuagint as *daimones* (demons).[79] Second Temple Jewish literature is replete with allusions to a variety of such forces of evil, and Josephus even claims that King Solomon was trained in the ways of fighting evil spirits, and that he "composed incantations . . . and left behind forms of exorcisms with which those possessed by demons drive them out, never to return."[80] Josephus himself testifies to witnessing the activity of an exorciser in the presence of Vespasian and his soldiers,[81] and of course the New Testament is replete with stories of people possessed by a variety of evil spirits.[82] Scholars have even noted distinct similarities in the import assigned to some terms that refer to a variety of spiritual forces in Palestinian sectarian literature with those found in Iranian terminology,[83] suggesting some sort of Iranian cultural impact on the religious thought and imagery embraced by certain Palestinian Jewish circles.[84]

It is hardly surprising, then, that the Palestinian rabbis were also party to this widespread belief in spirits; according to one opinion in the Mishnah, "the harmful spirits" *(mazikin)* were among the 10 things created on Sabbath eve at twilight.[85] Rabbi Shimon b. Yohai interpreted the word "all" in a particular scripture ("And *all* people of the earth shall see that thou art called by the name of the Lord"—Deuteronomy 28:10) to refer "even to spirits and even to demons."[86] Such beliefs found their way into halakhic discourse as well, and thus, for example, the Tosefta addresses the permissibility of whispering an incantation "about demons" on the Sabbath.[87]

The universality of belief in demons and spirits notwithstanding, it is nevertheless in the Babylonian rabbinic corpus that we sense a true affinity to specific demonological images prominent in Iranian religious thought. The pervasiveness of demons so common in Pahlavi literature[88] resonates clearly in the Babylonian Talmud:[89]

It has been taught: Abba Benjamin says: "If the eye had the power to see them, no creature could endure the demons." Abaye said: "They are more numerous than we are and they surround us like the ridge around a field." Rav Huna says: "Every one among us has a thousand on his left hand and ten thousand on his right hand." Rabba says: "The crushing in the Kallah [i.e., the gatherings for public learning among the Babylonian rabbis] is from them. The wearing out of the clothes of scholars is due to their rubbing against them. . . . If one wants to discover them, let him take sifted ashes and sprinkle them around his bed, and in the morning he will see something like the footprints of a cock."[90]

Another talmudic tradition describes the queen of demons—Igrath, the daughter of Mahalath—at the head of 180,000 "destructive angels." Originally, we are told, these forces had unbridled permission to wreak destruction, but their powers were curtailed following the decree of one of the rabbis[91] ordering her never to pass through settled regions. " 'I beg you'—she pleaded—'leave me a little room,' so he left her the nights of Sabbath and of Wednesdays." It is for this reason, the Babylonian Talmud warns, that "one should not go out alone . . . on the nights of either Wednesday or Sabbath" (BT Pesahim 112b). Yet another sage—Abaye—succeeded in limiting the activities of these angels to isolated areas, removing them by his decree from settled regions (BT Pesahim 112b). Not only are these allusions to such demonic forces introduced into the talmudic discourse without any sign of skepticism or inferred disbelief, but they actually suggest that the most noted legal scholars of the rabbinic world accepted the existence of such forces; however, the scholars were able to overcome their destructive powers either by some specific knowledge they possessed or by virtue of their own pious behavior. Prayer, we can assume, would be a particularly potent weapon in this confrontation, and thus we read the following story about "a demon" that haunted the schoolhouse of Abaye, so that whenever two disciples would enter the premises, even during daytime, they would be harmed. Upon the arrival of another sage—Rabbi Aha b. Jacob—in town, Abaye saw to it that none of the townsmen offered him hospitality, thereby requiring the rabbi to spend the night in the schoolhouse:

The demon appeared to him in the guise of a seven-headed dragon. Every time he [Aha] fell on his knees [in prayer] one head fell off. The next day he reproached [the men of the schoolhouse]: "Had not a miracle occurred, you would have endangered my life." (BT Kiddushin 29b)

Legal discussions and allusions to demons seem to merge effortlessly in the Babylonian Talmud, hardly leaving an impression that the world of halakhah—

rather than that of devils and spirits—is the "real" and exclusive environment in which rabbis function. The long discussion of demons, magic, and the like found in the Babylonian Talmud (Pesahim 109b–112b) is introduced through a question relating to the mishnaic stipulation that at the Passover seder one must drink four cups of wine: "How could our Rabbis enact something whereby one is led into danger? Surely it was taught: A man must not eat in pairs [i.e., eat an even-numbered amount of dishes] nor drink in pairs nor cleanse himself twice nor perform his requirements [a euphemism for intimacy] twice." All this, we are ultimately informed, is because—as the demon Joseph once told Rabbi Joseph—"Ashmedai[92] the king of the demons is appointed over all pairs" (BT Pesahim 110a).

What is striking, however, is not merely the credulity evinced by the Babylonian rabbis toward these phenomena but also their knowledge that such beliefs were not always shared by their Palestinian counterparts: "In the West [Palestine] they are not particular about 'pairs' " (BT Pesahim 110b).[93] Moreover, it appears that all sorts of Babylonian rabbinic customs are related to fears well established in Iranian demonology. For example, the care that the rabbis demand in not randomly discarding the parings of human fingernails—"One who buries them is righteous, one who burns them is pious, and one who throws them away is a villain"[94]—derives directly from Iranian fears about the powerful potential, for good as well as evil, found in nail-parings. According to the Vendidad (17.9), nail-parings should be dedicated to a particularly fabulous bird (known as "Asho.zushta" and identified as the owl) renowned for uttering holy words in its own unique tongue, thereby causing devils to flee. This bird was charged with guarding the parings, lest they fall into the hands of the devils who then turn them into hostile weapons.[95]

The rabbis of Babylonia were aware of potential danger lurking wherever the demons and their kind might be found, which was just about everywhere. Particularly susceptible moments were during the various functions connected with eating and drinking:

Abaye said: "At first I thought the reason why the last washing [of the hands after a meal] may not be performed over the ground [but only over a vessel] was that it made a mess, but now my master [Rabbah bar Nahmani] has told me it is because an evil spirit rests upon it [i.e., the water]." (BT Hullin 105b)

Abaye was also advised by his mentor not to drink water from the mouth of a jug but to pour off some water first and then drink, "because of evil waters"— that is, the fear that demons may have drunk from the water at the top of the jug

(BT Hullin 105b).[96] In general, demons rendered the drinking of water a potentially dangerous activity, and one had to know precisely when and where it was advisable to refrain from drinking: "A man should not drink water from rivers and pools at night, and if he drinks, his blood is on his own head, because of the danger."

What is the danger?—the Talmud asks, and responds by citing the name "Shaberiri," apparently the demon that causes blindness. Fortunately, the rabbis were also privy to the effective incantation that might ward off this particular spirit: "O So-and-so, my mother told me: 'Beware of Shaberire, berire, rire, ire, re; I am thirsty for water in a white glass' " (BT Pesahim 112a).[97]

Here too it was Zoroastrian literature that also warned against drinking water at night. In a collection of Zoroastrian traditions known as *Sad Dar* (lit. "The Hundred Subjects"),[98] we read that "it is not proper to swallow water at night, because it is a sin."[99] A Pahlavi fragment alludes to the contamination of well-water at night,[100] and yet another text[101] explicitly relates to the presence of demons and fiends who seize upon the wisdom of one who eats or drinks in the dark.

For Zoroastrians, however, demons did not only lurk in various locations and wait to pounce on some hapless innocent. Just as one's physical being might be assaulted by these forces, so others might lay siege to a person's moral nature and behavior.[102] Pahlavi texts describe various spirits taking over a man's personality: "A man whose body is inhabited by Akoman [Evil Mind], this is his mark: He is cool as regards good works, has bad relationships with the good, is difficult [in] making peace, is an advocate of the destitute good and is himself [miserly].[103] The same text goes on to describe a man "whose body is inhabited by Xesm [Anger]" and the negative impact on his behavior: "It is impossible to talk to him, when people talk to him he does not listen. . . . [H]e tells many lies to people and inflicts much chastisement on an innocent person."

This being the case, we can understand how all sorts of actions might be attributed to such demons who take control of a man's faculties, thereby controlling his deeds as well. Not only was this sort of compulsion known to the Babylonian rabbis, but they even attempted to define the legal ramifications of such behavior. In this context the Talmud cites the following halakhah: "If a man is compelled by force to eat unleavened bread [on Passover], he thereby performs his religious duty." The nature of this compulsion, however, is immediately addressed: "Compelled by whom? Shall I say by an evil spirit?" (BT Rosh Hashanah 28a). The conclusion, of course, might be to consider "sin" as well the result of various powers that have taken control of one's being, thereby possibly alleviating any moral culpability for such action. Although this was not addressed directly by the Babylonian rabbis, they nevertheless appear to have been familiar with the image of one whose actions seem to be directed, and indeed coerced, by some sort of invading demon. When asked why her children are so beautiful, a woman ascribes it to her husband's modesty, describing how her husband cohabits with her only at midnight, and even then "uncovers a hand-breadth and covers a handbreadth, and is as though he were *compelled by a demon*" (BT Nedarim 20b).[104]

The belief in demons and spirits demanded a powerful arsenal of protective measures to ward off potential dangers, and the ancient world produced an enormous variety of them. The Jews of Babylonia were no different in this re-spect from their brethren in Palestine and elsewhere, nor from the non-Jewish environment in which they lived. Amulets, incantations, and other measures were employed universally, but certain discoveries relating to this community would appear to shed some interesting light on one particular aspect of the rela-tionship between Jews and gentiles east of the Euphrates River.

During the past 150 years, hundreds of earthenware bowls, containing incan-tations primarily in Jewish Aramaic but also in Syriac and Mandaic, have been discovered in Mesopotamia and Iran, the areas that in Late Antiquity and the early Middle Ages constituted the regions of talmudic and gaonic Babylonia.[105] These bowls are usually dated between the fourth and seventh centuries C.E.— that is, the second half of the talmudic era and the immediate post-talmudic period. The vessels are inscribed in ink, usually on the concave side in spiral con-centric circles, but there are various exceptions to this pattern.[106] (See p. 250.) A large number of such bowls were found in 1888–89 at excavations at Nippur, where they were discovered *in situ* in private dwellings, usually in what is as-sumed to be their original position, upside down. Scholars have assumed that, positioned in such a manner, and given their contents, the bowls were intended to trap and imprison various demons. Although this interpretation is reinforced by the language frequently found in the bowls ("bound and sealed are all de-mons and evil spirits"),[107] other such vessels were intended to rid a person or a house of some evil spirit ("now flee and go forth and do not trouble Komes b. Mahlaphta in her house and her dwelling").[108] The removal of the spirit or demon was effected in a manner very similar to the dispatching of a writ of di-vorce, and indeed some of the bowls actually use the terminology of a Jewish *get*, except that in place of a woman being divorced, we encounter Lilith or some other demon as the object of the process:

> I, Komes bat Mahlaphta, have divorced, separated, missed thee, thou Lilith, Lilith of the Desert. . . .[I]t is announced to you, whose mother is Palhan and whose father [Pe]lahdad, ye Liliths: Hear and go forth and do not trouble

Komes bat Mahlaphta in her house. Go ye forth altogether from her house and her dwelling and from Kaletha and Artasria her children . . . for so has spoken to thee Joshua ben Perahya: A divorce has come to thee from across the sea.[109]

Even more striking is the fact that these "deeds of divorce" frequently adhere not only to the terminology of a *get* but to legal stipulations as well, such as the requirement that the document cite explicitly the full name of the intended divorcee, as well as the person charging the particular spirit with removal. Indeed, one bowl actually alludes to a previous case where the banned spirit was not named, thus rendering that earlier document invalid: "Just as there was a Lilith who strangled human beings, and Rabbi Yehoshu'a bar Perahya sent a ban against her, but she did not accept it because he did not know her name."[110]

The numerous references in the bowls to Yehoshua ben Perahya, the "rabbi" we encountered in a talmudic confrontation with "the queen of demons," is just one of many factors that support the widely—albeit not universally[111]—accepted theory that these bowls were inscribed not only by Jews but indeed by those Jews who had at least some access to rabbinic legal formulae. The language in many of the bowls has been definitively identified as Babylonian Jewish Aramaic, and the frequent quotation of biblical scripture in Hebrew lends further support for assuming that before us are the products of Jewish practitioners of magic.

But if the language and content all point to Jewish magicians, one factor in many of the bowls almost certainly suggests a non-Jewish involvement as well: the clients on whose behalf the bowls were produced very frequently go by decidedly Persian names, at times even Zoroastrian theophoric ones.[112] Some Jews may have adopted Persian names, but the preponderance of otherwise Jewish components in the vast majority of magic bowls found to date, alongside a decidedly non-Jewish nomenclature for the beneficiaries of the bowls, seems to point to a fascinating social and cultural reality in talmudic Babylonia. As a minority group, however self-assured, the Jews may have been considered by the indigenous population of Babylonia not only as "different" and even "outsiders" but, more important, as "others" who nevertheless have access to certain knowledge, or powers, that "we" locals are not privy to. In fact, societies frequently attribute such extraordinary talents precisely to groups living outside the mainstream, or on the fringes of society. It may very well be that the Jews of Babylonia were willing to offer their services in connecting with certain forces or spirits not readily accessible to the masses. And while this activity might have been frowned upon—at least in principle—by the rabbis themselves, they could not prevent their coreligionists from providing a service in great demand by neighboring groups who were not party to the same misgivings.

This last observation deserves some further explication. On the one hand, the

An example of Aramaic magic bowls, written by Jews but
possibly intended to heal non-Jews in Sassanian Babylonia.
(The Israel Museum, Jerusalem)

rabbis evinced enormous discomfort with all sorts of magical activities,[113] considering them an attempt at circumventing proper channels of prayer and behavior in the process of seeking certain benefits, and thereby constituting a
denial of the exclusive role of "the heavenly *familia*" in the granting of such re-
wards.[114] Yet, on the other hand, it is clear from what we have seen that the belief
in an army of demons and spirits was deeply embedded in the rabbinic mind
and that the rabbis did not shy away from addressing this "reality" with their
own unique recourse to a wide array of incantations and other activities, all
aimed directly at the threatening entity and forgoing supplication to the divine
protector or benefactor.

This seeming inconsistency characterizes the rabbinic position vis-à-vis
all sorts of popular beliefs and their attendant behavior. Among the most obvious examples of such fence straddling are the numerous rabbinic statements
addressing astrology. Here, of course, the barriers between Babylonia and the
rest of the Jewish world had long ago been removed. While the very phrase

"Chaldean" served in ancient times to link the land of Babylonia with a propensity for astrological activity,[115] astrology had become so popular by the Greco-Roman period that "scarcely anybody made a distinction between astronomy and its illegitimate sister."[116] For the rabbis, however, recognition of the efficacy of astrology placed in question not only man's freedom of choice but also the whole concept of Divine providence and its critical link with the principle of free will.[117] Recourse to astrological divination was tantamount to recognition that events were predetermined in the stars and not dependent on God's will, which properly should be influenced by man's behavior. Consequently the third-century sage Rav, in the name of one of the few second-century rabbinic authorities also of Babylonian origins (Rabbi Yosi of Huzal), declared: "How do we know that you must not consult Chaldeans [astrologers]? Because it says: 'Thou shalt be whole-hearted with the Lord thy God' (Deuteronomy 18:13)."[118]

But neither in Babylonia nor in Palestine could the rabbis bring themselves to deny outright the "science" of their day, "a science recognized and acknowledged by all the civilized ancient world."[119] Moreover, just as Jewish authors of the Second Temple period had already identified Abraham as one who "sought and obtained the knowledge of astrology and the Chaldean craft,"[120] so too did the Babylonian sages attribute to Abraham a belief in planetary influence. When he is promised by God that he will have an heir, he replies:

Sovereign of the Universe, I have looked at my constellation and find that I am not fated to beget a child. He [God] told him: "Leave your astrological calculation, for Israel is not subject to planetary influence [lit. 'there is no planet—mazal—for Israel']."[121]

God's response does not deny the power of the stars but claims that Israel—unlike the rest of humankind—has been removed from planetary control. Though clearly striving to maintain the theological purity of Israel's relationship with Divine providence, this somewhat contrived rabbinic compromise never really convinced the Babylonian sages that there was nothing in the stars for them. A passage in the Babylonian Talmud elaborates precisely what characteristics will adhere to people born on each of the seven days of the week (BT Shabbat 156a). The continuation of that same text notes how being born under the various planets also determines one's behavior:

He who was born under Venus will be wealthy and an adulterer. . . . He who was born under Mercury will be of a retentive memory and wise. . . . He who was born under Mars will be a shedder of blood. Rav Ashi said: "Either a surgeon, a thief, a slaughterer or a circumciser."

Elsewhere, Rava declares that "life, children, and livelihood" are not the consequence of one's merits but are "dependent on the planet" (BT Mo'ed Katan
28a). Yet another sage, Rav Papa, suggests that one should plan various activities
in accordance with the planetary constellation. Thus, for example, a person
should avoid litigation during the month of Av, "whose planet is pernicious," and
prefer instead the month of Adar, "whose planet is favorable" (BT Ta'anit 29b).

Even more telling is the foresight that the rabbis attribute to the various
"Chaldeans" that they themselves solicited for advice. Rav Joseph turned down
an offer to serve as head of the rabbinical academy "because the astrologers had
told him that he would be head for only two years." And so his colleague Rabbah
filled the position for 22 years, ultimately to be succeeded by Rav Joseph who indeed served for only two and a half years (BT Berakhot 64a).[122] Interestingly, a
later (tenth-century) version of this same story claims that it was Rav Joseph's
mother who had contact with the astrologers,[123] and we can only wonder if this
latter rendition is not something of a cleansed version intended to distance the
sage himself from behavior that does not quite conform to the standards set by
the rabbis themselves. Elsewhere in the Babylonian Talmud we do, in fact, find a
story describing contacts between the mother of a sage and Chaldeans, and
there, too, the prophesies of the astrologer are proven correct:

> Rav Nahman b. Isaac's mother was told by Chaldeans [astrologers]: "Your son
> will be a thief." She did not permit him to go bareheaded, telling him: "Cover
> your head so that the fear of heaven may be upon you, and pray [for mercy]."
> He did not know why she said this.
>   One day when he was sitting and studying under a palm tree, his garment
> fell from over his head, he raised his eyes, saw the palm tree, and temptation
> overcame him. He climbed up and bit off a cluster [of dates] with his teeth.
> (BT Shabbat 156b)

The Talmud cites this story to prove that Israel is *not* given to the influence of
planets, but, inasmuch as Rav Nahman's behavior until his "fall" overcame the
Chaldeans' prophesy, the bottom line of the story would appear to prove just the
opposite. Moreover, this is not an isolated case of a sage interacting with an astrologer, and in those other cases as well the pronouncements of the "Chaldeans"
invariably prove to be accurate.[124]

In sum, all of these sources seem to suggest a unique social and cultural
reality. The Babylonian sages knew quite well what a "perfect" Jewish world
ought to look like, and we would do well to interpret many of their program-
matic declarations as just that: idyllic guidelines for a world that could not possibly exist given the cultural milieu in which these rabbis functioned. And so,

theoretical declarations notwithstanding, in practice both the rabbis and their flock functioned as part of their social and cultural environment. Did these beliefs and their consequential behavior render the rabbis themselves "non-rabbinic"? Not really, if we accept the multiplicity of cultural influences all contributing to the uniquely Babylonian version of rabbinic society. In Jewish terms, much of their learning was nothing if not a continuation and intensification of Palestinian rabbinic teaching. Even here, however, they almost certainly grafted at least some aspects of the local Sassanian legal process to the mass of Palestinian material that they succeeded in co-opting and making their own.[125] As for popular culture, here too they forged an amalgam between ideas passed on from Palestine through the same rabbinic pipeline that transmitted legal materials and the surrounding Iranian environment that supplied them with a wealth of religious and spiritual imagery.

The genius of Babylonian rabbinic leadership, however, was not so much in the melding of such variegated influences into a broad cultural mosaic but rather in the creation and propagation of a self-image that would project this culture as being the embodiment of the one unique and ancient model of true, unadulterated Israelite tradition, with uncontaminated roots going back to First-Temple Jerusalem and the days of the prophets. Given all that we know about the diverse influences that left their mark on Babylonian Jewish culture prior to their establishment as a literary corpus, one undeniable fact remains. By post-talmudic times, the sages of Babylonia would not only assume the upper hand within the rabbinic world of their day but also ultimately succeed in securing a near-universal acceptance of their Talmud as the definitive expression of rabbinic Judaism. Having emerged out of almost total obscurity only a few centuries earlier, the communal success story of Babylonian Jewry would now be complete.

NOTES

1. The import of the names "Babylon" and "Babylonia" is far from consistent. Whereas the former is commonly employed as a designation of the ancient city, it (as well as "Babylonia") frequently refers to the vast territories between the Tigris and Euphrates rivers, south of Baghdad and constituting much of the southeastern areas of modern-day Iraq. In "Jewish geography," however, talmudic "Babylonia" usually includes all the Jewish communities east of the Euphrates, i.e., not only southeastern Iraq but also Mesopotamia to the northwest, as well as the Iranian territories east of the Tigris, such as Assyria, Media, and Elymais (Khusistan).

2. For surveys of the early Jewish captive community in Babylonia, see R. Zadok, *The Jews in Babylonia During the Chaldean and Achaemenian Periods According to the Babylo-*

nian Sources (Haifa, 1979), and E. J. Bickerman, "The Babylonian Captivity," in W. D. Davies and L. Finkelstein, eds. *The Cambridge History of Judaism,* vol. 1 (Cambridge, Engl., 1984), 342–58.

3. The Munich manuscript of the Babylonian Talmud reads "to her father's home," probably influenced by the allusion to the patriarch Abraham.

4. The date of the letter does not appear in chapter 29 of Jeremiah, but the passage seems to belong to the same historical context as the two previous chapters; see J. Bright, *Jeremiah,* 2d ed. (New York, 1984) 210–11.

5. The earliest successes of the Judaean captives in adjusting to their new land, while maintaining some degree of unique ethnic identity, are documented in the Murashu archives, discovered in 1893 at Nippur. See M. D. Coogan, "Life in the Diaspora: Jews at Nippur in the 5th Century B.C.," *Biblical Archaeologist* 37 (1974): 6–12, and S. Daiches, *The Jews in Babylonia in the Time of Ezra and Nehemiah According to Babylonian Inscriptions* (London, 1910).

6. BT Bava Bathra 55a and parallels; see J. Neusner, *A History of the Jews in Babylonia,* 5 vols. (Leiden, 1965–70), 2: 69. For the subsequent implications and various interpretations of the principle, see S. Shiloh, *Dina de-Malkhuta Dina* (Jerusalem, 1975). For a brief discussion of the principle's impact on Jewish communal development, see D. Biale, *Power and Powerlessness in Jewish History* (New York, 1986), 54–57.

7. This statement by Josephus (*Antiquities,* 11:133) seems to reflect a common general impression shared by other Jews in the west (see, e.g., Philo, *Legatio ad Gaium,* 216, 282) of vast numbers of Jews populating the lands beyond the Euphrates; in a way it also seems to highlight a shared ignorance of any real internal communal structures and cultural activities among those Jews.

8. Josephus, *Antiquities,* 15:14–15; here again Josephus relates that Hyrcanus II settled in Babylonia "where there was a great number of Jews."

9. For the role of Babylonian Jewry and Judaism in early modern Jewish scholarship, see I. Gafni, "Talmudic Research in Modern Times: Between Scholarship and Ideology," in A. Oppenheimer, ed., *Jüdische Geschichte in hellenistisch-römischer Zeit* (Munich, 1999), 134–48. For the place of Hillel in this dispute, see ibid., 145.

10. The formal reckoning of Parthian history begins with the uprising of Arsaces I and his brother Thiridates against the Seleucid Empire, circa 247 B.C.E. In effect, the beginning of Parthian rule in portions of Babylonia overlaps with the Seleucid era, but the main thrust of Parthian expansion at the expense of the Seleucid Empire, under King Mithridates I (171–138 B.C.E.) coincides with the Hasmonaean brother's rebellion against those very same Hellenistic rulers.

11. Parthian kings frequently attached titles such as "Philhellene," "Epiphanes," or "Euergetes" to their names, and Plutarch (Crassus 33) describes how one of Euripides' plays was being presented at the Parthian court when word was received there about the victory over Crassus at Charrae. Interestingly, the Babylonian Talmud (Bava Kamma 117a, according to most manuscripts) has the third-century sage Rav describe the Parthians—who had just

been defeated by the "Persians" (Sassanians)—as "Greeks." On Parthian attitudes toward Hellenism, see R. Ghirshman, *Iran* (Harmondsworth, 1954) 266–68, and R. Ghirshman, *Iran, Parthians and Sassanians* (London, 1962), 1–12, 257–81. Note also the title "The Adaptable Arsacids" for the Parthians, in R. N. Frye, *The Heritage of Persia* (Cleveland, 1963).

12. For general surveys of the Parthian Empire, see N. Debevoise, *A Political History of Parthia* (Chicago, 1938); A. D. H. Bivar, "The Political History of Iran Under the Arsacids," in E. Yarshater, ed., *Cambridge History of Iran*, vol. 3(1) (Cambridge, Engl. 1983), 21–99; and J. Neusner, "Parthian Political Ideology," *Iranica Antiqua* 3 (1963): 40–59.

13. *Antiquities*, 18:310–79 (the story of the brothers Asinaeus and Anilaeus); *Antiquities* 20:17–69 (the conversion of the royal family of Adiabene). Here, too, various nineteenth-century Jewish writers thought they might derive from these narratives solid information on the cultural and religious fabric of the Babylonian Jewish community in pre-talmudic times; however, see Gafni, "Talmudic Research," 144–45, esp. n. 59.

14. These identifications are in fact untenable. Borsif has been identified with the Burs mentioned by Yaqut and other Arabic sources (present-day Birs Nimrud) and is situated southwest of Babylonia, whereas the biblical text clearly refers to cities in Assyria; see A. Oppenheimer, *Babylonia Judaica in the Talmudic Period* (Wiesbaden, 1983), 104. The same is true for Perat de-Meshan, clearly in the vicinity of the Shatt al-Arab and consequently far removed from any Assyrian locality (ibid., 348).

15. BT Yoma 10a; Gen. Rabbah 37:4.

16. Yaqut and other Arab geographers have identified the three as islands in the Euphrates; see Oppenheimer, *Babylonia Judaica*, 28, 446.

17. BT Bava Bathra 91a; Kuta, or Kuta Rabbah, is the present-day Tall Ibrahim on the Habl Ibrahim canal, 30 kilometers northeast of Babylon; see Oppenheimer, *Babylonia Judaica*, 175, who notes that Arab sources also connect Kuta with Abraham.

18. A. Momigliano, *Alien Wisdom* (Cambridge, Engl., 1975), 116.

19. Apud Eusebius, *Praeparatio Evangelica*, 9.27.4.

20. BT Gitin 88a; see also Tanhuma Noah 3: "He [God] acted righteously with Israel in that He had the exile of Yekhoniah precede the exile of Zedekiah, in order that the Oral Torah not be forgotten by them."

21. All the attempts at identifying an exilarch in Babylonia prior to the third century C.E. are based on late and insufficient evidence; see J. Liver, *Toldot bet David mi-Ḥurban Mamlekhet Yehudah ve-ad le-aḥar Ḥurban ha-Bayit ha-Sheni* (Jerusalem, 1959), 41–46, and other literature cited in I. Gafni, *Land, Center and Diaspora: Jewish Constructs in Late Antiquity* (Sheffield, Engl., 1997), 55 n. 37. To be sure, given the overall paucity of information on the Babylonian Jewish community prior to the talmudic era, the existence of an early exilarchate cannot be dismissed out of hand and may actually have made sense within the political and social frameworks of the Parthian Empire.

22. *Iggeret Rav Sherira Gaon*, ed. B. M. Lewin (Haifa, 1921), 72–73. The antiquity of synagogues played a major role in Babylonian historical consciousness; see A. Oppen-

heimer, "Babylonian Synagogues with Historical Associations," in D. Urman and P. V. M. Flesher, eds., *Ancient Synagogues: Historical Analysis and Archaeological Discovery*, vol. 1 (Leiden, 1995), 40–48.

23. BT Kiddushin 69b, 71a; BT Ketubot 111a.

24. BT Kiddushin 69b.

25. Ibid.

26. BT Kiddushin 71b, and BT Gitin 6a; see also A. Oppenheimer and M. Lecker, "Lineage Boundaries of Babylonia," *Zion* 50 (1985): 173–87, and A. Oppenheimer and M. Lecker, "Burial Beyond the Euphrates," in S. Ettinger et al., eds., *Milet*, vol. 1 (Tel Aviv, 1983), 157–63.

27. See I. Gafni, "Reinterment in the Land of Israel: Notes on the Origin and Development of the Custom," *The Jerusalem Cathedra* 1 (1981): 96–104, and Gafni, *Land, Center and Diaspora*, 79–95.

28. *Avot de-Rabbi Nathan*, ed. S. Schechter, version A, chap. 26, p. 82.

29. Of course, the historicity of the story itself is not the issue here, but rather the self-image and political awareness that it reflects.

30. A frequent talmudic rendition of "herbad" or "erbad," one of several Persian titles for priests of the Zoroastrian church.

31. BT Gitin 16b–17a. For an exhaustive study of the talmudic source, its textual variants, and the wider religious realities and implications of the Zoroastrian priestly attempts at safeguarding the purity of fire and removing it from nonreligious contexts, see E. S. Rosenthal, "For the Talmudic Dictionary—Talmudica Iranica," in S. Shaked, ed., *Irano-Judaica*, vol. 1 (Jerusalem, 1982), Hebrew sec. 38–134, esp. 38–42, 58–64, and the notes on 75–84, 128–31.

32. For the nature of the Roman persecution of Jews during and following the Bar Kokhba uprising, see M. D. Herr, "Persecutions and Martyrdom in Hadrian's Days," *Scripta Hierosolymitana* 23 (1972): 85–125.

33. See J. Duchesne-Guillemin, "Religion and Politics Under the Sasanians," in E. Yarshater, ed., *The Cambridge History of Iran*, 3(2): 874–97.

34. BT Yevamot 63b.

35. See n. 11 above.

36. The text is quoted here according to almost all the important manuscripts of BT Bava Kamma and has undergone extensive scrutiny because of its obvious reference to the major political changes of the day. See Rosenthal, "For the Talmudic Dictionary," 54–58, 87, and D. Sperber, "On the Unfortunate Adventures of Rav Kahana: A Passage of Saboraic Polemic from Sasanian Persia," in Shaked, ed., *Irano-Judaica*, 1: 83–100.

37. BT Berakhot 56a; BT Sukkah 53a; BT Mo'ed Katan 26a; BT Sanhedrin 98a.

38. BT Berakhot 56a.

39. BT Sukkah 53a.

40. See D. Goodblatt, "A Note on the name 'ypr' / 'pr' hwrmyz," *Journal of the American Oriental Society* 96, 1 (1976): 135–36.

41. BT Ta'anit 24b; for the other stories, see J. Neusner, *Jews in Babylonia*, 4: 35–39.

42. BT Ketubot 61a–b.

43. BT Yoma 10a. Not all the Babylonians concurred with this prognosis, and in the continuation of this same source Rav predicts the opposite: Rome will defeat Persia. When asked how the destroyers will emerge victorious, the Talmud—anonymously—suggests that the latter were also guilty of destroying synagogues. (Rav himself is simply quoted as stating that this was God's wish—without elaborating.) This vague allusion to religious pressure on the part of the Sassanians might reflect the harsh reactions to some of the behavior attributed to the Zoroastrian priests, or possibly it was formulated during the few periods of outright persecution in Persia of minorities in general, not only Jews. These occurred in the late third century and again in the tumultuous days of the fifth century. For brief surveys of the attitude toward Jews under the Sassanians, see G. Widengren, "The Status of the Jews in the Sassanian Empire," *Iranica Antiqua* 1 (1961): 117–62; J. Neusner, "Jews in Iran," in Yarshater, ed., *The Cambridge History of Iran*, 3(2): 909–23.

44. BT Mo'ed Katan 26a.

45. See W. Wright, *The Homilies of Aphraates: The Persian Sage*, vol. 1: *Syriac Text* (London, 1869), 394. For literature on this relationship, see J. Neusner, *Aphrahat and Judaism* (Leiden, 1971), 7–12. The confidence of the Jews in their confrontation with Iranian Christianity may also be the result of superior numbers; see F. Gavin, *Aphraates and the Jews* (Toronto, 1923), 17. See also G. F. Moore, "Christian Writers on Judaism," *Harvard Theological Review* 14 (1921): 199.

46. See R. Brody, "Judaism in the Sasanian Empire: A Case Study in Religious Coexistence," in S. Shaked and A. Netzer, eds., *Irano-Judaica*, vol. 2 (Jerusalem, 1990), 52–61.

47. On this source, see M. Beer, "Notes on Three Edicts Against the Jews of Babylonia in the Third Century," in Shaked, ed., *Irano-Judaica*, 1: 25–37, and Brody, "Judaism in the Sasanian Empire."

48. For the rite of Zoroastrian exposure, see M. Boyce, *Zoroastrians, Their Religious Beliefs and Practices* (London, 1979), 14–15, 44–45, 120–21.

49. From Vendidad 6. The Vendidad, consisting of 22 sections, was most probably compiled in the Parthian period. It deals with a variety of legal topics and contains elaborate laws relating to purity. The translation here is from M. Boyce, ed. and trans., *Textual Sources for the Study of Zoroastrianism* (Manchester, 1984), 65.

50. The "Persians," in rabbinic imagery, "grow hair like bears" (BT Megillah 11a; BT Kiddushin 72a; BT Avodah Zara 2b), and in fact Sassanian art (coins and rock-carvings) almost always portray Persian rulers with grown beards, frequently in contradistinction to the Roman rulers shown in those same depictions.

51. It is not absolutely clear what aroused Zoroastrians to prohibit the slaughtering of animals by Jews; see Beer, "Notes on Three Edicts," 29–31. S. Shaked, "Zoroastrian Polemics Against Jews in the Sasanian and Early Islamic Period," in Shaked and Netzer, eds., *Irano-Judaica*, 2: 93, quotes certain Zoroastrian texts that advise "not to kill cattle before they reach

maturity" and claim that "Dahag"—the mythical representative of the negative views that oppose the true faith—"taught to kill cattle freely, according to the custom of the Jews."

52. See Brody, "Judaism in the Sasanian Empire," 61, and the literature cited in I. Gafni, *Yehudei Bavel bi-Tekufat ha-Talmud: Ḥaye ha-Ḥevrah ve-ha Ruaḥ* (Jerusalem, 1990), 49–51, 251.

53. S. Shaked, "Iranian Influence on Judaism: First Century B.C.E. to Second Century C.E.," in Davies and Finkelstein, eds., *The Cambridge History of Judaism*, 1: 308–25, esp. 309. A copious literature exists on the possible bilateral influences of the Jewish and Persian religions and cultures, alongside an equally elaborate bibliography denying the "influence" aspect and arguing for a more independent, albeit at times chronologically concurrent, development of similar ideas. See G. W. Carter, *Zoroastrianism and Judaism* (Boston, 1918); J. Barr, "The Question of Religious Influence: The Case of Zoroastrianism, Judaism and Christianity," *Journal of the American Academy of Religion* 53, no. 2 (1985): 201–35; J. Neusner, *Judaism, Christianity and Zoroastrianism in Talmudic Babylonia* (Lanham, Md., 1986); and M. Boyce and F. Grenet, *A History of Zoroastrianism*, vol. 3: *Zoroastrianism Under Macedonian and Roman Rule* (Leiden, 1991), 366–67, 392–440.

54. Shaked, "Iranian Influence on Judaism," 324–25.

55. S. Baron, *A Social and Religious History of the Jews*, vol. 2 (New York, 1952), 191.

56. J. Naveh and S. Shaked, *Magic Spells and Formulae—Aramaic Incantations of Late Antiquity* (Jerusalem, 1993), 21.

57. BT Shabbat 122b; Palestinian Talmud (henceforth: PT) Shabbat 16:15d. It is interesting to note that the gentile is referred to in the PT as "a Persian," whereas in the BT simply as "nokhri"—a gentile. It appears that the PT uses "Persian" as a generic term for gentiles in Babylonia, whereas the BT reserves the use of "Persian" to government or church officials (see Gafni, *Yehudei Bavel bi-Tekufat ha-Talmud* 153 and n. 18).

58. See also BT Avodah Zara 65a: Rabah sent a gift to one bar Sheshak.

59. Most of the relevant information has been gathered by M. Beer, *Amora'ei Bavel: Perakim be-Ḥaye ha-Kalkalah* (Ramat Gan, 1974), 207–11.

60. For the various Aramaic dialects found in Iran from the Achaemenid period and down to the talmudic era, see *Encyclopaedia Iranica*, vol. 2 (London, 1987), 251–56. On the use of Aramaic by Jews, from late biblical times and down to the present, see the concise overview by J. C. Greenfield, "Aramaic and the Jews," in M. J. Geller et al., eds., *"Studia Aramaica," New Sources and Approaches* (Oxford, 1995), 1–18.

61. From a responsa of Rav Hai, published by A. E. Harkavy in *Hakedem* vol. 2 (St. Petersburg, 1908), 82.

62. See the sources cited in J. N. Epstein, *Dikdut Aramit Bavlit* (Jerusalem, 1960), 17.

63. The question of Hebrew as a commonly spoken vernacular even in Second Temple Palestine, as well as the first centuries of the Common Era, has been heatedly debated for over 150 years, with accusations of "Zionistically inclined" Hebraism and tendentious romanticism frequently introduced into the polemic. See, for a brief discussion, E. Y. Kutscher,

A History of the Hebrew Language (Jerusalem, 1982), 115–19; much of the relevant research has been cited by S. D. Fraade, "Rabbinic Views on the Practice of Targum, and Multilingualism in the Jewish Galilee of the Third–Sixth Centuries," in L. I. Levine, *The Galilee in Late Antiquity* (New York, 1992), 253–86. For one historian's perspective of the debate, see S. Schwartz, "Language, Power and Identity in Ancient Palestine," *Past and Present* 148 (1995): 3–47. Whatever the reality might have been in Palestine, few would argue for any widespread use of Hebrew as a vernacular among Jews of the Babylonian Diaspora in Late Antiquity.

64. See E. Yarshater, "Zoroastrian Pahlavi Writings," in Yarshater, ed., *The Cambridge History of Iran*, 3(2): 1166–69.

65. This tendency to provide biblical etymologies for Persian words fits nicely with the rabbinic propensity in the Babylonian Talmud of linking biblical place-names with contemporary cities in the Iranian countryside.

66. Only 130 examples of Iranian loanwords were noted by S. Telegdi, "Essai sur la phonétique des emprunts iraniens en araméen Talmudique," *Journal Asiatique* 226 (1935): 177–256; see also S. Shaked, "Iranian Loanwords in Middle Aramaic," *Encyclopaedia Iranica*, 2: 259–61. Shaked notes that many of the Iranian loanwards that appear in Middle Aramaic (i.e., the Aramaic of the Babylonian Talmud) may have entered that language over a protracted period of time and would thus not necessarily attest to contacts between Jews and Iranians during the talmudic period alone. In contradistinction to the Babylonian Talmud, over 3,000 Greek and Latin loanwords were cited by S. Krauss, *Griechische und lateinische Lehnwörter im Talmud, Midrasch und Targum*, vols. 1–3 (Berlin, 1898–99). Notwithstanding the problems involved in portions of Krauss's lists (see D. Sperber, "Greek and Latin Words in Rabbinic Literature," *Bar Ilan* 14–15 [1977]: 9–20 [English sec.]), the discrepancy between the scope and nature of the influence of surrounding "official" languages on the literary production of the Jews of Palestine and Babylonia is undeniable.

67. See S. Lieberman, *Hellenism in Jewish Palestine* (New York, 1950), 100–114.

68. PT Megillah 1:2, 71c; see S. Lieberman, *Greek in Jewish Palestine* (New York, 1942), 17.

69. See A. Christensen, *L'Iran sous les Sassanides* (Copenhagen, 1944), 45.

70. See Shaked, "Iranian Loanwords," 260–61.

71. See B. M. Bokser, "Talmudic Names of the Iranian Festivals," *Journal of the American Oriental Society* 95 (1975): 261–62.

72. See Neusner, *Jews in Babylonia*, 2: 88, and J. Neusner, *Talmudic Judaism in Sasanian Babylonia* (Leiden, 1976), 142.

73. See Gafni, *Yehudei Bavel bi-Tekufat ha-Talmud* 157 n. 33.

74. In Achaemenian times, Noruz (lit. "new day") was celebrated in spring (March/April); in the early Sassanian period it was also celebrated in autumn, thus leading to a dual celebration. However, with the establishment by the first Sassanian king, Ardashir I, of a 365-day year with no intercalation, Noruz crept backward every year by one quarter of a day, and thus the autumn festival of Noruz was actually being celebrated by the fifth cen-

tury in July. Subsequent calendar reform resulted in multiple celebrations of the holiday during the year. See M. Boyce, *Zoroastrians, Their Religious Beliefs and Practices* (London, 1979), 72, 105–6, 124, 128–30. To this day, various Zoroastrian factions celebrate Noruz at different times of the year; see S. A. Nigosian, *The Zoroastrian Faith* (Montreal, 1993), 115.

75. See Neusner, *Jews in Babylonia*, 2: 88, and D. Goodblatt, "The Poll Tax in Sasanian Babylonia," *Journal of the Eonomic and Social History of the Orient* 22 (1979): 275–76, and nn. 111–14.

76. See Rosenthal, "For the Talmudic Dictionary," 39–42.

77. The most comprehensive argument for such influence was put forward by J. Scheftelowitz, *Die Alpersiche Religion und das Judendum* (Giessen, 1920); some criteria for identifying apparent influences, albeit not necessarily for Babylonian Jewry alone, have been presented by S. Shaked, "Qumran and Iran: Further Considerations," *Israel Oriental Studies* 2 (1972): 433–46. See also D. Winston, "The Iranian Component in the Bible, Apocrypha and Qumran: A Review of the Evidence," *History of Religions* 5 (1966): 183–216, and E. Spicehandler, " 'Be Duar' and 'Dina de-Magistha,' " Hebrew Union College Annual 26 (1955): 333–54.

78. For a general comparison of demonology in Judaism and the Iranian religion, see Scheftelowitz, *Die Alpersiche Religion*, 25–61. On Iranian demonology, see A. Christensen, *Essai sur la démonologie iranienne* (Copenhagen, 1941), and M. Boyce, *A History of Zoroastrianism*, vol. 1, 2d ed. (Leiden, 1989), 85–108.

79. See Deut. 32:17; Ps. 106:37.

80. *Antiquities*, 8:45; compare the Wisdom of Solomon 7:20 as well as rabbinic statements linked to Solomon in connection with Ecclesiastes 2:8. See also L. Ginzberg, *Legends of the Jews*, vol. 6 (Philadelphia, 1956), 291 and nn. 488–89.

81. *Antiquities*, 8:46; Josephus describes in great detail how a demon was removed "through the nostrils" of a man possessed, who proceeded to "speak Solomon's name and recite the incantations he had composed."

82. Matthew 8:28–34, 12:43–45; Mark 1:23, 5:1–20; Luke 8:26–38.

83. The various Palestinian uses of the Hebrew term *ruah* (spirit), especially those found at Qumran, dovetail with parallel meanings applied to the Iranian term *menog;* see Shaked, "Qumran and Iran," 434–37.

84. Scholars long ago recognized the similar use of the word "heaven" as a reference to the deity in both Iranian and rabbinic literature; see E. E. Urbach, *The Sages*, vol. 1 (Jerusalem, 1975), 70 and n. 11. Yet another parallel has been noted between the Pahlavi concept of "wrath" and the the rabbinic concept of *midat ha-din* (the attribute of justice), whereby a concept well established in Zoroastrian dualism was adapted by the rabbis as a means of attributing man's suffering to the omnipotent God; see S. Pines, "Wrath and Creatures of Wrath in Pahlavi, Jewish and New Testament Sources," in Shaked, ed., *Irano-Judaica*, 1: 76–82, and Urbach, *The Sages*, 1: 451, 460–61.

85. Avot 5:6.

86. PT Berakhot 5:9a.

87. Tosefta Shabbat 7:23; see BT Sanhedrin 101a.

88. See Boyce, *A History of Zoroastrianism*, 1: 85.

89. For some of the relevant sources and a brief discussion, see Neusner, *Jews in Babylonia*, 4: 334–38, and 5: 183–86.

90. BT Berakhot 6a. Iranian demonology in fact assigned the form of various birds to a number of fabulous creatures that composed the vast army of supernatural forces existing alongside human beings and playing destructive as well as beneficial roles in this world; see Boyce, *A History of Zoroastrianism*, 88–90.

91. The Babylonian Talmud identifies him as R. Hanina b. Dosa, actually a first-century quasi-rabbinic figure in Palestine, known for his wonder-working activity rather than for any halakhic teaching; see B. M. Bokser, "Wonder-working and the Rabbinic Tradition: The Case of Hanina ben Dosa," *Journal for the Study of Judaism* 16 (1985): 42–92 (esp. 42 n. 1, which provides a list of earlier studies on Hanina ben Dosa).

92. This particular demonic figure never appears by name in Iranian sources, although it is apparently a derivation of the Zoroastrian *Aeshma Daeva* (the demon of wrath); the Greek form—Asmodaeus—appears in the Book of Tobit (3:8), a Second Temple apocryphal work likely to have been written in Babylonia and in an obvious Iranian environment. See R. N. Frey, "Qumran and Iran," in J. Neusner, ed., *Christianity, Judaism and Other Greco-Roman Cults (Studies for Morton Smith at Sixty)*, vol. 3 (Leiden, 1975), 170. "Ashmedai King of Demons" is known only to the Babylonian Talmud, most notably in a highly detailed account of his relationship with King Solomon (BT Gitin 68a–b); parallel traditions in Palestinian rabbinic sources (PT Sanhedrin 2:20c) talk only about "an angel" who appeared in the image of King Solomon.

93. Scholars have in fact noted an Iranian propensity for considering odd numbers favorable and even numbers dangerous; see Scheftelowitz, *Die Alpersiche Religion*, 88–91. See also BT Gitin 68a for another example where the Babylonian Talmud admits to a demon-connected interpretation of scripture (Eccles. 2:8) while acknowledging that the Palestinian exegetes understood the same text differently.

94. BT Mo'ed Katan 18a.

95. Boyce, *A History of Zoroastrianism*, 1: 90. Boyce notes that the practice of dedicating nail-parings to this bird while uttering appropriate words from the Vendidad is still observed by strictly orthodox Zoroastrians.

96. Rabbis not only knew how to limit the danger from demons but at times even knew how to get them to do one's bidding. A demon employed by Rav Papa "once went to fetch water from the river but was away a long time. When he returned he was asked: 'Why were you so long?' He replied: '[I waited] until the evil waters [i.e., the water from which demons had drunk] had passed.' But when he saw them [R. Papa and friends] pouring off [some water] from the mouth of the jug, he exclaimed: 'Had I known you were in the habit of doing this I would not have taken so long' " (BT Hullin 105b–106a).

97. The demon is apparently overcome by hearing his name diminish letter by letter.

98. On the nature of this book, see E. W. West, introduction to *The Sacred Books of the East—Pahlavi Texts,* vol. 24, part III, ed. F. Max Mueller, 3d ed. (Delhi, 1970), xxxvi–xlv.

99. Ibid., 292. In another tradition on the same page we are told that "it is not proper to pour away water at night, especially from the northern side which would be the worst"; the reason for this is that demons are supposed to come from the north, and anything thrown out northward might be of use to them.

100. See *Sacred Books of the East,* vol. 37, part IV, 3d ed. (Delhi, 1969), 471.

101. *Shayast ne-Shayast,* ix, 8; *Sacred Books of the East,* vol. 5, part I, ed. F. Mueller (Oxford, 1901), 310; on this collection, see Yarshater, ed., *The Cambridge History of Iran,* 3(2): 1177–78.

102. Boyce, *A History of Zoroastrianism,* 87.

103. Denkard, Book VI, 78; quoted in Shaked, "Qumran and Iran," 437.

104. Although the woman referred to is Imma Shalom, wife of the late-first-century Palestinian sage Rabbi Eliezer b. Hyrcanus, the story and language are definitely of Babylonian rabbinic provenance. The Baylonian Talmud frequently tells stories using well-known Palestinian figures as its heroes, but these are frequently couched in local Babylonian reality as well as terminology and have no parallels in Palestinian rabbinic literature.

105. There is extensive literature on the ongoing publication of these texts; see, e.g., Neusner, *Jews in Babylonia,* 5: 217 n. 1; J. Naveh and S. Shaked, *Amulets and Magic Bowls—Aramaic Incantations of Late Antiquity,* rev. ed. (Jerusalem, 1998), 19–21; L. H. Schiffman and M. D. Swartz, *Hebrew and Aramaic Incantation Texts from the Cairo Genizah* (Sheffield, Engl., 1982), 17–18 and notes; and P. S. Alexander, "Incantation Bowls and Amulets in Hebrew and Aramaic," in E. Schuerer, *The History of the Jewish People in the Age of Jesus Christ (175 B.C.–A.D. 135),* a new English edition revised and edited by G. Vermes, F. Millar, and M. Goodman, vol. III, part I (Edinburgh, 1986), 352–57. For a recent publication of one major collection, see J. B. Segal, *Catalogue of the Aramaic and Mandaic Incantation Bowls in the British Museum* (London, 2000). Yet another study is D. Levene, *A Corpus of Magic Bowls* (New York, 2001).

106. See Naveh and Shaked, *Amulets and Magic Bowls,* 13 n. 1.

107. Ibid., 135.

108. J. A. Montgomery, *Aramaic Incantation Texts from Nippur* (Philadelphia, 1913), 191.

109. Ibid., 190–91 (quoted in Neusner, *Jews in Babylonia,* 5: 223).

110. Naveh and Shaked, *Amulets and Magic Bowls,* 159; see also Alexander, "Incantation Bowls," 354 n. 24, for an attempt at recreating the halakhic context for the situation described on the bowl.

111. The major doubt was cast by Montgomery, *Aramaic Incantation Texts,* 112–13, who claimed that the use of names such as "Moses" and "Yehoshua ben Perahya" had already found its way into an eclectic magical environment, thereby removing the certainty of a Jewish connection. Many of Montgomery's readings, as well as conclusions regarding the Jewish origins of the bowls, were challenged in a brilliant review essay by J. N. Epstein,

"Gloses Babylo-araméennes," *Revue des Etudes Juives* 73 (1921): 40–72. Montgomery's contention is further weakened not only by the quoting of Hebrew scripture in some of the bowls but also by the references to uniquely Jewish legal conventions in the production of divorce writs; see Naveh and Shaked, *Amulets and Magic Bowls*, 17–18. See also J. C. Greenfield, "Notes on some Aramaic and Mandaic Magic-Bowls," *The Journal of the Ancient Near Eastern Society of Columbia University* 5 (1973): 149–56; B. A. Levine, "The Language of the Magic Bowls," appended in Neusner, *Jews in Babylonia*, 5: 343–73; and Alexander, "Incantation Bowls," 353 n. 23.

112. Naveh and Shaked, *Amulets and Magic Bowls*, 18.

113. For an overview of rabbinic attitudes toward all manifestations of magical activity, see G. Veltri, *Magie und Halakha*, (Tübingen, 1997), 295–326 (containing a comprehensive bibliography on the subject and related issues). See also G. Veltri, "Defining Forbidden Foreign Customs: Some Remarks on the Rabbinic Halakhah of Magic," in *Proceedings of the Eleventh Congress of Jewish Studies*, Div. C, vol. 1: *Rabbinic and Talmudic Literature* (Jerusalem, 1994), 25–32. Veltri's work addresses primarily the rabbinic attitudes toward phenomena of the Greco-Roman world.

114. BT Sanhedrin 67b; for a brief overview of rabbinic attitudes toward magic, see Urbach, *The Sages*, 97–101. Urbach senses the fuzzy demarcation in rabbinic tradition between those statements that appear to prohibit any recourse to magic and others that clearly suggest the sages' own involvement in a variety of such magical practices (see 101–2). Note the statement by L. H. Schiffman, "A Forty-two Letter Divine Name in the Aramaic Magic Bowls," *Bulletin of the Institute of Jewish Studies* 1 (1973): 97: "It is also clear that these incantations and the attendant magical practices could not have had the approval of the rabbinic authorities." To this, Greenfield ("Notes on Some Aramaic and Mandaic Magic-Bowls," 150 n. 10) responded—accurately, to my mind—"But even if there was no approval, these practices were condoned and tolerated." For a brief survey on the growing scholarly recognition of "the extent to which magic was ingrained in the rabbinic milieu," see M. D. Swartz, *Scholastic Magic* (Princeton, 1996), 18–22 and the bibliography in nn. 58 and 63. See also the comments and literature cited in Y. Harari, "If You Wish to Kill a Person: Harmful Magic and Protection from It in Early Jewish Magic" (Hebrew), *Jewish Studies* 37 (1997): 111–42.

115. And thus Cicero felt required to point out that "Chaldaei" was not the designation for practitioners of a specific training, but rather the name of a tribe (*De Divinatione* I, 1, 2). Indeed, the Third Sybilline Oracle (227; see also J. H. Charlesworth, ed., *The Old Testament Pseudepigraphy*, 2 vols. (Garden City, N.Y., 1983–85), 1: 367) praises Israel as a race of righteous men who "do not practice the astrological predictions of the Chaldeans nor astronomy" (cited in S. Lieberman, *Greek in Jewish Palestine* [New York, 1942], 97–98).

116. F. Cumont, *The Oriental Religions in Roman Paganism* (New York, 1956), 146.

117. See Urbach, *The Sages*, 277.

118. BT Pesahim 113b.

119. Lieberman, *Greek*, 98.

120. Pseudo-Eupolemos, apud Eusebius, *Praeparatio Evangelica* 9.17.3 (Charlesworth, *Old Testament Pseudepigrapha*, 2: 880). The Egyptian-Jewish author Artapanus (third–second centuries B.C.E.) claims that Abraham actually taught Parethothes, the King of Egypt, astrology (ibid., 2: 897).

121. BT Shabbat 156a and parallels; later midrashim leave even less to the imagination: "You are Jews, the words of the astrologers do not apply to you, for you are Jews" (Tanhuma, Shofetim 10).

122. The reference to "Chaldeans" is missing in some manuscript versions and also in the parallel version in BT Horayot 14a.

123. *Iggeret Rav Sherira Gaon*, ed. Lewin, 85–86.

124. BT Yevamot 21b; BT Sanhedrin 95a.

125. The degree of Iranian legal knowledge possessed by the rabbis, and their willingness to apply this knowledge to their own deliberations, is still open to debate, but for one recent attempt to prove the feasibility of such a process, see M. Macuch, "Iranian Legal Terminology in the Babylonian Talmud in the Light of Sasanian Jurisprudence," in S. Shaked and A. Netzer, eds., Irano-Judaica, vol. 4 (Jerusalem, 1999), 91–101.

SELECTED BIBLIOGRAPHY

Barr, J. "The Question of Religious Influence: The Case of Zoroastrianism, Judaism and Christianity." *Journal of the American Academy of Religion* 53, no. 2 (1985): 201–35.

Beer, M. *Amora'ei Bavel: Perakim be-Ḥaye ha-Kalkalah.* Ramat Gan, 1974.

———. *Rashut ha-Golah bi-Yeme ha-Mishna ve-ha-Talmud.* Tel Aviv, 1970.

Brody, R. "Judaism in the Sasanian Empire: A Case Study in Religious Coexistence." In S. Shaked and A. Netzer, eds., *Irano-Judaica*. Vol. 2. Jerusalem, 1990.

Gafni, I. "Expressions and Types of 'Local-Patriotism' Among the Jews of Sasanian Babylonia." In S. Shaked and A. Netzer, eds., *Irano-Judaica*. Vol. 2. Jerusalem, 1990.

———. *Yehudei Bavel bi-Tekufat ha-Talmud: Ḥaye ha-Ḥevrah ve-ha-Ruah.* Jerusalem, 1990.

———. *Land, Center and Diaspora: Jewish Constructs in Late Antiquity.* Sheffield, Engl., 1997.

———. "Talmudic Research in Modern Times: Between Scholarship and Ideology." In A. Oppenheimer, ed., *Jüdische Geschichte in hellenistisch-römischer Zeit*. Munich, 1999.

Goodblatt, D. "The Poll Tax in Sasanian Babylonia," *Journal of the Economic and Social History of the Orient* 22 (1979): 233–94.

———. *Rabbinic Instruction in Sasanian Babylonia.* Leiden, 1975.

Naveh, J., and S. Shaked. *Amulets and Magic Bowls—Aramaic Incantations of Late Antiquity.* Rev. ed. Jerusalem, 1998.

———. *Magic Spells and Formulae—Aramaic Incantations of Late Antiquity.* Jerusalem, 1993.

Neusner, J. *A History of the Jews in Babylonia.* 5 vols. Leiden, 1965–70.

———. *Judaism, Christianity and Zoroastrianism in Talmudic Babylonia.* Lanham, Md., 1986.

———. *Talmudic Judaism in Sasanian Babylonia.* Leiden, 1976.

Oppenheimer, A. *Babylonia Judaica in the Talmudic Period.* Wiesbaden, 1983.

———. "Babylonian Synagogues with Historical Associations." In D. Urman and P. V. M. Flesher, eds., *Ancient Synagogues: Historical Analysis and Archaeological Discovery.* Vol. 1. Leiden, 1995.

Shaked, S. "Iranian Influence on Judaism: First Century B.C.E. to Second Century C.E." In W. D. Davies and L. Finkelstein, eds., *The Cambridge History of Judaism.* Vol. 1. Cambridge, Engl., 1984.

———. "Zoroastrian Polemics Against Jews in the Sasanian and Early Islamic Period." In S. Shaked and A. Netzer, eds., *Irano-Judaica.* Vol. 2. Jerusalem, 1990.

Abraham about to sacrifice his son Ishmael
(the Muslim version of the biblical "binding of Isaac").
(New York Public Library, Spencer Collection, Persian ms. 46)

JEWISH CULTURE IN THE
FORMATIVE PERIOD OF ISLAM

REUVEN FIRESTONE

The prophet Muhammad lived to witness the success of Islam in Arabia by the time of his death in 632 C.E. Initially, however, he failed to win his fellow Arabs to Islam in Mecca, the pagan city of his birth. In fact, Muhammad's prophetic activities and behavior made him persona non grata in his native city; he was forced out of town in 622 and found success only after having made his great *hijra* (emigration) from Mecca to Medina, a large agricultural settlement populated by many Jews as well as other inhabitants who practiced the indigenous religious traditions of Arabia. It would be Medina where Islam would take hold. Medina would also serve as the crucible wherein the complex relations between Jews and Muslims and between Judaism and Islam would be forged.

THE CONVERSION OF RABBI ABDULLAH

A story is told by Muhammad ibn Isḥāq, the eighth century biographer of the prophet Muhammad, of the latter's coming to Medina:[1]

This is the story of Abdullah ibn Salām, the learned rabbi,[2] that one of his kinsmen told me about his conversion to Islam. [Abdullah] said: When I heard about the Apostle of God, I knew from his description, name, and time [of his appearance] that he was the one we were expecting. I was overjoyed about this but kept it to myself until the Apostle of God arrived in Medina. While he was staying in [the Medinan neighborhood of] Qubā' among the Banū 'Amr b. 'Awf, a man came with the news of his arrival while I was working at the top of a date tree with my aunt Khālida bint al-Ḥārith sitting below. When I heard the news of his arrival I called out: *"Allahu Akbar!"* When my aunt heard this she said to me: "My goodness! If Moses ibn 'Imrān [that is, the Moses of the Bible—see Exodus 6:20] had come you would not have become more excited." I replied: "O aunt! By God, he is the brother of Moses ibn 'Imrān and of the same religion, having been sent on the same mission." She exclaimed: "O nephew! Is he the prophet whom we have been told will be sent at this hour?" I answered: "Yes!" and she responded: "Then this is it!" I immediately went to the Apostle of God and became a Muslim. Then I returned to my family and ordered them to become Muslims as well.

I kept my conversion hidden from the Jews and went to the Apostle of God and said: "O Apostle of God, the Jews are a people of lies. Will you take me into your house and hide me from them? Then ask them about me and they will tell you what they think of me before they know I have become Muslim, because if they know [that I converted], they will falsely denounce me." So the Apostle of God put me in a room. [Some Jews] entered and began chatting. He asked them: "In your opinion, what kind of a person is al-Ḥusayn ibn Salām?" They answered: "[He is] our master and prince, our learned rabbi." When they had finished I came out to them and said: "O Jews, be reverent to God and accept what has come from Him, for by God, you know that this is the Apostle of God. You have found his description and his name written in the Torah. I bear witness that he is the Apostle of God. I believe in him, pronounce him true, and acknowledge him." They said: "You are lying!" and slandered me. So I said to the Apostle of God: "Did I not tell you that they are a people of lies, deceit and perfidy?" I then publicly revealed my conversion and the conversion of my family, and my aunt Khālida also became a good Muslim.

Although this apocryphal story cannot be accepted without corroboration as an accurate witness to the particular event it describes,[3] it contains within it important incidental data about Jews living in the environs and period of emerging Islam. We learn that the Jews had scholarly religious leaders to whom they referred as *ḥaver* and who worked in the local economy. Jews were involved in the date agriculture of the region and worked alongside their extended family kin, including women. Our story, like many others about Arabian Jews of this period, teaches us that both Jewish men and women had Arabic names. It is likely that al-Ḥusayn was Abdullah's "Jewish" name before he became a Muslim and took on the epithet, "servant of Allah" *(Abdullah)*, a common Islamic "conversion name." Although Abdullah's expression of amazement, "Allah is most great!" *(Allahu akbar)* is most likely a later Islamic interpolation, it is possible that Arabic-speaking Jews in this early period as well as in later centuries referred to their God as *Allah*. (The famous Saadiah Gaon [d. 942], for example, the most brilliant scholar of the gaonic period, regularly referred to God in his Arabic commentary as Allah.) And perhaps of greatest interest here, as will become clearer below, is that Arabian Jews spoke of the coming of a "prophet," some even predicting the hour of his coming based on biblical interpretation.

This famous story of Abdullah ibn Salām's conversion to Islam, like many other stories about Muhammad and his interaction with Jews found in the earliest Islamic sources, is not an objective historical report but, rather, in the form we have it, a literary composition—a tale or legend. Despite its unreliability as a factual report of the specific event it purportedly describes, however, it and other such tales contain fine and often detailed historical and cultural information that is repeated with subtle and nuanced variations in a great many other early Arabic sources and references. This quality of the early Arabic sources allows, therefore, for a guarded confidence in the historicity of certain of the data contained within them.

Our tale, along with many others, depicts the Jews living in Arabia during Islam's emergence as veteran inhabitants of the peninsula and deeply integrated into Arabian culture and civilization. The Jews are described both as Jews and as Arabs, and they are depicted as having been organized and acting according to indigenous Arabian paradigms of social organization and behavior. It is not easy to define the boundaries of identification that separated Jews from other inhabitants of Arabia, because they not only lived among their own in "Jewish" tribes but were also members of tribes not referred to in the sources as being specifically Jewish. Moreover, the Jews of Arabia appear not to have been physically distinguishable from the indigenous Arabs, many of whom consider themselves to have derived originally from the biblical Ishmael.[4] Arabian Jews spoke Arabic even among themselves, although there is evidence that at least some of them spoke a particular Jewish dialect referred to in Arabic sources as "Jewish" (yahudiyya), perhaps a Jewish dialect of Arabic similar in role to Yiddish as a Jewish dialect of Medieval German. Jewish professions mirrored those of the larger civilization in which they lived, with Jewish farmers, craftsmen, and even Bedouin, and the Jews could arm and protect themselves just as other tribal groups in the region. In fact, the Jews of sixth- and seventh-century Arabia appear so highly integrated economically, ethnically, and geographically into the local culture that they must be considered culturally or ethnically Arab, just as the Jews of Babylonia, speaking Babylonian Aramaic, were so deeply integrated into their local culture that they would refer to themselves as Babylonians.

At the same time that the Jewish communities that penetrated Arabia became "Arabized" through language, customs, and even personal names, so too did indigenous Arabian civilization come under the influence of Judaism. One pre-Islamic term for a high god in the old Arabian pantheon, for example, was al-Raḥmān, "the Merciful One," exactly equivalent to the Jewish Aramaic Raḥmānā that occurs in the Babylonian Talmud more than 250 times. Christian communities also made their way into Arabia, and many religious or cultic terms that became a part of Islam derive from Aramaic Jewish or Christian religious terminology that was applied to pre-Islamic Arabian religion.[5]

As these and other examples to follow will make clear, the cultural and even religious influence between Jews and Arabs and Jews and Muslims flowed in both directions, but, despite this bi-directionality during the pre-Islamic period, the Jews were known as monotheists in an overwhelmingly polytheistic region. Whether or not these Jews practiced one or more expressions of Judaism found also in the Land of Israel, in Babylonia, or in highly Hellenized areas has not yet been determined. The sources do clearly differentiate Jewish Arabs from other pre-Islamic Arabs when concerned with religious beliefs and practice. Nevertheless, the relationship between Arabian Jewry and the still-mysterious and possibly monotheistic religion of the pre-Islamic Arabian ḥanīfs remains unclear.

Muhammad himself fully expected the Jews of Arabia to become Muslims as well—to be "submitters" (the meaning of the term, "Muslim") to the will of God as articulated in the qur'ānic revelations that he heard and recited. That most Arabian Jews did not submit was a shock to Muhammad, because he believed during his initial period in Medina that the religion he preached, in opposition to the indigenous Arabian polytheisms of his generation, was virtually synonymous with the monotheism of the Jews. In fact, the story of earliest Islam is, in large part, a story of an emerging identity constantly being tested by the tension between God's word and the reality of a world, including the world of Arabian Jews, not easily willing to accept it. The ambiguous cultural and religious boundaries between Arabian Jews and other Arabs in pre-Islamic and early Islamic Arabia, therefore, established a series of tensions that would epitomize the foundational relationship between Jews and Muslims. These tensions are the center point around which the cultural history of the Jews in Islamic lands must be written.

ARAB CONQUESTS FIRST, ISLAMIZATION AFTERWARD

As mentioned above, Muhammad was initially unsuccessful in Mecca, but he succeeded brilliantly in Medina, and his success eventually spread back to his hometown and to much of Arabia before his death in 632. This was followed in the century after his death by a series of brilliant and extraordinary military conquests that took the world by surprise. Rising up out of an obscure desert region—physically near to the world empires of Byzantium and Persia but light-years distant from their level of civilization—the Arabs overwhelmed both within a decade. From the first Byzantine defeat at Ajnadayn in 634 to the fall of Alexandria in 643 and the last of the great Persian cities in 644, the Arabs found themselves in control of the center of world civilization. They pushed through Damascus, Jerusalem, Caesarea, Edessa, Ctesiphon (the capital of Persia), and then to the east toward India, from Alexandria and Old Cairo (called Babylon of Egypt) westward across North Africa and, eventually, Spain, and north from Arabia to the very gates of Constantinople itself.

These were conquests by Arabs. Because Islam as a religious civilization was still in formation, it is uncertain what the first conquerors knew and believed of Islam. It would soon become clear to the world that the triumphant Arabs also represented a new religion that would forever change the entire world constellation of religious civilizations, but in the early conquests Arab believers, other followers of Muhammad, pagans, and even Arab Jews and Christians took part.[6] Islam was one of the powerful motivators of the huge movement of peoples and energy that would come to dominate much of world history for the next millennium, but it was still in the process of formation during the great Arab expansion. The Qur'an itself, for example, was not "collected" or canonized until the caliphate of Uthman (644–56), who rose to his position 12 years after Muhammad's death and only after the Arab conquest of most of the Middle East.[7] Nor had the great compendia of Islamic law and tradition been formulated or the theologies systematized during the first century or more after the death of Muhammad. Islam was in the process of emerging, and like the butterfly that emerges in glory from its cramped chrysalis, it would take time for the life-sustaining fluids to flow through the expanding arteries of the empire and bring the necessary energy and sustenance to allow it to take off.

This was the formative age of Islam, when Islam was busy not only managing an empire but also defining itself. During the two centuries following the death of the Prophet in 632, its major literatures, theologies, and institutions would be established. During this period, and especially during the early decades, Jews would have a profound impact on the emergence of Islam. Soon afterward, Islam would stamp its own legacy on the evolution of Judaism.

ANCIENT JEWS ENTER ARABIA

Exactly when Jews had penetrated the peninsula remains a mystery, but Arab legend suggests as early as the Exodus from Egypt when Moses sent a contingent of soldiers deep into Arabia to fight the Amalekites living there. According to the tenth-century *Kitāb al-Aghānī*, the Israelite soldiers destroyed their enemy and eventually settled in the west-central area known as the Hijaz, the very region in which the towns of Mecca and Medina are situated. Other legends place the migration of Jews to the region in the wake of Roman persecution, a far more likely scenario. Jewish communities were established not only in the oasis towns of the Hijaz but also in the southern region that is now within the borders of the modern state of Yemen. Yemenite Jews credit their origins to the famous story of King Solomon and the Queen of Sheba. According to this tradition, the queen returned to her native land, a region of Yemen that to this day is called Saba, with a son fathered by Solomon. The King, in turn, sent Jews to settle in Yemen so that his son might be properly educated.

The true origin of the Jewish communities of Arabia may never be determined, but we have noted from the story of Abdullah ibn Salām that they were a significant part of the Arabian landscape by the time Muhammad was born, in 570. The Jews of Medina, for example (which was called Yathrib prior to Islam), were the dominant community of the town until shortly before Muhammad's birth. In the town of Taymā', about halfway between Medina and the great Nabatean center of Petra in today's Jordan, the Jews are said to have been powerful enough to insist that non-Jewish Arab tribes interested in settling in the town adopt Judaism.

The Jews of sixth- and seventh-century Arabia were highly integrated into Arabian culture—so much so, in fact, that it is often difficult to determine whether a person referred to in the sources is Jewish or not unless this is specifically noted. Jews tended to take on Arab names and adopt Arabian cultural practices. The renowned poet al-Samaw'al b. ʿĀdiyā, who lived in the mid-sixth century, is a classic example. His own name, Samaw'al, is an Arabized form of Samuel, but the name of his father is purely Arabian. It is assumed by some scholars, therefore, that only his mother was Jewish, although many other Jews in the period seem to have taken on equally Arabian names. Al-Samaw'al's fame as a pre-Islamic Arabian poet denotes his deep integration into Arabian civilization, because this ancient art form is considered the most sublime form of indigenous Arabian culture. Unfortunately, considerable controversy remains regarding the poems attributed to him. Some contain material reflecting Jewish ideas, but these have not been considered genuine by many scholars. Other poems that seem more likely to have been composed by Samaw'al himself contain no indication of Jewish background. Yet tradition associates him quite strongly with Judaism, along with the tradition that his grandson converted to Islam after the rise of Muhammad as Prophet.

Al-Samaw'al's greatest fame, however, derives from his celebrated loyalty rather than his poetry. The legend of his absolute fidelity has become proverbial in Arabic: "more loyal than al-Samaw'al." According to the story, Imru' al-Qays, one of pre-Islamic Arabia's greatest poets and the youngest son of the last king of the Kinda, led an unsettled life as an adventurer. Among his exploits was the attempt to avenge the assassination of his father. He eventually lost his allies and sought refuge from his pursuers by appealing to the hospitality of al-Samaw'al, who lived in a famous and impenetrable castle called Ablaq (one legend claims that it was built by Solomon himself). Al-Samaw'al recommended Imru' al-Qays to an Arab client king of the Byzantine emperor, who received him. Imru' al-Qays asked al-Samaw'al to guard his daughter, his paternal inheritance, and his valuable and famous family armor for the duration of his journey, to which al-Samaw'al agreed. When Imru' al-Qays' enemies learned that his armor was under al-Samaw'al's protection, they besieged the castle with a great army. Al-Samaw'al refused to release anything of Imru' al-Qays to his enemies, even after they managed to capture al-Samaw'al's son and threatened to kill him. Al-Samaw'al persisted in refusing to betray his trust, though he witnessed the death of his own son before his very eyes. The besiegers eventually withdrew without achieving their purpose, and al-Samaw'al's fidelity became legendary.

Although the historicity of this legend must be regarded with skepticism, it provides interesting cultural information relevant to the period just prior to the emergence of Islam. Such traits as hospitality, loyalty, and betrayal, use of armor and fortified castles, political alliances, and expectations of vengeance all correspond quite well with other information representing the period. That a Jew should be located in the midst of such a legend is not surprising considering the Jews' level of integration into the pre-Islamic Arabian world.

Just as the Jews absorbed and assimilated Arabian culture prior to the emergence of Islam, so too did they infuse Jewish or biblical culture into the indigenous cultures. The nebulous boundaries between "Jewishness" and "Arabness" did not interfere with the transmission of culture in both directions. Perhaps the most profound example of Jewish cultural infusion is that of the many biblical legends, ideas, and personages that had penetrated deeply into Arabia already in pre-Islamic times. Biblical stories circulated among Jews and Christians living in the region and were naturally and unselfconsciously shared with neighbors who were unfamiliar with the Bible. Many of these stories, which themselves originated as oral midrashic interpretations of biblical texts, were told and retold as part of normal human interaction at trading fairs and tribal or regional gatherings and celebrations. They naturally evolved to fit the specific contexts of individual recitations as they were passed from person to person and place to place, thereby unfolding into forms that conformed to local traditions. Many of these stories, therefore, like their Jewish or Christian bearers, became "Arabized" as they blended into the local topography and folklore traditions. As a result, uniquely Arabian legends began to emerge that reflected both the biblical and the indigenous heritages. Some of these would be absorbed into the religious civilization of Islam, and some of the "Islamized" legends would eventually be reabsorbed into the literary corpus of Judaism.

THE LEGEND OF ABRAHAM VISITING ISHMAEL

One classic example of "Arabization" is the story of Abraham's visits to Ishmael, found in both Jewish and Islamic literature. In Genesis 21, Hagar and Ishmael are banished from the tribe of Abraham and left alone and defenseless in the desert. Such behavior, hardly befitting a Jewish patriarch known for his hospitality and care for the stranger, inspired a series of midrashim, narrative interpretations that tried to make sense of the difficult biblical passage. One reading suggests that Abraham did not really abandon his son but visited him regularly in order to ensure his viability and well-being:[8]

"And [Ishmael] lived in the wilderness of Paran" [Genesis 21:21]. Ishmael took a wife from Arvot Mo'av whose name was 'Ayefa.[9] After three years, Abraham went to see his son Ishmael and swore to Sarah that he would not dismount from his camel at Ishmael's abode. When he arrived there at midday, he found Ishmael's wife. He asked: "Where is Ishmael?" She answered: "He and his mother went to bring the fruit of date trees from the desert." He said: "Give me a little bread and water, for my soul is faint from the desert journey."[10] She answered: "There is no bread and no water." He then said to her: "When Ishmael comes [home], tell him this. Say that an old man came from the Land of Canaan to see you, and that the threshold of the house is not good." When Ishmael came [home], his wife told him what he said. [Ishmael then] sent her out, and his mother sent for a wife from her father's house, whose name was Fatumah.[11]

Again, after three years, Abraham went to see his son Ishmael and swore to Sarah as the first time that he would not dismount from his camel at Ishmael's abode. When he arrived there at midday, he found Ishmael's [new] wife. He asked: "Where is Ishmael?" She answered: "He and his mother went to tend the camels in the desert." He said to her: "Give me a little bread and water, for my soul is faint from the journey," so she brought it out and gave it to him. Abraham stood and prayed before the Holy One for his son, and Ishmael's home was filled with all good things and blessings. When Ishmael came [home], his wife told him what he said, and Ishmael knew that his father's compassion was still extended to him, as it is said: "As a father has compassion for his children" [Psalm 103].[12]

This legend depicts a compassionate Abraham who, unwilling to abandon his own flesh and blood to the vicissitudes of the desert (see Genesis 21), personally ensures the viability of his son and progeny. The threshold to Ishmael's home symbolizes Ishmael's wife, the mother of his offspring. Abraham, the father of many nations (Genesis 17:5–6), ensures through this story that Ishmael's wife is a fitting matriarch of the Arab line. The names of the wives clearly indicate Islamic influence because they each duplicate the name of one of Muhammad's wives or daughters. The Muslim names do not, however, prove an Islamic origin for this story; the nature of the tale indicates a Jewish concern, quite well represented in the midrash, to preserve the status of Abraham in the face of criticism for seemingly abandoning his own family in the desert.

Because of Ishmael's biblical as well as rabbinic association with Arabs, the context for the narrative extension naturally incorporated such motifs associated with Bedouin life as date agriculture and camel herding. It thus serves as a Jewish story of intersection with classic Arab life by acknowledging the proximity between the Genesis Abraham character and classical Bedouin life depicted by Ishmael. Such proximity was not lost on the Jews living throughout the Fertile Crescent: from ancient antiquity into the period of the Arab conquests, migrations and raids of camel-herding nomads regularly brought Arabs into the settled agricultural areas that surrounded the Arabian Peninsula.

Given the continual interaction between Jews and Arabs from biblical days to the present, it is not surprising that Arabic versions of this foundation story follow the basic Jewish narrative quite closely. Before examining them, however, it should be noted here that no pre-Islamic Arabian literature has been preserved in its pristine form. No manuscripts, for example, exist such as we have for ancient Judaism and Christianity with the Dead Sea Scrolls and early Christian papyri. We can only extrapolate, therefore, from our knowledge of literary history and methods to arrive at a theoretical pre-Islamic literary form. Everything we do have describing or reflecting pre-Islamic Arabia, from ancient legends to poetry and genealogies, can be found only in the form that was recorded by later Muslims, and these texts therefore strongly reflect the influence of Islam. The Arabic renderings of Abraham's visits to Ishmael are no exception. They epitomize the continued fusion of cultures.

In the Arabic versions found in many Islamic sources,[13] Abraham feels the need to visit his son but promises Sarah that he will not dismount. He arrives at Ishmael's home, meets the inhospitable wife, and delivers through her the coded message to change the threshold of the house. Ishmael understands, divorces her, and marries a woman who hospitably offers Abraham a feast on his subsequent visit. Certain aspects of the story, however, are now particular to an Arabian environment. The names and genealogy of Ishmael's wives derive from local tribal traditions, for example, and they are not the names of Muhammad's wife or daughter. When the good wife feeds Abraham, the food is the diet of the Bedouin, which Abraham blesses. This, it explains, is why agriculture is impossible in the desolate mountainous settlement of Mecca, because Abraham specifically blessed the food of pastoral nomads rather then oasis dwellers. It is assumed in the Arabic tellings that Ishmael is living in Mecca; medieval Arab geographers recorded the tradition that the Arabic equivalent to the Hebrew *paran* mentioned in Genesis 21:21 is *faran*, a reference to the mountains of Mecca.[14]

Ishmael's association with Mecca leads us to the Arabic extension of the story, not found in any Jewish sources, which brings Abraham there on a third and final visit to his beloved son. The following translation is from Muhammad b. Isma'il al-Bukhārī (d. 869), *al-Ṣaḥīḥ*.[15]

[Abraham] stayed away from them for a while, but then came while Ishmael was sharpening some arrows he had under a tree near the Zam-zam well.[16] When [Ishmael] saw him [approach], he arose and they greeted each other as a father would his son and as a son would his father. [Abraham] said: "O Ishmael, God has given me a command." [Ishmael] replied: "Then do as your Lord has commanded you." [Abraham] asked: "Will you help me?" He answered: "I will help you." So he said: "God has commanded me to build a house [*bayt*] here," and he pointed to a small hill raised up above what was around it. And with that, they raised the foundations of the Ka'ba [*al-Bayt*]. Ishmael would bring the stones and Abraham would build it. When the building was raised up high [so that Abraham had difficulty reaching up to place the stones, Ishmael] brought a certain stone and set it down for him. [Abraham] stood upon it and built as Ishmael would hand him the stones, both of them saying "O Lord, accept this from us, for You are the All-hearing, the All-knowing" [Qur'an 2:127].

The journey of this story of Abraham is striking. A biblically centered Jewish story evolves into an Arabian one as it journeys through the medium of oral tellings. It may have continued to be considered a "Jewish" legend as successive narrators began to incorporate local motifs, but it eventually moved across the boundary of Jewish particularity into generic Arabian culture. It became a legend that, for Arabian Jews, Christians, and pagans, provided meaning to local traditions.

Abraham is known in the Bible as a wanderer and founder of sacred places. From Ur of the Chaldeans he moves to Haran in northern Mesopotamia, and from Haran to the Land of Canaan. He sojourns in Egypt and returns to Canaan to build an altar at Beth El and another at the oaks of Mamre in Hebron. He plants a sacred tree in Beersheba and offers sacrifices in other places where God speaks with him directly. Such an important founder of sacred places would easily be associated with local Arabian sites as well. Why should he not have made his way into Arabia to found the Ka'ba in Mecca, an ancient religious shrine and place of sacrifice? Even before Islam, he was known to pagan Arabs. Ancient traditions recall that pictures of Abraham, Ishmael, and Mary, the mother of Jesus, were kept among the figurines and effigies of the pre-Islamic Ka'ba.[17]

Abraham, then, had become a generic hero known to all the pre-Islamic inhabitants of the peninsula. His name and image were shared, but his essence was not identical: to the Jews he was the originator of God's covenant with their people; to the Christians he was the first to acknowledge the truth of faith and spirit over the law;[18] and to the pagans he was the founder of the sacred shrines and cult places in Mecca. In the seventh century, however, as Islam came to dominate the peninsula, the Ka'ba and the sacred shrines in and around Mecca were shed of their idols and incorporated into Islamic tradition. The Islamizing process included an increasing association with the ancient and original monotheist Abraham, who naturally provided the proof of monotheistic authenticity as the *original* intent of the sacred sites. The Islamic Abraham cycle thus depicts the patriarch, with the help of his son, establishing Mecca as a purely monotheistic site. Only generations later did Ishmael's descendants gradually abandon the strict monotheism of their ancestors and degenerate into the state of religious anarchy known as pre-Islamic polytheism. The purpose of Muhammad's prophethood was to correct this error and reestablish Abraham's pristine monotheism. As the Abraham narrative journeyed through its Arabian environment from the pre-Islamic period into that of Islam, therefore, the *generic* or multiple Arabian associations with Abraham coalesced into an Islamic particularity. Abraham himself became Islamized.

The Qur'an, the very divine revelation of Islam, would claim Abraham as its own:

And when We made the House[19] a refuge and safe for humankind [We said]: Take as your place of worship the Place of Abraham [*maqam ibrahim*]. We made a covenant with Abraham and Ishmael [saying]: Purify My house for those who circumambulate, are engaged [with it], and bow and prostrate themselves. So Abraham prayed: Lord, Make this area safe, and bestow its people with fruits—those among them who believe in God and the Last Day.

[God] answered: As for the unbeliever, I will grant him a little happiness. Then I will force him to the punishment of the Fire and a horrible end. And when Abraham and Ishmael were raising up the foundations of the House [they prayed]: Our Lord, Accept [this] from us, for You are the Hearer, the Knower. Our Lord, Make us submitters [*muslimayn*] to You and our progeny a submissive people to You [*umma muslima laka*]. Show us the ritual places and turn toward us, for You are the One who causes to turn in repentance, the Merciful. (Qur'an 2:125–28)

Ironically, rather than serving as a unifying motif to bring the "Abrahamic religions" together in dialogue as is attempted in our day, the person of Abraham served at times as the center of polemic between them in Late Antiquity and the Middle Ages. The Qur'an itself bears witness to the controversy over Abraham:

O People of Scripture! Why do you argue about Abraham, when the Torah and the Gospel were not revealed until after him? Have you no sense? Do you not argue about things of which you have knowledge? Why, then, argue about things of which you have no knowledge! God knows, but you know not! Abraham was not a Jew nor a Christian, but was an early monotheist [*ḥanīf*], a muslim [i.e. one who submits to God's will], not an idolater. (3:65–67)

Our story of Abraham's visits to Ishmael thus turns full circle. A Jewish midrashic tradition became part of the pre-Islamic "public domain" as it was woven into the very fabric of generic Arabian culture. As Islam then absorbed relevant Arabian lore into its emerging ethos, the story became part of the legacy that would be Islam. What began, then, as a narrative interpretation of a biblical passage among Jews, ended as a narrative interpretation of a qur'anic passage among Muslims.

Is this Islamic "borrowing" from Judaism? Did Judaism provide the source for the qur'anic verses and the Islamic concepts? This is a classic question that has influenced the nature of research on Islam and its relationship with Judaism and Christianity. Classic Orientalist studies of Islam tended to assume *a priori* that Islam "borrowed" its ideas from the "original" ideas or beliefs of "Judeo-Christianity." They then set out to trace that history through textual analysis. As we have seen above, it is true that parallels may be found between Islamic and Jewish or biblical ideas and texts, and the parallels are many. But no religion is created *ex nihilo*. On the contrary, all scriptures and all religions combine *inspiration* (pure creativity), with *influence* (absorbing outside ideas). This includes the Bible. The many striking parallels between biblical *realia* and those of Canaanite culture and literatures demonstrate the heavy influence of Canaanite civilization. But because no human creation is absolutely without precedent, must every creation be assumed to be, at core, unoriginal and merely a result of borrowing? The answer is, of course, no, because the essence of creativity is inspiration within a context composed of preexisting realia—that is, influence. The question of borrowing, therefore, becomes beside the point, because no creation can consist only of inspiration without influence. Jews and Judaism indeed had a profound impact on emerging Islam, as did Christians and Christianity, pagan Arabs and pre-Islamic Arabian culture, and Persians and Zoroastrian traditions as well as those of Abyssinia, Greece, and so forth. But so, too, would Islam strongly affect those very evolving traditions that influenced it in its formative stages. Such fluidity might be considered "reciprocal influence": the commerce of cultures naturally ensures that they interact, absorb, discharge, and recombine as they contact one another through the ever-permeable boundaries of interethnic human contact and communication.

WHAT KIND OF ARABIAN JUDAISM?

A second classic question affecting Western students of Islam is why Islamic expressions of some themes that have parallels in Judaism and Christianity seem at times to be so contrary to Jewish or Christian expressions. Some Islamic parallels and references to Jewish tradition seem so odd that they are generally assumed by Westerners to have been misunderstandings or outright errors. The Qur'an, for example, claims: "The Jews say: Ezra ['uzayr] is the son of God, and the Christians say: The messiah is the son of God. This is what they say from their [own] mouths, resembling the speech of unbelievers of old. God fight them, for they lie!" (9:30). In another passage, the Qur'an asserts: "The Jews say: the hand of God is fettered. [But] their hands are fettered! And they are cursed for what they say!" (5:64).

From the perspective of Judaism in all of its extant forms, these verses seem to exhibit an extraordinary misunderstanding of Jewish belief. It is also possible that these qur'anic verses are polemical statements meant to discredit Judaism, because it is quite clear that the Qur'an, like other scriptures, is in part a polemical text. Rather than taking either of these approaches, we shall undertake to examine such Islamic records of Arabian Judaism from the hypothesis that they might in fact be accurate representations of Jewish ideas or practice.

The Qur'an represents itself as the word of God spoken through the prophet Muhammad to the people of seventh-century Arabia. However, because the Qur'an appears as if it were revealed in serial form during the 22 years of Muhammad's prophetic mission, it seems on many occasions to describe or respond to actual historical phenomena or situations that he encountered. Muslim Qur'an scholars have attempted to reconstruct the occasions of revelation based on their impression of Muhammad's biography, but little consensus has been reached among them. This, in part, has led some Western scholars to suggest that the Qur'an represents the thinking or history of an entirely different period and geography ranging from pre-Islamic Arabian tradition to heterodox Babylonian Jewish traditions of the eighth or ninth centuries. These views are interesting but not compelling, and they have not garnered enough support to merit abandoning the traditional chronographic and geographic setting for the contents of the Qur'an. The verses cited above therefore seem to reflect an observation of seventh-century Medinan Jewish belief.

It is clear that sixth- and seventh-century Judaisms were still in a state of flux as rabbinic Judaism was establishing itself as the dominant and soon to be virtual monopolistic expression of the religion of Israel. It would be a grave error to assume, *a priori*, that the kind (or kinds) of Judaism believed and practiced by seventh-century Arabian Jews was the same as that of Maimonides in twelfth-century Egypt. Despite its relative proximity to the Land of Israel, Babylon, and Egypt, the largely desolate Arabian Peninsula was not a regular stop for travelers moving within the "Fertile Crescent," and it cannot be assumed to have fallen under the influence of distant schools. In fact, the isolated peninsula served regularly as a refuge for people seeking freedom from outside influence. We know, for example, that early Christian communities found asylum from Roman persecution in various desert regions, and later groups of non-Orthodox Christians, to escape the theological compulsion of the Orthodox Byzantine Empire, sought sanctuary in Arabia. It is quite likely, although we have less documentation for Jews of this period than for Christians, that some nonrabbinic or marginal groups did the same when rabbinic proselytizing to them became more forceful.

Although perhaps surprising, some of the ideas attributed to the Jews by the qur'anic passages cited above are very much within the parameters of Jewish thinking in Late Antiquity, although they may not necessarily reflect what we would today call rabbinic Judaism. In relation to the passage suggesting that the Jews deify Ezra, for example, the originally Jewish books known as 4 Ezra (14:9, 50,[20] also known as 2 Esdras) and 2 Enoch (22:11) attribute a near-divine or angelic status to the biblical personages of Ezra and Enoch that could have been construed by early Muslims as compromising an austere and absolute conception of monotheism. The second qur'anic citation may in fact reflect a Jewish interpretive midrash on Lamentations 2:3: "He has withdrawn his right hand in the presence of the foe."[21] The text of 3 Enoch 48a actually reads, "R. Ishmael said to me: Come and I will show you the right hand of the Omnipresent One, which has been banished behind him because of the destruction of the Temple."[22]

If some Jews of the seventh-century Hijaz were familiar with these noncanonical compositions, it is likely that they were not all rabbinic Jews. The Qur'an itself seems to refer to different categories among those who accept the Torah as Scripture: "We have sent down the Torah [al-tawrāt] containing guidance and light, by which the prophets who surrendered [to God] judged the Jews [al-ladhīna hādū], the rabbāniyūn, and the aḥbār" (5:44). The latter two terms are generally identified in traditional Islamic scholarship as "rabbis" and "scholars," and there is indeed support for the singular form, rabbānī, deriving from the Hebrew rav, rabbi, or rabbān, and for the Arabic ḥabr or ḥibr, deriving from the Rabbinic title ḥaver. Yet this verse seems to posit three related but different groups who were judged by God through the Torah and the prophets. Another translation might read: "We have sent down the Torah containing guidance and light, by which the prophets who surrendered [to God] judged the Jews, the Rabbanites and those of the havurot."[23]

In another qur'anic passage, the same rabbāniyūn are described specifically as being very closely engaged in the study and teaching of Scripture: "Be rabbāniyūn by virtue of your teaching/knowing the Book, and in virtue of your studying it" (3:79). Might this be a reference to a distinctively rabbinic, text-centered Judaism, as opposed to other Judaisms—perhaps even a form that may have survived from the period before the destruction of the Temple? It is still impossible to arrive at any firm conclusions, but the evidence suggests that the Jews of Arabia at the birth of Islam were not all rabbinic and that a range of Jewish expression existed.

There is certainly evidence that at least some seventh-century Jews of the Hijaz went into trances and engaged in other mantic activities, perhaps even engaging in mystic journeys that parallel those of the Merkavah mystics of the Land of Israel. In one case, which appears to reflect at least an element of historical reality, Muhammad himself attempted to observe a Jewish practitioner engaged in mantic activity in Medina.[24] Muhammad, in fact, had a great deal of contact with a large and diverse Jewish community in Medina, and the relationship that ensued between them would have a tremendous impact on the future of world Jewry. But in order to make sense of this important period, we must first backtrack to the origins of Islam as understood by Islam itself.

EARLY ISLAM CONFRONTS MEDINAN JUDAISM

Muhammad received his first divine revelation in about 610 C.E. while meditating in a cave on the outskirts of his native town, Mecca. He shared his experience with his wife, Khadīja, and with his family and close friends, but according to the collective memory of Islam he refrained from preaching publicly until about three years later.

Islamic tradition describes Muhammad's prophetic mission in great detail, from the first words of revelation he received at that terrifying moment in the cave at Mt. Hira to the last words he uttered at the moment of his death. The general chronicle of his mission unfolds as a single narrative in the great biography of the Prophet known as the *Sīra*, but that composition is a result of the collecting and editing of thousands of brief, independent oral tellings, called *ḥadīth*, which depict discrete parts of his life. These ḥadīth are literary building blocks in the form of short, eye-witness reports describing various aspects of Muhammad's life, his habits, and his utterances. They existed in oral form for generations before being systematically collected and reduced to writing in a genre of literature called the Ḥadīth. Only after their collection into the large compendia, organized first by the names of those who told them and then by topics, were they rearranged into the linear narrative of the *Sīra*. Often consisting of only a dozen or so words, each ḥadīth focuses on one small item, ranging from how Muhammad cleaned his teeth to his very words describing his experience of God. As might be expected of such data, the ḥadīth often contradict one another. The ancient collectors of these traditions therefore faced a daunting task: evaluating and organizing the material into forms that would lend insight and provide spiritual and intellectual guidance to the community of believers.

The *Sīra*, composed by Muhammad ibn Isḥāq in the mid-eighth century, is the earliest and best-respected biography of Muhammad. However, it does not always agree with the parallel material found in such early historical works as al-Wāqidī's *al-Maghāzī*, Ibn Saʿd's *al-Ṭabaqāt*, or other early collections, and no corroborative record may be found outside the religious literature. The available narrative of Muhammad's prophetic career therefore represents the collective memory of Islam, and this memory includes a great amount of information about the Jewish communities and individuals among whom Muhammad lived. In fact, the *Sīra*, the Qur'an, and other early sources all openly acknowledge the major impact of Jews and Judaism on early Islamic history. Muhammad recited the divine revelations to Jews and expected them to join his religious fellowship. He spoke, argued, and fought with them, and he warmly accepted them as converts. But this period of intense interaction with Jews occurred only after he left Mecca.

After receiving the divine call, Muhammad preached openly in his native town and gained followers, but he also created enemies when he disparaged the old gods. For generations before the birth of Muhammad, Mecca had been a cultic center, a major place of pilgrimage for the idolatrous Arabs. Perhaps because of this idolatrous quality of Meccan life, there is no record of Jewish or Christian communities in the town, though biblical ideas were known in Arabia by the early seventh century and, as we have seen, biblical motifs had penetrated even into pre-Islamic cultic practices. While still in Mecca, according to an Islamic tradition accepted by most Western scholars, Muhammad recited revelations containing references to personages, occasions, and concepts found in the Hebrew Bible and New Testament. For example, Noah, the Flood, Abraham, Moses, Jesus, a day of judgment, and concepts of heaven and hell may all be found in what are generally considered the "Meccan" verses.

According to the Islamic sources, powerful Meccans had much at stake in the local religious tourism industry. Pilgrims needed food, lodging, and guides to take them to the shrines and direct them as to the most efficacious activities and offerings required at each sacred site, and these services were provided, for a fee, by families and coalitions in the town. When Muhammad denounced the idolatry that was at the base of this economy, he gained serious enemies. He was protected by powerful members of his extended family for a time, but his two most stalwart protectors died in the same year, leaving him in a position of great weakness. It was shortly thereafter that he received an invitation from Medina to arbitrate an intractable feud that had developed between the major tribal clans of that settlement. Muhammad made his hijra with his followers in 622, which marks the year zero of the Islamic or hijri calendar. It was in Medina that Muhammad would come into regular and ongoing contact with a substantial Jewish community.

Muhammad knew that he was a prophet of God sent to the Arab people. The Qur'an itself, narrated in God's words, proclaims that the divine revelations he received were sent to enlighten the Arabs: "By the Book that makes clear, We have made it an Arabic Qur'an, so perhaps you will all understand. It is [from] the Mother of Books,[25] in Our presence, exalted, wise. Shall We deny you the Word because you are a people of excess?" (43:2–5). He had been opposed by most of the Arabs in Mecca, but in Medina, he believed, the large Jewish Arab community, which had a long history of prophets and Scripture, would naturally flock to his divine revelations and prophecies. We have already learned the story of Abdullah ibn Salām, but he was not the only Jew to have awaited a messianic figure. Others seem to have expected a redeemer to arise from the south, which from the perspective of Medina was the direction of Mecca. The *Sīra* records the statement of Salama b. Salāma b. Waqsh:

> We had a Jewish neighbor among the [clan of the] Banu 'Abd al-Ashhal who came out to us one day from his home. . . . He spoke of the resurrection, the [divine] reckoning, the [heavenly] scales, the Garden and the Fire. . . . [They asked] "What would be a sign of this?" He said, pointing with his hand to Mecca and the Yemen [i.e., southward]: "A prophet will be sent from the direction of this land." They asked: "When will he appear?" He looked at me, the youngest person, and said: "This boy, if he lives his natural term, will see him." And by God, a night and a day did not pass before God sent Muhammad, His messenger, and he was living among us. We believed in him, but [the Jewish neighbor] denied him. . . . When we asked him, "Aren't you the man who said these things?" He said, "Certainly, but this is not the man."[26]

The expectation of a messiah arising from Arabia was widespread enough to have attracted some Jews to the area from the Land of Israel and its environs. The following statement is cited on the authority of a leader *(shaykh)* of the Jewish tribe in Medina known as the Banū Qurayẓa:

> A Syrian Jew[27] named ibn al-Hayyabān came to us a few years before Islam and lived with us. . . . When he was about to die, he said: "O Jews, what do you think made me leave a land of bread and wine to come to a land of hardship and hunger?" We answered: "You know best." He said: "I came to this town to see the emergence of a prophet whose time had come. This is the town to which he will migrate."[28]

Such traditions are clearly made to prove, from the Islamic perspective, the authenticity of Muhammad's prophethood, but they correspond with Jewish ideas and are found so frequently that they seem to reflect a genuine expectation among at least some Jews. The irony of this is clear from another tradition found later in the *Sīra:*

> 'Āṣim b. 'Umar b. Qatāda said on the authority of some elders of his tribe, who said: When the Messenger of God met them he said: "Who are you?" They answered: "From the Khazraj [tribe of Medina]." "Are you allies of the Jews?" "Yes," they answered. So he said: "Will you not sit with me so I can talk with you?" "Of course," they replied. So they sat with him, and he called them to

God, expounded to them Islam, and recited for them the Qur'an. Now God had prepared them for Islam in that the Jews, who were People of the Book and knowledge while they themselves were polytheists and idolaters, lived with them in their towns. They used to raid [the Jews] in their settlements, and when [bad feelings] arose between them the Jews would say: "A prophet is being sent soon. His time has come. We will follow him and kill you with his help [just as] 'Ad and Iram were destroyed."[29] So when the Messenger of God spoke with this group and called them to God, some of them said to the others: "By God, this is the very prophet about which the Jews had threatened us. Do not let them get to him before us!" So they responded to his call, believed him, and accepted his teaching of Islam.[30]

Given the messianic expectations of at least some Jews in Medina, it may seem surprising that, with few exceptions, the Jews did not flock to Muhammad's teachings despite the general acceptance of his leadership among many non-Jews within a few years of his arrival. With the highly Arabized nature of the Jewish community of Medina and at least a certain amount of common Arabized biblical culture shared between Jews and pagans, one might expect a more equal response to the option of joining the Arabian monotheism being introduced by Muhammad. But he seems not to have fit the specifically Jewish cultural paradigm of the Expected One closely enough, and the revelations and prophecies he recited in the squares of Medina, though parallel to many in the Hebrew Bible, seem not to have satisfied Jewish expectations. The community chose not to follow him, and it eventually suffered exile, slavery, and destruction as a result.

The Qur'an innocently provides some specific information about the way Jews responded to Muhammad's teachings in Medina. It expresses bitterness and disappointment at their refusal to accept the new divine dispensation. Yet it notes with some consolation that this behavior was not new, because the Israelites were a stiff-necked people who did not fully follow Moses, nor were they true to their own covenant. "Remember: We made a covenant with you and raised up the mountain over you [saying]: 'Take hold firmly of what We have given you and remember what is in it. Perhaps you will be pious.' But you turned away after that. If it were not for God's grace and mercy toward you, you would have been among the losers" [2:63–64, directed as if to Jews].[31] This image of God threatening the Israelites with death under a mountain if they will not accept the Torah finds a parallel in pre-Islamic rabbinic tradition,[32] demonstrating the Qur'an's intertextual relationship not only with biblical lore but with rabbinic tradition as well.

Most Medinan Jews did not accept Muhammad's revelations as accurate

statements of Scripture. The Qur'an observes that they would note the discrepancies between his renderings of biblical themes and those with which they were
already familiar. It therefore accuses them of distorting their own scriptural
record from the original revelation they received at Sinai. The pure and undis-
torted Sinaitic revelation would have been consistent with that of the new revelation given to Muhammad, and indeed, according to later Islamic tradition, it
even included prophecies of the coming of the Arabian prophet. "There are
some among [the People of the Book] who distort Scripture with their tongues
so that you would think it is from Scripture, but it is not from Scripture. They
say: 'This is from God' though it is not from God. They knowingly speak false-
hood about God" (3:78). Because the Hebrew Bible, like the Christian, is considered to have been tampered with, neither are accepted by Islam as dependable
sources of divine revelation. Yet the Qur'an also notes that some Jews did indeed
believe Muhammad's words of prophecy: "There are some among the People of
the Book who believe in God and in what He revealed to you and what has been
revealed to them, humbling themselves to God." (3:199).

Jews also challenged Muhammad to demonstrate the truth of his prophethood according to biblical precedents such as that of Elijah, who in 1 Kings 18
had his sacrifice consumed by a heavenly fire. "[There are] those [Jews] who say:
'God has obligated us not to believe in a messenger until he offers a sacrifice that
the fire will consume' " (3:183).

The Qur'an remained an unwritten oral text throughout Muhammad's lifetime, which proved a difficulty for him, because he was challenged by the Jews to
confirm his prophecy by showing them that he was in possession of a physical
book of Scripture: "The People of the Book ask you to bring down to them a
Book from heaven" (4:153). It is quite clear that the Jewish rejection of Muhammad was not a polite refusal to accept his authority and program but rather a serious and proactive resistance. "Many of the People of the Book want to make you
unbelievers again after your having believed" (2:109). Why, we might ask, would
the Jews take such an active stand against Muhammad and his community?

The answer to this question lies both in the distinct nature of the Jews' cultural identity and in their particular political and religious standing in Medina.
The Jewish community had recently lost its absolute political dominance in the
town but remained a powerful force, and the three major Jewish tribes were al-
lied with the now dominant non-Jewish factions in a complex set of political
and kinship relationships. That is, not only did Jewish tribes have alliances and
pacts of nonaggression with non-Jewish tribes, but there were also Jewish clans
or factions that were members of tribes not identified specifically as Jewish. It
was therefore not uncommon for Jews and non-Jews to belong to identical kin-

ship groups, suggesting that intermarriage between kinship groups probably also occurred.

Medina suffered from a great deal of tension and violence between competing tribes and kinship groups just prior to Muhammad's immigration there; he was actually invited to Medina to arbitrate and resolve the rampant factionalism of the town. His main strategy to this end was to create a trans-tribal organization of believers whose loyalty to God (and God's religious community) would transcend loyalty to tribe. The traditional tribal system of relationships upon which the Jewish community depended was therefore beginning to give way to Muhammad's super-tribe, which threatened the Jews in three ways. First, their protective alliances began to unravel and become meaningless as the Muslim community grew. Second, by claiming to be God's prophet and spokesman, Muhammad threatened the important and prestigious standing of the Jews as representatives of ancient monotheism in a region dominated by pagan idolaters. And third, as more and more Medinans were influenced by Muhammad and his message, the very essence of the Jews' distinct Jewish-Arab identity was threatened by the likelihood that there would be no role for them in a Muslim Medina. In their opposition to Muhammad, therefore, the Jews were guarding their political position, their religious tradition, and their identity within the larger fabric of Arabian culture.

The Jews therefore sought to prevent Muhammad's rise to dominance in the city, and in doing so they engaged in tactics that fully reflect Arab cultural norms and expectations. The composition and public recitation of poetry, for example, was used to discredit or humiliate enemies as well as enhance the status and pride of one's own community in pre-Islamic Arabia, and poetic satire was used in Muhammad's day as well in order to demean or humiliate one's enemy. Medinan Jews such as Abu 'Afak, Ka'b b. al-Ashraf, and 'Asmā' bt. Marwān are cited in Islamic sources as having written poems criticizing Muhammad and his followers and even inciting people against him. Women as well as men engaged in this activity on both sides. The Muslim poetess Maymūna bt. 'Abdallah, for example, is said to have answered Ka'b al-Ashraf's negative verse in kind. And 'Asmā' bt. Marwān, who may have been a convert to Judaism, was considered such a threat that Muhammad asked for a volunteer to silence her. The great Ḥassān b. Thābit, sometimes referred to as the "poet laureate" of the Prophet, threatened her with death in a poetic retort to her poem discrediting Muhammad's leadership and calling on her fellow Medinans to attack him. As the conflict intensified, the stakes grew higher. Some of the incendiary poems and their responses are reproduced in the *Sīra,* and all three Jewish poets mentioned here were eventually assassinated by Muhammad's followers.[33]

The Qur'an and *Sīra* bear witness to this war of words and its effect on the people of Medina. One difficult and somewhat obscure qur'anic verse, for example, seems to allude to an attempt by Jews to humiliate Muhammad in public. It reads,

> There are some Jews who change the words from their places by saying: "We hear and disobey" [*sami'nā wa'aṣaynā*] and "Listen, you who are not listened to," and "Look at us," twisting their tongues and speaking evil of religion. If they had only said, "We hear and obey" [*sami'nā wa'aṭa'nā*]... it would be better for them and more upright. But God cursed them for their unbelief, and they do not believe, except for a few. (4:46)

Three incendiary remarks are made by the Jews in relation to Islam and the Prophet, and the Qur'an corrects them by stating what they *should* have said.

It is impossible to reconstruct the original context of any ancient text with confidence, and this certainly includes the Qur'an. Nonetheless, we can imagine the satirical power of such gibes if we sketch a context for this particular passage given other information we have regarding the cultural history of seventh-century Medina. The Qur'an depicts Muhammad publicly reciting and interpreting the divine revelations to his followers and other interested onlookers. One of the Jews in the crowd publicly calls out to Muhammad *"Sami'nā wa'ṣaynā, ya Muhammad! Sami'nā wa'aṣaynā!"* The phrase is immediately recognizable to a Jew familiar with biblical recitation in Hebrew, because, although it is Arabic, it *sounds* virtually like a quote of Deuteronomy 5:24: "*Shamā'nū ve'asīnū* [We hear and we obey]." In the Arabic, however, it means the opposite: "We hear and disobey." To the Jewish bystander, the phrase would be understood according to its bilingual meaning with the full force of the double entendre: "We hear and obey *our* religious tradition, O Muhammad [Hebrew meaning] but we hear and publicly acclaim our *disobedience* to *your* religious preaching [Arabic meaning]!" This clever taunt would undoubtedly elicit a laugh among the Jews, whereas the Muslims and other non-Jews would simply fail to understand the humor. Muhammad and his followers would be confused, and embarrassment and humiliation would attend their confusion and the mockery of their opponents—always the goal of effective public satire.

This passage portrays the Jews of Medina as being familiar with Arabian linguistic, literary, and cultural norms yet loyal to their particular identity as Jews. Despite their deep and successful acculturation, their Jewishness seems not to have been determined only by religious beliefs. They are sometimes described in the sources as a *jummā'* (meaning "aggregate" or "collective"). This could be a reference to a certain range of religious expressions within a collective identity of Jewishness, or it could refer to a trans-tribal "ethnic" Jewish subculture, not based on a genetic or biological distinction but rather on a transcendent sense of peoplehood that could include a variety of subsumed expressions of practice or beliefs within it. Either of these possibilities might seem to contradict the earlier observation that Medinan Jews were not above the tribal factionalism that plagued the city. In fact, however, the two trajectories of identity may have lived quite intimately together. Highly integrated into the tribal system of Arabian society, Jews naturally identified closely with their kinship groups though they still retained a super-tribal sense of Jewish identity, even if they did not always share every detail of religious belief. The Islamic sources are certainly not consistent in their descriptions of Medinan Jews, suggesting that the community was layered—that it was not monolithic politically, economically, socially, or religiously. Although the Medinan Jews are identified as a "collective," they are described as speaking, looking, dressing, and acting like other Arabs. Sometimes they are portrayed as identifying themselves as Jews and being identified by others as such. At other times, they are portrayed acting exactly like any other Medinan Arab and without any hint of their Jewish identity.

The Medinan Jews failed to prevent Muhammad's rise in influence and power. Instead, they were successfully divided and conquered by the Prophet and his followers. Two of the three powerful Medinan Jewish tribes were exiled, and, of the third, the Banū Qurayẓa, the women and children were taken as booty and the adult males were killed. This important episode of Jewish and early Muslim history has been of some interest to Western scholars, which has in turn stimulated a reexamination by Muslims, and the entire issue has become controversial.[34] Western scholars have tended to condemn the Muslims' treatment of the Jewish tribes, and particularly that of the Banū Qurayẓa, as cruel, unnecessary, and unethical. Muslims in turn condemn the Jews as treacherous in aiding the enemies of Muhammad, conniving against him, and murderous, thereby deserving of such draconian measures. What both viewpoints omit is the observation that both Muhammad and the Jews were acting according to the cultural expectations of their time and place. It should only be expected that the nature of politics is informed by culture. The two sides were both working under the same basic "rules of engagement," according to which factions at the time jockeyed for dominance when the stakes were high. The competition between Muhammad and the Medinan Jews was a "zero-sum game" in which there could be only one winner—and both sides seem to have known that.

By the time of Muhammad's death in 632, there were only a few Jews still living in what had by then become known as *Madīnat al-Nabī*, the "City of the

Prophet." The conflict was immortalized in the Qur'an as well as the Ḥadīth, and anti-Jewish sentiment based on this conflict has become canonized as Scripture. However, some (though far fewer) qur'anic passages demonstrate a sense of openness and toleration of Jews and other Peoples of the Book: "Those who believe [in Islam], the Jews, Christians, and Sabians—whoever believes in God and the Last Day, and has acted uprightly, have their reward with their Lord. They shall not fear nor grieve" (2:62).

In the aftermath of the great Arab Conquest, the many Jewish communities that suddenly came under the hegemony of Islam did not fare any worse than they had under the Christians and Zoroastrians, and in most cases it appears that they fared significantly better. It should be remembered that, during the first century or more, Islam was continuing to define itself, so its influence and pressure was negligent in the immediate wake of the conquests and then increased over the years. It must also be remembered that the official Muslim policy toward "Peoples of the Book"—that is, Jews, Christians, and other religious groups that could claim a divine Scripture—was quite different than it was toward polytheists. According to the Qur'an: "[T]hen kill the polytheists wherever you find them, and seize them, beleaguer them, and lie in wait for them everywhere; but if they repent, and establish prayers and pay zakāt [a required tax distributed to the needy], then open the way for them: for God is forgiving, compassionate" (9:5). This verse became the authoritative source for the absolute outlawing of idolatry within the Islamic world. Polytheists were to be given the choice of conversion or death.

The policy toward peoples of Scripture was based on Qur'an 9:29: "Fight against those who do not believe in God or in the Last Day, and do not forbid what God and His messenger have forbidden, and do not practice the religion of truth among those who have been given the Book, until they pay the jizya, off hand, humbled." Scripturaries were to be fought until they accepted the hegemony of Islam but were then free to practice their religions without interference on the condition that they pay a special tax (jizya) and submit to a secondary societal status.

Eventually, most Jews living in the Islamic world did become Muslim, and an even higher percentage of Christians converted.[35] The debate over the reason for this has also raised controversy, with one view claiming that Muslims forced conversion either outright or through "cultural imperialism," whereas the other suggests that conversion is a natural, voluntary response of subdominant groups to the attraction of a dominant one, allowing for relatively porous boundaries between the cultures of the rulers and the ruled.

It would take at least three centuries for the majority population of the Islamic Middle East to become Muslim. Certainly in the earliest period, most Jews seem to have remained faithful to their ancestral traditions. A few key converts, however, had a profound effect on emerging Islam. The first, as noted above, was Abdullah ibn Salām, who became an exemplar in Islamic tradition of the few Jewish scholars who would admit that Muhammad was indeed referred to in the Torah as the final prophet of God. Another early convert, who was extremely influential in the developing methodologies and contents of Islamic exegesis and tradition, was a Yemenite Jew named Abū Isḥāq Ka'b b. Matī', but known more commonly as Ka'b al-Aḥbār, meaning roughly, "Ka'b, the religious scholar."[36]

KA'B AL-AḤBĀR: FROM FAME TO NOTORIETY

Ka'b and the tale of his conversion and subsequent influence on the early caliphs and other Muslim leaders are enveloped in legend. Nevertheless, we shall observe how his story, even with its marbled layers of fact and fiction, sheds important light on aspects of the complex relationship between Jews and early Muslims and between early Medieval Judaism and the emergence of Islam.

Ka'b was from southern Arabia, which, in the sixth and seventh centuries, had a large Jewish and Christian population. Very little is known of his life before he converted, but the sources suggest that he derived from a well-known tribe, perhaps even from the great one of Ḥimyar, which produced kings that ruled much of southern Arabia for centuries and may have converted as a collective to Judaism in the early fifth century. Ka'b was greatly revered by his Muslim contemporaries for his wisdom and scholarship. He counted among his students two of the most important early Muslim scholars and traditionists: Abdullah ibn 'Abbās, who is known as the originator of Islamic exegesis; and Abdullah Abū Hurayra, one of the most prolific sources of ḥadīth on the behavior and sayings of Muhammad.

Like other Yemenite Jews and non-Jews, Ka'b did not become a Muslim during Muhammad's lifetime or even during the reign of the first caliph, Abū Bakr. He was born before Muhammad, and it is curious that he seems to have changed his mind about Islam only when he was in his seventies or perhaps older. What exactly inspired him to convert is unknown, but he made his way as a Jew to Medina during the reign of the second caliph, 'Umar ibn al-Khaṭṭāb. When he arrived there in 636, he found few Jews remaining in the town; most had been exiled or had converted to Islam. Ka'b became close to the caliph and attracted pious Muslims to him because of his knowledge of the Bible and its midrashic interpretation. This period in Medina is quite interesting because, according to the histories, Ka'b lived there as a Jew for some two years before becoming a Muslim.

Ka'b is described as teaching from a Torah scroll in the mosque, according to the Muslim traditionist Ḥusayn b. Abī al-Ḥurr al-Anbārī, and famous scholars are described as asking him to interpret difficult verses from the Qur'an, which, typically, he would interpret from the context of biblical stories. In a tradition found in the famous Ḥadīth collection of Mālik b. Anās, Ka'b is said to have observed a man who took off his shoes in a mosque. Ka'b turned to the man and said: "Why did you remove your shoes? Was it because you were interpreting the [Qur'an] verse: 'Take off your shoes, for you are in the holy valley, Tuwa?' [20:12]."[37]

This scriptural verse is part of a qur'anic narrative parallel to Exodus 3, in which Moses sees a burning fire out of the midst of which his name is called. Ka'b then asks the man who had removed his shoes: "And do you know of what Moses' shoes were made? They were made from the leather of a dead donkey." It is clear from both Exodus 3:5 and Qur'an 20:12 that God demanded of Moses that he remove his shoes. Both scriptural texts associate the removing of shoes with Moses being in a sacred place, but neither explains exactly what the reason was for removing shoes in such circumstances. Ka'b fills in the gap with the explanation that Moses' shoes were made from the skin of a dead donkey (jild ḥimār mayyit). The exact significance of this fact has been lost to us, but it was obvious enough in Ka'b's day that the listener did not need further explanation. Could the issue have been that shoes made of donkey leather were considered defiling and therefore must be removed when one is in a sanctified place?[38] Was his point that any clothing made of animal skin was forbidden in such a place, or was he simply suggesting a reason for an old local custom?

Because Ka'b's explanation is found in Islamic literature, he is portrayed as making his point about the *Islamic* custom of removing one's shoes when entering a place of prayer, and he does so by anchoring it to a scriptural text in typical exegetical fashion, Muslim or Jewish. In doing so, however, he refers to a reason that is no longer remembered, perhaps reflecting an old *Jewish* Arabian custom no longer practiced today in a Jewish context but now standard practice in Islam. Ka'b cites the Qur'an, but he may well be citing it as a parallel to the Exodus text, subsequently applying a Jewish explanation to the qur'anic verse in order to make his point. The comment that Moses' shoes were made of the skin of a donkey cannot be found in extant Jewish sources, but, given Ka'b's acknowledged Jewish background, he may have been articulating an old interpretation that has since been lost from Jewish tradition.

Ka'b is typically portrayed as using biblical and midrashic literature as the basis for his views on Islamic doctrine and tradition. His Jewish knowledge seems to have served him well, and he was well respected by his Muslim peers, who often consulted him. One tradition, found also in Malik's collection,[39] has the famous Muslim scholar Abū Hurayra recount his meeting with Ka'b:

I sat with him. He told me about the Torah and I told him about the Apostle of God. One of the things I told him was that the Apostle of God said: "The best of days upon which the sun ever arose is Friday. Adam was created on that day, was brought down from the Garden on that day, was pardoned on that day, and died on that day. The [final] Hour will occur on that day ... and there is a time during that day when a Muslim does not pray [formally, but if] he asks something of God, he is granted it." Ka'b said: "This is [but] one day of the year." I answered: "No, every Friday." So Ka'b consulted the Torah [tawrāh] and said: "The Apostle of God is correct."

Later, Abu Hurayra related this conversation to Abdullah ibn Salām.

I told [Abdullah] that Ka'b said: "This is [but] one day of the year." Abdullah ibn Salām replied: "Ka'b is lying!" I then told him that Ka'b consulted the Torah and agreed that it was every Friday. So Abdullah said: "Ka'b is correct." Abdullah then said: "I know which time it is [that a Muslim will receive anything he requests from God]." [Abu Hurayra] said to him: "So tell me and do not hold back." So Abdullah ibn Salām said to him: "It is the last hour of Friday."

This exchange raises a number of issues related to the intersection of customs and traditions between Judaism and early Islam. Ka'b's "one day of the year" may have referred to Yom Kippur, but he later revises his statement after "consulting the Torah," thereby agreeing with Muhammad's teaching. Abdullah becomes quite angry when hearing Ka'b's initial statement of what would appear to be the normative Jewish view, but he is satisfied when learning that Ka'b revised his position, perhaps drawing on the Jewish tradition that many extraordinary things were created at the last hour of the Friday of creation.[40] Because of the divine wonders associated with that hour, it could have been considered a particularly auspicious time for personal supplication.

This story of Ka'b, Abū Hurayra, and Abdullah, with Muhammad's statement about the merits of Friday a constant referent, serves as an important foundation story to justify the Islamic day of religious congregation on Friday, in juxtaposition to the Jewish Saturday or Christian Sunday. It is impossible to reconstruct what Ka'b was thinking or reading when he gave his view on Muhammad's wisdom as told him by Abu Hurayra, but the "Torah" that he consulted was certainly not the Five Books of Moses. It was, rather, the extended Jewish meaning of Torah as "Jewish learning," because the legend of the special creations on Friday afternoon are found only in the Midrash and Talmud. We also observe in this story about Ka'b al-Aḥbār that he had the temerity to question a statement of the Prophet and, after consulting his Jewish sources, was bold enough to say, "The Apostle of God is correct."

This story again raises the question whether it reflects a true historical occasion. We know that many Islamic traditions of this nature were fabricated, and it is possible that this one was, too. A number of factors, however, strongly suggest that its core indeed reflects history. The most striking is that the story depicts Ka'b as unwilling to accept the word of the prophet Muhammad without corroboration, and that he consults the Torah to confirm a prophetic statement. Such behavior would probably not have been fabricated by Muslims, who would strongly criticize Ka'b for this in later generations.

According to the tradition, Ka'b accompanied the caliph Umar northward into Palestine and Syria during the Arab conquests, and was with him upon his first visit to Jerusalem. Ka'b, who is quite moved by Jerusalem, tells the caliph about a Jewish prophecy that Arabs would conquer the city from the Romans (which in Arabic parlance includes the Byzantine Roman Empire). His particular reverence for Jerusalem seems to have landed him in a bit of trouble, however.

When the Arabs capture the city, they discover that the site of the ancient Temple had been turned into a garbage dump. This was fully in keeping with Byzantine Christian doctrine, which sought to demonstrate through its imperial policies that the old divine covenant with the Jews was no longer valid after the appearance of Jesus. Henceforth, the only valid covenant would obtain with those who believe in the saving grace of Christ. As the primary symbol of ancient Judaism, the Temple and its environs were purposefully desecrated by the Byzantine authorities. Both Muslim and Jewish versions of the story depict the Arab conquerors proceeding directly to the Temple Mount, which they thoroughly cleanse. Umar himself is often featured in these accounts as the leader of the clean-up.

Umar wanted to build a mosque on the Temple Mount, and he asked Ka'b's advice. According to an early version in the great universal history of Muhammad ibn Jarīr al-Ṭabarī (d. 923),[41] Umar asked him:

> "Where do you think we should put the mosque?" "By the rock," answered Ka'b. "By God, Ka'b," said Umar, "you are following after Judaism. I saw you take off your sandals." "I wanted to feel the touch of it with my bare feet," said Ka'b. "I saw you," said Umar. "But no. We will make the forepart the *qibla* [the direction of prayer], as the Prophet of God made the forepart of the mosques their *qibla*. Go along! We were not commanded concerning the rock, but we were commanded concerning the Ka'ba!"

The rock here is the portion of bedrock that protrudes slightly from the surface of the level of the Temple Mount, known in the Mishnah (Yoma 5:2) as the "Foundation Stone" *(sh'tīyāh)* upon which the Holy of Holies, the most sacred part of the Temple, stood. When Ka'b came to the Temple Mount, he immediately removed his shoes, clearly in response to entering a holy place. As in the previous narrative, we must ask if removing his shoes was a Jewish act or a Muslim act. Whichever it was, he was criticized by the caliph for doing it *there,* which clearly indicates a Jewish response to entering into the sacred area of the Temple.

The last part of the story is a bit confusing in this version. To clarify: the *qibla* is the direction of Islamic prayer. It always faces toward the Ka'ba in Mecca, the most sacred and central religious shrine of Islam, and from Jerusalem and its environs, Mecca is due south. There is evidence in the Qur'an and early Islamic tradition that the qibla, like the direction of Jewish prayer, was toward Jerusalem for a brief period when Muhammad first came to Medina. Shortly after his arrival, however, the qibla was turned toward Mecca. The controversy becomes clear in another version of the story:[42]

[T]he caliph himself went there, and Ka'b with him. Umar said to Ka'b: "O Abū Isḥāq, do you know the position of the Rock?" Ka'b answered: "Measure from the well which is in the Valley of Gehenna so and so many ells; there dig and you will discover it," adding, "at this present day it is a dungheap." So they dug there and the rock was laid bare. Then Umar said to Ka'b: "Where do you say we should place the sanctuary, or rather, the *qibla?*" Ka'b replied: "Lay out a place for it behind [that is, to the north of] the Rock and so you will make two qiblas: that, namely, of Moses and that of Muhammad." And Umar answered him: "You still lean toward the Jews, O Abū Isḥāq. The sanctuary will be in front [that is, to the south of] the Rock." Thus was the Mosque [of al-Aqsa] erected in the front part of the *Haram* [Temple Mount] area.

Ka'b is accused here of trying to insert Jewish religious ideas into Islam. Yet in the previous story, he was not criticized for confirming a statement of Muhammad by consulting the Torah, an act that could have been considered just as egregious as regarding the Temple Mount a sacred site. Ka'b even refers to the Torah as the Book of God, despite the fact that Islam does not consider the Torah an accurate divine revelation. He is depicted elsewhere as counseling Umar to refer to Jerusalem not as Aelia, the name applied to it by Hadrian in the second century in order to dissociate the holy city from its Jewish heritage, but as Bayt al-Maqdis, the exact Arabic equivalent to the Hebrew "Beyt Hamiqdash," the Jerusalem Temple.

In a story told by Ibn 'Abbās's student 'Ikrima,[43] a man says to the great scholar and exegete,

> "O Ibn 'Abbās, I heard something remarkable from Ka'b the *ḥabr* about the sun and the moon." [Ibn 'Abbās] had been reclining, but he sat upright and said, "What is it?" [The man went on], "He claims that the sun and the moon will be brought on the Day of Resurrection as if they were castrated bulls and thrown into hell."[44] One of Ibn 'Abbās's lips flew up in anger and the other dropped. Then he said three times, "Ka'b lies! Ka'b lies! Ka'b lies! This is Judaism that he wants to insert into Islam! God is too great and honorable to punish the obedient. Have you not heard God's word: "He has made the sun and the moon work for you diligently?" [Qur'an 14:33].

Ibn 'Abbās, agitated and upset, finally cites traditions on the authority of Muhammad himself that contradict Ka'b's teaching. 'Ikrima then decides to tell Ka'b what has been said.[45]

> I got up with those who had been told [the story]. We came to Ka'b and told him Ibn 'Abbās's reaction upon hearing [Ka'b's] statement and what he reported [in response] on the authority of the Apostle of God. So Ka'b arose and accompanied us to Ibn 'Abbās. [Ka'b] said: "I heard your reaction to my statement. I ask God's forgiveness and repent. I simply reported from a book of midrash that was in circulation.[46] I did not know that there were Jewish changes [*tabdīl al-yahūd*] in it."

Ka'b was actually citing a midrash containing material that would be considered outside the parameters of normative rabbinic tradition. His final comment suggests, interestingly enough, that he may have ultimately realized this. From the standpoint of Islam, however, such distinctions were irrelevant (nor is it clear how fixed was the midrashic canon at this time). In this story, Ka'b is condemned for attempting to insert "Jewish teachings" into Islam, yet we noted previously that he was not condemned in other tales for doing exactly that. On the contrary, he was sought out by early Muslims exactly because he had access to ancient monotheistic lore that could lend insight into God's word and will as expressed in Islamic Scripture and tradition. Why was he so harshly condemned here and so welcomed in other contexts?

The definitive answer may never be known, but two aspects of Ka'b's situation provide significant clues. Although it was known to all that Ka'b was knowledgeable, the Jewish nature of his knowledge seemed to matter little if at all. What was important was that he had access to ancient monotheistic wisdom. Because Islam was only in formation during Ka'b's lifetime, it was not yet clear exactly where it fit in relation to Judaism and Christianity. Most of what would become Islamic dogma simply had not been established at this point. Ka'b, for example, could question and then find Jewish confirmation of Muhammad's statement about the status of Friday. Later, however, the belief developed that the word of the Prophet was infallible, after which Ka'b's behavior could no longer be considered acceptable. While he lived, however, Ka'b was regularly consulted both for his access to divine wisdom and, like other scholars of Holy Scriptures either Jewish or Christian, for his ability to predict future events based on his knowledge of divine revelation.

More significant than this, however, is the fact that Ka'b's reputation declined in subsequent generations as Islam began increasingly to view itself as an independent religious civilization. Material attributed to Ka'b was tainted by his unabashed association with Judaism. Islam provided the ideological basis of the largest and most successful empire of the age, and any hint of dependence or subordination to another tradition would have been considered at the least impolitic. By the end of the eighth century, it became improper to consult Jews about problems of religion and belief. In later texts Ka'b was occasionally accused even of surreptitiously attempting to corrupt Islam from within while masquerading as a convert.

One may detect the change in Ka'b's status by examining the sources of tradition in which he is cited by name. In the canonical collections of Ḥadīth, the most highly respected sources, his name cannot be found at all. Many of the traditions attributed to him in extra-canonical literature, however, can be found also in the Ḥadīth collections, although there they are attributed not to him but to his students. He himself was too tainted to be included in the Ḥadīth by the time of its assembly in the ninth century. Some of the information he brought was too important to be excluded from it, however, so it is found attributed to students of his such as Ibn 'Abbās, who is not suspected of being too closely associated with Judaism or other foreign religious traditions. Ka'b's stories and teachings may be found in his own name, however, in the popular literature of the story-tellers, or quṣṣāṣ, who told tales of ancient prophets and patriarchs. Reflecting popular culture that transcended religious affiliation, these "Stories of the Prophets" (qiṣaṣ al-anbiyā') preserve much of the aggadic material for which Ka'b was famous.[47]

The story of Ka'b al-Aḥbār reflects aspects of Jewish culture and civilization of seventh-century Arabia just as it reflects aspects of emerging Islam. The midrashic traditions Ka'b cites sometimes lie outside of the canon of rabbinic

Judaism that we know today, suggesting that the religious ideas and practices of ancient Arabian Jews may have been somewhat different from what we know from the Talmuds of Babylon and the Land of Israel. Ka'b partially judaized the very religion into which he assimilated. He is not unique, of course; proselytes often contribute something of their prior religious ideas and practices as they integrate into the systems of new religions.

In fact, the Islam that Ka'b knew must have looked quite different from later forms. It was most certainly less distinct from Judaism than it is today. As Muhammad's expectations that the Jews of Medina would follow him suggest, the boundaries between the two systems were simply not so clear. One tradition even states that a group of Jews who had embraced Islam asked (but did not receive) Muhammad's permission to observe the Jewish Sabbath and to study the Torah at night.[48] Early Muslims came to Jews like Ka'b and to Christians for monotheistic wisdom and lore that would help them understand their own revelation and the acts of Muhammad. But as Islam developed, as its tenets and practices became more standardized and unified, its adherents came to see themselves as distinct, unique, and different from other religious civilizations.

During Ka'b's lifetime, rabbinic Judaism itself was still emerging and its boundaries were still permeable. Some of Ka'b's teachings may have since fallen out of Judaism because they became irrelevant and were forgotten, or because they were rejected. In a fascinating reversal, however, some of Ka'b's and other Jews' traditions, preserved in Islamic literature, would reappear in Jewish literature when, by the tenth century, Jews began to absorb and appropriate aspects of the powerful and attractive Islamic religious, intellectual, and cultural civilization.

NOTES

1. *Al-Sīra al-Nabawiyya* (Beirut, n.d.), 1: 516–17; translated by Alfred Guillaume as *The Life of Muhammad: A Translation of Ibn Ishaq's Sirat Rasul Allah* (Karachi, 1955), 241–42.

2. Ḥabr 'ālim. The Arabic term, *ḥabr*, *is simply the Arabic pronunciation of the talmudic title,* ḥaver, *or learned scholar (Bava Batra 75a: "*ḥaverim *are none other than* talmidey ḥakamim*").*

3. Its strongly polemical nature should immediately raise caution regarding its historicity. See A. J. Wensinck, *Muhammad and the Jews of Medina* (Berlin, 1982); R. Firestone, "The Failure of a Jewish Program of Public Satire in the Squares of Medina," *Judaism* (Winter 1997): 438–52; W. M. Watt, "The Condemnation of the Jews of Banū Qurayẓah," *Muslim World* 42 (1952): 160–71; and G. Newby, "The Sīrah as a Source for Arabian Jewish History: Problems and Perspectives," *Jerusalem Studies in Arabic and Islam* 7 (1986): 121–38.

4. According to classical Arabian genealogies, the "original Arabs" (*al-'arab al-'āriba*)

have died out, whereas the "arabized Arabs" (*al-'arab al-musta'riba*) derive from nonindigenous tribes who assimilated Arabian culture and language after migrating into the Arabian Peninsula; see G. Rentz, "Djazirat al-'Arab," in *Encyclopaedia of Islam,* 2d ed. (Leiden, 1: 543–46. 1983), Many contemporary Arabian tribes, including the Quraysh tribe from which Muhammad derived, trace their ancestry to Ishmael, whom Abraham brought to Arabia (see Gen. 21).

5. Many of these terms were absorbed into Islam. For a listing of foreign religious vocabulary found in the Qur'an, see Arthur Jeffery, *The Foreign Vocabulary of the Qur'ān* (Baroda, India, 1938). Christian communities also lived in Arabia during this period, and they too contributed cultic and religious terminology to what would emerge as Islam. See Spencer Trimingham, *Christianity Among the Arabs in Pre-Islamic Times* (London, 1979).

6. S. D. Goitein, "Jewish Issues in *Kitab Ansāb al-Ashrāf* of al-Balādhurī" (Hebrew), *Zion* 1 (1936): 76.

7. Earlier attempts at establishing an authoritative text may have occurred, such as the "collection" under the first caliph, Abu Bakr, but even that under Uthman was not conclusive. The primitive nature of Arabic orthography and various "readings" or different ways of pronouncing the words continued to plague the Muslims, and some modern scholars question the traditional account of the collection and canonization of the Qur'an altogether. For a synopsis of the traditional Islamic view with minor criticisms, see Richard Bell and W. Montgomery Watt, *Introduction to the Qur'ān* (Edinburgh, 1970).

8. The earliest complete narrative, reproduced here, is found in *Pirqē Rabbi Eli'ezer* (Warsaw edition with commentary of David Luria), chap. 30, a work that was redacted in its present form after the emergence of Islam and that contains Islamic influence but is made up mostly of pre-Islamic material. An English translation (of a different manuscript) of *PRE* was made by Gerald Friedlander, *Pirkē De Rabbi Eliezer* (London, 1916; reprint, New York, 1981), 218–19. A more embellished rendering may be found in the later *Sefer HaYashar* (Tel Aviv, 1980), 55–56.

9. The *Targum Pseudo-Yonatan* (Gen. 21:21) has " 'Adisha." Most likely added to an earlier narrative core, these allusions to the name of Muhammad's beloved wife, 'Ayyishah, date its final redaction to after the emergence of Islam.

10. Note the double entendre in the words, *'ayefā nafshī* ("my soul is faint") in relation to the name 'Ayefa.

11. *Targum Pseudo-Yonatan* (Gen. 21:21) has Fatima, which was the name of Muhammad's daughter.

12. In the continuation of this story, Abraham also demonstrates his continuing love for Hagar by taking her back after Sarah's death. Traditional commentaries from the targums to Rashi suggest that Abraham's wife, Qeturah, named in Genesis 25:1, was none other than Hagar.

13. For a synopsis of 17 versions of this story in Arab sources, see Reuven Firestone, *Journeys in Holy Lands: The Evolution of the Abraham-Ishmael Legends in Islamic Exegesis* (Al-

bany, N.Y., 1990), 76–82. See also Aviva Schussman, "Abraham's Visits to Ishmael—The Jewish Origin and Orientation" (Hebrew), *Tarbiz* 49 (1980): 325–45.

14. Yaqūt b. 'Abdallah al-Rūmī (d. 1229), *Mu'jam al-buldān*, 7 vols. (Beirut, 1990), 4: 255.

15. *Al-Anbiyā'*, #583. This work is one of the two most highly revered Islamic religious books after the Qur'an, so such a narrative remains of great importance in contemporary Islam.

16. The Zam-zam well is the sacred well in Mecca, only a few steps away from the Ka'ba, from which Muslim pilgrims still drink.

17. See, e.g., Bukhārī, *Ṣaḥīḥ, anbiyā'* 9:23, 24.

18. See, e.g., Romans 4:9–25 and Galatians 4:21–31.

19. The qur'anic term for the Kaaba in Mecca. In qur'anic discourse, capitalized "We" refers to God, who is the divine narrator of the Qur'an.

20. This verse is found only in the Oriental (Syriac, Ethiopic, Armenian, and Arabic) recensions, not in the Latin.

21. Lamentations Rabbah 2:6, as suggested by David Halperin and cited indirectly in Gordon Newby, *A History of the Jews of Arabia* (Columbia, S.C., 1989), 59.

22. Cited in Newby, *History,* 59. See also David Halperin, *The Faces of the Chariot* (Tübingen, 1988), 467–68.

23. Or, "those of the *haverīm.*" See, however, Qur'an 5:63.

24. David J. Halperin, "The Ibn Sayyad Traditions and the Legend of al-Dajjal," *Journal of the American Oriental Society* 96 (1976): 213–25.

25. This common idiom means, in essence, the "essential divine word" or divine source from which all revelation comes.

26. *Al-Sīra al-Nabawiyya* (Beirut, n.d.), 1:212/Guillaume 93–94.

27. The common designation for the Land of Israel in medieval Arabic texts is (greater) Syria (*al-shā'm*).

28. *Sīra* 1:213–14/Guillaume 94.

29. 'Ād and Iram are names of ancient Arabian tribal groups that had disappeared long before the emergence of Islam but that still lived in the memories and oral traditions of the Arabs.

30. *Sīra* 1:428–29/Guillaume 197–98.

31. The theme of the Israelites breaking their own covenant is repeated in the Qur'an: 2:84, 93, 100; 3:187; 5:12–13.

32. See, e.g., BT *Shabbat* 88a, Avodah Zara 2b. *Tanḥuma, Bereshit* 58:3. The motif is also repeated in the Qur'an: 2:93; 4:154.

33. *Sīra* 2:51–58, 635–38/Guillaume 364–69, 675–76; Wensinck, *Muhammad and the Jews of Medina,* 110–12; Michael Lecker, *Muslims, Jews and Pagans: Studies on Early Islamic Medina* (Leiden, 1995), 38–48; W. Montgomery Watt, *Muhammad at Medina* (Oxford, 1956), 15, 18, 178–79, 210.

34. See, e.g., Wensinck, *Muhammad and the Jews of Medina;* Watt, *Muhammad at Me-*

dina; W. F. Arafat, "New Light on the Story of Banu Qurayza and the Jews of Medina," *Journal of the Royal Asiatic Society* (1976): 100–107; and Barakat Ahmad, *Muhammad and the Jews: A Re-examination* (New Delhi, 1979). M. J. Kister summarizes the various views in his "The Massacre of the Banu Qurayza: A Re-examination of a Tradition," *Jerusalem Studies in Arabic and Islam* 8 (1986): 61–96.

35. Richard Bulliet, *Conversion to Islam in the Medieval Period* (Cambridge, Mass., 1979).

36. Literally, "Ka'b of the *haverim.*" *Al-ahbār* is a plural form of *hibr,* the Arabic equivalent of the talmudic title, *haver.* Although in early Islam the term is usually applied to a few pious and learned Jewish converts, it was sometimes also associated with exceptional Muslims lacking any known Jewish lineage.

37. *Al-Muwaṭṭa', K. al-libās* 16 (Cairo, n.d), 916.

38. See Exodus 13:13 and the extended discussion in BT *Bekhorot* 1.

39. *Al-Muwaṭṭa', K. al-Jum'a* 16 (p. 108).

40. BT *Pesahim* 54a. See Louis Ginzberg, *The Legends of the Jews,* trans. from German by Henrietta Szold, 7 vols. (Philadelphia, 1968), 1: 83, 5: 103.

41. Muhammad ibn Jarir al-Ṭabarī, *Ta'rīkh al-rusul wal-mulūk,* ed. M. J. De Goeje (Leiden, 1964), 1: 2408–9, translation in Bernard Lewis, *Islam from the Prophet Muhammad to the Capture of Constantinople,* vol. 2 (New York, 1974), 3.

42. F. E. Peters, *Jerusalem: The Holy City in the Eyes of Chroniclers, Visitors, Pilgrims, and Prophets* (Princeton, 1985), 189.

43. Al-Ṭabarī, *Ta'rīkh,* 1: 62–63, and translated in *The History of al-Ṭabarī,* vol. 1 (Albany, N.Y., 1989), 233. Translated and annotated by Franz Rosenthal; editor, Ehsan Yar-Shater.

44. *Thawrān 'aqīrān.* See D. Halperin and G. Newby, "Two Castrated Bulls: A Study in the Haggadah of Ka'b al-Aḥbār," *Journal of the American Oriental Society* 102, no. 4 (1982): 631–37.

45. Al-Ṭabarī, *Ta'rīkh,* 1:74, translation in *History of al-Ṭabarī,* 1: 243.

46. *Kitāb dāris,* which is generally translated as "well-worn book." Halperin and Newby ("Two Castrated Bulls," 632–33) correctly translate *dāris* through its meaning as study or reading, equal to the Hebrew *midrash.*

47. One of these collections has been translated into English by Wheeler Thackston, *The Tales of the Prophets of al-Kisā'ī* (Boston, 1978). A great deal of this material may also be found in the first few volumes of the recently translated *History of al-Ṭabarī* (variable dates as volumes are translated).

48. Kister, "*Ḥaddithū 'an banī isrā'īla wa-lā ḥaraja:* A study of an early tradition," *Israel Oriental Studies* I (Tel Aviv University, 1972), 238.

SELECTED BIBLIOGRAPHY

ARABIC SOURCES IN TRANSLATION

Guillaume, Alfred. *The Life of Muhammad: A Translation of Ibn Ishaq's Sirat Rasul Allah.* Karachi, 1955.

Ṭabarī, Muhammad ibn Jarir al-. *The History of al-Ṭabarī.* Vol. 1. Albany, N.Y., 1989. Translated and annotated by Franz Rosenthal; ed., Ehsan Yar-Shater

Thackston, Wheeler. *The Tales of the Prophets of al-Kisā'ī.* Boston, 1978.

SECONDARY STUDIES

Firestone, Reuven. "The Failure of a Jewish Program of Public Satire in the Squares of Medina." *Judaism* (Winter 1997): 438–52.

———. *Journeys in Holy Lands: The Evolution of the Abraham-Ishmael Legends in Islamic Exegesis.* Albany, N.Y., 1990.

Halperin, David. *The Faces of the Chariot.* Tübingen, 1988.

Lecker, Michael. *Muslims, Jews and Pagans: Studies on Early Islamic Medina.* Leiden, 1995.

Newby, Gordon. *A History of the Jews of Arabia.* Columbia, S.C., 1989.

Peters, F. E., ed., *Arabs and Arabia on the Eve of Islam.* London. 1998.

Trimingham, Spencer. *Christianity Among the Arabs in Pre-Islamic Times.* London, 1979.

Watt, W. Montgomery. *Muhammad at Medina.* Oxford, 1956.

Wensinck, A. J. *Muhammad and the Jews of Medina.* Berlin, 1982.

CONCLUSION

DAVID BIALE

In the chapter on the Bible with which this cultural history began, Ilana Pardes portrayed the first Jews imagining their formative years as a collective biography:

> The nation—particularly in Exodus and Numbers—is not an abstract detached concept but rather a grand character with a distinct voice (represented at times in a singular mode), who moans and groans, is euphoric at times, complains frequently, and rebels against Moses and God time and again. Israel has a life story, a biography of sorts. It was conceived in the days of Abraham; its miraculous birth took place with the Exodus, the parting of the Red Sea; then came a long period of childhood and restless adolescence in the wilderness, and finally adulthood was approached with the conquest of Canaan.

How can this model help us conclude our journey through three millennia of Jewish cultures? At its very origins, the nation is not heroically united but rent with divisions and doubts. It moves from the primordial Exile in Egypt to the Promised Land, but the threat of future exiles hangs over it like an inescapable shadow. It wishes to establish its own individuated identity, but the fleshpots of Egypt beckon it back while the gods of Canaan lie in wait ahead.

So, too, in all the varieties of Jewish culture we have visited, diversity and interaction have been as much the rule as unity and isolation. At times, the narrative that the Jews tell about themselves speaks of "a nation dwelling alone and not counted among the other nations," as we remember from the prophecy of Balaam. But the story also contains fissures and factions, as well as bold crossings of borders.

The biblical narrative supplies all of the elements of later Jewish history—homeland and exile, fidelity and betrayal, divine revelation and the eclipse of God—but the one thing it does not provide is finality. To paraphrase the nineteenth-century philosopher of Jewish history, Nahman Krochmal, the nation goes through a natural cycle of birth, maturation, and old age—only to be born again and repeat the cycle. Every age of Jewish history may be seen as a collective biography.

Where, we might ask, is the present moment in the collective biography of the Jews in the cycle of life? Before attempting to answer this question, we must take note of how Volume III ends: with American Jewish culture. The contributors to this work debated long and hard about whether the final chapter should be on the State of Israel or the largest contemporary Diaspora community. Each suggests a certain goal, as if all that has preceded must point ideologically toward the final chapter. And, yet, we intend no such teleology, for we start with the assumption, as Stephen Whitfield says, that the future remains to be written. Rather than try to defend the particular way this history ends—and, of course, it had to end with one or the other—it may be more fruitful to think about these two largest communities as siblings in the collective family history of the Jews.

A century ago, the largest centers of Jewish culture lay in Europe, both East and West. Numerically, the Jewish communities of North Africa, of the Middle East, and of North America were relatively small and peripheral. Even farther to the periphery were the much smaller communities in South and Central America, Ethiopia, India, and China. Over the course of the past hundred years, the demography of the Jewish people has undergone a radical change and, with it, so has Jewish culture. The tiny community of Ottoman Palestine is now the State of Israel, which, demographers tell us, may soon contain the plurality of the world's Jews. The North American Jewish community, which had already begun to swell with immigrants in the year 1900, has probably reached its peak population, with demographers predicting a slow but steady decline, because of intermarriage and low fertility, in the decades ahead. Meanwhile, the great population centers in Europe, particularly in the East, were decimated by emigration and the Holocaust. A much reduced (though by no means dead) Jewish community exists in the former Soviet Union, as it does in other European countries, numbering altogether around one and a half million. Little is left of the Jewish communities in North Africa or the Middle East, with the exception of the State of Israel, just as little is left of the much smaller Indian or Ethiopian diasporas. Only in South Africa, Australia, Argentina, and Brazil do populations of 100,000 or more remain, but all are declining.

Our concern here is not with numbers, but with culture. After all, the tiny Ashkenazic communities of France and the Rhineland in the High Middle Ages rarely contained more than a few thousand souls and yet produced a powerful culture whose echoes still resonate today. The current demographic decline of the North American Jewish community comes at a time of cultural innovation and vitality, and we should be cautious about correlating one with the other. Is this community in its cultural adolescence or senescence? Its origins lie in the same mass migration out of Eastern Europe that also fed the Zionist settlement in the Land of Israel. In terms of the length of Jewish history, a century is culturally a very short time. Both Israel and the United States are young cultures that are still undergoing rapid changes. World-wide trends, such as feminism, and new media, such as film, have had enormous impacts on both cultures. The globalization of culture is likely to create both the greatest challenge and greatest stimulation to each of these communities.

Because the process of Jewish immigration is not yet complete for either Israel or America, cultural change may also come about from new immigrants. Although the dominant culture in Israel is in the Hebrew language, itself growing and changing with the rapidity of youth, there is now a flourishing Russian Jewish subculture there, with newspapers, books, theater, radio, and television all in the language of Israel's most recent immigrants. Whether this culture will have any more lasting power than did Yiddish culture in America (or, for that matter, in Israel itself) remains unknown. But even if it is ultimately translated into Hebrew, this immigrant culture will no doubt have an enormous impact on Israeli culture as a whole. Similarly, a vigorous Israeli subculture exists within—or beside—American Jewish culture, especially in New York, Los Angeles, and the Silicon Valley of the San Francisco Bay Area. Here, too, it remains to be seen what impact this subculture will have on American Jewish culture as a whole, which has always been a composite of many Jewish immigrations.

Indeed, from its earliest origins, the history of the Jews has been one of migrations, and Jewish culture has always been the product of the intense interactions with the new cultures in which the Jews found themselves. In this sense, Jewish culture has always evolved on a global stage, whether that of the empires of the ancient Near East, the Greco-Roman Mediterranean, or the later worlds of Islam and Christianity. Jewish culture itself frequently had a global reach as well: rabbis moved back and forth from Babylonia and Palestine; medieval legal authorities from France ventured into Spain; Polish rabbis wrote commentaries on Joseph Karo's Sephardic law code, written in Safed; and, on the level of popular religion, Jewish women and men shared similar customs in Yemen, Kurdistan, and Germany.

Jewish culture at the present moment has something of this global quality, but, with the transformations of modernity, it lacks the unifying force of rabbinic authority and a shared popular culture that characterized it for much of the past millennium and a half. Even if the authoritative Babylonian Talmud was modified by custom in many communities, or even rejected by a group like the Karaites, most Jews followed practices that were recognizable throughout most of the Jewish world. Today, Jewish culture bears a greater resemblance to the

Greco-Roman period of factionalism and competing claims of authority before the ascendancy of the rabbis. Then, too, a global culture called Hellenism laid claim as the "universal" culture against the "parochial" claims of ancestral Jewish custom. Then, too, Jerusalem was the religious and political center of a widely scattered Diaspora that recognized its centrality but also felt at home in foreign lands.

That world underwent a great crisis with the destruction of the Temple and, some centuries later, with the decline of the political and religious institutions of Palestine. Today, the situation is reversed in some ways, with the State of Israel ascendant as a center of Jewish culture. The great crises of this age are not the destruction of the Temple but the Holocaust that eradicated the cultures of Jewish Europe and, more broadly, the cultural pluralism ushered in by modernity. We stand at the threshold of an entirely new era, just as did the generations after the destruction of the Second Temple.

But one might go even further back for a historical analogy to the present moment: to the period of the Bible itself, not so much the Bible as it was finally edited and canonized but, rather, the many conflicting cultural threads from which it was woven. The formative years of ancient Israel were a period of extraordinary ferment in which those who would become Jews struggled to draw the ethnic and religious boundaries between themselves and their Canaanite, Egyptian, and Mesopotamian neighbors. A certain "orthodoxy" emerged at the end of this process and put its seal on the sources that recorded this struggle, but it is the cacophony of voices preserved in the Bible—the complaints of the people vs. the admonitions of Moses—that most resembles the state of Jewish culture today. There is, of course, a world of difference between the modern age and the ancient, but the problems of Jewish identity remain startlingly similar.

The Bible, like Homer's *Iliad* and Virgil's *Aeneid,* was an ancient attempt to imagine the origins of the nation. It is the foundational text on which all later Jewish culture—a culture quintessentially of commentary—was built. Jewish culture today is perhaps less closely tied to the biblical text as its source, but in one sense it is not entirely divorced from its predecessors. If the Bible is read not as one voice speaking but as many, so, too, all the cultures of the Jews described in these volumes represent many voices, responding, in myriad ways, to both text and context, each seeking to integrate a historical tradition with a specific cultural environment. Perhaps all these disparate voices from three millennia, assembled together under this literary roof, constitute the collective biography of Israel.

INDEX

Page numbers in *italics* refer to illustrations.

ABOUT THE EDITOR

David Biale is the Emmanuel Ringelblum Professor of Jewish History at the University of California, Davis. He is the author of *Power and Powerlessness in Jewish History* and the editor of *Insider/Outsider: American Jews and Multiculturalism*. He lives in Berkeley, California.